STUDIES IN AUGUSTINE
AND ERIUGENA

John J. O'Meara

❧

STUDIES IN AUGUSTINE AND ERIUGENA

edited by Thomas Halton

The Catholic University of America Press
Washington, D.C.

B
655
.Z7
O28
1992

Copyright © 1992
The Catholic University of America Press
All rights reserved
Printed in the United States of America

The paper used in this publication meets the minimum requirements of
American National Standards for Information Science—Permanence of Paper
for Printed Library Materials, ANSI Z39.48-1984.
∞

Library of Congress Cataloging-in-Publication Data
O'Meara, John Joseph.
   Studies in Augustine and Eriugena / John J. O'Meara.
     p. cm.
   Includes bibliographical references and index.
   1. Augustine, Saint, Bishop of Hippo. 2. Erigena, Johannes
Scotus, ca. 810–ca. 877. I. Halton, Thomas. II. Title.
B655.Z7O28 1992
ISBN 0-8132-0768-1 (alk. paper)
92-7188

Contents

Acknowledgments vii
Abbreviations xi

Introduction 1

I. CONFESSION AND HISTORICITY

1. The Historicity of Augustine's Early Dialogues 11
2. "*Arripui, aperui, et legi*" (*Confessions* VIII, 12, 29) 24
3. Patrick's *Confessio* and Augustine's *Confessiones* 31
4. Augustine's *Confessions*: Elements of Fiction 39

II. AUGUSTINE ON LOVE AND SEXUALITY

5. Augustine the Artist and the *Aeneid* 59
6. Virgil and Augustine: The Roman Background to Christian Sexuality 69
7. Augustine's Attitude to Love in the Context of His Influence on Christian Ethics 88
8. Virgil and Augustine: The *Aeneid* in the *Confessions* 103

III. AUGUSTINE, PLOTINUS, AND PORPHYRY

9. Neoplatonism in the Conversion of Augustine 121
10. A Master-Motif in Augustine 132
11. Augustine's View of Authority and Reason in A.D. 386 140
12. Augustine and Neoplatonism 146
13. Porphyry's *Philosophy from Oracles* in Eusebius's *Praeparatio Euangelica* and Augustine's *Dialogues of Cassiciacum* and *City of God* X 166
14. Plotinus and Augustine: Exegesis of *Contra Academicos* II, 5 195

15.	The Neoplatonism of Augustine	209
16.	Parting from Porphyry	219

IV. AUGUSTINE AND ERIUGENA

17.	Augustine's Understanding of the Creation and Fall	233
18.	Eriugena's Use of Augustine in His Teaching on the Return of the Soul and the Vision of God	244
19.	Eriugena's Use of Augustine in His Teaching on the Soul-Body Relationship	255
20.	Eriugena's Use of Augustine's *De Genesi ad litteram* in the *Periphyseon*	269

V. METHOD AND CRITICISM IN THE STUDY OF AUGUSTINE

21.	Research Techniques in Augustinian Studies	287
22.	Studies Preparatory to an Understanding of the Mysticism of Augustine and His Doctrine on the Trinity	294
23.	The Conditions of Controversy	305

Afterword by Louis J. Swift	311
Notes	315
General Index	357
Index of Augustinian Texts	361

Acknowledgments

Grateful acknowledgment is made to the publishers and editors for permission to reprint [with slight alterations]:

I. CONFESSION AND HISTORICITY

1. "The Historicity of Augustine's Early Dialogues." Under title: "The Historicity of the Early Dialogues of Saint Augustine," *Vigiliae Christianae* 5 (1951) 150–78.
2. "'*Arripui, aperui, et legi*' (*Confessions*, VIII, 12, 29)." Under title: '"Arripui, aperui, et legi,"' in *Augustinus Magister* I (Paris, Etudes Augustiniennes 1954) 59–65.
3. "Patrick's *Confessio* and Augustine's *Confessiones*," in *Latin Script and Letters* A.D. *400–900. Festschrift Ludwig Bieler,* ed. J. J. O'Meara and B. Naumann (Leiden: Brill, 1976) 44–53.
4. "Augustine's *Confessions*: Elements of Fiction," in *Augustine: From Rhetor to Theologian,* ed. J. McWilliam (Waterloo, Ontario: Wilfred Laurier University Press, 1992) 77–95.

II. AUGUSTINE ON LOVE AND SEXUALITY

5. "Augustine the Artist and the *Aeneid*," *Mélanges offerts à Christine Mohrmann* (Utrecht: Spectrum, 1963) 252–61.
6. "Virgil and Augustine: The Roman Background to Christian Sexuality." Under title: "Virgil and Saint Augustine: The Roman Background to Christian Sexuality," *Augustinus* (Madrid), XIII (1968) 307–26.
7. "Augustine's Attitude to Love in the Context of His Influence on Christian Ethics." Under title: "St. Augustine's Attitude to Love in the Context of His Influence on Christian Ethics," *Arethusa* II (1969) 46–60.
8. "Virgil and Augustine: The *Aeneid* in the *Confessions*," *Maynooth Review* 13 (1988) 30–43.

III. AUGUSTINE, PLOTINUS, AND PORPHYRY

9. "Neoplatonism in the Conversion of Augustine." Under title: "Neoplatonism in the Conversion of Saint Augustine," *Dominican Studies* 3 (1950) 331–43.

10. "A Master-Motif in Augustine." Under title: "A Master-Motif in St. Augustine," in *Actes du premier Congrès de la Fédération Internationale des Associations d'études classiques* (Paris: C. Klincksieck, 1951) 312–17.
11. "Augustine's View of Authority and Reason in A.D. 386." Under title: "St. Augustine's View of Authority and Reason in A.D. 386," *Irish Theological Quarterly* 18 (1951) 338–46.
12. "Augustine and Neoplatonism," *Recherches Augustiniennes* 1 (1958) 91–111.
13. "Porphyry's *Philosophy from Oracles* in Eusebius's *Praeparatio Euangelica* and Augustine's *Dialogues of Cassiciacum* and *City of God* X," *Recherches Augustiniennes* 6 (1969) 103–39.
14. "Plotinus and Augustine: Exegesis of *Contra Academicos* II, 5," *Revue internationale de philosophie* 24 (1970) 321–37.
15. "The Neoplatonism of Augustine." Under title: "The Neoplatonism of Saint Augustine," in *Neoplatonism and Christian Thought*, ed. D. J. O'Meara (Albany: State University of New York Press, 1982) 34–41, 233–34.
16. "Parting from Porphyry," Congresso Internazionale su *S. Agostino nel XVI Centenario della Conversione, Roma, 15–20 settembre 1986*, Atti 2 (Roma: Institutum Patristicum "Augustinianum," 1987) 357–69.

IV. AUGUSTINE AND ERIUGENA

17. "Augustine's Understanding of the Creation and Fall," *Maynooth Review* 10 (1984) 52–62.
18. "Eriugena's Use of Augustine in His Teaching on the Return of the Soul and the Vision of God," in *Jean Scot Erigène et l'Histoire de la Philosophie*, ed. R. Roques (Paris: Centre national de la recherche scientifique, 1977) 191–200.
19. "Eriugena's Use of Augustine in His Teaching on the Soul-Body Relationship." Under title: "Eriugena's Use of Augustine," *Augustinian Studies* 11 (1980) 21–34.
20. "Eriugena's Use of Augustine's *De Genesi ad litteram* in the *Periphyseon*." Under title: "'Magnorum Virorum Quendam Consensum Velimus Machinari' (804D): Eriugena's Use of Augustine's *De Genesi ad litteram* in the *Periphyseon*," in *Eriugena: Studien zu seinen Quellen*, ed. W. Beierwaltes (Heidelberg: Carl Winter Universitatsverlag, 1980) 105–16.

V. METHOD AND CRITICISM IN THE STUDY OF AUGUSTINE

21. "Research Techniques in Augustinian Studies," *Augustinian Studies* 1 (1970) 277–84.

22. "Studies Preparatory to an Understanding of the Mysticism of Augustine and His Doctrine on the Trinity." Under title: "Studies Preparatory to an Understanding of the Mysticism of St. Augustine and His Doctrine on the Trinity," *Augustinian Studies* 1 (1970) 263–76.
23. "The Conditions of Controversy," review of François Decret, *Aspects du Manichéisme dans l'Afrique Romaine* (Paris: Etudes Augustiniennes, 1970). In *Augustinian Studies* 4 (1973) 199–204.

Abbreviations

WORKS OF AUGUSTINE

C	Confessiones
CA	Contra Academicos
CF	Contra Faustum
DBV	De beata vita
DCE	De consensu evangelistarum
DCD	De civitate Dei
DDC	De doctrina christiana
DGnL	De Genesi ad litteram
DI	De immortalitate animae
DLA	De libero arbitrio
DME	De moribus ecclesiae
DOR	De ordine
DQ	De quantitate animae
DT	De trinitate
DUC	De utilitate credendi
DVR	De vera religione
E	Epistulae
R	Retractationes
S	Sermones
SO	Soliloquia

GENERAL WORKS

ACW	Ancient Christian Writers
AEPHE	Annuaire. Ecole pratique des hautes études
APhC	Annales de philosophie chrétienne
ArPh	*Archives de philosophie*
AS	*Augustinian Studies*
AugM	*Augustinus Magister*
BA	Bibliothèque Augustinienne
CM	*Classica et Mediaevalia*
CSEL	Corpus Scriptorum Ecclesiasticorum Latinorum
DThC	*Dictionnaire de Théologie Catholique*

EThL	*Ephemerides Theologicae Lovanienses*
HThR	*Harvard Theological Review*
IER	*Irish Ecclesiastical Record*
IThQ	*Irish Theological Quarterly*
PG	Migne, Patrologia Graeca
PL	Migne, Patrologia Latina
RBi	*Revue Biblique*
REAug	*Revue des études Augustiniennes*
RechAug	*Recherches Augustiniennes*
RECA	*Real-Encyclopädie der classische Altertumswissenschaft*
REG	*Revue des études grecques*
REL	*Revue des études latines*
RicSRel	*Ricerche di Storia Religiosa*
RIPh	*Revue Internationale de Philosophie*
RThAM	*Récherche de Théologie ancienne et médievale*
TAPA	*Transactions of the American Philological Association*
VigChr	*Vigiliae Christianae*

STUDIES IN AUGUSTINE
AND ERIUGENA

Introduction

The main themes of the papers collected here are Augustine's approaches to love (including sexuality) and Neoplatonism. These are important themes and have been constant in the study of Augustine throughout the passing century. The former of these has, rightly, received increasing attention in a wider context in recent years—as one is reminded by such books as Peter Brown's *The Body and Society* and— even if unsound on Augustine—Elaine Pagel's *Adam, Eve and the Serpent*. To both themes I have made a modest contribution in these papers and elsewhere.

It is the nature of such papers as are reproduced here to attempt to put their points in context, so that, since the papers are prepared for different occasions and audiences, there is much inevitable repetition of relevant background material. Since, moreover, Augustine himself tended to return again and again in an obsessive way to ideas to which he attached overriding importance in his own life and in the lives of others, there creeps in here additional repetition; for prominent among such ideas were those of love and Neoplatonism. It is hardly necessary to say that my views have developed and changed on particulars over the years.

The consideration of any treatment by any author of any theme must first take account of the extent to which the documents in which the theme occurs are more or less historical or more or less fictional. This is especially true of Augustine, who penned for us the immortal and alluring, but by no means uncomplicated, *Confessions*. We need to be able to tease out the historical from the fictional in it. Its frequent use of quotations from Scripture, for example, in lieu of the straightforward recital of fact, can be less helpful in conveying this fact than one too easily assumes—just as, by the way, the presence of some of the same scriptural phrases in St. Patrick's *Confessio* and Augustine's *Confessions* to "describe" similar experiences cannot in itself establish their connection. Writers of this time fell back on a well-known text from Scripture as one might on a proverb, only much more frequently. With this minor point

I begin. Then I proceed to attempt to distinguish between event and make believe in the artist that was Augustine.

This leads in to the treatment of women and love, which has to be seen against the background of the Greek and Roman—but especially Roman—world and also, in Augustine's later life, of Hebraic Revelation. Here I focus on Virgil, partly because he is for me the most sensitive and imaginative of all poets (as he may well also have been for Augustine), but also because his *Aeneid* was truly the Epic of Rome—and Rome was the context of Augustine's life. Its central theme, that one's personal desires must yield to the service of the Fatherland no matter how painful the cost, had been lived fully by so many Roman worthies whose names were glorified down through the centuries—Brutus, Torquatus, Curtius, the Decii, Regulus, Cincinnatus, and so on. While they were imitated—it was the thesis of Sallust that impressed Augustine enormously—Rome would continue to live in immortal glory. Their names decorate the pages of Augustine's *City of God* as exemplars worthy of imitation especially by Christians. Augustine chose for himself the ideal of following the first of all these worthies, Aeneas.

Like Virgil, if not Aeneas, Augustine was susceptible to an intense and refined sensuality and expressed this with much feeling. Exceptionally in his generation of Christians he insisted even to old age that the term *amor* for love should be used not only of human love but also as equivalent to *dilectio* or *caritas*, which was applied to the divine. Thus he not only remained loyal to human love but elevated it beyond reckoning. It is not generally realized how much honor Augustine does to love and, for him, as a matter of course, sexuality. Nevertheless, as for Virgil, Aeneas, and the antique heroes of Rome, love for him too must yield to duty—duty to God. Love was, in fact, a merciless destroyer, as could be seen especially in the case of Dido, driven to suicide in choosing love instead of duty. "And so two loves have made two cities: namely, love of self even to the contempt of God, the earthly, but love of God even to the contempt of self, the heavenly." Augustine was above all else a Roman, partly in birth, wholly in education, particularly in profession as a rhetor and, I would say, even by cast of mind. With his Roman predecessors he took his stand on *moribus antiquis*.

He took hard decisions on love. Unlike other Fathers, he insisted that "man" was created animal, and was then equally male and female, who could have blamelessly exercised their sexuality even in Eden. Nor did he accept that the original sin had anything to do with sex: it was a sin, he said, of disobedience. Yet he uniquely associated the transmission of that sin to all mankind with concupiscence, which, again, while not itself a true sin, was yet, he says, a sin in a manner of speaking (*modo quodam loquendi*). One sorrowful line from Virgil haunted him even late in life: it describes the emotional turmoil in Aeneas's mind as he abandons Dido and follows Jupiter's command: "His resolution abides; unavailingly the tears roll down." There is the paradox of Augustine, the man, as he calls himself, who had been in love with love. Here Augustine shows himself voluntarist above all, and less an intellectual. Here he was an inheritor of ancient Rome, creating a new, a Christian empire.

To have a fuller understanding of Augustine's complex attitude to sexuality and women, one must read his mature work *Genesis Understood Literally*, which I examine in *The Creation of Man in de Genesi ad litteram*. Here the Bible is helped out with Neoplatonism. One again, love, irresistible, is the destroyer.

From Boissier and Harnack in 1888 until Alfaric in 1918, the view had on the whole prevailed among scholars that Augustine's conversion in 386 had been rather to Neoplatonism, especially to the teaching of Plotinus, than to Catholicism. It was even contended by Gourdon that Augustine did not fully embrace Catholicism until a few years after he became a bishop in 396—not an impossibility at that time in North Africa. As this century proceeded that view was more and more challenged, until in 1950 Courcelle demonstrated that just precisely in Milan, when Augustine was there, and precisely with a lead from Ambrose, his proclaimed spiritual father, a *synthesis* of Catholicism and Neoplatonism was available to him. Augustine's own earliest writings were optimistic on the extent of the role Neoplatonic philosophy could play in such a synthesis: the few who were capable of following the independent way of reason could hope to understand whatever was taught by faith; and they especially could exploit fully the teachings of revelation. If, however, there should appear to be a conflict between faith and reason (for there could not really be, since the one God was the source and illumination of both) Augustine clearly proclaimed that he would take the side of Christ over that of Plato. An emphasis on liberal arts as necessary, not for the practice, but for happiness in understanding faith, was especially associated with Porphyry, as I indicate.

By 1954 when the centenary of Augustine's birth was celebrated in Paris—the heyday of Augustinian scholarship in this century—the question of Augustine's Neoplatonism occupied, in the opinion of some, excessive attention. In spite of such attention there was considerable vagueness on the question. The point, for example, of how Augustine reconciled the "immaterialism" of Neoplatonic eschatology with the "materialism" of Catholicism, although a crucial matter, was little addressed. And although Theiler had given his vote for Porphyry as the Neoplatonist who influenced Augustine's conversion almost exclusively, and Henry rather favored Plotinus, even scholars who would allow a role to both seemed to acquiesce in the proposition that Plotinus played the greater part in that event. This was assumed in spite of Augustine's clear estimate (however inappropriate this seems to us) that Porphyry was the greater philosopher and the more influential among his contemporaries, and in spite of the fact that Porphyry received far more attention from Augustine. Moreover the whole passage in the *Confessions* (VII, IX, 13ff.), where Augustine compares what he found and did not find in certain Neoplatonist books with what was to be found in the Prologue to St. John's Gospel, has a close parallel in *City of God* X, where Porphyry is explicitly in question.

My Oxford thesis (1945), the *Young Augustine,* and papers published over many subsequent years (including some collected here) kept hammering at the claim of Porphyry to the critical, but not exclusive, role in Augustine's conversion. The refusal of the "Neoplatonists" to accept that Christ was the Mediator between God and man is central to the passage in the *Confessions* where the Neoplatonist books are in question. I made the case that the Neoplatonist involved is Porphyry, and that Augustine's rejection of Porphyry, who refused to accept the Incarnation, triggered, so to speak, his conversion. Support for my view in relation to Augustine's parting from Porphyry on the question of Christ's Mediation has grown—from G. Madec, for example, more recently.[1]

I had assumed, with Courcelle, for example, that the work of Porphyry that had the critical influence on Augustine's conversion was one known as *"De regressu animae,"* a title mentioned only by Augustine and by him only twice—in the tenth book of the *City of God*. I gradually began to suspect that this was, as often happened, no more than a descriptive title. Lewy, writing independently, came to the same conclusion. I soon felt that the passages attributed to the *"De regressu animae"* were to be related in some way to the *Philosophy from Oracles* of Porphyry, well known from Eusebius and explicitly mentioned by Augustine in a later book of the *City of God* itself. The prevailing opinion on the *Philosophy from Oracles,* however, was that it was an early work, characterized by belief in theurgy, and did not (however odd that might seem) include any oracle from a famous collection known as the *Chaldaean Oracles*, made well before the time of Porphyry. The *"De regressu animae,"* by contrast—it was supposed—had serious philosophical reflection (and so must have been written late in Porphyry's life, after he had been the disciple of Plotinus) and did contain some of the *Chaldaean Oracles*: its *ton* was irreconcilable with that of the *Philosophy from Oracles*. It is well to bear in mind, however, in connection with the question of *ton*, that in both cases we are dealing with some, perhaps quite few, fragments only. And as a matter of fact the preface to the *Philosophy from Oracles* states that it treats for the most part of *philosophical* themes and only a little of oracles; and Lewy and I quite independently have shown that it did contain some of the *Chaldaean Oracles*.

Porphyry's *Philosophy from Oracles,* unlike the *"De regressu animae,"* was very well known indeed. It was a bitter attack on Christianity and the followers of Christ, although it accepted that Christ was a good man: but he was not divine. It was answered by, for example, Eusebius of Caesarea, from whom we derive most of its fragments, and Arnobius. I have made the case in my *Philosophy from Oracles in Augustine* and *Charter of Christendom*, for example, that Augustine's *City of God* is very much a reply to this work of Porphyry.

In my *Philosophy from Oracles in Augustine* I argue that Porphyry's *"De regressu animae"* is part of, or to be identified with, his *Philosophy from Oracles*. This argument is entirely independent of the question of Porphyry's role in Augustine's conversion: *both* works are Porphyry's. The argument, as conducted, is, on the positive side, wholly internal to the works of Augustine. It tries to demonstrate that whole themes in many works of Augustine are related to the *Philosophy from Oracles*. While this method is dictated by Augustine's obsessional use and re-use, often with modification, of themes that made a deep impression on him, it is cumbersome inasmuch as it does not allow the use of the technique of parallel passages, where the phrase is the unit. Here the theme must be our concern. If the proceeding is to be scientific, it must be comprehensive and involve the repetition of similar passages requiring some comment however, necessarily, brief. I can hardly believe that many would have the courage to expose themselves sufficiently to such tedious argument. Nevertheless my argument was well received by many and described in the best modern commentary on the *City of God* as well defended. But Pierre Hadot, who in a very long review showed himself generous in his appreciation of the nature of the argument, was not convinced. Recent treatment of the point by A. Smith, however, does not accept Hadot's position.[2] Most recently Pier Franco Beatrice accepts my "demonstration."[3]

My detailed exegesis of *Contra Academicos* II.5 issues in balancing more evenly the claims on Augustine of the Scriptures—St. Paul especially—and the Life of Anthony with those of the Neoplatonists at the moment, so to speak, of his conversion. This text had been interpreted (also by me) as referring principally, if not exclusively, to the Neoplatonists—reflecting the tendency since Harnack and Boissier (which even still continues) to see Neoplatonism everywhere in the early *Dialogues* of Augustine, and by implication to call into question in varying degrees the historicity of the *Confessions*. It is hard to shake off Plotinus! I think I show that this text is in fact in accord with the *Confessions* and underscores the point that at his conversion Augustine accepted not just the Incarnation (which, for a Neoplatonist, involved materialism) and Mediatorship of Christ, but fellowship with Christians and the ideals of Christian living. As he remained, nevertheless, as he says, expectant of enlightenment from the Neoplatonists,[4] this involved for him some Roman eclecticism which—in this matter—remained with him to the end of his days.

I was not unduly surprised to find that the Platonist themes that Aquinas explicitly or demonstrably related to Augustine are in the main the very themes the latter discusses in the tenth book of the *City of God*, where he is measuring up to Porphyry. They constitute, in my belief, a major, if not the major, part of Augustine's experience of the Neoplatonists.

That Augustine departed from the Neoplatonists in most important matters and thereby, in his commanding position, filtered little Neoplatonism into the West is readily seen in the consideration of his influence on Johannes Scottus Eriugena (ninth century). Eriugena is aghast at Augustine's "materialism," especially in relation to the resurrection of Christ's and our own bodies, and the vision of God in the afterlife. Here, to excuse Augustine, Eriugena supposes that, perhaps, Augustine had one teaching for the intellectual few (who could appreciate a purely intellectual existence) and a quite different one for the materially minded mass of men (who could understand only fleshly things). Had not St. Paul said that milk was given to infants, but a stronger food to the grownups? As it happens, Augustine himself was more than a little given to such suppositions in relation to others who might seem to disagree with him. Without going so far as believing that Augustine, like Pilate, despaired of truth and was, therefore, pragmatic, it is clear that he could bring himself on occasion to take short cuts. The Romans were above all interested in happiness, in morals, in the practical running of life, and made unembarrassed profession of this. So, ultimately, was Augustine. Eriugena, no Roman, was not so much a voluntarist.

Eriugena's determined efforts to interpret Augustine as being on his, very Neoplatonic, side has the welcome result of reminding us that Augustine was sometimes undogmatic, even on occasions profoundly aporetic. He might for the most part take what seem definite positions—and in due course his later followers represented them as even more definite. But precisely on the question of the resurrection of the body he does at least once state plainly that he doesn't think that the soul will have "some kind of a body" when it has departed from this earthly body. But this—and some other phrases of wider application in this kind of context—is at variance with his views as normally expressed and as his followers have passed them on. But from it one sees the persistence, even to the end of his life, of the Augustine who relished the rational speculation of the Neoplatonists. We should never forget this side of Augustine too.

Pierre Hadot, following on from the approach of my *Philosophy from Oracles in Augustine* wrote: "Je dirais que le livre de M. O'Meara me fait souhaiter une étude génétique des schémas augustiniens." I comment on, among other matters in the last papers given here, his own subsequent use of such a more formal, "genetic" method, and also of its use by O. du Roy and, to some extent, by A. Mandouze. Nevertheless, I am only too well aware that actual demonstration by such a method is not often possible, especially when one is dealing with fragmentary material: one hopes only to advance a better-working hypothesis. *En passant*, I note that Hadot later evinced a greater appreciation of Porphyry as a philosopher, if also less affected by Plotinus, and that it was his influence, rather than that of Plotinus, that was more likely to be exercised by Victorinus on Augustine. This last contention was the burden of my *Young Augustine*. I have to observe that in some of the last papers included I follow with perhaps excessive zeal my counsel, given there, not to translate certain kinds of texts.

JOHN J. O'MEARA

PART I

CONFESSION AND

HISTORICITY

1

The Historicity of Augustine's Early Dialogues

❧

Statement of the Problem

The question of the historicity of the *Dialogues of Cassiciacum*, composed by Augustine shortly before his baptism, is of considerable interest and importance, not only because of the peculiar character of the works themselves,[1] but also because it is maintained by many scholars that the *Dialogues* are not only at variance with, but also more reliable than, the *Confessions* in their account of Augustine's mental outlook in A.D. 386.

D. Ohlmann, J. Van Haeringen and R. Hirzel,[2] among others,[3] have examined this matter. Ohlmann and Van Haeringen hold a brief for the historicity of the *Dialogues*. Opposing Ohlmann and Van Haeringen is R. Hirzel, who treats of the question only in a passing way in his large work on the Dialogue. He maintains, not that the *Dialogues* are entirely fictional, but that there is a considerable element of fiction in them. In particular the claim that a *notarius* or reporter was present during the disputations he regards, in direct opposition to Ohlmann, as fictional. In this article an attempt is made to weigh the evidence in favour of the historicity and then to urge the case for the opposition.

The Evidence For

I

Ohlmann[4] maintains that Augustine's *Dialogues* were something new in the genre: the conversations did take place; they were duly recorded by "*notarii*"; the *Dialogues* as we have them, apart from stylistic modifications and omissions, are faithful reports of the disputations actually held. In short what we read was actually said by the person to whom it is attributed, though not perhaps in exactly the same form of words,[5] or in such a summary manner. There was no fiction employed, or practically[6] none. This is what we shall mean by the term *historical* and this is the position in defence of which Ohlmann argues as follows:

There are the many assurances of Augustine himself[7]—those within the *Dialogues* for example; but the greatest stress must be placed on those which are given by Augustine many years after the composition of the works. Ohlmann places much emphasis on these latter. These read as follows:

> 1. C IX, 7:
> "ubi quid egerim in litteris iam quidem seruientibus tibi, sed adhuc superbiae scholam tamquam in pausatione anhelantibus, testantur libri disputati cum praesentibus et cum ipso me solo coram te; quae autem cum absente Nebridio, testantur epistulae."
>
> 2. R I, 2:
> "librum de beata uita non post libros de Academicis, sed inter illos ut scriberem contigit. ex occasione quippe ortus est diei natalis mei tridui disputatione conpletus, sicut satis ipse indicat. in quo libro constitit inter nos, qui simul quaerebamus, non esse beatam uitam nisi perfectam cognitionem dei."

Ohlmann allows that the testimony of the first of these passages is not decisive.[8] The evidence given so far, he thinks, finds its true interpretation in the passage from the *Retractationes*. At the end of his life, and in an independent book, Augustine affirms the general historicity of *De beata vita*: "sicut satis ipse indicat." Ohlmann is satisfied that his case is as good as proven.[9]

Ohlmann then proceeds to give another line of argument already presented by Bindemann.[10] If the *Dialogues* are not what they profess to be, *viz.* touched-up records of actual conversations, then we must conclude that Augustine's first attempts in the dialogue form were a dismal failure. This, however, cannot be allowed.[11] Therefore, Ohlmann argues, the *Dialogues* are what they profess to be. Ohlmann examines the argument of *De ordine* to demonstrate his contention that it could not have been the composition of Augustine writing by himself. He has no difficulty in pointing out what would be defects in the work[12] if it were considered as being just another dialogue in the traditional mould, but which he regards as the highest art in a new type of dialogue. He writes enthusiastically: "ejusmodi dialogos quis unquam veterum philosophorum finxit? Singula ipse velim inspicias insignemque in omnibus leporem agnosces . . . atque novum dialogorum genus idque summa magni scriptoris arte excultum ab Hirzelio non agnitum esse mecum miraberis."[13]

Ohlmann draws a contrast between the *Contra Academicos*, *De beata vita,* and *De ordine* on the one hand, and the *Soliloquia* and the other *Dialogues* of this early period on the other. The latter are entirely fictitious: there is no mise-en-scène, no prologue, no epilogue, and no interruptions. The *Retractationes* refer to them in a way which marks the distinction: Augustine does not, so Ohlmann asserts,[14] use such a term of them as *"quaerebamus."* In one place in the *Retractationes* Augustine recants something attributed to Evodius in the *De libero arbitrio*: that is only proper—"cum dialogus *fictus* sit."[15] The conclusion is that the former group of *Dialogues* is historical.[16]

The discussion about the dates on which the three *Dialogues* took place has some relevance to our question. If the various indications given in the *Dialogues* and the *Retractationes*—many of them clear in their import—all point to one definite sequence, then this would be a confirmation of the historicity of the *Dialogues*[17] as understood by Ohlmann. After an examination of the matter Ohlmann elects for the order found in Table 1.[18]

Table 1

Date (A.D. 386)	Dialogue
November 10th	Contra Academicos I, 5–11
11th	Contra Academicos I, 11–16
12th	Contra Academicos I, 16–25
13th	De beata vita 7–17
14th	De beata vita 17–23
15th	De beata vita 23–26
16th	De ordine I, 6–27
17th	De ordine I, 27–33
18th, 19th	—
20th	Contra Academicos II, 10–14; 14–24[19]
21st	Contra Academicos II, 25–30
22nd	Contra Academicos III, 1–7; 7–45
23rd	De ordine II, 1–19; 19–54[20]
(vel paulo post)	

Finally, Ohlmann insists that only a Dialogue as historical as he claims the *Dialogues of Cassiciacum* to be, could descend to such unusual[21] and tedious[22] detail. In no fictitious dialogue could the author give himself such generous praise as is found of Augustine in the *Contra Academicos*.[23]

II

We shall now examine what J. H. Van Haeringen has to offer by way of special contribution to the evidence for the historicity of the Dialogues.[24]

Van Haeringen immediately fixes upon Augustine's "invention" in the dialogue form: the actual employment of the *"notarius"*[25] who took down everything as spoken[26] and from whose record the *Dialogues* were later written up.[27] Not everything was included in the written *Dialogues*.[28] There was, however, little departure from the account given in the notes.[29] If there was any departure, it was for the most part concerned with style.[30] It is clear that he understands the question of the historicity of the *Dialogues* in the same way as does Ohlmann.

Van Haeringen appears to agree with Ohlmann in his main arguments, but he offers as against Tillemont[31] and Ohlmann a completely new order for the *Dialogues* (found in table 2). He suggests[32] that we should distinguish between the order in which the disputations *occurred*, and the order in which they were *written*. The two orders do not coincide.

Table 2

Order of	
Occurrence	*Composition*
Contra Academicos I	Contra Academicos I
Contra Academicos II, III	De beata vita
De ordine I	De ordine I, II
De beata vita	Contra Academicos II, III
De ordine II	

Van Haeringen adopts this rejected theory in order to overcome the difficulties which stand in the way of Ohlmann's view,[33] and which, he believes, Ohlmann has not explained away. He contends that the *"otiosi"*[34] must be understood in a full sense; that is, no disputation took place between the first and second books of the *Contra Academicos*.[35] On the other hand, it could be said that the *De beata vita* and the *De ordine* I and II were *composed* or *written up* between the composition of the first and second books of the *Contra Academicos*.[36] Moreover, this order explains a number of other difficulties overlooked by Ohlmann.[37]

The Evidence Against

I

The first serious objection to the historicity of the *Dialogues* arises naturally from the form in which we find them—the dialogue form.

Augustine edited and published the *Dialogues* and always regarded them as *his* books.[38] These are indisputable facts. That he regarded them—and the *Contra Academicos* in particular—as serious and important[39]—is equally certain. There is no question here of retrospective publishing of work carried through without any eye on publication.[40] There is a deliberate choice of the literary form and attention paid to models.[41] It is clear that Augustine was intent on producing literary works.

That Augustine had ambitions, through, if not in, the literary field is beyond a shadow of doubt. These ambitions his parents and benefactor, Romanianus, had encouraged from his earliest years.[42] Later on he himself attempted to win the recognition of Hierius and Rome with his *De pulchro et apto*, dedicated to Hierius, "quem non noueram facie, sed amaueram hominem ex doctrinae fama . . . et quaedam uerba eius audieram, et placuerant mihi . . . et magnum quiddam mihi erat, si sermo meus et studia mea illi uiro innotescerent . . ."[43] This was about five or six years before his conversion. In the meantime he came to Rome, managed to attract the notice of Symmachus, and by his aid became Master of Rhetoric at Milan.[44] Before a year had elapsed he had delivered a panegyric on the occasion of the consulship of the all-powerful Bauto (A.D. 385).[45] He was also, it would appear, chosen to deliver another panegyric before the young Emperor.[46] Such distinctions would lead to the highest offices of the Empire.[47] At this period—that is, immediately before he retired to Cassiciacum—Augustine was consumed with anxiety over success, and overworked both in his profession and in canvassing influential supporters.[48] He says himself that he could easily have won office.[49] Already, however, his conversion was making worldly success less attractive. But there is no evidence that his conversion affected his interest in writing. On the contrary, his conversion seems to have directed all his energies into writing. He cemented his relations with the Christian-Neoplatonist writer Flavius Mallius Theodorus of Milan, by addressing to him *De beata vita* and by referring in *De ordine*[50] to his works as models which he himself could follow in his own *Dialogues*. He embarked upon a series of writings,[51] and although it was never completed, he did not lay down his pen until his death. When he came to write his *Retractationes* he did not draw any distinction between his earlier *Dialogues* and his later works in the point of authorship. They were all *his*: his συγγράμματα not his ὑπομνήματα.[52]

In *Contra Academicos, De beata vita,* and *De ordine* Augustine followed a well established and popular model: the dialogue form, known best to him probably from Plato and Cicero.[53] In doing so he inevitably committed himself to certain conventions which his public would demand, and which would certainly cause him to modify the accuracy (that is, on the supposition that the discussions were held) of his picture.[54] The closer, moreover, a dialogue approaches the traditional type, the more conscious, it may not unreasonably be argued, the imitation; and the more conscious the imitation, the more suspect the historicity. Consequently, it is necessary for us to determine the extent to which the conventions of the dialogue form are found in the works under consideration. We shall on this point *here* confine ourselves to the *Contra Academicos*.

By the time Augustine had set about publishing the *Contra Academicos*, not only had there been many models of the dialogue form, but these models had been discussed. There were definitions of the dialogue and classifications[55] of its different types. Cicero was undoubtedly Augustine's chief model; his *Academica* cannot have been far from Augustine's mind while the *Contra Academicos* was in process of composition.[56]

It will be sufficient for our purpose here to indicate the prominent features which the *Contra Academicos* (and the two other *Dialogues of Cassiciacum*) share in common with other well-known dialogues.

There is the division of the work into Books, a commonplace of the dialogue-form. In the *Contra Academicos* each of the first two books has a preface.[57] This is said to be an Aristotelian feature.[58] This preface is often an introductory letter addressed to the person to whom the work is dedicated. It is usually of some length and is often autobiographical. Such prefaces are found in Cicero's *De natura deorum, Tusculanae disputationes, De finibus,* and *De oratore*. The prefaces to the *Dialogues of Cassiciacum* have these features.[59]

We must note, however, the intrusion of another, though related, genre into each of the two prefaces of the *Contra Academicos*—the protreptic. The prose protreptic developed out of maxim-poetry,[60] and the Sophists were chiefly responsible for its creation. In its usual form it is an earnest exhortation addressed, and in Hellenistic times, dedicated, to some person whom, it is supposed, the author wishes to convert to a way of life. The protreptic was sometimes cast in dialogue form.[61] There was a continuous line of protreptics right from the fourth century B.C. to the period of Augustine's life.[62]

Augustine had Cicero's *Hortensius*, a dialogue-protreptic, close to his thoughts when the *Contra Academicos* was being proposed. He used it as a kind of text book for the debate.[63] We cannot wonder then, if the force of this type of writing is felt not only in the introductory letter to Romanianus, but also in the disputations in which the young men engage.

It is important to insist upon the "schoolroom" atmosphere of the *Contra Academicos*, for this mise-en-scène precisely was used in many dialogues which make no claim to be in any sense historical. Such are the *De finibus*[64] and the *De oratore* of Cicero and, among others, the *Charmides, Euthydemus, Lysis, Phaedo, Philebus*,[65] and *Theaetetus*[66] of Plato. In the *Contra Academicos* discussions open with a reference to one preceding[67] and close with a determining of what is to follow.[68] A summary of what had been said in the absence[69] of one of the interlocutors is given to him when he is present again. One feels that one is present at a set course of instruction, conducted, however, by a master who is deeply interested in the *spiritual* welfare of his charges.[70] Augustine's attitude to Licentius and Trygetius is always that of a master[71] and never anything else. Even, as is the way in some such dialogues, if he be appointed referee,[72] he is always director[73] also. And when one of the youthful interlocutors says something which a reader would feel to be beyond that interlocutor's capacity, there is the usual refuge in the expression of utter astonishment.

Next comes for discussion the guarantee usually given in dialogues that the reader is presented with a faithful report of what actually took place. In the course of the *Contra Academicos*, *De beata vita* and *De ordine* there are twenty such references. We are told that a *notarius* took down every single word that was said;[74] the entrance of an interlocutor was noted;[75] we have the actual words—at least in the *Contra Academicos* I[76]—of Augustine and Alypius, if not, sometimes at any rate, those also of the other members of the group;[77] in any case we are given the gist of each speaker's contribution.[78]

There is nothing peculiar in the character of the guarantee of historicity here given. The purporting to furnish absolute accuracy is not new.[79] Nor is the further assertion that such accuracy is based on notes made, not *after,*[80] but *during* the debates. Hirzel[81] appeals to a second-century gnostic text, the *Pistis Sophia* which could have been known to Augustine. It is not, however, likely to have been read by him, at any rate before A.D. 386. But we can instance at least one case of a guarantee similar to that given in the *Contra Academicos*. No one would maintain that the *Epinomis* is historical; yet there we read:

> Θεογονίαν τοίνυν καὶ ζωογονίαν ἀναγκαῖον, ὡς ἔοικε, πρῶτόν μοι κακῶς ἀπεικασάντων τῶν ἔμπροσθεν βέλτιον ἀπεικάσαι κατὰ τὸν ἔμπροσθεν λόγον, ἀναλαβόντα ὃν πρὸς τοὺς ἀσεβεῖς ἐπικεχείρηκα λόγους, φράζων ὡς εἰσὶ θεοὶ ἐπιμελούμενοι πάντων, σμικρῶν καὶ μειζόνων, καὶ σχεδὸν ἀπαραμύθητοι τῶν περὶ τὰ δίκαιά εἰσι πράγματα, εἰ δὴ μέμνησθέ γε, ὦ Κλεινία · ἐλάβετε μὲν γὰρ δὴ καὶ ὑπομνήματα. καὶ γὰρ ἦν τὰ ῥηθέντα τότε καὶ μάλα ἀληθῆ. 980 C-D.

It may be that ὑπομνήματα does not extend to the fullness claimed for the records of the *notarius* in the *Contra Academicos*,[82] though we cannot deny that it might.[83] There is this other point too, that the ὑπομνήματα are here supposed to have been taken during, probably, the *Laws*, and do not supply the material for either the *Laws* or the *Epinomis*. All the same, the record-taking in the *Contra Academicos* is not less likely to be a fiction than the note-taking of the *Epinomis*. This is especially true when we recall that record-taking was very common in the fourth century A.D.[84] Unless we deny all originality and intelligence to Augustine, we must suppose that he was capable of employing a fiction which was as plausible in his day as the taking of notes, if not actual records, was in the time of Plato.

We might indicate another instance—and a very remarkable one—of record-taking. This time also it is unquestionably a fiction. One Thessalos in a document of the first century A.D.[85] tells us that he took an accurate record of the revelation which was afforded him: "de mon côté, toujours prévoyant, j'avais apporté, sans le dire au prêtre, du papier et de l'encre pour prendre note, le cas échéant, de ce qui serait dit."[86] Indeed this provision of paper and ink for seances of all kinds was a commonplace.[87]

For the reasons we have advanced, then, we conclude that there is no trust whatever to be placed in the claim that the historicity of the *Dialogues of Cassiciacum* is guaranteed by the alleged records of a notary who was present.

One must note too how traditional is the range of τόποι treated of in the *Contra Academicos* and the other *Dialogues of Cassiciacum*. Apart from the more general questions of knowledge, happiness, and the order of the universe—questions which constantly recur, of course, in philosophical dialogues—there occur here many of the τόποι that are so common in the spiritual-guide-and-disciple type of dialogue. We instance the soul's return to God, the necessity for self-knowledge, for knowledge of God, and for knowledge by revelation; the motifs of philosophy as a harbour, of corporal life as a prison, of the activity of demon-spirits of the air, of the masses who are sunk in ignorance and the few who are wise.[88] Present too are the warnings against a *lis de verbis*[89] and the insufficiency of definitions.[90] And finally, there are the usual commendations of dialectic.[91] There is indeed very little that is new in the *Dialogues* of Augustine.[92]

Lastly, there are points of detail in the *Dialogues of Cassiciacum* which can be attested elsewhere. The occasion of the *De beata vita* was supposed to be Augustine's birthday. The traditional dialogue was often associated with feasts[93] and it was the custom in the Neoplatonic schools to celebrate birthdays especially.[94] Another point which deserves some attention is the inspiration which is attributed to Licentius. Such inspiration or possession, especially where poets are concerned, is a common feature and a useful *deus ex machina* in the traditional dialogues.[95] It was not uncommon for the last speaker in a Socratic debate to express the opinion that, of course, his opponent will easily refute him some other time.[96] And naturally many dialogues end with a prayer to a deity.[97]

It is obvious, then, that both in broad outline and also in detail Augustine's early dialogues conform consciously and very closely to the traditional type. Such close approximation naturally arouses suspicions in our minds. We cannot place confidence in any claim made in the works themselves unless there is extrinsic support—*nosti morem dialogorum*.[98]

II

A second serious argument against the historicity of the *Dialogues* is suggested by the change from a dialectical method of enquiry to what amounts almost to a formal lecture—a change which happens both in the *Contra Academicos* and the *De ordine*.[99] This is common in earlier dialogues.[100] Indeed, few authors could attain to the same dramatic power that pervades the dialectical arguments in some of Plato's works, and it was but a question of time until the "Aristotelian" dialogues of set speeches became the usual type.[101] These are seen, for example, in the works of Cicero. It looks as if Augustine tried to do what Plato did, and failed. The first book of the *Contra Academicos*, for example, makes an honest attempt at being dialectical. It succeeds in this, but it fails to stir one's interest or advance the argument. The second book begins to introduce set speeches,[102] but it is still marred, as is the first, by frequent interruptions. The debate on the questions at issue has not got far beyond the introductory stage even at the end of the second book.[103] It is only when set speeches are developed that something is achieved, and in both the *Contra Academicos* and the *De ordine* the set speech extends to one-third of the whole work.

The introduction of set speeches, and particularly the longer speeches at the end of both the *Contra Academicos* (running to some six thousand words and without any interruption), and the *De ordine* (somewhat longer and with only slight interruption), while it helps the *Dialogues* in interest and argument, cannot but shake our confidence in the historicity claimed. In this matter we cannot ignore the fact that Augustine never again attempted dialogues either in the Platonic, "dialectical," or Aristotelian "expository," manner; the works soon to follow on the *Dialogues of Cassiciacum* are written, as were some of Porphyry's, in the manner of a catechism. The first step in the direction of the catechism was taken early in the second book of the *Contra Academicos*.[104] And just as the later dialogues are almost certainly fictional, so at least the second, longer, and more important sections of the *Contra Academicos* and *De ordine* arouse our deepest suspicions.[105]

III

A third difficulty against the historicity of the *Dialogues* is the improbability of certain episodes. The clearest instance is to be found in the first book of the *De ordine*.[106]

Even Ohlmann, following the suggestion of Kaibel, is prepared to admit that Augustine may have "invented" the mouse which disturbed Licentius.[107] Van Haeringen conjectures that some of the ideas attributed to Trygetius could not have been his: "quippe cum maiora sint, quam ut iuvenili menti congruant." He suggests, however, that Trygetius was more likely to be capable of such ideas than was Licentius.[108] Yet here in the *De ordine* Licentius is made to present doctrine which far transcends anything that Trygetius is represented as giving. We see then that even the exponents of the historicity of the *Dialogues* are somewhat embarrassed when confronted with the *De ordine*.

The first thing which causes some surprise is the time of the debate. The indications given suggest strongly that it started before midnight and continued until the morning.[109] None of the three participants would appear to have had any sleep at all. That Augustine should so unseasonably force upon them a debate in the early hours of the morning is not easily to be believed.

The second item on this point is connected with the choice of the chief speaker—Licentius. A discussion "de ordine" had been on demand by Zenobius, a friend of Augustine, for some time.[110] Augustine himself had always been agitated by this very question. Yet it is not Augustine who supplied the characteristically[111] Augustinian doctrine in this earlier portion (which is to be sent to Zenobius),[112] but Licentius, who, we are told, up to this showed not the slightest interest in the question,[113] nor had ever discussed it with his "tutor" Augustine.[114] It is to be noted that the debate is supposed to have arisen by accident. It was a too convenient accident! Augustine also is supposed to send an account of it to Zenobius.[115] The *De ordine* I was, in fact, published, and published in Augustine's name. Licentius' ideas, indeed, were deserving of attention. The attribution of such ideas to a youth, probably in his teens,[116] who for all his possible precocity and poetic temperament was so unlikely to have them, cannot but cause surprise. On Augustine's own showing Licentius seems to have had no previous experience in philosophy or philosophical debate. He had just read the *Hortensius*,[117] and had yielded a fickle allegiance to Philosophy. He had not read, we gather, Cicero's *Academica*.[118] We can hardly believe that Licentius really said what he is reported as saying.

Apparently Augustine expected that his readers would be surprised at such an improbable attribution;[119] for both himself and Trygetius are depicted as being amazed at the behaviour and knowledge of their companion.[120] Our suspicions are to that extent justified. But Augustine's explanation of what must be called a "phenomenon" does not allay our doubts. Licentius is said to be in some way inspired—much as Socrates was in the *Phaedrus*.[121] We can hardly believe that Licentius was really so inspired. It is something more than what we expect to happen in an exalted mood.[122] Augustine may have had some reason for employing what looks very like a "deus ex machina," but a "deus ex machina" sounds the knell on historicity.

All three factors, the time of the debate, the person who supplies the doctrine, and the means by which the incapacity of that person is overcome, together with a detail or two noted by others, combine to justify us in our belief that the account of the night debate in *De ordine* I is not historical. It is too improbable. No analysis can succeed in giving the impression of improbability which the text itself conveys.[123]

There are many other minor improbabilities occurring here and there through the *Dialogues*. Now it is a forced melodramatic passage which in its every detail provokes suspicion:[124] again, it is a defence of his (Augustine's) procedure in his treatment of the dialogue form.[125] There are other instances, too, where we feel that the speakers were hardly capable of enunciating the doctrines attributed to them.[126]

IV

A final difficulty against the historicity of the *Dialogues* is the fact that in spite of the alleged guaranteed accuracy of the records there are many discrepancies. This is immediately seen in the varying theories as to the dates and sequence of the *Dialogues*. The peculiar feature in this case is that each theory has to attempt to explain away clear evidence of equal authenticity with that on which itself is based: for all evidence is traced to the *notarius*. The theories cannot of their nature be reconciled. Either Augustine made a mistake in interpreting the records, or deliberately altered them as he pleased, or there were no records kept.

Conclusion

It is admitted by all that the *Dialogues of Cassiciacum* are not entirely fictional. They are to some extent, at any rate, related to facts. It is true that the interlocutors were such as they are represented to be, and at the time in question were actually in Cassiciacum, engaged in exercises such as are described in the *Dialogues*. So much can be gathered from the *Letters* and *Confessions*. The *Retractationes*, moreover, almost certainly guarantee the historicity of two details indicated in the *Dialogues*. From this we suppose that other details may be generally "historical," unless they give serious grounds for suspicion or contradict direct evidence.[127]

But the *Dialogues of Cassiciacum* are emphatically not reliable. They are written compositions of Augustine, and consciously follow closely, in outline and in detail, the form and matter of previous models. The internal assurances as to their "historicity" are worthless. A certain change in form of the *Contra Academicos* and the *De ordine*; the improbability of certain episodes; and the presence of discrepancies, remind us forcibly that Augustine availed himself freely of his privilege—claimed by himself and admitted by everybody—to employ fiction.

We cannot assess the extent to which fiction was employed. Very much could have been invented. At any rate there is ground for believing that the element of fiction is far from negligible.

2

"Arripui, aperui, et legi"
(*Confessions* VIII, 12, 29)

≥●

M. Pierre Courcelle in his *Recherches sur les Confessions de saint Augustin* (Paris, 1950, p. 190) says à propos of the garden scene in the conversion of St. Augustine: "Au cours de cette scène se produit une sorte de miracle; une voix jeune crie: '*Tolle, lege.*' Augustin considère ces paroles comme un avertissement divin, prend les *Epîtres* de saint Paul, jette les yeux sur le premier verset venu et décide d'y conformer sa vie. Ni dans ce que j'ai appelé les '*premières Confessions,*' ni par la suite, Augustin ne rappelle cet épisode."

Few readers of the *Confessions* will fail to single out the garden scene as being at least one of the high points of the whole book. The intensity of the drama represented there is so great that they will remember it long after other episodes described in the book have been forgotten. Augustine himself was doubtless aware of the overwhelming power of the passage, and even if it had little or no historical background—but, of course, all the more so if, as I believe, it was on the whole historical—he was not likely to let it slip from his memory. In point of fact Augustine shows a distinct tendency to repeat topics that have seemed to him important, and one could say almost *a priori* that this very garden scene, whether historical or not, was bound to be used by him again and even more than once or twice: for in many ways it was the central crisis of his whole life. Courcelle's assertion, if true, must startle and surprise. But is it true? I shall give reasons here for believing that it is not.

Augustine refers to his conversion a number of times in the *Dialogues* written before his baptism. The very first such reference not only uses some of the actual phrases later used in the relevant passage in the *Confessions* (VIII, 29), but also is invested with the same highly charged emotion. The passage is as follows:

"Cum ecce tibi libri quidam pleni, ut ait Celsinus, bonas res Arabicas ubi exhalarunt in nos, ubi illi flammulae instillarunt pretiosissimi unguenti guttas paucissimas, incredibile, Romaniane, incredibile et ultra quam de me fortasse et tu credis—quid amplius dicam?—etiam mihi ipsi de me ipso incredibile incendium concitarunt. Quis me tunc honor, quae hominum pompa, quae inanis famae cupiditas, quod denique huius mortalis uitae fomentum atque retinaculum commouebat? Prorsus totus in me cursim redibam. Respexi tamen confitebor, quasi de itinere in illam religionem, quae pueris nobis insita est et medullitus inplicata; uerum autem ipsa ad se nescientem rapiebat. Itaque titubans properans haesitans arripio apostolum Paulum. Neque enim uere, inquam, isti tanta potuissent uixissentque ita, ut eos uixisse manifestum est, si eorum litterae atque rationes huic tanto bono aduersarentur. Perlegi totum intentissime atque cautissime." (CA II, 5)

This first description of his conversion by Augustine is brief to the point of obscurity. Courcelle does not fail to notice this and proposes his own elucidation. The passage, however, is not so difficult to interpret if we remember its relation to the fuller account of the same incident in the *Confessions*. The text in the *Contra Academicos* describes three separate stages in the conversion: the reading of Neoplatonist books, the comparing of their teaching with that of the Scriptures and especially of St. Paul, and finally his consultation of St. Paul in obedience to the command of the *tolle lege*. These three stages are described separately but successively in the *Confessions* also. In the *Contra Academicos* the description of the first of the three stages is completed with the words: *"prorsus totus in me cursim redibam."* But the other two stages are telescoped in what remains; and it is the third stage, the ever memorable *tolle lege*, which dominates—*as far as the expressions and emotion go*. The *content*, however, belongs mostly to the second stage, his reading, that is, through *all* of St. Paul and comparing it with Neoplatonism.

Augustine has here allowed his memory of the *tolle lege* scene to intervene and come to the forefront of his mind so as to overshadow his memory of his more prolonged study of St. Paul. So vivid in fact was his recollection of that excited reaching out for the volume of the Apostle at the bidding of the *tolle lege* that in this place—and elsewhere—he uses not only *itaque*, but also *arripere*, and always with words denoting great expectation. His words graphically reproduce the dramatic motions of getting up from the ground where he was lying, and seizing St. Paul's text from the table—motions which are particularly if not exclusively applicable to the garden scene. In short, in this passage from the *Contra Academicos* he is covering the same ground as he was to cover later in the

Confessions, and inasmuch as the expressions and emotion of this passage are distinctly echoed again in the *Confessions,* this is one instance where Augustine quite clearly recalls the episode of the garden scene.

Coming to the expressions themselves—it is undeniable that the phrases: *"itaque titubans, properans, haesitans, arripio apostolum Paulum . . . perlegi totum intentissime atque cautissime,"* of the *Contra Academicos* are but echoed in the *"itaque concitus redii . . . arripui (codicem apostoli), aperui, et legi in silentio capitulum"* of the *Confessions.* In both the *Contra Academicos* and the *Confessions* at this point he refers not only to the light which dawned upon his mind after the sudden consultation of St. Paul, but also to the fact that the thought of Antony, his monks and their lives occurred to him at the moment of the *tolle lege* (*tunc uero quantulocunque iam lumine asperso, tanta se mihi philosophiae facies aperuit . . . neque enim uere, inquam, isti tanta potuissent uixissentque ita, ut eos uixisse manifestum est* and *luce securitatis infusa cordi meo . . . audieram enim de Antonio . . . vade vende omnia*). The expressions are by no means close: but the items they describe are identical. There is one other expression, however, which may be of the greatest significance. In the *Contra Academicos* we read: *"respexi tantum, confitebor, quasi de itinere in illam religionem, quae pueris nobis insita est et medullitus inplicata; uerum autem ipsa ad se nescientem rapiebat."* Is this echoed in the corresponding passage of the *Confessions* in the words: *"et ecce audio uocem de uicina domo . . . quasi pueri aut puellae, nescio . . ."*? I do not suggest, as Courcelle seems to think,[1] that the *pueri* is the same in both cases: one clearly refers to Augustine's own childhood; the other refers, I believe, not to the children of Continence, but to the child who spoke the *tolle lege*. Nevertheless I feel that it was because he was under the influence of his recent conversion and remembering especially the words of the child in the garden that Augustine, when he came to describe his conversion *en passant* in the Preface to the second book of the *Contra Academicos,* introduced, because of his mental absorption with it, the figure of a child. A child beckoned to him in both cases, and in both cases he was unconscious of what was happening: *"pueris . . . nescientem"* (CA), *"pueri . . . nescio"* (C). The most natural explanation of the heightened emotion and the occurrence of the figure of a child in the *Contra Academicos* (where, because of the necessary brevity of the reference, it is not clearly developed) and the *Confessions,* is not that in both cases Augustine is employing the same literary device at an interval of some thirteen years, but rather that he is referring to an historical event: he seemed to hear some child say *tolle lege*, and the memory of that child possessed his mind whenever he thought of the final stage of his conversion.

If what I have suggested is true, it is favourable to the historicity of the *tolle lege* scene in the garden. My present purpose however is concerned rather with indicating that Augustine did treat of the episode elsewhere than in chapter XII of the eighth book of the *Confessions*. Whatever about the *pueri*, the recurrence of the mention of the followers of Antony, the mention of the light that dawned upon his mind, a few other smaller items such as the presence of *intentissimus* in one passage and *intentissime* in the other, but above all the phrases: "*Itaque titubans, properans, haesitans, arripio apostolum Paulum* and *itaque concitus . . . arripui (codicem apostoli), aperui, et legi,*" are to my mind the clearest evidence that what one would have supposed to be true is true: that Augustine did more than once refer to the episode of the scene in the garden.

To mention another instance, also from the *Dialogues*—the memory of that excited seizing of St. Paul consequent on the child's *tolle lege* was so great that, when in the *De beata vita* he is even more briefly than in the *Contra Academicos* referring to his recent conversion, the note of excitement creeps in again and some of the expressions are used in a strange way. He writes:

> "Lectis autem Platonis [Plotini?] paucissimis libris, cuius te esse studiosissimum accepi, collataque cum eis, quantum potui, etiam illorum auctoritate qui diuina mysteria tradiderunt, sic exarsi, ut omnes illas uellem ancoras rumpere, nisi me nonnullorum hominum existimatio commoueret. Quid ergo restabat aliud, nisi ut immoranti mihi superfluis tempestas, quae putabatur aduersa, succurreret? Itaque tantus me arripuit pectoris dolor, ut illius professionis onus sustinere non ualens, qua mihi uelificabam fortasse ad Sirenas, abiicerem omnia, et optatae tranquillitati uel quassatam nauem fissamque perducerem." (DBV I, 4)

Here there is the same heightened emotion described in terms of a fire of flame: *sic exarsi* (cf. *incredibile incendium* of the *Contra Academicos* and the *aestus* of the *Confessions*), and the same reference to ambition and success (*honor, hominum pompa, inanis famae cupiditas: immoranti superfluis . . . Sirenas* and the many references to pride and ambition in the *Confessions*); here again the main topic is his prolonged study of St. Paul; and here again the emotion of the *tolle lege* scene breaks through into the expressions: *itaque . . . arripuit*. And as before the issue to the storm (*tempestas*) is peace.

This passage, addressed to a friendly philosopher, Mallius Theodorus, turns the account in a way which that Platonist might be supposed to appreciate: the passage has Neoplatonic echoes. In addition it is somewhat less intimate than the passage in the *Contra Academicos* which is addressed to his friend and patron Romanianus, and so he gives Theodorus the ostensible (but also a true) reason for his resigning from his profession and retiring to the country—his illness—and not the more important and personal one—his conversion to Christianity. In effect Augustine is not giving a formal account here any more than in the *Contra Academicos*—of the garden scene; but for all that it seems plain to me at least that again, when he was writing those lines, the memory of the garden scene was in his mind and has left its trace quite clearly on the passage.

Coming to the *Confessions* themselves—one can see the influence of the garden scene upon two passages at least, that is to say, apart from the formal description of the event itself.

The first is his account of the impression the *Hortensius* of Cicero made upon him. Scholars have been puzzled to understand how such a book should have had such an effect upon him. Part of the explanation, doubtless, is that the book came his way just when such a book was likely to have such an effect upon him: many other philosophical treatises could have had the same effect. But it is nonetheless true that his description of the effect that the book did have upon him is strangely emotional. I feel, in fact, that once again the emotions of the *tolle lege* scene worked themselves into the account he gives us of this early and significant experience in his life. In other words, he over-rates the effect that the *Hortensius* did have on him, and in his account is using his memory of the *tolle lege* scene.

> "Et usitato iam discendi ordine perueneram in *librum quemdam* Ciceronis . . . uiluit mihi *repente omnis uana spes*, et immortalitatem sapientiae concupiscebam *aestu* cordis *incredibili*; et surgere coeperam ut ad te redirem . . . ardebam reuolare a terrenis ad te; et *nesciebam* quid ageres mecum . . . accendebar et ardebam; et hoc solum me in tanta flagrantia refrangebat, quod nomen Christi non erat ibi . . . hoc nomen . . . in ipso adhuc lacte matris, tenerum cor meum praebiberat, et alte retinebat . . . *itaque* institui animum intendere in Scripturas sanctas . . . *et ecce uideo* rem non compertam superbis, neque nudatam pueris . . . ego dedignabar esse *paruulus*." (C III, 7f.)

The occurrence here of the words italicized suggests very strongly that the same memory was in Augustine's mind when he was writing these words as was there when he was writing the passages referred to in the *Contra Academicos*, the *De beata vita* and the *tolle lege* of the *Confessions*: the memory of the garden scene. It is another instance of Augustine's recalling that famous event. Apart however, from the question that arises as to the actual effect that the reading of the *Hortensius* had upon him at the time—as opposed to his account of it subsequent to his conversion and influenced by the memory of that conversion—the question arises as to the significance of the reference in this passage to his own childhood and the *paruulus*. Was it true that Augustine *at the time* was dissatisfied with Cicero's *Hortensius only* because there was there no reference to Christ? If we take the view that that was so, then we will have a very strong and additional reason for holding that Augustine was always primarily interested in religion or the religious side of philosophy rather than philosophy itself. But if we feel that Augustine at the time was not so upset at the absence of the name of Christ, then we have to account for the prominence of this point here. In either case it remains possible that this prominence is influenced by the association in his memory of child and conversion, an association based upon the events described in the *tolle lege* scene. That Augustine connected the two episodes, the *Hortensius* experience and the final conversion, in his mind is quite clear from his own reference to the *Hortensius* episode in his description of the final scene (C VIII, 7, 17).

The second instance: Courcelle suggests the possibility that the *tolle lege* scene is a doublet of the conversion of the two men at Trier which had just been recounted to Augustine by Pontitianus. The implication is that the story told by Pontitianus and retold to us by Augustine is historical, while the story told by Augustine to us of his own conversion is, being a doublet, a fiction or, in part, fictionally adapted to the story of Pontitianus. On the contrary I feel sure that if the description of one of these scenes is adapted to the events of the other, it is the story of Pontitianus that is adapted to that of Augustine. Is it to be argued that Augustine's account of what he heard from Pontitianus is historical, and his account of what he experienced himself so intensely is unhistorical, on the ground that the description of the second account comes after and is like the first? Once again I would say that the impression of his own conversion affected him so profoundly that when he recounts Pontitianus' story of the men of Trier, he allows the memory of his own conversion to creep in. This does not mean that he invented much in the story of Pontitianus—for there are extraordinary coincidences in the details of mental crises in the cases of men greatly separated in age and character, e.g., the conversions of Newman and Rousseau, which in some ways approximate so closely to the conversion of Augustine—it merely means that his account of their conversion was coloured by his remembrance of his own. The entry of Pontitianus is no sooner mentioned than he is described as reaching for the book on the table before him, and we are told, in words by now significant: *tulit, aperuit, inuenit apostolum Paulum*.

It is suggested here that not only is it not true that Augustine did not recall again the episode of the *tolle lege* scene but that he did so more than once—in no formal way, it is true, but nevertheless quite definitely. There is a proverb, in English at any rate, that the criminal returns to the scene of his crime. Augustine, although no criminal, shows a remarkable fondness for returning to topics and events which have meant much to him. It would indeed be remarkable if he did not revisit again and again in his mind the scene of the most momentous crisis of his life. Some instances have been given here where it is contended there is such a return; but there are others.[2] The passages in his works where he speaks of Platonist pride and Christian humility, of the way of authority for the many and the way of reason for the few and some other related topics—all in some way derive from his experience during the final stages of his conversion.

Although it is not immediately relevant to our present purpose, we may ask the question if this does not make the historicity of the account of his conversion in the *tolle lege* scene less improbable? It is true that even a pure fiction can leave a strong impression; but if Augustine, when he came to describe the garden scene in the *Confessions*, reverted to the phrases which he employed for the first time in the *Contra Academicos*, then the continuing recollection of a real event is a more likely explanation than the continuing recollection of a fiction. Moreover, while one can have reserves about the general historicity of the *Contra Academicos*, one can have little doubt about the historicity of most of the points mentioned in the prefaces—and his first description of his conversion is one of them. The accord between the *Contra Academicos* and the *Confessions* on this matter is indeed remarkable. It is, I feel, based on fact.

3

Patrick's *Confessio* and Augustine's *Confessiones*

೩

Pierre Courcelle, in *Les Confessions de saint Augustin dans la tradition littéraire*,[1] writes:

"Cette *Confessio* a suscité récemment des recherches attentives, mais contradictoires dans leurs conclusions sur le rapport avec les *Confessions* d'Augustin. M. Bieler a cru remarquer divers emprunts textuels aux *Confessions*.[2] M. O'Meara, au contraire, nie que les rapprochements allégués par M. Bieler soient probants.[3] Il faut lui concéder que bon nombre sont peu sûrs. Même le fait que Patrick, comme Augustin, joigne à la confession d'action de grâces l'auto-défense et la confession des péchés, peut sembler insuffisant. Pourtant, certains des parallèles établis par M. Bieler me semblent valables, même s'il est vrai, comme objecte M. O'Meara, que le passage augustinien repose lui-même sur un texte scripturaire, qui risque ainsi d'être leur source commune. De telles rencontres sont, en réalité, plus nombreuses et plus précises que ne le signalait M. Bieler."

Courcelle then quotes and examines a number of parallels which I shall discuss presently. His final conclusion is:

"L'influence des *Confessions* sur Patrick me semble d'ailleurs ne pas être seulement d'ordre littéraire, mais toucher plutôt à la formation spirituelle intime."[4]

Again he writes:

"Patrick . . . semble avoir été touché intimement par le maître."[5]

The intervention of Courcelle in this debate invites a brief assessment of his contribution which may suitably be done here.

It must first be stated that Ludwig Bieler in the article in question was mainly quoting the views of P. Grosjean and H. Misch, which he describes as "certainly *suggestive* of literary dependence." He manifests his detachment, however, not only by drawing attention in the same article to the difference between the two works,[6] but also when he reports the matter as an hypothesis:[7] "*If* Patrick did study St. Augustine . . ." Accordingly at the beginning of my discussion of the matter I drew attention to Bieler's clear reserves.[8] Since then Bieler has dismissed the case first put forward seriously by Misch.[9]

Although Courcelle does refer in a note[10] to Professor Christine Mohrmann's *The Latin of Saint Patrick*,[11] he does not manifest any appreciation of how she widened and strengthened the attack on the thesis that literary dependence of the *Confessio* on the *Confessiones* could be proved. She draws attention to the fact that *confessio* may well not be a title for Patrick's letter; that in any case it does not cover the same range of meaning as does the title (real and contemporary) of Augustine's work; that the use of the Bible in both works may seem superficially similar, but is in fact quite different; and finally that "there is not a single passage which can be proved to be a quotation from or an allusion to Augustine's *Confessions.*"[12] But her whole characterization of Patrick's Latinity is such as to make the literary dependence of the one on the other almost, if not quite,[13] impossible.

It can be seen, then, that Courcelle misrepresents the extent of Bieler's advocacy of Misch's thesis; did not perhaps have the opportunity of noting Bieler's withdrawal from Misch's point of view; and did not draw sufficient attention to the seriousness of the further atack by Mohrmann. In these circumstances, doubtless, he did not forbear to use the technique of comparing parallel passages to improve on Misch. I had indicated the "possibility" and likely fruitlessness of this.[14]

The great uses and equally great abuses of employing the comparison of parallel passages to establish literary dependence were fairly comprehensively expounded, for example, by A. Mandouze[15] and discussed by others and by Courcelle, Mohrmann, and myself[16] (but in another context) at the Congrès International Augustinien in 1954. There is much that one could recall from that discussion that would be useful in the present context, but brevity compels me to give one excerpt only—but one indispensable here—from Mohrmann's contribution on that occasion:

"1. Là où il s'agit de textes techniques, rédigés dans la langue spéciale et technique d'un groupe bien défini, une identité de mots et de tournures nous donne, en général, le droit de conclure à un emprunt. Mais il s'agit d'un emprunt au groupe, on n'a pas encore prouvé, sans plus, un emprunt à tel ou tel auteur de ce groupe."

"2. La situation change foncièrement dès que l'on quitte le domaine technique. Si l'on constate des ressemblances, voire des identités tex-

Confessio and Confessiones   33

tuelles là où il s'agit d'éléments de la langue courante qui décrivent des situations générales de la vie de tous les jours, il faut être très prudent. Une dépendance réelle, un emprunt est loin d'être établi par le seul fait d'une ressemblance ou d'une identité des mots employés. Voyons la chose de plus près.

"Il ne faut jamais oublier que telle ou telle situation suscite presque invariablement tels ou tels mots. Les possibilités de l'expression linguistique sont loin d'être illimitées, comme d'ailleurs les ressources créatrices de l'esprit humain. Une situation définie inspire des mots définis et l'identité des mots ne présuppose pas, dans ce cas, une dépendance, une relation de source.

"Il faut encore ajouter que dans chaque langue existent des tournures toutes faites s'appliquant à telle situation, des clichés qui s'emploient presque automatiquement. La phraséologie toute faite des faits divers de nos journaux n'est pas une innovation des nos jours. Les procédés de la rhétorique antique aboutissaient également à une langue banale où abondaient les clichés.

"Dans le domaine de la langue littéraire, de la prose et de la poésie, la situation est encore plus compliquée par la relation qui existe entre langue poétique ou littéraire et langue courante. Les jeux de mots de la langue populaire par example, sont repris à des époques très diverses par des auteurs de caractère très différent . . ."

. . . "D'innombrables mères répètent chaque jour à leur enfant: Sois sage. Des centaines de maîtres d'école, à tel élève: tiens-toi tranquille. Il suffit de trois petits mots, intercalés entre ces expressions, et voici le vers de Baudelaire:

"Sois sage, ô ma Douleur, et tiens-toi plus tranquille."

"Il y a ici une différence à la fois minime et capitale qui distingue de l'idiome courant celui de la poésie, mais qui montre combien devient délicate cette science des sources dès qu'on se trouve dans le domaine de la littérature et de la langue courante.

"Le danger est particulièrement grand pour nous autres qui travaillons dans le domaine du monde antique: nos connaissances de la langue courante latine sont extrêmement restreintes. Presque tous les textes qui sont parvenus jusqu'à nous sont d'un caractère nettement littéraire. Que savons-nous du latin parlé dans la vie de tous les jours?"[17]

Armed with the sobriety that is indispensable let us scrutinize the additional parallel texts between the *Confessio* and the *Confessiones* now advanced by Courcelle.[18]

AUGUSTIN, C X, 3, 4, 16, p. 243:
"Indicabo me talibus (= animis fraternis) . . . Tu autem, domine . . . , consumma *imperfecta* mea. Hic est fructus confessionum mearum, non qualis fuerim, sed *qualis sim, ut* hoc confitear non tantum coram te secreta exultatione *cum tremore* et secreto maerore cum spe, sed etiam in auribus credentium filiorum hominum . . . Hi sunt servi tui, *fratres* mei."

X, 27, 38, I, p. 268:
"*Sero* te amaui, pulchritudo tam antiqua et tam noua! Et ecce intus eras et ego foris et ibi te quaerebam et in ista formosa, quae fecisti, deformis inruebam."

IV, 1, 1, 25, p. 67:
"Sed *inrideant* nos fortes et potentes, nos autem infirmi et inopes confiteamur tibi."

IX, 4, 12, 2, p. 218:
"Nec oblitus sum *nec silebo* flagelli tui asperitatem et misericordiae tuae *mirabilem* celeritatem."

IV, 16, 31, 4, p. 88:
"Sed sic eram *nec erubesco*, Deus meus, *confiteri tibi* in me misericordias tuas."

XI, 25, 32, 8, p. 319:
"Ecce, Deus meus, coram te, quia non mentior (*Gal.* I, 20.)"

PATRICK, *Conf.*, 6, p. 60, I:
"Tamen etsi in multis *imperfectus* sum, opto, *fratribus* et cognatis meis scire *qualitatem meam, ut* possint perspicere uotum animae meae . . . Vnde autem uehementer debueram *cum* timore et *tremore* metuere hanc sententiam."

2, p. 57, 14:
"Et ibi dominus aperuit sensum incredulitatis meae, ut uel *sero* rememorarem delicta mea et ut conuerterem toto corde ad Dominum deum meum."

45, p. 83, 13:
"*Rideat* autem et insultet qui uoluerit, ego *non silebo* neque abscondo signa et *mirabilia* quae mihi a Domino monstrata sunt."

44, p. 83, 9:
"Sed *confiteor Domino meo* et *non erubesco* in conspectu ipsius, quia non mentior (*Gal.*, I, 20)."

The first of these sets of parallels is concerned with the inescapable task of an autobiographer: he must tell what manner of man he is (*qualis sim, ut; qualitatem meam, ut*) if he has a purpose (*ut*) to achieve. Furthermore while he may have to address himself to his enemies he is likely also to address himself to his friends ("brothers") around him (*fratres* and *animis fraternis*—a phrase fabricated with possible, but not total, justification from a long paragraph preceding—*fratribus*). The recurrence of *cum timore* from the New Testament in both texts in this context would be natural in authors at all familiar with the Scriptures. I would regard all of these parallels in the contexts of the works as, in Mohrmann's term, banal and without any significance in relation to proving literary dependence. The suggestion, however, of a connection between *imperfecta* and *imperfectus* is quite unacceptable: the first refers to God's completion of things yet unperfected in Augustine (*nequaquam deserens coepta tua, consumma imperfecta mea*); the second refers to Patrick's failings (Bieler translates: "although I am imperfect in many things").[19]

The second instance depends entirely on the recurrence of the one word *sero* in Patrick. In Augustine's case it refers to his *loving* God late. In Patrick's case (Bieler: "that I might at last remember my sins and be converted with all my heart to the Lord my God"), it refers to a late *repentance* and (probably) *conversion* to God. (Courcelle fails to draw attention to the idea common to both texts that God had care of the authors, who were themselves unaware of this.) While the word *sero* can have for those who know Augustine's *Confessiones* a special association which they apply (but only, of course, from time to time), when occasion offers, it is an almost inevitable word when one sets out to describe doing anything late, or too late. Any good Latin dictionary gives instances of its use in the sense of "too late" and this, inevitably, has its own sense of regret quite independently of its use in one place in Augustine's *Confessiones*. Virgil (to give but one example) too has his own haunting use of the word:

> Libertas, quae sera tamen respexit inertem,
> candidior postquam tondenti barba cadebat,
> respexit tamen et longo post tempore uenit.[20]

And there is an old proverb: *sero sapiunt Phryges* which sums up the banality and universality of the experience implied in *sero*.

The next item is made up of two quotations from Augustine and one from Patrick. The Augustine quotations are taken from books of the *Confessiones* as far apart as IV and IX, which destroys the notion of a parallel text. In any case the recurrence of *inrideant* and *rideat* has Biblical reference. There are some 18 instances of *irrideo* and 20 of *rideo* in the Bible, a number of them, in both cases, in the subjunctive mood and with the meaning "scoff." Patrick's *non silebo . . . mirabilia* is referred by Bieler, properly, to Psalms 71, 17. Augustine's text from *Confessiones* IX *could* indeed have the same reference—but this would be no proof that Patrick depends on Augustine: there are over 100 uses of *mirabilis* and associated words in the Bible, and 35 of *mirabilia* in the *Psalms* alone. There are over 40 uses of *sileo* in the Bible, and several similar to *non silebo*—e.g., *Ezech.* 24.27: *et loqueris et non silebis ultra*; 33.22: *non silui amplius*; *Ps.* 39.12: *ne sileas*; 49.3: *Deus . . . non silebit.*

The final instance given by Courcelle, likewise, has such strong Biblical reference that it is without use to prove dependence of the one text on the other: I have already indicated that *confiteor* occurs over 160 times in the Bible, *erubesco* 52 times, and that both words are connected in meaning.[21]

Courcelle concludes: "Quelle que soit la distance entre la culture d'Augustin et l'inculture de Patrick, il me paraît comme à M. Bieler que la *Confessio* de l'un suppose les *Confessions* de l'autre. J'inclinerais même à croire que Patrick conçoit et décrit ses ''voix'' à la manière et sous l'influence d'Augustin.[22] Enfin, l'emploi d'un registre analogue de citations scripturaires est tout de même un indice sérieux de parenté littéraire. L'influence des *Confessions* sur Patrick me semble d'ailleurs ne pas être seulement d'ordre littéraire, mais toucher plutôt à la formation spirituelle intime."[23]

The reader should note carefully the escalation that occurs in this final conclusion. It is implied that Bieler felt that the *Confessio* of the one *supposes* (that is, has demonstrable literary dependence on) the other: this is, as we have seen, untrue. Courcelle's daring *inclination* (*J'inclinerais même*) to connect the description of the voices is, on the face of it, an admission that he has not proved it.[24] The use of the same Biblical texts in the *Confessio* and the *Confessiones* can certainly indicate that both authors depend on the Bible, or on readings (liturgical, for example) from it, or common quotations from it—but practically all ecclesiastical writers and preachers of every age depend on the Bible in this way. It could not possibly be proved that Patrick got his quotations from the Bible from Augustine's *Confessiones only*. Finally, it *seems* to Courcelle that the influence of the *Confessiones* on Patrick is *rather* in the area of intimate spiritual formation. At this point this idea is said to occur to Courcelle himself only—later in the book, however, it is implied that it is entertained as likely by others.[25]

While it must remain *possible* that Patrick read the *Confessiones* before he wrote the letter now called *Confessio*, and that consciously or unconsciously he could in a literary or spiritual sense be dependent on that work, there is no proof within the documents that this is so.

Up to this point, as on the previous occasion when I examined this topic, I have confined myself narrowly to the two works involved. I might now, however, be allowed to make some few remarks on the implications for the Patrick question in general of the negative results here indicated.

Courcelle himself[26] gives us sufficient guidance as to the extent to which Augustine's *Confessiones* were known and used in the century which, on any reading of the Patrick question, is relevant, that is the fifth century A.D.—and in the geographical areas again most relevant, that is Gaul and, to a lesser extent, Italy and Africa.

Although it might seem surprising that St. Jerome implies that he had not known of the *Confessiones* some four to seven years after they were written around 400, we have sufficient evidence that they were known and used before 422 by some people closely associated with Augustine—Paulinus of Nola, Evodius of Uzala (near Hippo), the Spaniard Orosius (who was at Hippo in 417), Paulinus of Milan and Augustine's biographer Possidius.

Of people not so immediately connected with Augustine, Prosper of Aquitaine, who lived at Marseilles up to 440, mentions Germanus and Palladius, and died after 455, is of clear interest in a Patrician context. His *Liber Sententiarum ex operibus sancti Augustini delibatarum* affords incontrovertible proof of his use of the *Confessiones*. The relevance of Paulinus of Pella (died after 459) to the present topic is not proved, and in any case would at most but confirm that the *Confessiones* were known in Marseilles at a possibly relevant date. Claudianus Mamertus, a priest from Vienne in Gaul who died about 474, appears to know the *Confessiones*. Ennodius of Pavia (who however was writing at the end of the century and from Italy) definitely knew the *Confessiones* and indeed wrote in their manner what Courcelle calls "un pastiche assez médiocre." Eugippius (who was also writing from Italy even later in the century, if not in the next) clearly knew the *Confessiones* since he published excerpts (doctrinal, however, rather than autobiographical) from them. Finally Fulgentius of Ruspe (in Africa), who died in 533, cites the *Confessiones*.

The hard evidence given by Courcelle, therefore, of the knowledge of the *Confessiones* in Gaul in the fifth century can be reduced to, perhaps significantly, Prosper at Marseilles. We could possibly add Paulinus (also at Marseilles) and Claudianus Mamertus from Vienne, about 150 miles to the North. This is not to say that it is unlikely to have been known to others in that area of Gaul or elsewhere—especially because of Augustine's prominence in relation to all aspects of Pelagianism. Nevertheless, whatever *our* views of the fame of the *Confessiones*, our certain knowledge of its fame in Gaul in the fifth century seems disappointing.

The conclusion that Patrick's *Confessio* shows no reliable indication of literary dependence on Augustine's *Confessiones* could be interpreted (though I do not do so) as confirmation that the latter work was not after all very famous. One would then be free to suppose that Patrick could have spent a lengthy sojourn in Gaul without showing evidence of dependence on the *Confessiones* in his *Confessio*. This may be so. But it would seem to the present writer that, so far as literary[27] (as distinct from linguistic and other) evidence is concerned, the testimony of the *Confessio* is almost decisively against Patrick (who was clearly no dullard) having been exposed over a long period, not only to the *Confessiones*, but to any literary influence in any relatively cultured ecclesiastical centre such as existed at the time in Gaul. In coming to this conclusion I am not ignoring irony and both traditional and personal humility in Patrick's references to his own rusticity.

4

Augustine's *Confessions*
Elements of Fiction

❧

Some readers were somewhat scandalized when Pierre Courcelle wrote that the *tolle lege* episode, the description of Augustine's actual conversion, in the *Confessions* (VIII, 28f.) contains "de fiction littéraire et de symbolisme." He indicated the Plotinian allusions; the reminiscence of the famous story of Prodicus, according to which Heracles as a young man, on reaching a crossroads alone, hesitated between the appeal of Pleasure and that of Virtue, each represented by a woman proposing her own way to him; the opposing invitations to Augustine of the Vanities on the one hand and Continence on the other to follow them, presented in the form of a rhetorical *controuersia*; reminiscences of Persius—and more besides. From which Courcelle concluded that the scene, purporting to describe the hour, so to speak, of his actual conversion, *"fourmille d'intentions littéraires."* As for the fig tree under which Augustine cast himself in the agony of mind that immediately preceded his sudden yielding to Christ, it could have only a symbolical meaning: it recalled the fig tree under which, according to the Gospel of St. John (I, 48), Nathanael sat, a tree which is constantly interpreted by Augustine as symbolizing the mortal shade of sin that spreads over the human race. Literary forms and symbolism were only half the story: with the exception of the item of the fig tree, the whole scene of the garden in Milan, according to Courcelle, is explained by the influence of the *Life of Anthony* by Athanasius, a life referred to, just before the conversion scene, by Augustine himself.[1]

If one accepts these affirmations of Courcelle on the most critical details recounted in the *Confessions,* one feels invited perhaps to treat more items indicated in the *Confessions* as being possibly fictitious in the same sense. To do this would not necessarily impugn the truthfulness of Augustine, unless one insisted, wrongly it may be, that "truth" and "fiction" were always mutually exclusive. All description, it might be contended, is to some extent fictitious. All of us, when we set out to describe an event, tell a story—narrate. There is no way we can choose words that correspond exactly to what actually happened; at best they will convey approximately the most objective version to which we can consciously discipline ourselves. This does not make for fluent expression or easy reading. And so we embroider upon our message, we tell a story, we narrate.

The description we give is the description we must choose. Here we are limited, so to speak, by the materials available to us. What we choose at any one time, moreover, will be affected by our present purposes and interests. These purposes and interests will tend to vary as we proceed through life and adjust our picture of it. But for all that, it must be added, there may well be an underlying consistency of purpose and interest reflecting our psychological make-up. What we choose will also depend upon our models—for there is usually some model or some convention. A lawyer will have one way of presenting an account—representing an event; a civil servant, gobbledegooking his way around bills with their sections and sub-sections, another; a guru a third. We speak within conventions.

Autobiography, for example, in the nature of things must compose a story, even more than some other forms of writing. At first blush this seems paradoxical: is it not the autobiographer's sole task to tell the truth, the whole truth and nothing but the truth about himself? He cannot, of course, tell the whole truth: this would yield *à la rigueur* tedious life-long documentation. This is not acceptable. So choice creeps in. I must choose what I shall recount. Correspondingly I must choose what I shall omit: "I brush them away . . . until what I want is unveiled" (*Conf.* X, 12).[2] By the very choice there is already necessarily misrepresentation, that is, in so far as there is non-representation. But there is something more significant—and it is unavoidable—I choose acording to some canon, some pattern, some ideal; otherwise I could not choose at all. Thus, for example, Augustine recounts the story of his stealing pears that he did not need, only because it was symbolical of wilful sin: it was the *symbol* that justified the inclusion of the event, not the event itself, which was trivial. This is tantamount to admitting that in autobiography one is creating oneself anew: one is painting an image of oneself. One chooses, among the events of the past that one can recall, those that seem significant *now,* those that bear some relation, not excluding opposition, to one's present picture of oneself then. This implies that one's earlier view of oneself, then, is identical with one's present view of what one was like then—which is unlikely. One can never recover exactly one's view of oneself at any particular time in the past. We can reconstruct it, but we do so only with the help of our more or less faithful memories and our imaginations, which must start from the present. Augustine tells us explicitly that the account he gives of his babyhood and even later childhood in the *Confessions* (I, 8) is conjectured.

Telling the truth and nothing but the truth is, at best, an exercise in approximation. Words are never adequate to describe reality. They are a *pis aller*! Fiction is a frequent vehicle for alleged truth.

Bearing such ideas in mind, we may approach the question of the fictional elements in the *Confessions* of Augustine. It is emphasized here that our purpose in this paper is not to attack in any way the general historicity of the *Confessions*; it is rather to draw attention to the considerable element of fiction in the narrative in which this historicity is conveyed.

First it is important to insist that the *Confessions* does not purport to be, nor does it issue in being, so to speak, a "proper" autobiography. One has only to observe that its last three books are mostly concerned with the interpretation of Genesis to come to the conclusion that they at least have little pretence at constituting any part of a strict autobiography. The intrusion of *so much* confession of faith in, and praise of, God, so important for the purposes of the book, tells us something, it is true, but disproportionally little about Augustine's life. The use of Scripture, and especially the Psalms, leaves the reader too often baffled. The opening of the book dilates upon God and the soul, God's omnipresence, his immensity, and his attributes. It is a slow and indirect beginning.

Georg Misch, the specialist in the genre of autobiography, noted that the project of telling the story of his life yielded in Augustine's *Confessions* to metaphysical and religious preoccupations, to the exercise of his religion, and to the awakening in others of the religious sentiment he himself felt. If the *Confessions* is an autobiography, it is an autobiography of an entirely new form: the story of his past is far from being Augustine's only aim.[3]

But there *is* direct description of events in the *Confessions*. Augustine does give us information on his life, even if he omits many things that he remembers: "I pass over many things because I hasten to those which most urge me to confess to you, and there are many things that I do not remember" (III, 21). One must realize that he never set out to give an account of his whole life: he concentrates in fact for the most part on episodes, and even these are diluted with prayers and demonstrations of doctrine (which are reflected in works contemporary with the *Confessions*) on original sin, conversion of the sinner, and the operation of the will. Added too are the heretical opinions of the Manicheans, and a number of other matters, such as the Neoplatonic theory of the beautiful, his views on baptism, marriage, love and friendship, and a host of other topics. What he set out to write was not so much an autobiography as a *uita*, a "Life," a tale with a moral for others.

The *Confessions* contain not just one *uita*, but many. There are, for example, the "lives" of his mother, of his friend Alypius, of Victorinus, of the public officials of Trier and of St. Anthony—all of these lives feature a sudden conversion of some sort, due usually to some intervention of Providence. Monica, while still a young girl, had succumbed to the love of wine. One day a maidservant, quarrelling with her, called her a winebibber: "wounded through and through by this taunt," Augustine tells us solemnly, "she beheld her foul state, and immediately condemned it and cast it off . . . But you, O Lord, by means of madness in one soul, even heal another" (IX, 18). Alypius was converted from an infatuation with the circus by a sarcastic remark of Augustine's about the circus, which Alypius heard on entering his class: "Upon hearing those words he burst forth from that deep fit in which he had willingly plunged himself. He shook his mind with a vigorous self-control. All the filth of the circus fell off from him, and he never returned there again" (VI, 12). Augustine remarks that God had worked the transformation through himself, though he did not know it. Victorinus, from being a demon-worshipper, had been convinced of Christianity, but was afraid to become formally a Christian for fear of offending his demon-worshipping friends. The old Neoplatonic-Christian priest, Simplicianus, told him that he would not reckon him among Christians unless he saw him in the Church of Christ. This he kept repeating; suddenly and unexpectedly Victorinus said to Simplicianus, "Let us go to the Church. I wish to become a Christian" (VIII, 4). Augustine attributes this conversion to the grace of Christ. The public officials of Trier chanced to come upon the life of St. Anthony and one of them began to read it; suddenly in anguish he said to his companion, "I have determined to serve God, and from this very hour and in this very place I make my start" (VIII, 15). In his story of the moment of his own conversion Augustine appeals to the experience of Anthony: "For I had heard how Anthony had been admonished by a reading from the Gospel at which he chanced to be present, as if the words read were addressed to him: 'Go, sell what you have, and give to the poor . . . and come, follow me,' and by such an oracle (*tali oraculo*) he was immediately converted to you" (VIII, 29).

These and other rudimentary lives, such as those of Nebridius (VI, 17; IX, 6) and Verecundus (IX, 5), also given in the *Confessions*, were much appreciated in the early Christian Church, not least of all in North Africa in the time of Augustine. Apart from any inspiration from pre-Christian sources, there were many descriptions in Christian literature of the search for truth, of the confession of sins, conversion by grace (here the story of St. Paul's sudden and astounding conversion and reversal of roles from enemy to defender of Christianity was dominant), and the recital of visions and revelations experienced, which must have been to some extent models for Augustine. In his case the influence of the *ad Donatum* of Cyprian of Carthage, where Cyprian gives a brief account—of which there are a number of surprising reminiscences in the *Confessions*—and the *Passiones* of such African martyrs as Perpetua, Marian and Cyprian are of particular interest. The *Confessions* too tells us of exhortations, terrors, consolations, directions, dreams, oracles, miracles and admonitions which issued in the dramatic scene of Augustine's sudden conversion in the garden—itself reminiscent too of Christ's agony in the garden and the submission of His will to the Father. Mixed in with all these are the themes of the Prodigal Son, the wandering of Virgil's Aeneas, and—this reflecting Augustine's philosophic interests and experiences—the Neoplatonic theme of return, *regressus*, to the Father and the Fatherland.

The overall theme of the *Confessions*, transcending its very many digressions, is not simply Augustine's life, but his life insofar as it illustrates an idea that was uppermost in his mind, as it must be in the mind of anyone who feels that he has been entrusted with a mission, the theme of conversion. It is a salvational theme, one common to Christianity and Neoplatonism and many other religious or philosophical systems of the time. It applied to man as an individual and all men as a race. It was a near-obsession in Augustine's mind.

Augustine had learned from Plotinus that the most fundamental—in the literal sense of that word—fact and origin of existence lay in conversion—ἐπιστροφή.[4] According to Plotinus the first being, Intelligence, came into existence in its turning towards the One to see it: τῇ ἐπιστροφῇ πρὸς αὐτὸ ἑώρα· ἡ δὲ ὅρασις αὕτη νοῦς.[5] That was the philosophical fundament of philosophical, religious, mystical and all experience. In the very first paragraphs of his first extant work, the *Contra Academicos* (386), Augustine bids his old friend and patron Romanianus to wake up under the providential buffetings of fortune and give himself to philosophy, to which indeed his son, Augustine's student, Licentius, had already been "converted" from the snares and pleasures of youth. The preface to the contemporary *De beata uita* again dilates at length on the function of what appears to be misfortune in bringing us—and Augustine himself—to the beloved Fatherland. And likewise the notion of conversion is very much present in the other contemporary dialogue— the *De ordine* (I, 23; X, 28).

In passing one should observe that the great contrast between the *Confessions* and the *Dialogues of Cassiciacum* arises not only from their different purposes—the one a story of ultimately religious conversion, the other concerned primarily to expound philosophical themes in the forms of Platonic-type dialogues—but also in the more religiously oriented presentation in the one and the more philosophically oriented in the other. The description of his conversion in *Contra Academicos* II 5 ends in indicating that he discovered that philosophy and religion were at one, but leads to the recommendation of *philosophy* as illuminated by St. Paul: *tunc uero quantulocumque iam lumine asperso tanta se mihi philosophiae facies aperuit.* Similarly in the *De beata uita,* the comparison of the teachings of the Neoplatonists and the divine mysteries is made, but the issue of the event is presented as an escape from the world into the harbour of philosophy: *ergo uides, in qua philosophia quasi in portu nauigem.*[6] There is not only not a conflict between the reports of his conversion as given in the *Dialogues* and the *Confessions*—there is in fact close correspondence: but whereas in the beginning, while preferring the authority of Christ over all other, he saw no conflict of any substance between the Neoplatonist doctrine that he read and the teachings of St. Paul and, moreover, expected to understand Christian teaching through Neoplatonist reasoning, by the time of the *Confessions* he had discovered the irreconcilability of both positions on major issues and had elected unambiguously for Christianity, for the Incarnation and the Crucifixion, which were outlandish doctrines to the Neoplatonists. In other words the conversion syndrome that always affected him expressed itself in the earlier professedly philosophical works as conversion to a religion for the understanding of which he embraced a philosophy; in the *Confessions* it expressed itself in terms of embracing a religion in relation to which a certain philosophy could be both a serious help and a serious hindrance.

There can be no doubt but that Augustine's initial expectations from Neoplatonism in relation to Christianity were very high. But from an early stage his enthusiasm for the Neoplatonists was diminished, even if never altogether abandoned.

Augustine, then, although presenting the same material without deliberate falsification in the *Dialogues* and the *Confessions*, had not only different purposes—he had different models. The "life," the *uita*, that he gave of himself in the *Confessions* appears, according to the very plausible view of Courcelle,[7] to have been written in response to an interest shown in him by Paulinus of Nola. Augustine's friend Alypius had written to Paulinus in A.D. 395 to request from him a copy of the *Chronicles* of Eusebius of Caesarea: by way of *douceur* he enclosed five works of Augustine against the Manichees. Paulinus complied with the request but in turn asked Alypius to write for him an account of "the whole story of his holiness's life"[8] and to send it to him. He wanted to know, in the words of Virgil's *Aeneid*, "of what race he was, where was his home," *qui genus, unde sis domo* (VIII, 114), a ritual formula to designate an "autobiography." He was especially interested in his vocation to the ascetic life, and if he had been converted and ordained to the priesthood by Ambrose, as he had been himself. Alypius's reply is not extant, but Courcelle supposes that Alypius asked Augustine to fill Paulinus's request. Augustine wrote to Paulinus in the summer of 396 saying that he was completing the life of Alypius requested and that, among other things, he offered himself fully to Paulinus to be known to him—since each so much desired to know the other.[9] The life of Alypius would appear to have been completed—some of it, as we have already indicated, is incorporated in the *Confessions* (VI, 7–10, 11–16). Courcelle supposes that Paulinus received it and, impressed by it, requested Augustine to do in relation to his own life what he had done for Alypius—where he was born, what was his vocation to the ascetic career, had he been converted and ordained by Ambrose, and so on. Here, it would seem, was given the outline plan of the *Confessions*. In this context one can easily understand why such a large proportion of the book was taken up with Augustine's period in Milan (V, 13–IX, 16), where he was finally converted to the ascetical life and baptized by Ambrose. This Milan period amounts to thirty-eight per cent of the first nine books that constitute the substance of the *Confessions* and corresponds to three years, or nine per cent, of his life to that date. Clearly the conversion episode is the centre of interest of the book and does actually comply with what appears to have been Paulinus's request. Although he omits to speak of his ordination—which Paulinus had requested in the case of Alypius—we know that he had originally planned to describe this.[10]

We should take note too of the audience Augustine had in mind for his book: it was not God only or Paulinus—*non enim a te solo illa legerentur:* "for not by you alone will those things be read" (E XXVII, 5); it was in general the *spiritales* (V, 20; X, 6), those given to the spiritual life within the Church who, like Paulinus, would be avid to read of the *uita* and especially the conversion of such a prominent and distinguished convert—the public orator at the Imperial Court, one who could well have aspired to the governorship of a province, a former Manichee, one who presumably had the intellectual equipment and sophistication to champion the cause of Christianity with and against the Neoplatonists, one baptized by the great Ambrose, and one finally who had had a dramatic conversion. He tells us plainly (XI, 1, 3) why he recounts so many things—not that God should know them, but that he should excite his own love for God and the love of his readers so that they would cry out, "The Lord is great and greatly to be praised." But his critics, indeed his detractors, would read the book too and would not derive profit from such a moral tale.

I shall now enter into some detail on what I may call the fictional context or elements of the *Confessions*. The first I want to discuss is his use of Scripture, and especially the Psalms, to convey thoughts and information: this is a very indirect, analogical, and to that extent fictional, way of recounting events, and leaves us frequently without any clear idea of the details of what in fact happened.

Take for instance the celebrated passage (VII, 13–15) in which Augustine describes what he read in the Platonist books. He does not say for example, "I read in some of the *Enneads* of Plotinus, or in the *De regressu animae* (or *Philosophy from Oracles*) of Porphyry, or in these works of both philosophers, translated by Victorinus, of the Father, and Intelligence, and the soul of man and their relations. This enabled me to conceive of a spiritual deity, which released me from a block until then insurmountable to me. It seemed to me as it had seemed to others, that there was a correspondence between these Principles and the Father and the Word of the Christian Trinity." Such a statement would have given us direct information on a crucial episode in Augustine's life where, because of the indirect telling, in spite of the concentrated attention of scholars for a century, obscurity remains. He described the episode indirectly, using the words of the Prologue of St. John's Gospel to indicate what he had read—and what he had not read—in the books of the Platonists, the *libri Platonicorum*. In the end we are left with little more than questions: Did he read something of Plotinus or Porphyry or, as may seem likely, of both? What books or portions of books did he read? In view of Augustine's general obsession with Porphyry (as seen throughout his works and especially books X and XIX of the *City of God*); his omission of mention of the third Neoplatonist hypostasis here in the *Confessions* and his report in the *City of God* (X, 23) that Porphyry does not at all or does not clearly speak of this third hypostasis; his accusation of Porphyry of idolatry, usually with the quotation of Paul's Epistle to the Romans (I, 21f.): "They changed the glory of the immortal God for images resembling mortal man or birds or animals or reptiles"—the text used at this point in the *Confessions* to describe some of what he did read in the Platonist books but did not accept; his indication that these books did not have—or at any rate that he did not read there—the Incarnation and Crucifixion; and finally his report that after reading these books he shared the Porphyrian-Photinian view that Christ was a good man, body and soul, but was not God—it is impossible to exclude Porphyry's *De regressu animae* (or *Philosophy from Oracles*) from the Platonist books read at this juncture. If this were so, then the appositeness of the text of Romans XIII, 14: "Put on the Lord Jesus Christ," which, according to Augustine, wrought his conversion, would become manifest, for it would represent his humble acceptance of the Incarnation against Porphyry's prideful contempt of it. But, alas, the process of using Scripture to inform leaves us groping for hypotheses which are only more or less to be approved.

In this passage of the *Confessions* to which I have been referring, Augustine uses not only the indirectness of Scripture to impart crucial information, he confuses things further by using rhetoric. He sets up a contrast between "what he read" in the Platonist books (*et ibi legi, legebam ibi, inueni haec ibi*), and "what was in them" (*est ibi*) and "what he did not read" (*non ibi legi*), and "what was not in them" (*non est ibi, non habent illi libri*). At first blush the phrases *non ibi legi, non est ibi,* and *non habent illi libri* seem to refer to the *absence* of reference to the Incarnation and Crucifixion in the Platonist books; but for all that it is impossible altogether to exclude the idea that these books explicitly rejected the doctrines of the Incarnation and Crucifixion, as did Porphyry:

"not *there* did I read," "not *there* is found," "*those* books do not have . . . ," in the perfectly good sense that these books would be the last place where Augustine, in addition to the teaching on the Principles, would find also the teaching on the Incarnation and Crucifixion, since they explicitly rejected these doctrines. One should not press this point too far, but it illustrates the obscurity of the indirectness of the use of Scripture to describe something else, especially when reinforced by rhetoric.

There is also the question of the poet that Augustine was. He tells that he composed poems and entered poetical competitions (III, 14; IV, 1) in his early manhood. And although we have no extant poem of his, F. Van der Meer has written finely of his poetry—perhaps, indeed, too finely:

> He was an *homme de coeur*. . . . When one studies Augustine's arguments one is impressed not so much by his powers of reasoning as by the personal passion that lies behind the arguments. One can always sense the man who dared to say to God: It was your *beauty* that drew me to you. . . . Few saints illustrate so overwhelmingly the thesis that in the existential order of things *prière et poésie* stand next to each other, the one being perhaps simply the continuation of the other. Augustine is the greatest poet of Christian Antiquity, without ever having written any poetry worth mentioning. . . . He possesses the fifth talent, the most valuable of all, the gift of endless wonderment, remaining in this like the little children to whom the Kingdom of Heaven was promised.[11]

Again Van der Meer appeals to Pascal that, like Jesus Christ and St. Paul, Augustine exists in the order of love, not in the intellectual order— for they all aimed to bring fire, not to teach. As we quoted from the *Confessions* already, his aim in writing the *Confessions* was to excite his own affections and those of his readers to God, to declare, "The Lord is great, and exceedingly to be praised" (XI, 1).

The poetic qualities of the *Confessions* are from time to time distinctly obtrusive. With regard to theme, it is possible to compare, as Augustine does himself, his wanderings in search of God with the wandering of Aeneas in search of Italy and great Rome; Augustine's theme is to that extent compared by him to the Roman epic. The *Confessions* and the *City of God*, both proceeding from considerations of Roman institutions and Greek philosophy to Hebrew Revelation, in the one as applied to the individual Augustine, and in the other as applied to the history of mankind, represent each in its own way a view of the mission of Christianity, and each contains distinct reminiscences of the *Aeneid*. The *City of God* in its first paragraph compares Rome's mission as expressed by Virgil: *Parcere subiectis et debellare superbos* (VI, 853) to the Hebrew and Christian: *Deus superbis resistit, humilibus autem dat gratiam* (Prov. 3, 34; Jas. 4, 6; I Pet. 5, 5)—and there are other significant reminiscences of the *Aeneid*.

The poetry of the diction in the *Confessions*, however, is much more obvious. It is a long time since J. Finaert studied this in his *Évolution littéraire de Saint Augustin*,[12] and I do not propose to repeat his conclusions here. Anyone who has read the *Confessions* in Latin will recall the lyricism caused by the extensive use of the Psalms, and how rhetoric is frequently transformed into poetry. That is why, for example, the translation done into French by E. Tréhorel and G. Bouissou often employs the form of free verse. One might reasonably contend, I think, that sometimes the poetry barely escapes, if it does escape, being a rhetorical jingle:

> *Veni Carthaginem, et circumstrepebat me undique sartago flagitiosorum amorum. nondum amabam et amare amabam et secretiore indigentia oderam me minus indigentem. quaerebam quid amarem, amans amare, et oderam securitatem et uiam sine muscipulis* . . . (III, 1)

This passage is given a verse translation by Tréhorel and Bouissou, not surprisingly. It borders on an excess of rhetoric: the word *sartago*, although expressive enough, might well not have been chosen if it had not occurred to Augustine as paralleling *Carthago*. The passage is an illustration, although not the only or even the most obvious one, of what I call the incantatory style of the *Confessions*. This passage is not and does not pretend to be a recital of the concrete facts that happened to Augustine on his coming to Carthage: these are *not* detailed, but instead there is conjured up for us an emotional tumult which was of importance in suggesting a state of soul, itself relevant to a moral tale. What is said is, doubtless, true, but it is also an imaginative *reconstruction*; it is partly a fiction.

The influence of the parataxis of the Bible much enhances the lyrical character of the *Confessions*: *et ibam longius a te* . . . *et sinebas et iactabar et effundebar et diffluebam et ebulliebam* . . . *et tacebas* (II, 2). One feels that Augustine's love of such diction arises, not merely from rhetoric and the Bible, but from a strongly artistic temperament which was preoccupied more with artistic truth than a banal account. A. Solignac, in the course of discussing the style and poetic elements of the *Confessions*, draws attention also to what he terms the "colour and the ornaments" of its style.[13] The book is full of the poetry of images. Comparisons, metaphors, personifications emerge from Augustine's pen, sometimes as fugitive sparks, sometimes under the guise of small charming *tableaux*, and sometimes as long-continuing frescoes. Sometimes there is a strange realism: the soul is described as having a head, eyes, a back, flanks and a belly. Always there is antithesis which emphasizes the difficulty of stating truth in words: *in istam dico uitam mortalem* an *mortem uitalem . . . nescio* (I, 7).

There is, moreover, an additional consideration which is rather difficult for us to appreciate. Augustine had a profound belief in the workings of Providence. One's actions or words might have the most surprising and even improbable results. We have already seen the instance recounted by Augustine of Alypius—Augustine had seen Alypius enter his classroom, and thereupon illustrated a text on which he was engaged by a biting sarcasm at the expense of the circus, to which his audience (and Alypius) were captive: "You know, O my God, that at that time I had no thought of curing Alypius of his disease. But he applied it to himself, and believed that I had said it only because of him. . . . I had not rebuked him, but you (God) who make use of all men, both the knowing and the unknowing, in the order that you know . . . out of my mouth and tongue made coals of fire by which you cauterized a mind of such high promise and healed it" (VI, 11, 12). There was the taunt of the maid-servant that converted Monica (IX, 18), and the taunt of Simplicianus to Victorinus: "I will not reckon you among Christians, unless I see you in the Church of Christ," that was followed by conversion: "Suddenly and unexpectedly he said to Simplicianus: 'Let us go to the church, I wish to become a Christian'" (VIII, 4). Any word might be an oracle: the "Go, sell what you have . . . and come follow me" that converted Anthony (*tali oraculo confestim ad te esse conuersum*), and the "take up and read" that brought Augustine himself to the point of conversion (VIII, 29). That latter phrase had seemed to Augustine at the time as likely to be no more than a banal instruction in a children's game. But he took it to be a command of God: *diuinitus mihi iuberi*. As Augustine frequently called the Scriptures "oracles" as he does in the *Confessions* (XII, 22) and especially in the second half of the *City of God*, to be matched, but in their superiority, with the pagan oracles as appealed to by such as Porphyry, so he reveals himself as a man of his times more profoundly affected than we are likely to be by a sensitivity to possibly oracular expressions. This might extend not only to normal sources for such expressions, but to one's own casual words and writings too.

Augustine held very open views on the interpretation of Scripture. Various meanings might be found in its words, *all* of which were true: "While every man tries to understand in Holy Scripture what the author understood therein, what wrong is there if anyone understands what you, O light of all truthful minds, reveal to him as true, even if the author he reads did not understand this, since he also understood a truth, though not this truth" (XII, 27). Once again in the *Confessions* he asserts that an abundance of meanings can be taken out of the words of Scripture, and that it would be rash to affirm which of them Moses chiefly meant: this would be to offend against charity, for the sake of which Moses spoke what he spoke (XII, 35). He even considers what he himself would have done if he had been Moses: "I should have wished . . . that such power of eloquence be given me, and such ways to fashion words that . . . they who can understand, no matter what true interpretation they have arrived at in their thought, would not find it passed over in (my) words: and if some other men by the light of truth had perceived a further meaning, it should not fail to be understood from these same words" (XII, 36). He is careful to tolerate for readers who are sense-conscious only a gross sensible understanding of Scripture: that God, for example, like a man, by some new and sudden decision, operating outside of himself and, as it were, in distant regions, made heaven and earth, two great bodies in which all things would be contained. Such readers are like fledglings in a nest who must be content as they are until they can fly: otherwise they may fall from the nest and be trampled on (XII, 37). As we saw from an earlier remark of his, we must always employ charity—for the sake of which Moses spoke what he spoke.

This reflection on how he would have hoped to write, if he had been Moses (see also XII, 41–43) must suggest that he might have entertained similar purposes in relation to his own actual writing: this too could be interpreted in a way that he did not have in mind when he was writing. This is not surprising, for it is at root a commonplace in relation to the interpretation of all authors that are of universal appeal: his own favourite poet Virgil was a case in point. But Augustine speaks with an unusual intensity on this matter, not only in the *Confessions*, from which we have been quoting, but elsewhere. Thus in the *Usefulness of Believing* he asserts that a reader can sometimes usefully understand the contrary of what the writer intended (10f.)

The combination of what we may call this openness to what writing may mean on the one hand, and charity in allowing understandings that elsewhere one might characterize as puerile on the other, cannot but have resulted from time to time for Augustine in what one might call "detachment" from the actual words that he was writing. He allowed Providence, the Spirit, to supplement his words. He had the authority of Paul for this, who wrote that the "Spirit helps our weakness" (Rom. 8, 26), this in relation to what words we use in prayer. And so we find an extraordinary number of indefinite phrases in the *Confessions*. We should have a brief look at some of these.

One is a linguistic usage which suggests that Augustine occasionally wished to weaken a reference that one would expect to be particular. He speaks of Aeneas for example, as *nescio quis*, "some Aeneas or other" (I, 20), when it is evident that he knew precisely who Aeneas was. Similarly with regard to Joshua (XI, 30), and St. Paul (XII, 20) he uses the term *quidam*, "a certain person," when equally he knew precisely who was involved. Likewise in his description of the fig-tree in the conversion-scene (VIII, 28) and the window at which his mother and he stood during the "Vision of Ostia" (IX, 23) he employs the term *quaedam*, "a certain fig-tree," "a certain window," when there is no evident need for the indefinite term at all. Attempts have been made to account for such uses of *quidam* by Augustine, but without convincing success.[14] I myself believe that Augustine's use of such terms is intended, as I said earlier in a similar connection,[15] to take the emphasis and concentration off the nouns to which they are attached, in order to heighten the Providential in the scene.

And then there is the concentration on indefinite terms in the conversion scene itself. Here is the passage in Latin:

> *nescio quid* enim, *puto,* dixeram, in quo apparebat sonus uocis meae iam fletu grauidus, et sic surrexeram. mansit ergo ille ubi sedebamus nimie stupens. ego sub *quadam* fici arbore straui me *nescio quomodo* . . . et *non quidem his uerbis,* sed in hac sententia multa dixi tibi . . . et ecce audio uocem de uicina domo cum cantu dicentis et crebro repetentis *quasi* pueri an puellae, *nescio*: "tolle lege, tolle lege." (VIII, 28f.)

It is obvious that this scene is described in terms that convey great emotion, emotion that affects the descriptions of the same event in the

Dialogues of Cassiciacum, the description of Augustine's first conversion to philosophy by the *Hortensius* of Cicero, and the description in the *Confessions* of the conversion of the public servants at Trier (VIII, 15). It is part of Augustine's psychology not only to have almost an obsession with the same theme of conversion, but equally to employ the same emotional terms in his description of it. The indefinite phrases not only heighten the emotion of the description of the *tolle lege* scene: they are a kind of *incantation*. They deliberately take the emphasis and concentration, nay more, the precision, off the words that are used—for some words must be used—and heighten the supra-rational, the marvellous, the Providential in the scene.

This impressionism is marked in Augustine. In spite of the picture of him as the great definer of doctrines in the West, he was also profoundly questioning, profoundly aporetic. He professes this openly and constantly, especially in his mature and non-controversial work (he tended to be dogmatic in controversy) the *De Genesi ad litteram*. Hence it is that texts from him have been confidently used on both sides in the bitter theological conflicts of later ages. Yet even in connection with the question of the origin of the individual soul—how it is found in the body and whether or not it comes through Adam—he had to write at the end of his life: "I did not know this then, and I still do not know it now."[16] Similarly in relation to the beatific vision, when he was discussing it at the very end of the *City of God*, he countenanced two possibilities, one more Platonic and one more Scriptural, which latter he said, was easier to hold. But he declares that, to tell the truth, he must confess his ignorance on the topic.[17]

The charity, moreover, for which he appealed in dealing with those less able to reason and understand, increased, as did his approbation of miracles, as life went on. Thus the belief, based on a fundamentalist reading of Scripture, that in the beatific vision we would see God with corporal eyes, which he appears to favour in the *City of God*, had been simply put aside in correspondence of the year 408;[18] But by the year 413, although he still maintained this position, he allowed for the anthropomorphic views on the matter held by a fellow-bishop.[19]

Some of his tolerance for the less intelligent he could relate to his understanding of the esoteric and exoteric doctrines practiced by the philosophers. He had a real *penchant* for attributing to those whose opinions he controverted their actual lack of belief in the doctrines they espoused. There are many instances of this, which I have detailed elsewhere,[20] in, for example the first half of the *City of God*: Posidonius in V, 2 is represented as not likely to have been sincere in a certain astrological explanation. Varro in VI, 4 and 9 is said not to have spoken his mind plainly on the matter of religion in Rome; Apuleius is also said in IX, 8 to have concealed his full opinion—and so on. It is ironic that Johannes Scottus Eriugena, when he encounters in Augustine a doctrinal opinion which does not accord with one accepted by himself from a Greek Father, attributes to Augustine the process of concealing his true opinion: "And so," he says, "it is more credible that (Augustine) wrote according to the capacity of his audience than to have disagreed with Ambrose. . . ."[21]

The most significant case of this presumption by Augustine that authors might not believe what they explicitly teach is found in his very first extant work, the *Contra Academicos*: there (III, 43) he supposed that the professedly sceptical New Academy was not only not sceptical at all but preserved within itself the true doctrine of Plato. He immediately adds a phrase that may tell us a great deal about him: *hoc mihi de Academicis interim probabiliter, ut potui, persuasi. Quod si falsum est, nihil ad me*—"this opinion about the Academics I have meanwhile adopted, as far as I could, as probable. If it is false, it does not affect me." It is difficult not to judge his attitude as more than a little debonair.

Augustine, then, indulged from time to time in a measure of make-believe, accommodation, detachment—whatever one cares to call it. It arose to some extent from a profound belief in Providence which he felt had been significantly at work in his own life—"You (God) worked within me so that I might be persuaded to go to Rome. . . . The most hidden depths of your providence must be proclaimed" (V, 14). When in turn he left Rome for Milan and all that was to follow, neither his Manichean friends in Rome nor he himself knew the significance of what was happening (V, 23). Likewise God had ordained in His secret ways that he and Monica should commune together at Ostia on a day before she died: "A day that you (God) knew, although it was unknown to us" (IX, 23). There are innumerable instances in the *Confessions* of Augustine's professions of one's unawareness of the secret workings of Providence. One did not know what apparently chance word would work some unexpected and significant result. Hence it was perhaps unnecessary to insist overmuch on precise formulation of what one might say in any conjuncture: "The Spirit helps our weakness" (Rom. 8, 26). Is there some explanation here of Augustine's bias against nature in favour of Grace?

The *Confessions* has also its share of credit in dreams, visions and miracles. He urged his mother to discover in a vision his future marriage: "both at my pleading and by her own desire, each day with a mighty cry from her heart she besought you (God) to give her in a vision some sign as to my coming marriage" (VI, 23). But the vision never came, although she did have some revelations on that occasion which she discerned as not coming from God. The extent of Augustine's belief in Monica's visions cannot be determined[22] but he evidently had some belief in them (III, 19). Likewise he had reason to report that she could dream what was to be. Augustine's belief in miracles at this time is also clearly demonstrated.[23]

In short the necessary indirectness of poetry, and particularly of the use of the Psalms and Scriptures generally to describe things, added to cultivated detachment from particulars, leaves one frequently uninformed where one might very much wish to be informed. What was the name of Augustine's mistress? What was the name of the friend of his early youth who died and left him disconsolate? What Platonist books or excerpts did he read? Did he get to know Ambrose at all well? The method of the *Confessions* is not that of even direct narrative.

The accumulation of the considerations that I have advanced to show how qualified must be our expectation of strict historicity in the *Confessions* does not mean that Augustine tells untruths. Much of what he wants to say has reference to states of soul rather than to any particular facts, and these states of soul involve imaginative reconstruction and for him imaginative, indeed emotional and poetical expression. Much of the description is borrowed from the Psalms and so is indirect and unclear as to its precise intent. In view of the scope of the work, relatively few precise facts are conveyed. The aim of the work is not to inform, but to arouse the minds and hearts of his readers. Some of the states of soul described are perceived by him, as he would say, in his inner ear.[24] Is the scene of his conversion in the garden simply deeply affected by fiction in *its expression*, as Courcelle would have it? Or is it wholly fictional, both as to expression and fact? Has it been sufficiently noted that, when he writes of his sorrow immediately on his mother's death (IX, 29) he again speaks of a youthful voice, his heart's own voice: "Something childish in me was by a youthful voice, my heart's own voice, checked"? This voice was clearly internal to him. What he heard in his inner or interior ear had to be bodied forth in some way: Did he invent this? Or did it "occur" to him much as he described it?

There are innumerable records of alleged experiences similar to that of Augustine's hearing the *tolle lege* in the garden in Milan. Many are recounted with explicit guarantee of their total truth—that is, of the total authenticity of the agent's perception. Take this one for example, told by a recent English Poet Laureate, C. Day Lewis. He had been speaking with unusual fervour and eloquence at a meeting in London. Halfway through his speech, he tells us: "I seemed to detach myself from the man who was so eloquently holding forth, to hover above my own shoulder, and with x-ray eyes to look penetratingly down. I heard myself speaking with sincerity and fervour . . . to my detached self up there it was as though reality had evaporated out of the performance. When I sat down, all in one piece again, I distinctly heard above the applause a small voice saying three or four times within my head, 'It won't do, it just won't do.'"[25] Day Lewis is clear that the small voice spoke its short and repeated instruction *within his head*. If one followed Courcelle in preferring in the conversion scene in the *Confessions* the reading *de diuina domo*, "from the divine house," from Heaven, that is from the invisible God, in his inner ear, one would have an interestingly close correspondence in the case of Augustine—but this raises a difficult question.

If experience of this kind, proceeding from highly emotional states, are to be described, they can be described only in terms of a subjective internal perception. Augustine, interestingly enough, reports that he sought at the time of the experience to relate it to an external objective circumstance: was *tolle lege* used in some children's game? He could not verify that it was. It seems unlikely that Augustine "invented" the scene. Conversions of the kind described involve a long gestation, but a moment does come when, to use Augustine's own constantly repeated word, suddenly all is changed. But as the experience is a mental one, so its process has no external dimension. Yet the converted can have a perception which, and which only, he can describe. The truth is a subjective truth and the reader cannot control it.

It has not been the purpose of this paper either to attack or to defend the historicity of the *Confessions*. What I have tried to do is to draw attention to the extraordinary amount of "fiction" or fictional elements used as a vehicle in the narrative. There still remains the task of assessing the historicity of each episode in the light of outside evidence, Augustine's other works, and his techniques and purposes.

PART II

AUGUSTINE ON LOVE AND SEXUALITY

🙵

5

Augustine the Artist and the *Aeneid*

₴

"Autre difficulté, propre à Augustin . . . Augustin, lui aussi, se répète beaucoup. Plus exactement, il emploie avec constance les mêmes schémas . . . on ne peut s'empêcher de penser à la nécissité d'une étude historique et génétique de ces schémas augustiniens. Ce serait une contribution importante à l'histoire de la pensée augustinienne . . . Autrement dit, il faudrait une étude des méthodes de travail d'Augustin . . . une extraordinaire puissance d'assimilation . . ." (P. Hadot, "Citations de Porphyre chez Augustin," REAug VI, 3 (1960), pp. 217f., 244.)

"There was never absent in him a certain magic and brilliance, for he was fundamentally an artist; he was, moreover, essentially an artist in sympathy, and that is why he never failed in charm . . . In his writings he remained till the day of his death one of the world's greatest artists in thought . . . He was also one of the most intuitive of poetical minds, for whatever one may say of him and in whatever mood we encounter him, the mark of the artist is palpable and unfailing." (F. Van der Meer, *Augustine the Bishop* [London 1961], pp. 21, 16.)

It seems altogether suitable that a Dublin contribution to these studies should concern itself with the artistry—to say nothing about the sympathy and charm—so unerringly discerned in Saint Augustine by Professor Mohrmann's colleague Van der Meer. Others more qualified will offer gifts more philological to our *docta*; one from Joyce's city proffers a fragment of *A Portrait of the Artist*:

[ἢ δέον ἀ]ιέν, ἀοιδέ, τὸ μὲν θύος ὅττι πάχιστον
[ἄμμι φέρει]ν, μοῦσαν δ'ὦ 'γαθέ, λεπταλέην.
　　　　　Callimachus, Πρὸς Τελχῖνας 23f.

One of the disconcerting features in Augustine is his tendency to attribute to his sources ideas which suit his present purpose, when there seems to be no objective ground for such an attribution. Even more—he frequently interprets an author as intending the very opposite of what he clearly says. He is, of course, fully aware of what he is doing, and there is no intention to deceive. He finds justification for this procedure in the existence of Providence in which he had a particularly lively belief:

> tertium est, cum ex alieno scripto intelligitur aliquid ueri, cum hoc ille qui scripsit non intellexerit. In quo genere non parum est utilitatis, imo si diligentius consideres, totius legendi fructus est integer; hic error non modo humanus est, sed saepe etiam homine dignissimus. (DUC X)

He goes on to say in the following paragraph that the reader may *usefully* understand the contrary of what the writer meant. It is not our purpose here to examine if such an attitude was determined to some extent by the circumstances of his conversion, and perhaps particularly by his attitude to certain Neoplatonists. Here we are concerned solely with the fact and an *additional* explanation of it, one rooted in his character and temperament as an artist. We are, to use Hadot's phrases, dealing with his *méthodes de travail,* his *puissance extraordinaire d'assimilation.*

But first one should look at a few preliminary instances of this phenomenon.

The first that is notable occurs at the end of Augustine's first extant work, the *Contra Academicos.* There he interprets the Academic principle *nihil posse percipi* as having been purely political and meant to conceal the fact that the Academy continued to preserve the true Platonic teaching. He then goes on:

> Hoc mihi de Academicis interim probabiliter, ut potui, persuasi. Quod si falsum est, nihil ad me, cui satis est iam non arbitrari, non posse ab homine inueniri veritatem (43).

It is very clear that Augustine has not only no confidence in his interpretation of the matter, but that he is not even greatly concerned whether it is true or not: his confidence reposes elsewhere.

It will not be necessary to do more than give a few other instances from a later work, a major work, say the *City of God.* A quick glance at the first half of this provides all that we shall need.

Posidonius in V.2 is represented as not likely to have been sincere in a certain astrological explanation. More seriously Varro in VI.4 and 9 is said not to have spoken plainly his mind on the matter of religion in Rome: *neque hoc aperte dicere uoluisse, sed intelligentibus reliquisse . . . ciuilem (religionem) uero reprehendere quidem non audeat.* Numa in VII.34f. is described as wishing to *conceal* the sources of his religious ordinances rather than *destroy* them so that they might providentially be discovered in due time: *sed occulta Dei ueri prouidentia factum est, ut et Pompilio amico suo illis conciliati artibus, quibus hydromantia fieri potuit, cuncta illa confiteri permitterentur, et tamen, ut moriturus incenderet ea potius quam obrueret, admonere non permitterentur.* In VIII.3 Socrates' moral approach to philosophy is said not to be clearly accounted for on the ground of the impossibility of arriving at rational truth and it is hinted that another explanation may be possible: *non mihi autem uidetur posse ad liquidum colligi . . . sicut de illo quidam beneuolentius suspicantur.* Apuleius in IX.8 is also said to have concealed his full opinion: *quamuis et eorum malitiae liberius exprimendae pepercerit, non tam ne ipsos, quam ne cultores eorum, apud quos loquebatur, offenderet: significauit tamen prudentibus, quid de illis sentire deberent . . .*

Interestingly enough Augustine goes on actually to consider the use of "opposites" *from an artistic point of view* in relation to God's providential design. God deals with antitheses in creation as a poet does in his poem: "ita ordinem saeculorum tamquam pulcherrimum carmen etiam ex quibusdam quasi antithetis honestaret. Antitheta quae appellantur in ornamentis elocutionis sunt decentissima, quae Latine ut appellentur opposita, uel, quod expressius dicitur, contraposita, non est apud nos huius uocabuli consuetudo . . . ista contraria contrariis opposita sermonis pulchritudinem reddunt (XI, 18). Venena ipsa, quae per inconuenientiam perniciosa sunt, conuenienter adhibita in salubria medicamenta uertantur . . . Vnde nos admonet diuina prouidentia non res insipienter uituperare, sed utilitatem rerum diligenter inquirere, et ubi nostrum ingenium uel infirmitas deficit, ita credere occultam, sicut erant quaedam, quae uix potuimus inuenire: quia et ipsa utilitatis occultatio aut humilitatis exercitatio est aut elationis adtritio" (22). He continues in this strain, referring to God as an *artifex magnus in magnis* and relating beauty to proportion and correspondence of parts.

Not only Numa, then, is willing to suppress knowledge (even if it be false) and even fear to publish it: *quod scire neminem uoluit, ne homines nefaria doceret, uiolare autem timuit, ne daemones iratos haberet* (VII.34); not only Varro likewise believes that it is useful that the general mass of people should sometimes have the truth withheld from them: *de religionibus loquens multa esse vera (dicit), quae non modo uulgo scire non sit utile, sed etiam, tametsi falsa sunt, aliter existimare populum expediat* (IV, 31); but even God's providence justly conspires in men being deceived: *decipi iustum est* (VII, 35).

To these instances many more, of greater or lesser consequence, dealing with the attitudes of Varro or Porphyry or Providence, might be added—but perhaps a sufficient range of examples has been given to suit our present purpose. It can be seen immediately that the possibilities for "comprehension" (in the strictest meaning of that word) provided by such a preoccupation with a Providence that reconciles all things, even what appear to be opposites, are very great and are exploited by Augustine. The artist in Augustine, however, felt free to combine, to assimilate, things that might seem to have no apparent connection—and even things that were clearly contraries: *tamquam pulcherrimum carmen etiam ex quibusdam quasi antithetis honestaret.* Indeed one may feel that the artist in Augustine, when it came to composition, tended to take over from the theologian. It might have helped sometimes to have kept in mind that the artist can gain the ascendant in Augustine's words and phrases; that the artist has his own daring, takes his material very often from where he wills, and uses it often with little reference (and even at variance) to its original use. The artist at times can often seem almost irresponsible in his real or assumed vagueness towards his material: *illae quibus tenere cogebar Aeneae nescio cuius errores* (C I, 13, 20). Who can possibly believe that Augustine was uncertain as to the identity of Aeneas? If he says something similar of Cicero or some other person or event about whom or which we have controlling information we are saved from deception: but this should serve as a useful reminder that we should always remember that we are dealing in Augustine's case with an artist who does not always resist the demands of his *métier.*

The element of "make-believe" is strong in any artist; it was strong in Augustine. The images of his past reading and experience kept beckoning to him as he composed, inviting him to use them. He tells us for all practical purposes so himself:

> uenio in campos et lata praetoria memoriae, ubi sunt thesauri innumerabilium imaginum de cuiuscemodi rebus sensis inuectarum. Ibi reconditum est quidquid etiam cogitamus, uel augendo uel minuendo, uel utcumque uariando ea quae sensus attigerit; et si quid aliud commendatum et repositum est, quod nondum absorbuit et sepeliuit obliuio. Ibi quando sum, posco ut proferatur quidquid uolo, et quaedam statim prodeunt; quaedam requiruntur diutius, et tamquam de abstrusioribus quibusdam receptaculis eruuntur; quaedam cateruatim se proruunt, et dum aliud petitur et quaeritur, prosiliunt in medium quasi dicentia, ne forte nos sumus? et abigo ea manu cordis a facie recor-

dationis meae, donec enubiletur quod uolo, atque in conspectum prodeat ex abditis. . . . (C X, 8, 12)

For the moment this passage, which may owe something to Virgil as we shall see, reveals the artist at work, moulding his material with a full artistic consciousness. It is not his *mind* which finally judges the image to be accepted or rejected; rather it is his heart—*abigo ea manu cordis a facie recordationis meae*—a conceit which is certainly more literary than philosophical or theological.

In seeking to interpret such a writer one cannot have full confidence in the efficacy of scientific methods which, whatever their value when soberly applied to texts written by authors less artistic than Augustine, may fail to do justice to him. It is not merely that Augustine will combine two or several ideas coming from different places and even different authors; that he will combine ideas that would seem to have little to do with one another, or are in fact strictly incompatible; he will, temporarily at least, advance solutions which the neatness of construction suggest to him, even if one knows that he cannot really believe in them. Above all, the same themes are being endlessly combined and expressed in phrases partly the same and partly different. He is essentially the artist moulding his clay. To discern the different elements in his composition is no easy task and requires equipment that is more than purely scientific. Here proof cannot always be demanded. Here familiarity and sensitivity can be of great use. Above all they can be useful, if not in proving some point, at least in getting to know Augustine.

As a brief exercise in trying to discover the genesis of Augustine's ideas, his methods of work and assimilation, and his repetition of themes, it may be of some use to consider the influence that the *Aeneid*, and particularly Aeneas himself, had upon him, especially in the *Confessions*. This on the face of it is a fairly neutral topic, not involving theological or Neoplatonic controversies. This is an advantage. On the other hand one must forego in such a proceeding the advantages given by aiming at a particular point to be "proved"; even if proof is not achieved, a straight thrust through a tangled field of scholarship can yield sometimes fine vistas and considerable results.

It might be well to draw attention very briefly at this stage to a certain similarity between Augustine and the creator of the *Aeneid*. Both spent their childhood in small towns and went to local schools; both subsequently went to greater centres of learning and studied rhetoric; and both later developed a serious interest in philosophy. Both enjoyed some patronage, and both retired from public careers, partly through physical infirmity. These factors, however, are purely external, not to say accidental. The same may be true of what similarities one may choose to discover in the earliest iconographical representations we have of them. But their literary temperaments and approach, their profound preoccupation with religion and man's sad destiny, their consciousness of being the witnesses and interpreters of new eras, these are bonds more intimate and of greater consequence.

That the *Aeneid* was the book of all others that affected and was loved by the growing Augustine is beyond question. But the intensity of this influence and its persistence right up to the time of his conversion at least is not always kept in mind. Yet it is important that we should remember the active hold this poem had upon him, and what such a hold implies about the literary cast of his mind:

> adamaueram enim latinas (litteras), non quas primi magistri, sed quas docent qui grammatici uocantur ... tenere cogebar Aeneae nescio cuius errores, oblitus errorum meorum; et plorare Didonem mortuam, quia se occidit ob amorem ... quid enim miserius misero non miserante seipsum, et flente Didonis mortem, quae fiebat amando Aenean ... flebam Didonem 'exstinctam ferroque extrema secutam' ... et si prohiberer ea legere, dolerem, quia non legerem quod dolerem ... non clament aduersus me uenditores grammaticae uel emptores: quia si proponam eis, interrogans utrum uerum sit quod Aenean aliquando Carthaginem uenisse Poeta dicit; indoctiores nescire se respondebunt, doctiores autem etiam negabunt uerum esse ... peccabam ergo puer cum illa inania ... amabam ... dulcissimum spectaculum uanitatis equus ligneus plenus armatis, et Troiae incendium, atque ipsius umbra Creusae. (C I, 13, 20f.)

One should note that here he refers to the *Aeneid* not by its title, but by the descriptive phrase *Aeneae errores* which became for him symbolical of his own wanderings and of the wanderings of mankind on its way to its destiny. One should also not underrate the special appeal of the poem to a North African boy, because of Aeneas's coming to Carthage. But the episode of Dido seems to have made an appeal to Augustine which was also very personal: her death for the love of Aeneas is contrasted with the death of his soul for want of the love of God.

After his conversion and on the eve of his baptism Augustine, who must have continually used the *Aeneid* in his profession as rhetor, was still reading Virgil. In DOR I, 26 we are told that he read half a book of

Virgil before supper at Cassiciacum with his young charges there. For a period of seven days no discussions were held: *cum tres tantum Virgilii libros post primum recenseremus, atque ut in tempore congruere uidebatur, tractaremus. Quo tamen opere Licentius in poeticae studium sic inflammatus est* . . . (CA II, 4, 10; cf. III, 1, 1). Perhaps Licentius' passion owed something to Augustine's own. In the contemporary *De beata uita* there is a very puzzling preface, which is in part at least autobiographical, which has an allusion to the Sirens, but which may well be inspired to some extent by the wanderings of Aeneas. The possible echo of words, phrases and sentiments here from the fourth book of the *Aeneid* especially need not detain us here. We should note, however, how Augustine, whatever his literary source or sources for this preface, employs great freedom of assimilation, going so far as to include a reference to the specific point of the influence of the reading of books in the matter of conversion: this must be founded more directly on his own experience than on any literary source—and yet he generalizes it.

Even at the later stage of the composition of the *De ciuitate Dei* the *Aeneid* continued its hold upon Augustine. In the very preface the city of the Scriptures is compared to the city of Virgil: rex enim et conditor ciuitatis huius in scriptura populi sui sententiam diuinae legis aperuit, qua dictum est: "Deus superbis resistit, humilibus, autem dat gratiam." Hoc uero, quod Dei est, superbae quoque animae spiritus inflatus adfectat amatque sibi in laudibus dici: "parcere subiectis et debellare superbos." Augustine in effect puts forward his *Ciuitas Dei* as the Christian prose epic of Rome, in which the presence of the *Aeneid* is often felt. Apart from the fact that allusion to Virgil's poem is sustained throughout DCD (especially *Aeneid* I, II, IV, VI and VIII and especially in DCD III and IX) the underlying theme of the *peregrinatio ad patriam* is as dominant as in the *Aeneid*: *Italiam quaero patriam* (I.380). The theme of the fall of Troy is answered by the "fall" of Rome in book II of DCD, and the use of the theory of metempsychosis in *Aeneid* VI, especially ll.719–67, is paralleled by its use in DCD in connection with the central problem of the return of the soul and Christian immortality: *quae lucis miseris tam dira cupido?* (*Aen*. VI.721). The part of oracles, pagan and Christian (i.e., the Scriptures), is prominent in both works as is that of peace as the ultimate end in both: *pacis imponere morem: pax Romana* and *pax Christiana*.

But it is in the *Confessions* that the presence of the *Aeneid* is most felt. The circumstance of the alliterative parallel between the names Augustinus, Alypius, Adeodatus (Iatanbaal) and Aeneas, Achates and Ascanius (Iulus) is an odd accident. But it is no accident that Augustine thinks of the wanderings up to his conversion at times in terms of Aeneas, and most particularly of his own dallying with the flesh and postponement of vocation to Aeneas lingering in Carthage: the temptation was ended in both cases by an order from on high. Augustine had, as a matter of fact, entered deeply into sympathy on the side of Juno, Africa and Dido against Aeneas' duty in the exercise of ἠθοποιία which he had carried out with great success (C I, 17, 27 referring to *Aen.* I.32–35). One might ask here if anything of the sense of the mission that he had was communicated to Augustine in his thinking of the mission of his literary exemplar, Aeneas? One cannot know, of course. But it is difficult not to suspect that there must have been some influence here as well.

At any rate the literary overtones, conscious or unconscious, from *Aeneid* IV upon the *Confessions* may be discerned in the description of the enticements of Carthage to the young boy (III, 1, 1: *oderam securitatem et uiam sine muscipulis*), the painful wrenching of himself from the allurements of women: antiquae amicae meae succutiebant uestem meam carneam . . . discedentem quasi furtim uellicantes, ut respicerem. Retardabant tamen cunctantem me abripere atque excutere ab eis et transilire quo uocabar; cf. VIII.5.12. As Aeneas, so Augustine had considered the possibility of reconciling marriage with the mission which he knew was his—but this had to be rejected (C VI, 12, 21):

> fata obstant placidasque uiri deus obstruit auris
> mens immota manet, lacrimae uoluuntur inanes.
> (*Aen.* IV.440, 449)

In DCD (IX, 4) this last line easily came back to Augustine's mind to point the moral that, however harrowing the experience, we must forego all to do our duty. When the bidding came from above, both Aeneas (*Aen.* IV. 265ff.) and Augustine (C VIII, 12, 29) straightway overcame all obstacles: *attonitus tanto monitu imperioque deorum; diuinitus mihi iuberi.*[1]

Characteristically enough Aeneas's separation from Dido is used nevertheless also for the separation of Augustine from his mother, Monnica. Naturally suggestions might have come to him from many literary models, notably the story of the abandonment of Ariadne by Theseus; but it is impossible to exclude the episode of Dido and Aeneas from consideration. The purpose of Providence had to be carried out and Monnica, when the dawn came, found that her son had flown (*Aen.* IV.576ff.; 584ff.; C V, 8, 15). Nor should it occasion us any surprise if at times we feel that Monnica is thought of not only as Dido but, perhaps, more suitably as Aeneas's mother Venus, who had taken an active part in helping her son to fulfill, however reluctantly at times, his destiny.

The sixth book of the *Aeneid* is, of course, likely to have affected the *Confessions* in one way or another. In the *Aeneid* Aeneas is finally confirmed in his vocation by experiences in an underworld which has many Platonic touches. Augustine likewise (but there is no suggestion that this was not historical), was brought to the point of conversion by certain Platonic doctrines. Curiously, and again characteristically, the same journey to the underworld possibly lies behind the eloquent description in the *Confessions* of the *campos memoriae* with which we have already dealt: Aeneas discovers in Elysium not only Anchises but also the Roman worthies that were yet to be born:

> At pater Anchises penitus conualle uirenti
> inclusas animas superumque ad lumen ituras
> lustrabat studio recolens, omnemque suorum
> forte recensebat numerum . . .
> (*Aen.* VI.679ff.)

The passage from C X, 8, 12 already quoted, containing such terms as *campos, reconditum, repositum, obliuio, proferatur, abstrusioribus receptaculis, in conspectum prodeat ex abditis*, goes on as follows: "grandis memoriae recessus, et nescio qui secreti atque ineffabiles sinus eius . . . ibi et ipse mihi occurro; . . . atque ex his etiam actiones et euenta et spes, et haec omnia rursus quasi praesentia meditor . . . dico apud me . . . O si esset hoc aut illud! Auertat Deus hoc aut illud." Have we an echo here of that famous and pathetic line: "heu, miserande puer, si qua fata aspera rumpas . . ." (*Aen.* VI.882)? This brief and inadequate exercise helps us to see that Augustine was an artist and how he works. He was interested intensely in the processes of his own life, but he was also deeply involved in mankind; as he tried to discern the future plan of his own life, so he had a constructive and interpretative interest in the destiny of mankind at large. It was natural that with these preoccupations he tended to think of types, as himself as a type of man, such as Aeneas or the new man of Christian Rome. Literary characters all contained some message for him—he saw himself in all of them; all men were in him. This was the product of an unusually highly developed literary sensibility and natural taste for literature. This in turn was connected with, if not dependent upon, a memory that was, as he says himself, vigorous and tenacious.

This memory was not wholly unconscious: it was led by the mind as well as the heart. It surveyed its material and then chose and moulded it according to his desires and purposes. In forming his themes he took his details not from one source only, but from several—some of them in other circumstances unlikely to be combined. With the theological doctrine of Providential economy to support him, his artist's mind conflated, altered, reinterpreted, attributed alleged meanings to, and understood even the opposite of what an original source might have supplied. He does not do justice to Augustine who denies him inventiveness and free association, even if he must recognize that occasionally Augustine's syntheses were more neat than probable (of which he himself was fully aware). He was not consistent in his use of the same material: none of it was left inert within his mind, whether its source was the Bible, the thinking of the Platonists, or the literature of Rome,[2] especially the *Aeneid*. Nor was his art entirely predictable, entirely a matter of clean lines and neatly fitting elements.

And if his theology affected his art, so—even if we often forget it—did his art affect at least the formulation of his theology. Augustine was no scientific historian, or philosopher, or theologian. This is not to say that he is the less reliable as historian, philosopher or theologian: it is rather to say that the purely and exclusively scientific approach to Augustine is not sufficient. In itself such an approach will not allow us to follow the whole drift of his meaning. Here familiarity with even a fragment of the portrait of the artist will be of some aid.

6

Virgil and Augustine
The Roman Background to Christian Sexuality

ଌ

Status Quaestionis

In the autumn of 1963 there appeared an article by L. Janssens[1] which asserted that the pessimistic and rigoristic tendencies that determined the outlook of the Stoics, Neo-Pythagoreans, Essenes, and Gnostics on the moral evaluation of the marriage act and sexual[2] pleasure passed into western theology especially through the writings of St. Augustine. His authority was so great that for centuries his influence was paramount.

Janssens asserted that Augustine introduced a dualism into married life: his pessimistic attitude to sexual pleasure demanded that he should find justification for its use—this was found both in the need for procreation (*bonum prolis*) and precaution against a partner's adultery (*bonum fidei*). On the other hand true conjugal love was a *purely spiritual thing* (*bonum sacramenti*) in regard to which sexual relations could have no positive signification whatever. In fact carnal desire was for him an evil (*malum*) and a disease (*morbus*) and could only be an obstacle to the flowering of conjugal love. The more desire is repressed, the stronger is the *caritas coniugalis*. Hence Augustine, according to Janssens, wishes that all Christian couples could practice complete continence so as to be united not in the flesh but in *caritas*.

Janssens is careful to point out some of the sources of these ideas: Stoics, Neo-Pythagoreans, Essenes, and Gnostics. He is also careful to state that, although he was the principal agent in the transmission of these ideas into Christian theology, Augustine was not the only Church Father responsible. There were also Justin Martyr, for example, Athenagoras, Clement of Alexandria, Origen, Ambrose, and Jerome. All of these were determined that the Christian view of marriage would be no whit less ascetical than the Stoic or Neo-Pythagorean or what you will. He notes too that of the three great controversies that dominated Augustine's life—with the Donatists, the Manicheans, and the Pelagians—

the two latter provided him with a field only too favorable for the development of such pessimistic ideas.

Augustine's responsibility for the *transmission* of such attitudes on sexuality is, therefore, sufficiently clear. Unfortunately the account in his *Confessions* of his own earlier sexual life is so exposed to misconstruction,[3] in the sense that he had been a profligate in this regard, that more popular authors with insufficient knowledge of the question rationalize by saying simply that Augustine was a rigorist in sexual matters, precisely because he was reacting against his own earlier (alleged) behaviour. Augustine is thus becoming *the evil genius* of Christian Puritan morality, not only the transmitter, but largely the origin also.[4]

Since 1963 another source for Augustine's pessimism on sexual matters has been discovered, this time further back in Lucretius. D. R. Dudley asks: "Is it not possible that this passage[5] (the *innumerabilia mala* that attend hopeless love) was given an extended application by Augustine? And that it played a part in shaping that obsessive horror he came to feel for all the processes of sex and generation: *inter faeces et urinam nascimur*? If so, then the ἀταραξία of Epicurus is an ingredient in that Augustinian puritanism which has held such long sway.[6] Dudley draws timely attention to the passage in the *Confessions*[7] where Augustine reports of the period shortly before his conversion that, from his discussions with his friends Alypius and Nebridius, he would then have considered Epicureanism to have scored over all other systems, except that it did not admit any life after death nor any rewards or punishments, which he did.

Here then we are presented with Augustine the arrested enthusiast of Epicurean philosophy and transmitter of Lucretian pessimistic attitudes on sexual matters. Dudley, moreover, accepts the views of Quinn[8] and Allen[9] that Lucretius's attitude to love blighted the whole of Roman love poetry as seen in the coarseness and frivolity of Horace and the cold professional competence of the sensuality of Ovid. Catullus and Propertius alone, according to them, escape this frightful blight.

Virgil's Influence on Augustine

We can accept, I believe, the reality of the pessimistic contributions of the Stoics, Neo-Pythagoreans, Lucretius, and other Roman poets through Augustine to Christian sexuality. To this extent we already *have* a Roman background to it, a background that appears to me to have overshadowed in some ways the Christian message itself, so that at times it has been mistaken for it. It is curious, however, that in discussing the contrasting attitudes of Catullus and Propertius on the one hand and Lucretius "and the whole of Roman love poetry" on the other, Dudley does not mention Virgil at all, although he does Horace and Ovid.

Yet Virgil was greatly and consciously dependent on Lucretius (even if to a degree also on Catullus), wrote much on the theme of love and had strong, if not actually dominating, Epicurean connections. Virgil is, moreover, of special interest in relation to Augustine, for not even Cicero, whose influence in the intellectual formation of Augustine was fundamental, played as living a role in his conscious and subconscious mind as did Virgil. I have written something on this elsewhere,[10] and I shall not now repeat what I said then except in the most summary way.

Augustine as a boy had loved the story of the wooden horse, the burning of Troy and the "shade" of Creusa. He had entered deeply into the exercise of ἠθοποιία in connection with portraying the anger of Juno at her failure to prevent Aeneas and his companions from coming to Italy.[11] In his profession of rhetor he must continually have used the *Aeneid*. When he retired to Cassiciacum shortly after his conversion in 386 A.D. he read half a book of Virgil before supper with his charges Licentius and Trygetius every evening. His *Dialogues* reflect his interest in Virgil. In his *Confessions,* the story of his life's search for God, the presence of Aeneas and the *Aeneid* are strongly felt: his own wanderings, his dallying with the flesh and postponement of resolution reminded him of Aeneas's experience with Dido.[12] In both Aeneas's case and his own, when the trials of their formation had reached a climax, the deity had suddenly intervened. Augustine's sense of mission—and he had it in a profound degree—encountered the same opposition within himself as did Aeneas's, but won through:

> mens immota manet, lacrimae volvuntur inanes.

In the preface itself to the *City of God,* Augustine compares the city of the Scriptures which he is about to defend to the city of Rome: the ideal of the one is given as *Deus superbis resistit, humilibus autem dat gratiam.* The parallel ideal of the other is given in the words of the *Aeneid*: *parcere subiectis et debellare superbos.* Augustine in effect aims in the *City of God* to write the Christian prose epic of Rome. Allusion to the *Aeneid* is sustained throughout Augustine's great work, the underlying theme of which—*peregrinatio ad patriam*—dominates it, as does *Italiam quaero pa-*

triam the *Aeneid*. The theme of *the fall of Troy* in Virgil's work is answered by *the fall of Rome* in the second book (*also*) of the *City of God*. The use of the theory of metempsychosis in the *Aeneid*[13] is paralleled by its use in the *City of God* in connection with the central problem of the return of the soul and Christian immortality: *quae lucis miseris tam dira cupido?* The part of oracles is prominent in both works, as is that of peace as the desired end of both cities; *pacis imponere morem: pax Romana; pax Christiana*.

In the preceding we have been considering Augustine, the artist, revealing a deep sensibility and response to Virgil and his great theme. One element in that theme, one which we know strongly affected Augustine, was Aeneas's regretfully, but with relief, rejecting an appealing love at the bidding of a deity—to carry out a purpose judged higher and more worthy of pursuit than love. It is, therefore, necessary to indicate not only that the Stoics, the Neo-Pythagoreans, and Lucretius affected Augustine's attitude to love, but to examine also Virgil's attitude to love: for this certainly influenced Augustine, probably even more profoundly, and through him western theology.

Background to Virgil's Attitude to Love

The study of Virgil's attitude to love has been comparatively neglected by scholars. The background to this attitude is made up of various elements: with three of these, the contemporary moral, literary, and philosophical we shall immediately concern ourselves. These, of course, only partly reflect a much wider range of thought and experience. But it will be useful to glance at them briefly in turn.

Saara Lilja in *The Roman Elegists' Attitude to Women*,[14] although rather drastically restrictive in both material and approach to it, has many useful things to say of the contemporary moral background to love poetry in Rome in the years before 18 B.C.[15] The νεώτεροι had begun to put a serious valuation on free love and to prefer it to marriage, the sole object of which had been of old to produce new citizens.

"The new attitude to love adopted by the *poetae novi* clashed with public opinion, according to which an individual had to sacrifice all else to the welfare of the nation. One of the contemporaries of Catullus who defended the conventional view most strenuously was Cicero; and at the same time, Lucretius,[16] in the closing part of Bk. IV of his *De rerum natura*, condemned blind passion as a threat to the Epicurean peace of mind."[17] Those who defended the new attitude frequently admitted that in placing love and poetry—the *vita iners*—before all other pursuits they were doing something morally reprehensible:

> Otium, Catulle, tibi molestum est:
> otio exsultas nimiumque gestis:
> otium et reges prius et beatas
> perdidit urbes.[18]

But they couldn't help it: love was a slavery, a disease, madness. Their opponent Lucretius could not but agree to that.

Lilja has this to say of Virgil: "Let us pay attention to a marked resemblance between the notion of love as madness in Roman elegy and Virgil's description of Dido's demented love in the fourth book of the *Aeneid*. Virgil composed his epos in the years 29–19 B.C. and, according to Donatus, he did not do it systematically from the first book to the last. It is inviting to imagine that Dido's story may have been the first thing to inspire Virgil, whose tenth *Eclogue*, which is concerned with Gallus, praises the supreme power of love with the words *omnia vincit Amor: et nos cedamus Amori*" (69).[19]

Enough[20] has been written on the topic to make it unnecessary to do more than say that Dido's story, however, derives largely from the Medea[21] of Euripides who with his other creation Phaedra dominated the literary and male treatment—outside of satire—of woman in love in antiquity and long after. There was tenderness in Homer, although Helen was for him too ἑλέναυς ἕλανδρος, ἑλέπτολις[22]—the destroyer of ships and men and cities—and in Sappho, and even Archilochus. There was a philosophy of Aphrodite in the Homeric Hymns. But in general there was a growing tendency within Greek literature to think of love as a pleasure indeed, but even more a source of pain invincible,— a madness, leading women (good or bad), if scorned, to frightful revenge procured even, if necessary, by magic and spells. It is no wonder, then, that men sought an escape in philosophy and mutual friendship of one kind or another. Plato influenced men strongly in this direction.

From a literary point of view, therefore, Virgil, although he was responsive to all the various influences playing upon him, had to choose between the conventional attitudes towards marriage, love, and friendship on the one hand and the earlier and contemporary literary influences on the other—but whatever his ultimate choice, he had sympathy for all. One's scepticism in fully accepting easy categories of love in Rome as Lucretian (i.e., coarse and blighting) and Catullan (tender and idyllic) would be more than justified in the case of the maturing and more enigmatic Virgil. In any case Virgil was clearly influenced by both Lucretius and Catullus—but he chose to be an apostle of Righteousness.

In some ways philosophy helps to clarify the matter more, for there can be little doubt that Epicureanism did influence Virgil greatly in his youth and continued to do so for long after, if not in fact until the end.[23] The Donatus-Suetonius *Life* of Virgil reports that Virgil received the *toga virilis* on the very day on which Lucretius died—suggesting thereby that to some he seemed Lucretius's heir—as indeed he so clearly is in so many respects.

He moved, moreover, in the Epicurean circle near Naples that centred around Philodemus of Gadara and with which Horace and Varius Rufus among his poet friends were associated. Philodemus wrote epigrams dealing with erotic themes that are to be found in the *Greek Anthology*, but also others on friendship, moderation in pleasure and Epicurean themes. Another Epicurean in whose *hortulus* at Naples Virgil spent some of his impressionable years was Siro, of whom, however, we know practically nothing. Siro was also frequented, it is said, not only by the poets Quintilius Varus, Varius Rufus and Plotius Tucca, but also by Julius Caesar, Piso, Hirtius, Pansa, Dolabella, Cassius, Trebatius, Atticus, Paetus, and the soldier-poet Gallus.

Epicureanism was formally against marriage and love—both being judged inimical to peace. Friendship on the other hand was an *end* in the Epicurean thinking: it was achieved in living together under spiritual guidance in philosophic pursuit of the common goal: *happiness*. "Friendship calls us all to wake up to make one another happy." "Rather than a doctrine," writes Festugière, "Epicureanism was a spirit which realized itself in close fraternities where one preserved scrupulously the Word of the Sage and made profession of friendship."[24]

It can be seen that the influences, contemporary moral, literary, and especially philosophical, playing upon Virgil came both from the remote past and were a living and pressing reality upon him in Naples and in Rome. Donatus-Suetonius' *Vita* purports to fill in the facts of his life insofar as love in a general way is concerned: libidinis in pueros pronioris . . . vulgatum est consuesse eum et cum Plotia Hieria. sed Asconius Pedianus adfirmat, ipsam postea maiorem natu narrare solitam, invitatum quidem a Vario ad communionem sui, verum pertinacissime recusasse.

cetera sane vitae et ore et animo tam probum constat, ut Neapoli Parthenias vulgo appellatus sit.[25]

The influences I have described certainly must have disposed Virgil towards the cultivation of friendship in a philosophic and more specifically Epicurean vein. Although Virgil has sometimes been thought of as a Stoic and his creation Aeneas as a θεῖος ἀνήρ, V. Pöschl[26] seems to the present writer to be nearer the truth in regarding Aeneas and Virgil as approaching the Christian ideal of the hero: they have the power to save us from sentimentality, while having compassion on others, and raise us to resignation: this is far from a Stoic ideal.

At any rate Virgil's certainly known first body of poetry extant, the *Eclogues*, is a book involving a circle of friends—Quintus Cornificius, Cornelius Gallus, Alfenus Varus, Quintilius Varus, Asinius Pollio, and Lucius Valerius Messalla, a number of whom had shared with Virgil life in an Epicurean circle in or near Naples. But the *Eclogues* do not eschew the topic of love: on the contrary, *pace* Perret,[27] love is at least one of the dominating themes:

omnis vincit amor; et nos cedamus amori.[28]

Virgil on Sexuality

Here, since I must confine myself, I shall draw attention to just three passages representative of Virgil's attitude towards sexuality, one from each of his three works (dwelling, however, principally on the first)— *Eclogues* VI 41–81; *Georgics* III, especially 242ff., and *Aeneid* IV in general. I do not contend that these passages are in themselves wholly representative of Virgil's outlook on sexuality; but they are generally so.

Eclogue VI 41–81

The sixth *Eclogue*, according to Holtorf,[29] comes chronologically about halfway in the series, between *Eclogue* I and *Eclogue* IV. It holds, therefore, a central position amongst the ten. It has been preceded by *Eclogue* II, *The Passionate Shepherd to his Love*, which has the moral that physical love, here among men, is to be avoided or at least controlled, since it is without hope and destructive.

Next comes *Eclogue* III, the theme of the contest in which is love (*ho-*

mosexual and heterosexual), and which sings the praises of love's ineffable sweetness, speaks of its sadness in separation and angers, and again concludes that this fearful bittersweet experience destroys men and beasts: *idem amor exitium est pecori pecorisque magistro.*

Then comes *Eclogue* V, which celebrates Daphnis, the *inventor* and principal hero of pastoral poetry: Daphnis is distinctly an exotic figure being portrayed as a lover of one kind or another in Timaeus, Hermesianax, Sositheus, and Theocritus,[30] where he angers Aphrodite by claiming to be the equal of Eros himself. Virgil laments that with the death of Daphnis all nature dies. Daphnis symbolizes fertility—as does Venus at the beginning of Lucretius' poem[31]—the goodness of reproduction. *Eclogue* IX touches casually on the same subject of Daphnis, and *Eclogue* I speaks of freedom (*libertas*) which refers to politico-social matters but possibly also has overtones on the freedom from the bonds and cares of love[32] conferred by philosophy.

Eclogue VI, the *Song of Silenus*, introduces philosophy boldly and with unusual solemnity, a philosophy incontrovertibly Lucretian. The Silenus of the poem is himself a symbol of philosophy. His usual representation as intoxicated is understood to refer to his mysticism, which, being a fat and jolly old man riding on an ass and crowned with flowers, he apparently took lightheartedly.[33] Silenus describes in exact Lucretian terms the physical constitution of the universe for ten lines (31–40). Then, when he comes to describe the origin of man, Silenus abruptly has recourse to mythology: as Servius says, *relictis prudentibus rebus de mundi origine, subito ad fabulas transitum fecit:*

> hinc lapides Pyrrhae iactos, Saturnia regna,
> Caucasiasque refert volucris furtumque Promethei.
> his adiungit, Hylan nautae quo fonte relictum
> clamassent, ut litus "Hyla, Hyla" omne sonaret;
> et fortunatam, si numquam armenta fuissent,
> Pasiphaen nivei solatur amore iuvenci,
> a, virgo infelix, quae te dementia cepit!
>
> Tum canit Hesperidum miratam mala puellam;
> tum Phaethontiadas musco circumdat amarae
> corticis atque solo proceras erigit alnos.
> tum canit errantem Permessi ad flumina Gallum
> Aonas in montis ut duxerit una sororum,
> utque viro Phoebi chorus adsurrexerit omnis;
>
> quid loquar aut Scyllam Nisi, quam fama secuta est
> candida succinctam latrantibus inguina monstris

> Dulichias vexasse rates et gurgite in alto,
> a, timidos nautas canibus lacerasse marinis,
>
> aut ut mutatos Terei narraverit artus,
> quas illi Philomela dapes, quae dona pararit.
> quo cursu deserta petiverit et quibus ante
> infelix sua tecta super volitaverit alis.[34]

It has generally escaped notice that this version of man's origins implies a far more pessimistic view of women than even that given in Genesis: for it is a list mainly composed of the enormities of women in love.

From the general structure of this passage as a whole, where no item is dealt with in less than a line, I am inclined to think that the first two lines refer as one unit merely to the time of the creation of *women* by Pyrrha[35]—for women are to be the subject of the passage. In any case the chronological confusion of placing Pyrrha before her uncle, Prometheus, and even Saturn, can be justified only by the emphasizing of Pyrrha over Saturn and Prometheus—which has the result of focusing the light especially on the creation of women. The reference to Hylas recalls the incident when on the voyage of the Argonauts he was abducted by the lustful water-nymphs.

The next is the shocking story of the love of Pasiphae, wife of Minos of Crete, for a white bull. Virgil dwells on this episode for sixteen lines stressing the mad infatuation (*dementia*) of her love, which was greater than that of the daughters of Proetus, who, even though they were wholly persuaded that they were cows, still did not wish to do as she did. He stresses too the lack of interest of the bull and the likelihood of his distraction by Cretan cows. Virgil has gone near to the grotesque at this point, presumably to horrify us with how far a woman's love can go. At the same time these lines are notable for their sympathetic tenderness towards Pasiphae: twice he apostrophizes her, *a virgo infelix*. He thinks of her painful and vain wanderings in pursuit, of her distraction so that she calls out to the nymphs to help her, and of her destined disappointment. And it is significant that Dido should echo the words, *fortunatam si numquam armenta fuissent*, as she commits suicide on her desertion by Aeneas.[36] It is a useful reminder that Virgil enters deeply into the lot of women in love.

Next on the list is Atalanta, a woman of a totally different kind—but still not admirable. Her problem was that she was determined like her counterpart Hippolytus to live in perpetual celibacy. She cruelly killed the suitors who could not outrace her. But she too had to yield to a suitor,

Hippomenes, who had profited by the wiles of Venus. The particular point made against her here is in *miratam*: her greed for the apples of Hesperides was the undoing of her resolution to be celibate—she could be corrupted. The sisters of Phaeton were examples of such stubborn and vain[37] devotion to a brother's tomb that they brought death upon themselves, being changed into trees. It is impossible to account for the sudden intrusion at this point of Virgil's friend Cornelius Gallus—but one can say that Virgil makes a practice in the *Eclogues* of doing this kind of thing—so that we are not too surprised by it. On the other hand an explanation that might readily occur to the friends of Virgil and Gallus might easily escape us—and might conceivably fit into the context of the list of women—since we know that Gallus was eminent for his love poetry.

The story of Scylla, the daughter of Nisus, resumes the list of unfortunate women involved in love. She betrayed her father through desire to marry his enemy Minos. But Minos deceived her, whereupon she drowned herself. It is clear from the passage, however, that Virgil applies to her some of the story of Scylla, daughter of Typho, who scorned the love of Glaucus. Glaucus asked Circe for a love philtre so that he might win Scylla, but Circe, who had become infatuated with him, gave him instead a poison which changed Scylla below the waist into frightful barking monsters. She was so terrified that she threw herself into the sea between Italy and Sicily and became transformed into rocks that endangered ships and caused the destruction of sailors. Virgil in his conflation of the versions of the story of Scylla has chosen the details that put women in the worst possible light. Finally there is the gruesome story of Philomela (in the version told here) serving up as a meal to Tereus, her husband, the flesh of their son Itys, and then presenting him with Itys's head, hands, and feet in revenge for Tereus's affair with her sister. Once again there is compassion for Philomela who had loved her home.

Silenus did not stop there. He continued to sing the songs sung by Apollo to the Spartan youth Hyacinthus whom he loved—songs of love, perhaps. But these songs are not given. In what he has given, however, Virgil has painted a sombre but sympathetic picture of women in love—lustful, unnatural in lust, cruel and greedy and corruptible, stubborn, treacherous and disloyal and suicidal, ruthless even to the destruction of themselves and their children in jealousy and revenge. Philomela is very much a Medea-figure. It is a picture of woman's love that is very forbidding indeed. It is also, significantly, given as the history of mankind from its beginning. Women may cause all that is evil but they are not entirely to blame.

To summarize briefly the remaining *Eclogues*:

Eclogue IV commends marriage and procreation as the only way of renewing the world and ourselves.

Eclogue VIII deals with love among shepherds, of one's hopelessness in resisting or satisfying[38] it. *Nunc scio quid sit amor.*[39] Damon sings that Love is *indignus*, deceives one, brings death, gives one sorrowful complaint, is without hope, is unnatural, is unscrupulous, can be bound by no vows, is immediately fatal, induces evil derangement, is born of the rocks and has no blood, is cruel, is remorseless, and turns everything upside[40] down. There is emphasis again on the destructiveness of love especially through women:

> saevus Amor docuit natorum sanguine matrem
> commaculare manus; crudelis tu quoque, mater:
> crudelis mater magis, an puer improbus ille?
> improbus ille puer; crudelis tu quoque, mater.[41]

Love is first to be blamed—then women. The song of Alphesiboeus in response speaks of love depriving one of one's senses, fastening one in chains, burning one with fire, binding one by spells and magic, destroying one so that one hasn't even the will to be cured, perfidious and untrustworthy. But men rejoice at the advent of love, just the same.

Whereas *Eclogue* VIII gives a pretty comprehensive summary of Virgil's strictures on love, *Eclogue* VII sings, but with less emphasis, of the small joys of love.

Eclogue X celebrates Gallus's *Troubled Loves*.[42] Love is unworthy, destructive, deranging, disloyal, beyond control, uncaring, cruel, insatiable, saddening, a frenzy, hard, incurable, unpitying, robs one of one's interest, is unbending: *omnia vincit amor; et nos cedamus amori.*[43] Love is invincible. Virgil concludes by protesting that he loves Gallus hourly more and more.

Although philosophy and peace are prominent themes in the *Eclogues*, it would be impossible to say that the theme of love—and here physical love is almost always involved—is less dominant except in the sense that the elimination or control of love is essential for the philosophical life and peace. Love, in fact, is the enemy and occupies most of Virgil's attention. The enemy, naturally, is described in hostile terms, and woman, who for most men represents the enemy, fares badly in the account. In brief, marriage and procreation are to be commended, love of any kind but especially of women is to be avoided even if it may prove impossible to do so, and peace in a simple philosophical life is to be preferred above all. Virgil speaks with accents strongly Epicurean.

Georgics III esp. 242 ss.

We can look even more briefly at the passages from *Georgics* III and *Aeneid* IV; otherwise we would involve ourselves in much useless repetition. Only the essential points that cannot be presumed to be commonly known will be discussed.

The theme of the *Georgics* as a whole is the good of fertility, in crops, trees, cattle and bees:

> vere tument terrae et genitalia semina poscunt.
> tum pater omnipotens fecundis imbribus Aether
> coniugis in gremium laetae descendit, et omnis
> magnus alit magno commixtus corpore fetus.
> avia tum resonant avibus virgulta canoris,
> et Venerem certis repetunt armenta diebus.[44]

Once again one is reminded of Lucretius' invocation to Venus at the opening of a work which at the end of its fourth book savagely attacks love. Neither Lucretius nor Virgil have any doubts about the good of procreation. Chaste family life is blessed in terms this time clearly borrowed from Lucretius.

> interea dulces pendent circum oscula nati,
> casta pudicitiam servat domus.[45]

In *Georgics* III 64ff. there is a strong undertone suggesting that what is said of the breeding of cattle is true of reproduction in men: but Virgil declares this openly in due course, and there could be nothing more explicit or revealing:

> Omne adeo genus in terris hominumque ferarumque
> et genus aequoreum, pecudes pictaeque volucres,
> in furias ignemque ruunt: amor omnibus idem.[46]

All animals and men rush to the fire and frenzy of physical love—a *blandus labor* for the male.[47] The females should be kept spare and far from lethargy so that they may greedily seize deeply upon Love. Virgil, as always, speaks lovingly of the progeny—*dulces natos*.[48]

Nevertheless love—and here physical love is of course meant—is described as weakening and, through the female's allurements, destructive. There is a powerful picture of the effect of blind love on animals, how the female feeding in the pasture drives two males to fight for her until one is vanquished and retires unhappily undone. And then the climax comes: *amor omnibus idem*. Instances of the uncontrollable frenzy of love in lionesses, bears, boars, and tigresses are graphically given. The lioness forsakes her cubs and becomes savage; bears deal out wholesale death and destruction; the boar is morose; the tigress wicked; the horse ignores the bridle, blows, precipices.

The story of Leander is given, who in his passion brought death upon himself and his girl, Hero. And so the list goes on: lynxes, wolves, hounds, even the unwarlike stags. But the frenzy of mares is the most remarkable—they dare everything and will conceive, even if only of the wind. Their frenzy stops only when the hippomanes oozes from their groins.

Virgil ends this remarkable and beautiful passage by admitting that he is dwelling too long on this theme of desire. But he loves it:

> Sed fugit interea, fugit inreparabile tempus,
> singula dum capti circumvectamur amore.[49]

This is indication enough, perhaps, that Virgil knew that he was preoccupied with the theme of love.

Georgics IV deals with bees who do not indulge in physical love, and concludes with the moving story of Orpheus and Eurydice. But this love story has little new to tell us. Orpheus suffered the pangs of love, braved hell for Eurydice, but a sudden frenzy, an unconquerable urge seized the unguarded lover—he looked back and so lost his love. Thereafter he resists all women, all love, all marriage. And so Thracian Bacchants, scorned by him, tore his body to pieces and scattered it over the land, his tongue still calling "Eurydice."[50]

Aeneid IV in general

The broad outline and much of the story of Dido and Aeneas is too well known to need even a general description here. In brief, Aeneas was tempted to love and marriage by Dido: he succumbed to the one, and at the bidding of Jupiter avoided the other. It would be too much to say that he was infatuated with Dido. Dido on the other hand was infatuated with him, and when she could not win him by any means, including magic, destroyed herself and her work while cursing him and his descendants.

It is not necessary here to enter into the responsibilities of the gods and more particularly the mutually jealous, powerful and vindictive goddesses, Juno and Venus. They played with Dido's heart as if it were of no account. Thus Venus:

> quocirca capere ante dolis et cingere flamma
> reginam meditor, ne quo se numine mutet,
> sed magno Aeneae mecum teneatur amore.[51]

Love deceives, binds and holds Dido mightily.

Before she is aware of it, Dido is possessed by the hidden fire; the poison leaves her mind open to folly. Unhappy, she is in the prey of the disease and cannot satisfy her desire which grows even as she looks. Dido is unaware, is destined to unhappiness, is ambushed by the God of Love:

> Infelix Dido longumque bibebat amorem.[52]

In *Aeneid* IV the tragic overtones of love mount to a *crescendo*: love wounds, consumes with a blinding fire, deceives, makes insane. Dido weakens and falls. Even as she is falling she protests that she will not: she will observe *pudor*:

> ante, pudor, quam te violo aut tua iura resolvo.[53]

She will carry her fidelity to her former husband to the tomb. The mention of *pudor* (αἰδώς) at this point initiates the real drama; the traditional conflict between *pudor* and *amor* (ἵμερος)[54] is quickly resolved, and soon Dido rids herself of *pudor*:[55]

> impenso animum flammavit amore
> spemque dedit dubiae menti solvitque pudorem.[56]

The die is cast and from this point on Dido is no more in control of her passions than the animals in *Georgics*:[57] *amor omnibus idem*. Having given herself wholly to love, she can rid herself of it only in death. The *solvit pudorem*[58] inevitably leads to *me solvat amantem*[59] when she has chosen to die. The climax comes with their *conubia* in the cave:

> ille dies primus leti primusque malorum
> causa fuit; neque enim specie famave movetur
> nec iam furtivum Dido meditatur amorem:
> coniugium vocat, hoc praetexit nomine culpam.[60]

Whatever be the technical connotations of *conubium* and *coniugium*, in the use of both in this passage all aspects of civil and physical wedlock are covered. But it is to be noted that it is Dido who insists on the union being called formally "marriage." Her insistence on this can only mean that she was unsure of Aeneas' attitude on it. She wanted, moreover, to have their guilty union—for neither was in fact free, whatever the machinations of the gods—technically at least correct. Her crime was not her furtive love, but her proclamation that it was marriage.[61] Aeneas denies that he married her:

> nec coniugis umquam
> praetendi taedas aut haec in foedera veni.[62]

Virgil of course is so full of sympathy for Dido that his picture of Aeneas inevitably suffers. Aeneas can claim no great virtue—he too is caught with base desire and forgets his mission. He is pictured as uxorious and even effeminate. But when Jupiter commands him peremptorily to sail (*naviget!*), off he goes with perhaps some relief, but no excessive grief:

> ardet abire fuga dulcisque relinquere terras.[63]

His mission must take precedence over his love:

> Italiam Lyciae iussere capessere sortes:
> hic amor, haec patria est[64]
>
> Italiam non sponte sequor.[65]
>
> multa gemens magnoque animum labefactus amore
> iussa tamen divum exsequitur.[66]

Dido humiliates herself, begging him at least to wait until she learned to endure his absence: But Aeneas will go:

> mens immota manet, lacrimae volvuntur inanes.[67]

Nothing remains for Dido but to think of trying magic, regretting that she had not indulged her love—as would a beast, while keeping her vow to her former husband—and playing with the idea of cutting Aeneas into pieces, as Medea did to her brother, and scattering them on the waves. She thinks also of killing Aeneas's son and serving him as a meal to his father. Dido has become the complete Medea.

In Hades Dido joins the company of women who had suffered from love—too much or too little—Phaedra, Procris, Eriphyle, Evadne, Pasiphae, Laodamia, and Caeneus (now a woman).[68] Once again we encounter in Virgil a list of fateful women.

There is much more in the story of Dido and Aeneas and in the *Aeneid* as a whole which might be added to fill out Virgil's attitude to love. Much of this—indeed much of Book IV—is derivative, but hardly less significant for that, since the poet chooses to use it. Moreover, to bring out the sensitivity of Virgil's mind on this theme, so much of interest to him, one would have to examine the words and situations at greater length, with greater subtlety and greater sensibility. But once again whatever sympathy Virgil has for Dido or Aeneas in love, marriage for him is one thing, love another: nor are the claims of love superior to duty. Love remains a dangerous and destructive enemy.[69]

The imagery of love in *Aeneid* IV is the imagery of war. In the *Eclogues, Georgics* and *Aeneid* I–VI love is most often described as folly or madness, fire or destruction. It is also described as an enemy, a wound, a plague, a disease, an evil, a poison. It is painful, sad, unhappy, anxious, hopeless, fearful, weakening, exposed to separation and quarrels. It is cruel, savage, deceitful, hard, intolerable, shameful. It ambushes one, binds in chains, binds one by magic, it leads to unnatural acts, it knows no measure or reason. It is a slavery, it is blind, it is incurable, it is invincible, it is bittersweet. Women in love are lustful, the cause of evil, can be unnatural, ruthless, vengeful, unfaithful, self-deceiving, given to magic, abusive, given to tantrums, debase themselves, potentially inimical, unreliable and changeable, uncontrolled.

Virgil has little to say of the good side of love or of men's behaviour when under its power. There are descriptions of happy married couples, and the sweetness of children, and indeed how ineffable love is. But on the whole Virgil's attitude to love is fearful and pessimistic.

Conclusion

Enough, however, has been said to allow us to state a few preliminary conclusions. It is clear that Virgil was responsive to love and deeply felt its power. He could enter into the emotions of women, and had rare sympathy with them. Equally clearly his very preoccupation with love and sensibility in it made him fearful of it. The inherited literary picture of women tended to make him shy away from having serious relationships with them. So did the teaching of Epicurus. The circumstances of his *milieu*—philosopher-poets—provided a sufficient counter-attraction. And so he protested, perhaps by way of self-justification, that love was a wound, a disease, madness and all the rest. Likewise he protested, perhaps to confirm his resolution against them, that women were to be pitied, but were fatal—when they were not in fact bad. Philosophy excused him from marriage—marriage, however, was socially good, was justified in the procreation of children, and (here he may have been political) had to be treated seriously. But physical love in itself was fraught with danger, was without hope, and was destructive:

> idem amor exitium pecori pecorisque magistro.[70]

This pessimistic picture of physical love is sustained right through Virgil. It is no wonder that love cannot compete with duty, or philosophy, or marriage. All far transcend love in their claim upon men. And all are less to be feared.

The young Augustine was likewise fascinated by the theme of love and love itself. "To Carthage I came, where there sang all around me in my ears a cauldron of unholy loves: I loved not yet, yet I loved to love, and out of a deep-seated want, I hated myself for wanting not. I sought what I might love, in love with loving, and safety I hated, and a way without snares. To love, then, and to be beloved, was sweet to me; but more, when I obtained to enjoy the body of the one I loved, I defiled, therefore, the spring of friendship with the filth of concupiscence, and I beclouded its brightness with the hell of lustfulness. I fell headlong into love, wherein I longed to be ensnared."[71]

These words were written by a repentant and moralizing bishop long after the event. For all that, Augustine did not aim to deceive, and we may take it that he had feared love, as a snare, but still had hoped for it.

His conversion to philosophy at nineteen years of age is, however—and was for him—very significant: "This book (the *Hortensius* of Cicero) altered my affections and made me have other purposes and desires . . . to embrace wisdom herself."

We note too that he began to be the centre of a circle of young men all interested in serious studies.[72] Whatever the rhetoric of the *Confessions* and the facts of his *liaison* and son, Augustine had started on a way of life in communion with others which developed more and more like a philosophic enclave and ultimately affected the quality of religious living in the West. Moreover, as a Manichean he undertook, not very successfully it would seem, to cultivate chastity.

Eventually Augustine renounced marriage and ambition and attempted formally to set up a philosophic circle. But still he was preoccupied with the problem of the flesh: "I had now found the goodly pearl, which, selling all that I had, I ought to have bought, and I hesitated."[73] He was like Aeneas at Carthage and like him was delivered from the allurements of women only by intervention from above—in Augustine's case this is described in the *tolle lege* scene.[74]

When Augustine retired with his friends and pupils to a villa outside Milan in the autumn of A.D. 386, there to discuss philosophy, he spent, as we have seen, much of his time reading and discussing Virgil. Some of the preoccupations of these days are reflected not only in the *Dialogues* then written, but also in a poem by one of his pupils then present, Licentius, composed nine years later. Licentius' poem not only clearly echoes Virgil[75] and the *errores Aeneae*, the ideals of celibacy and the unambitious life, but also something of the Lucretian influences in *Eclogue* VI.

By this stage, at any rate, Augustine had already developed what has been called his obsessive horror of sex. In the *Soliloquia*, composed at that time, he asks himself what his attitude towards marriage is. He answers that however attractively for him the picture of a wife is painted: *nihil mihi tam fugiendum quam concubitum esse decrevi.*[76] He could think of nothing, he said, which so degraded a man's mind as womanly blandishments and such bodily contact. And so if it is the duty of a wise man (and he hadn't found out that it was) to provide for children, then he admired the men who for this reason alone used marriage, but he wouldn't imitate them: *nam tentare hoc periculosius est quam posse felicius.* He even recalled such love only *cum horrore atque aspernatione.*[77]

Augustine had developed this attitude, therefore, by the time he was thirty-two years of age and long before the Pelagian controversy; even before he engaged as a Christian in controversy with the Manicheans. Up to that time the influences upon him were partly Manichean (which did involve, in theory at least, the avoidance of reproduction) and partly professional—mostly authors such as Cicero and Virgil, and doubtless Lucretius.

The present author is sceptical of the "profligacy" of Augustine in his teens. Augustine was a serious youth and felt the need for a philosophical life at nineteen years of age. But he was temperamentally, as was Virgil, preoccupied with the problem of love. If by the early thirties he had to the extent we have described developed certain ideals and accepted certain pessimistic attitudes on sexuality, and if Virgil, his favourite author, inculcated similar ideals and attitudes, it cannot seem unlikely that Virgil, as well as, if not more than, Lucretius and the Stoics and Neo-Pythagoreans, formed some part of the Roman background of Christian sexuality so largely determined by Augustine.

7

Augustine's Attitude to Love in the Context of His Influence on Christian Ethics

St. Augustine has sometimes been described as the first "modern" man, and sometimes as a man standing between the world of antiquity and the world of today. Of the two descriptions the second is at least chronologically true. It is, given his special and important position in the Christian Church in Africa at the beginning of the fifth century, also in fact inevitably true. St. Jerome called him the best-known bishop in the whole world, *episcopus in toto orbe notissimus* (*Epist. ad Augustinum*, 75); his correspondence was read by high and low with avidity throughout the Latin world; his sermons reached a far wider audience than his sometimes impatient listeners at Hippo; but above all the fame of his conversion as described in his *Confessions*, and the great works that issued from his controversies with the Manichees, Donatists, and especially the Pelagians—among them the *City of God*—ensured that the Christian Church in the West, finding its way towards a philosophical and theological system adequate to its actual dominating role in the Roman Empire, spoke henceforth with the mind and often in the accents of Augustine. To St. Jerome, who was his not uncritical admirer, Augustine was "the oracle of the law, the sanctifier of justice, the initiator of spiritual glory and the dispenser of eternal salvation," *oraculum legis, sacrator iustitiae, instaurator spiritalis gloriae, dispensator salutis aeternae* (*Epist. ad Augustinum*, 260).

We may take it that St. Jerome knew the truth of what he was saying: he could never have known how true it was to remain. Augustine did literally become the oracle of the law, was held to have established the relations of Church and State, was a major source and inspiration behind the monastic and ascetic movements in Europe, and—alas—was considered by many to have closed the gates of heaven on the majority of mankind, past, present and to come. The very recital of these words conveys, I fear, the impression of a dominating and—as we might now say—Puritan power. It is, however, the context in which we must place our consideration of St. Augustine's attitude to love: the attitude *he* adopted was all influential, and this attitude was closely related to his life and to his general philosophical and theological views.

To revert briefly to my first words: if Augustine seems "modern" to some it can only be because his mind has so significantly contributed to the formation of the "modern" mind. If he seems more "modern" to us than some of his contemporaries or successors, it can only be because of the richness of his personality in the ever relevant and deservedly famous *Confessions*. But it is a total and dangerous illusion to imagine that Augustine was in some way or another a twentieth-century man set down in North Africa some sixteen hundred years too soon and—this is the important point—holding views *greatly* in advance of his contemporaries. The truth rather is that his views then are still to a considerable extent our views now. There are signs over the last two hundred years or so, increasing every day in this rapidly expanding and technological world, that Augustine's influence will be less—and less in the domain of ethics. But it is well to realize that some of the attitudes being discarded were attitudes already old when Augustine, the *pontifex*, the bridge-builder, carried them from the world of Greece and Rome into the Christian West.

We must now narrow our consideration to the problem of St. Augustine's attitude to love. I do not propose to define love, since I am pessimistic about the ultimate possibility of verbal definition—and what other kind of definition is there? But I shall indicate my general meaning. By "love" I mean any movement towards union between a person and another person, thing, or even abstraction. I do not in fact divide the person into body and soul, flesh and spirit—a division inherited by us from the Greeks and especially the Platonists—but I will in practice speak as if I did: for we mostly do so, and so did Augustine with whose attitude we are concerned here. To simplify matters, however, I shall be speaking a little of personal relationships, whether physical or mental, on the one hand, but more of love of an ideal, whether considered as existent outside of oneself or not, on the other. Briefly I shall be speaking of love of men for men, women, and especially self-perfection or God.

St. Augustine was brought up in a system of education which has been most competently and sympathetically described (following on the lead of Werner Jaeger) by H. I. Marrou. His *History of Education in Antiquity* stresses the central fact that from Homeric times to the period of Augustine, education centered around the relationship of men—particularly of a younger man with an older man who provided him with a model life to imitate and with a set of moral values. It is important to avoid regarding such relationships as either entirely innocent or entirely (in our sense) perverted. They were intended to be, and often were, noble *and* passionate. This practice resulted, of course, in the exclusively male character of Greek society; and to the extent that this exclusive maleness dominated and persisted in ideal and practice, family life and heterosexual relations took only the second, and sometimes conflicting, place. Marrou is tempted to see the endurance of these ideals in the exclusively male public boarding schools and university colleges of, say, the time of Newman. At any rate the hundred or so ephebic gymnasia of the Hellenistic world were like the public schools in this, that children's names were put down for acceptance shortly after birth—if not, for all we know, before.

It would be wrong to think of such a system of education as concerned with personal and moral relationships only: by the time of Empedocles and Socrates, when schools of a more formal kind took shape, the content of education became intellectual, dealing with poetry, rhetoric, politics, and the pursuit of truth in mathematics and philosophy. Education indeed, to the exclusion of other interests and activities (including family life), became such a dominating thing among the leading classes that one's whole life almost was given to it. Marrou quotes Malraux as saying that it takes fifty years to make a man. The ideal in Greece at the time of which I am speaking was that from the age of twenty to thirty a man should study various sciences, from thirty to thirty-five dialectic, from thirty-five to fifty he should expose himself to the experience of life; then at fifty he was considered fit to contemplate. This ideal is not as remote from life, even our life, as it may seem. We can observe certain tendencies in post-graduate and research institutes. If slavery made education an actual occupation for the Greek—πρὸς τὴν ἐν αὐτῷ πολιτείαν . . . τὰ αὐτοῦ πράττων (Plato, *Rep.* 591c, 496d), "towards the management of one's own polity," "doing one's thing,"—automation may do so again, but for a wider and more disguised elite.

Education was the *heart* of Hellenistic Civilization, which, since there was no strictly autonomous Roman education or indeed civilization, it remained right up to the days of Augustine. Education, *paideia, humanitas,* was a fair substitute for the departed gods and decayed city—so much so that as a Christian might now have his tombstone surmounted by a cross, so then some had inscribed upon their graves that they were devotees of the Muses. For many, too, conversion to philosophy meant in psychological terms very much what conversion to religion has meant for such as Newman—I do not say Augustine, for in his case the two conversions, if two, were closely related. Philosophy for many implied a μέθοδος βίου, a way of life approximating to the plain living and high thinking of religious monastic communities, which later were to be their inheritors in the West. This kind of conversion was not always the result of a personal revelation: there were manuals and treatises written to convince and move men to philosophy and the philosophic life. Such a treatise was Aristotle's *Protrepticus,* and such was the *Hortensius* of Cicero which moved Augustine to his first conversion—to philosophy—when he was nineteen years of age. Later Christians, such as Clement of Alexandria, continued to use the title *Protrepticus* or Exhortation when they had religion in mind, not philosophy.

I have entered into details of this system of education, because without such details it is impossible to understand certain features of the ancient world and Augustine's own experience, which had much to do with his attitude to love. Having given these details, I may now be permitted to confine myself to little more than a mention of these features, which are too well known to require exposition here. One of these is the attitude to love in the philosophical schools of Greece and Rome. Take the case of Plato's *Symposium,* which discusses love formally: the subject is approached at various levels of increasing seriousness and always from the corporal towards the abstract and finally the spiritual. The speech of Diotima represents Plato's attitude to love, an attitude which was honored in the schools that looked upon him as their founder.

> He who would proceed rightly in this business must not merely begin from his youth to encounter beautiful bodies. In the first place, indeed, . . . he must be in love with one particular body, and engender beautiful converse therein; but next he must remark how the beauty attached to this or that body is cognate to that which is attached to any other, . . . and so, . . . he must make himself a lover of all beautiful bodies, and slacken the stress of his feeling for one by contemning it and counting it a trifle. But his next advance will be to set a higher value on the beauty of souls than on that of the body, so that however little the grace that may bloom in any likely soul it shall suffice him for loving and caring, and for bringing forth and soliciting such converse as will tend

to the betterment of the young; and that finally he may be constrained to contemplate the beautiful as appearing in our observances and our laws, and to behold it all bound together in kinship and so estimate the body's beauty as a slight affair. From observances he should be led on to the branches of knowledge, that there also he may behold a province of beauty, and by looking thus on beauty in the mass may escape from the mean, meticulous slavery of a single instance, . . . and turning rather towards the main ocean of the beautiful may by contemplation of this bring forth in all their splendour many fair fruits of discourse and meditation in a plenteous crop of philosophy; until with the strength and increase there acquired he descries a certain single knowledge connected with a beauty which has yet to be told. . . .

When a man has been thus far tutored in the lore of love, . . . in the right and regular ascent, suddenly he will have revealed to him, as he draws to the close of his dealings in love, a wondrous vision, beautiful in its nature; and this, Socrates, is the final object of all those previous toils. First of all, it is ever-existent and neither comes to be nor perishes, neither waxes nor wanes; next, it is not beautiful in part and in part ugly, nor is it such at such a time and other at another, nor in one respect beautiful and in another ugly, nor so affected by position as to seem beautiful to some and ugly to others. Nor again will our initiate find the beautiful presented to him in the guise of a face or of hands or any other portion of the body, nor as a particular description or piece of knowledge, nor as existing somewhere in another substance, such as an animal or the earth or sky or any other thing; but existing ever in singularity of form independent by itself, while all the multitude of beautiful things partake of it in such wise that, though all of them are coming to be and perishing, it grows neither greater nor less, and is affected by nothing. . . . In that state of life above all others . . . a man finds it truly worth while to live, as he contemplates essential beauty. . . . Tell me, what would happen if one of you had the fortune to look upon essential beauty entire, pure and unalloyed; not infected with the flesh and colour of humanity . . . ? What if he could behold the divine beauty itself, in its unique form? Do you call it a pitiful life for a man to lead—looking that way, observing that vision by the proper means, and having it ever with him? Do but consider . . . that there only will it befall him, as he sees the beautiful through that which makes it visible, to breed not illusions but true examples of virtue, since his contact is not with illusion but with truth. So when he has begotten a true virtue and has reared it up he is destined to win the friendship of Heaven; he, above all men, is immortal. (Plato, *Symposium* 210a–212a, tr. Lamb, LCL)

One can see this in Plotinus, a Neoplatonist who influenced Augustine at the time of his conversion.

> Therefore we must ascend again towards the Good, the desired of every Soul. Anyone that has seen This, knows what I intend when I say that it is beautiful. Even the desire of it is to be desired as a Good....
>
> And one that shall know this vision—with what passion of love shall he not be seized, with what pang of desire, what longing to be molten into one with This, what wondering delight! If he that has never seen this Being must hunger for It as for all his welfare, he that has known must love and reverence It as the very Beauty; he will be flooded with awe and gladness, stricken by a salutary terror; he loves with a veritable love, with sharp desire; all other loves than this he must despise, and disdain all that once seemed fair.
>
> This indeed is the mood even of those who, having witnessed the manifestations of Gods or Supernals, can never again feel the old delight in the comeliness of material forms: what then are we to think of one that contemplates the Absolute Beauty in Its essential integrity, no accumulation of flesh and matter, no dweller on earth or in the heavens—so perfect Its Purity—far above all such things in that they are non-essential, composite, not primal but descending from This?
>
> Beholding this Being, ... resting rapt, in the vision and possession of so lofty a loveliness, growing to Its likeness, what Beauty can the soul yet lack? For This, the Beauty supreme, the absolute, and the primal, fashions its lovers to Beauty and makes them also worthy of love. And for This, the sternest and the uttermost combat is set before the Souls; all our labour is for This, lest we be left without part in this noblest vision, which to attain is to be blessed in the blissful sight, which to fail of is to fail utterly. (Plotinus, *Enneads* 1.6.7, tr. MacKenna)

One can see it in the ecstasies described by Augustine himself in the *Confessions*.

> And I wondered not a little that I was now come to love thee, and no phantasm instead of thee: nor did I delay to enjoy my God, but was ravished to thee by thine own beauty; and yet by and by I violently fell off again, even by mine own weight; rushing with sorrow enough upon these inferior things. This weight I spake of was my own fleshly custom. Yet had I still a remembrance of thee; nor did I any way doubt, that there was one to whom I ought to cleave.... For studying now, by what reasons to make good the beauty of corporeal things, either celestial or terrestrial, and what proof I had at hand solidly to pass sentence upon these mutable things, ... I had by this time found the unchangeable and true eternity of truth, residing above this changeable mind of mine. And thus by degrees passing from bodies to the soul, ... and from thence to its inner faculties, ... and so forward, ... I passed on to the reasoning faculties.... This also finding itself to be variable in me, betook itself towards its own understanding ... that so it might find

out that light, which now bedewed it . . . thus by a flash of the twinkling eyesight it came so far as that which is. (C VII, 17, tr. Watts, LCL)

Fleshly love, with male and even more with female, was hardly worthy of one's attention—except for social reasons. One may recall Montaigne's distinction between marriage, love, and friendship: marriage was a social contract involving neither love nor friendship and of course possible only with a woman; love was intense but of short duration; friendship was the finest achievement and woman was too weak to support so exalted a relationship. The distinction is hardly a popular one nowadays—but it reveals how a relatively modern man could carry on the ideals of the pagan into the Christian world without much self-questioning—or, to put it another way, how paganism has continued to persist in Christianity.

Coming nearer to Augustine one might draw attention to the attitude of Roman followers of Epicurus to love. It is important to remember that Augustine shortly before his conversion to Christianity in 386 refrained from accepting the Epicurean view on human destiny only because he could not accept Epicurus' doctrine that nothing of the human soul survived bodily death (C VI, 26). Certain it is that at this time Augustine and some ten of his friends were planning to live a community life—such as later he was to realize at Cassiciacum after his conversion and before his baptism; and later still in his monastic communities at Thagaste and Hippo. Their ideal was to escape from the bustle of life. But, significantly enough for our present topic, the project became impossible because of their wives (C VI, 24). Dudley, in the book on Lucretius which he edited in 1965, suggests that the Epicurean recoil from love, as savagely and to that extent unconvincingly instanced by Lucretius (4.1141ff.), is the source of what is taken to be Augustine's obsessive horror of all the processes of sex and generation:

> Atque in amore mala haec proprio summeque secundo
> inveniuntur; in adverso vero atque inopi sunt,
> prendere quae possis oculorum lumine operto,
> innumerabilia; ut melius vigilare sit ante,
> qua docui ratione, cavereque ne inliciaris.
> nam vitare, plagas in amoris ne iaciamur,
> non ita difficile est quam captum retibus ipsis
> exire et validos Veneris perrumpere nodos.

"And more, these evils are found in a love that is successful, and when all goes passing well; but in love that is unhappy and helpless, evils there are that you can see with your eyes shut, innumerable: so that it is better to be on guard betimes as I have explained, and to take care that you be not enticed. For to avoid being cast into the snares of love is not so difficult, as when you are caught in the toils to get out and break through the strong knots of Venus" (Loeb tr. by Rouse). I have myself little doubt but that such vivid passages in Lucretius did affect to some extent at least the young impressionable Augustine. I am inclined, however, to trace what I would consider Augustine's less savage but no less convincing horror of physical love to the abiding influence upon him of Virgil.

I have discussed this matter to some extent elsewhere[1] and will not repeat what I said then. Suffice it to say that Virgil, following Lucretius, reacted against a neoteric movement in poetry in which a life given to the pursuit of love was commended. He inherited rather and passed on the themes of the greatly attractive and greatly destructive heroines of Greek literature—Helen, the Greek Eve, and above all Medea, the prototype of Dido who made such a profound impression upon Augustine.[2] Aeneas, Virgil's hero, is sensitive to the appeal of love, for him indeed a great temptation, but he steels his heart and gives himself to a nobler destiny.

> mens immota manet, lacrimae volvuntur inanes.
> (*Aen.* 4.449)

Virgil himself shared the friendship of many Epicureans in Naples: something of that life and friendship is to be seen in his *Eclogues* where the compelling power of love is sometimes praised but mostly feared:

> idem amor exitium est pecori pecorisque magistro.
> (*Ecl.* 3.101)

To complete our brief sketch of the aspects of his educational and philosophical background that affected Augustine's attitude to love,[3] one should draw attention to the archaic moralism of the Roman patriotic ideal summed up in Ennius' famous line

> moribus antiquis res stat Romana virisque.
> (Cic. *De Rep.* 5.1)

The persistent inspiration of the great moral heroes of Rome, whose praise was sung by Sallust, is strongly present in the *City of God* where Brutus, Torquatus, Curtius, Regulus, and others are held up as models for Christian imitation. Finally, but not least significantly, the tradition of the Roman mother-figure, the great moulder of her sons, Cornelia, the mother of the Gracchi, Aurelia mother of Caesar, Atia mother of Augustus, cannot but have strengthened the mother-figure that was Monnica in the psychological makeup of Augustine. These moral influences, strongly tinged with ambition as they were, tended if not to be actually hostile, to put the sentiment of love very much in second place.

It is to be noted that the educational background which I have indicated is not just historical in the sense of being the background to any well educated man born in the Roman Empire towards the middle of the fourth century: all its details are known to have deeply affected Augustine—the living together of males in friendship in the pursuit of the higher ideals of the philosophic life; the attractions of Epicureanism in this connection; the deep influence of the enigmatic Virgil whose hero resists an almost compelling love; and the rather Stoic moral idealism of the Roman tradition where Rome's great passion (according to Augustine)—*laudum immensa cupido* (Virgil, *Aen.* 6.823)—overbore all other loves and desires.

When we go on to look at the main evidence for Augustine's attitude to love, the *Confessions*, we must be extremely careful how we interpret that document. It is not in any normal sense a mere autobiography. The work is a confession, indeed a profession to God of sin, of praise, and especially of faith. The bishop speaks to God but before men and for their edification. And so at one time his language follows his mind in its aspirations towards ecstasy, and at another elaborates upon an incident from his past or present to drive home a moral lesson on his readers. Augustine when he wrote the *Confessions* was a bishop much accustomed to preaching; and the *Confessions* is an extended sermon where prayer and moralization are more developed and refined than was normally possible in his basilica. But Augustine had also been a professional rhetorician who automatically employed the elaborate techniques of rhetoric and special pleading. The reader of the *Confessions* must therefore be careful to bear in mind that in both the selection and description of any episode Augustine was normally affected by moralizing and rhetorical considerations. One must make proper allowance for these in the assessment of the probable historical fact of any particular event described.

With these and other such considerations in mind I have given my reasons elsewhere[4] for refusing to accept with any confidence that Augustine was a roué in his youth. He was, as a matter of historical fact, a serious-minded and ambitious young man who kept faithful all through his late teens and twenties to one woman, the mother of his son Adeodatus. He put her away with painful sorrow only when his mother and his own ambitions made her presence undesirable, as marriage with a woman in her social condition was impossible.[5] Indeed Augustine tells us that he had to pretend to keep up with his youthful friends in wrongdoing (C II, 79).

> To Carthage I came, where there sang all around me in my ears a cauldron of unholy loves: I loved not yet, yet I loved to love, and out of a deep-seated want, I hated myself for wanting not. I sought what I might love, in love with loving, and safety I hated, and a way without snares. To love, then, and to be beloved, was sweet to me; but more, when I obtained to enjoy the body of the one [gender unspecified] I loved. I defiled, therefore, the spring of friendship with the hell of lustfulness. I fell headlong then into love, wherein I longed to be ensnared. I was both beloved, and secretly arrived at the bond of enjoying. (C III, 1, Pusey's translation, contracted)

This is one of the passages which appears to suggest that Augustine was a roué. To some (in conjunction with the *variis et umbrosis amoribus* of an earlier passage in the *Confessions* [II, 1]) it suggests all sorts of sexual excesses and especially homosexuality—a construction on these texts which with Legewie and Marrou[6] I question. But when one has subtracted the rhetoric (e.g., *Carthago—sartago*) one is left with no more fact than that he wanted to love, did experience sensual love, and was loved in return. There is nothing to indicate the scale or intensity of these experiences. But since the language is highly rhetorical on the one hand, and this experience is compared inevitably to its disadvantage with fair friendship and the love of God on the other, it would be surprising if even a modest experience of sensual love was not painted by the repentant moralizing and rhetorical bishop in even blacker and more exaggerated colors than are actually found here. Indeed the dominating and important theme in this famous passage is: *fames mihi erat intus ab interiore cibo, te ipso, deus meus*. His confused unconscious passion for God could be released at this time only on sensible things. Even then, he says, his real love was for God—and this seems to me, taking account of the background I have sketched, the words of this text, his early "conversion" to philosophy at the age of nineteen, and the tenor of his life as a whole, to be absolutely true.

At the same time one must acknowledge the fact that the last obstacle to his final conversion was the inability of his will to accept chastity:

> But still I was enthralled with the love of woman, nor did the Apostle forbid me to marry, although he advised me to something better. But I, being weak, chose the more indulgent place; and because of this alone, was tossed up and down in all beside. (C VIII, 2)

This passage reveals fairly clearly that for Augustine the choice was not between a sensual life outside of marriage or one in it, but rather between a sensual life at all and a life of the spirit. Both the exaggerated standards of chastity professed by the Manichees, with whom he had spent his twenties, and the ascetical purgation demanded by the Neoplatonists, who brought him intellectually to the point of final conversion, undoubtedly had the result of placing the question of continence very much to the fore in the mind of this man now seeking to embrace perfection. Hence one of the last scenes in his description of his conversion in the *Confessions* (VIII, 27) is the characteristically rhetorical and dramatized encounter of his Sensual Passions already described as former friends, on the one hand, and Continence beckoning him on the other. It is another version of his old problem—"give me chastity, Lord—but not yet"; another version of the two laws, that of the flesh and that of the spirit. The outcome although made to center positively on the acceptance of Christ involves the abandonment of the flesh: the text of Scripture which finally converts Augustine reads: "Put ye on the Lord Jesus Christ, and make not provision for the flesh in concupiscence" (Rom. 13.13ff.).

It would be foolish and unscientific to claim that Augustine was insensitive, either when he was young, or even when he was well on in life, to the appeal of the flesh. He does not pretend this himself for a moment. After his conversion he still oscillated between considering the embrace of a woman as most degrading to a man's mind, horrible and to be contemned, and, within twenty-four hours, being titillated by the blandishments and sweetness of woman's love (SO I, 17, 25). It is as unnecessary as it would be wrong to dehumanize Augustine, to ignore the evidence that he was a warm and passionate man, fully alive to and allured by the delights of love and the virtues and satisfactions of marriage. Augustine is not simply reacting against his own excesses in love. He (Augustine) is not *against* love. But he prefers to it the life of the spirit; and since the flesh is a threat to that life—as his whole education and his own experience had deeply convinced him—*Augustine is afraid of love*—of any love but what he considered the highest, the love of God. In this, his own life and experience but takes its place within the long tradition of most literary, but especially philosophical prejudice in fear of love. This prejudice he in his turn has passed on to us.

The influence of Monnica, his mother, upon Augustine's attitude to love is impossible to fathom, but so far as one can judge from the evidence, is not unlikely to have influenced Augustine away from the love of women. It is inevitable that he was psychologically involved with her and seems almost always to have responded, not always without rebellion, in the end to her masterful wishes on his behalf. Her ambitions were worldly but were also moral and directed towards Christian perfection. It is arguable that with such a woman so strongly active in his life Augustine could not but be embarrassed about woman's love. It would, however, be dangerous to seek to specify too precisely the nature and extent of her influence in this regard, especially since the *Confessions*, on which such an analysis must be based, can be treated as an intimate journal only with the greatest reservations.

From the time of his conversion onwards for the rest of his days, Augustine, more than ever before, led his life in a community of friends engaged in asceticism and the pursuit of perfection. If now such a life was animated by the Christian theological ideal (and distracted by various overwhelming obligations), still it was in many respects a continuation of an earlier more literary and philosophic ideal (which also had been subject to distractions of another kind). It was an adaptation of the pagan notion of *otium* to Christian purposes. To this extent Augustine helped to introduce into Christian monasticism an intellectual character which has greatly enriched it. Père Festugière lays the responsibility for this development upon Augustine in the West.[7] While Festugière says explicitly that the kind of spirituality so introduced is not positively anti-Christian, he is at great pains to point out that it is in its origins and structure independent of Christianity. This view, even if it may be somewhat oversimplified, underlines the continuing influence on Augustine and on our contemporary Christianity, as indeed is but natural, of his educational formation and aspirations to the philosophic life led as far as possible with males.

It can hardly be denied that for all his personal attractions Augustine was strongly combative when he was engaged—as he mostly was after his conversion—in controversy. Nor can it be denied that in argument he was sometimes ruthless and immoderate. He knew this himself and could not but regret it: *atrociter disputavi,* he says of his controversy with the Pelagians. These controversies tended to make him adopt intransigent positions that made no allowance for another point of view. And so we have the theme of the two cities based on two loves, the love of self to the *exclusion* of God, and the love of God to the *exclusion* of self. By the time he was a bishop Augustine had committed himself wholly to the service of the love of God and, to that extent, had cut himself personally off from human—and especially female—love as far as possible. But it was the Pelagian controversy particularly that brought him to make his more illiberal formulations against human love. These views had been in fact in his mind long before. In the *Confessions* (VI, 11, 20) he had written that he had believed, in his stupidity, that continence was within one's own powers: he had not known that it had been written that no one can have continence unless God gives it. It was precisely his own experience at the time of his conversion that only God's grace had broken the bond of incontinence that held him back from conversion. The Pelagians, therefore, were flatly contradicting the truth of an experience of the greatest intimacy and consequence to himself. This had the unfortunate result in Augustine's mind of inducing him to elaborate the enormities of the flesh and man's inevitable submission to them in order to make more evident the power and generosity of God's delivering grace. And the more bitter the controversy became, the more extreme became the formulations, until in the end concupiscence in itself was pronounced sinful and therefore horrible and to be avoided: these positions are in themselves extreme; but they were expressed in the heat of controversy in language still more extreme and indeed inhuman.

Various texts support the views that Augustine considered the carnal appetite as a cause of sin, or itself a sin.[8] In 1963 Janssens[9] asserted that Augustine was responsible not only for transmitting to the Christian West pessimistic and rigorous views on sexuality, but introduced even into married life a dualism whereby the married might act rightly in procreation but would act wrongly if they sought pleasure in the act: the ideal even within marriage was union in that form of love called *caritas*. There is no doubt that Augustine, because of the importance of his influence, is responsible for the transmission of these ideas—and I am making no effort to deny this. But it is important to bear three things in mind in this connection: these ideas have their source in pre-Christian philosophies; they did *not* arise in Augustine for the first time *only* in reaction to his supposed excesses in youth; and Augustine's more extreme formulations of these ideas have not been generally accepted by the Christian Churches, and they meet with less support than ever now.

It is curious that Augustine should have invoked love itself to justify everything, including presumably such a rigorous doctrine as I have just indicated: *dilige et quod vis fac (Tractatus in Johannis Epistulam,* PL 35.2033), "love and do what you will." On the face of it this should mean that the goodness of anything is determined by the love that seeks it. This might seem a very permissive doctrine indeed. But for Augustine the formula held no danger—for him God was love. There could be only one love and one kind of loving—God and His love. This is a characteristically absolute position in Augustine. Elsewhere I have drawn attention to his treatment of justice in the same way.[10] His vision of life was so flooded by God's light that no other light that was truly light could exist separately.

We are familiar with the statement "God is love." Augustine in his *Tractatus in Johannis Epistulam* (PL 35.2052) can say "Love is God," *dilectio Deus est:* "therefore whoever loves his brother loves God," *necesse est ergo ut Deum diligat quisquis diligit fratrem.*

It can be seen from all of this that love is central to Augustine's theology and view of life; but the love is a spiritual love primarily related, even if through man, to God. The measure of his "deification in leisure" (E X, 2) reduces or seems to reduce his interest in and care for men. But this *is* an absolute position, absolutely true and absolutely misleading. Augustine's whole life was caught up with the service of God in men. His ardent sensibility ran to excesses of love and, as in Catullus, following, indeed, a common pattern in physical love, it ran to excesses of hate. These excesses led him to inhuman denunciation on the one hand and superhuman love on the other. Catullus behaved more humanly when he prayed the Mother Goddess to put far from him the excesses of her service: *Dea, magna dea, Cybele, dea domina Dindymi, / procul a mea tuus sit furor omnis, era, domo: / alios age incitatos, alios age rabidos* (63.91ff.). "Goddess, great goddess, Cybele, goddess, lady of Dindymus, far from my house be all thy fury, O my queen; others drive thou in frenzy, others drive thou to madness" (LCL tr. by Cornish). Augustine made no such prayer, nor could he. In the Donatist controversy he is said to have resorted to every means necessary to defend the Church; in the Pelagian, he did everything to defend God: one might ask if *man* too did not equally need defense. But Augustine's whole life from the beginning to the end inexorably drove him to love God to the *contempt* of his human self: this is the *real* explanation of the sad paradox of a loving saint who in his more absolute pronouncements seemed intent upon destroying all that was human in human love.

8

Virgil and Augustine
The *Aeneid* in the *Confessions*

From the composition of Virgil's *Aeneid* towards the last quarter of the last century B.C. to that of Saint Augustine's *Confessions* around A.D. 400 there was the passage of some four hundred years. During that time Rome, from being Pagan, became Christian. The *Aeneid* and the *Confessions* represent, as well as any work of literature could be said to represent them, the high periods in which these two great works were written—the ripeness of Pagan Rome and the opening of the Christian era. They are related to one another by Augustine himself who compared explicitly the "wanderings of one Aeneas," a principal theme in the *Aeneid*, with his own wanderings. I hope to show here some of the ways in which the *Aeneid* influenced the *Confessions*.

First it is necessary to say something of the special interest and importance of the *Aeneid* for such as Augustine. H. I. Marrou, a sensitive and enlightened critic, has spoken of Virgil as modeling "the categories of Roman thought, the forms of Roman sensibility, the imperatives of the Roman moral conscience . . . the most profound aspirations of Roman personal religion."[1] Virgil was, Marrou averred, "an interpreter at once indispensable and privileged." Apart from its expression of the individual Roman's outlook, the *Aeneid* makes manifest the extraordinary vitality of Rome itself. On the face of it the *Aeneid* may appear to be, if more sophisticated, at least less spontaneous than the *Iliad*; but in fact it is tense from beginning to end with nervous energy. Rome's early site, Rome's many battles and alliances, Rome's nourishing ethic, Rome's descent from great Troy, are paraded before us so that we see justice in the claim that her mission is to rule the world:

> Tu regere imperio populos, Romane, memento,—
> hae tibi erunt artes—pacisque imponere morem
> parcere subiectis et debellare superbos.[2]
>
> "remember, Roman, thou,
> To rule the nations as their master; these

103

> Thine arts shall be, to engraft the law of peace,
> Forbear the conquered, and war down the proud."
> (James Rhoades's translation)

Virgil lived and died in a most significant period in the history of Rome, one rendered peculiarly important to Christians, because about then Christianity had its origin. In this connection the Messianic interpretation of Virgil's Fourth *Eclogue* as introducing a new Golden, the Christian, Age was particularly inspiring to them. This impressed later people so much that they invested Virgil with extraordinary religious, philosophic and general wisdom. His poem was as the Bible, a source on which lots were drawn.

That the *Aeneid* seemed, as I have just suggested, more than merely symbolical of the Rome of Virgil, but also a book of transcending wisdom, can be seen from the estimation of it and its author in the works of a near-contemporary of Augustine—Macrobius. In Macrobius's *Saturnalia* Virgil's many-sided erudition—especially his learning in philosophy and astronomy but also in law, rhetoric, and much else—is praised. Virgil to Macrobius was omniscient and infallible—in Dante's phrase, the master of them that know. As creator of the *Aeneid* he was likened to the Creator of the universe.

The extraordinary popularity of Virgil and his *Aeneid* at the time of Augustine is further evidenced by the fact that the manuscripts on which modern editions are ultimately based come from the time of Augustine, and that, whereas we have no fragments of the translations of other Latin authors such as Horace and Juvenal done for Greek-speaking children, the sands of Egypt have yielded for this purpose no less than six copies of the *Aeneid*. The *Aeneid*, then, was not only a symbol of great Rome: it was also the lifeline of culture in the Latin and Christian West.

That Augustine knew Virgil's *Aeneid* well hardly needs demonstration. Not only have we the evidence of the many actual quotations by him from the *Aeneid* collected, for example, by Harald Hagendahl,[3] but we know that as a schoolboy, later as professional rhetor for many years, and finally even in the space between his conversion and baptism in A.D. 386–87, Augustine devoted much of his time to studying Virgil and the *Aeneid*, in school and later with his own students. It is inconceivable that Schelkle's idea, rejected by Hagendahl, that Augustine did not know Virgil's text *directly* should be correct. Jacques Fontaine, indeed, has written[4] finely of Augustine's passionate admiration for Virgil's poetry, and of how a clear quotation (of which there are *many* in Augustine and some extensive) in this case is of less value than an allusion—than the use, hardly conscious, of a *word charged with poetry*. Augustine's literary sensibility, Fontaine asserts, owes to its long *impregnation* by Virgil: *le ton recueilli* of many of his images, their discreet fulness, and that savour of dramatic interiority that often makes of a landscape of Virgil a state of soul. Without Virgil, Fontaine asserts, Augustine could not have conceived those "interior landscapes" of the *Confessions*, which seemed to him the most faithful expression of certain states of soul on its way to conversion.

One should say something of Augustine's sympathy with Virgil. This is very marked. The "dramatic interiority" of which Fontaine speaks is but one instance in which the later writer reaches back to his predecessor, in order to develop and manifest this characteristic more powerfully in himself. Some of this interiorisation in both of them must either derive from their Platonism or account for it—for Platonism and its immaterialism had an enduring influence on both. To Macrobius[5] Virgil seemed firstly to have taught the truth of philosophy and then transmuted it with fiction. Dante took a similar view of Virgil's handling of philosophy.[6] Augustine, reflecting the *Zeitgeist* of Macrobius, is more a philosopher (though not formally or extensively) than a poet—but though he did not write poetry he is judged to be a poet too. The *Confessions* has been called a sublime poem, and many of its prose passages have demanded renderings in verse when translated into other languages. Philosophy for Virgil and Augustine had a quasi-mystical dimension.

Both were profoundly affected by a strong belief in Providence, and that Providence was seen by both of them as operating through Rome. *Fata uiam inuenient.* Jupiter proclaims that his will will find a way. Virgil's vision of the course of Roman history, as revealed to Aeneas in the sixth book of the *Aeneid*, reaches its culmination in the reign of Augustus: for this all had been suffered; in this all was fulfilled. *Tantae molis erat Romanam condere gentem.* Augustine took a wider perspective which is made explicit in the *City of God*, a book which applies Augustine's personal experiences, recounted in the *Confessions*, to the canvas of all mankind:

> "the *way* which God built for us in the segregation of
> the Patriarchs, the bond of the Law, the foretelling of
> the Prophets, the sacrament of the Man assumed, the
> testimony of the Apostles, the blood of the martyrs and
> the entering into possession of the gentiles"[7]

all in unfaltering succession manifested this providence. To this Biblical account Augustine added a strong *Roman* component. He declares that God in his providence helped the Romans in creating their city and Empire and let them have sovereignty when and for as long as it was His pleasure. God in fact resolved, he says, to erect Rome in the West to be superior to the monarchies of the East in greatness and dignity. As it happened, it was Rome's opposition to evil that brought about so much of Rome's conquest, so that through wars that were honest, upright, and just, Augustine says, Rome was *providentially* compelled to grow. The fulfilment of the mission of pagan Rome was to be seen, he asserts, in its furnishing what should be an irresistible stimulus to Christians to be more virtuous for an immeasurably greater reward: "meditating long and seriously on [the great examples of Roman worthies] they could understand, he suggests, what love of their heavenly fatherland should be inspired by everlasting life, since a fatherland on earth has been so much loved by citizens inspired by human glory."[8] *Hic amor, haec patria est* were the words of Aeneas. Rome's destiny, in Augustine's view, lay in Christianity.

Both Virgil and Augustine had a deep religious feeling. Apart from his loving evocation of local gods and shrines, Virgil had a strong sense of the oneness of the community of men and gods and of the Platonic perception of the Beautiful, the source of all being. In practice he thought of Rome as a community living under the special design of God—a veritable City of God. Augustine's preoccupation with religion is more constant and manifest, since it was professional. But his most religious synthesis was in fact named the *City of God,* the community of angels and of all men, that ever were or will be, that are to be saved. Both Virgil and Augustine were conscious of being the heralds of new eras—the new Augustan age on the one hand, the Christian era on the other.

If sublimity, as Longinus argues, is the principal and irresistible quality of great writers, the product of a great soul which is deeply moral and deeply understanding of the self and the human condition, then we may safely look to both the *Aeneid* and the *Confessions* to see its presence. In both we can see impressive thoughts and strong emotion manifested in unusual arrangements of words, unusual expressions of thought, nobility of diction and metaphor, suitably elevated word order and rhythm.[9] This last is as true of the prose of the *Confessions* as the poetry of the *Aeneid*:

Sero te amaui, pulchritudo tam antiqua et tam noua, sero te amaui! et ecce intus eras et ego foris et ibi te quaerebam et in ista formosa, quae fecisti, deformis inruebam. mecum eras, et tecum non eram. ea me tenebant longe a te, quae si in te non essent, non essent. uocasti et clamasti et rupisti surditatem meam, coruscasti splenduisti et fugasti caecitatem meam, fragrasti, et duxi spiritum et anhelo tibi, gustaui et esurio et sitio, tetigisti me, et exarsi in pacem tuam.[10]

Too late loved I Thee, O Thou Beauty of ancient days, yet ever new! too late I loved Thee! And behold, Thou wert within, and I abroad, and there I searched for Thee; deformed I, plunging amid those fair forms, which Thou hast made. Thou wert with me, but I was not with Thee. Things held me far from Thee, which, unless they were in Thee, were not at all. Thou flashedst, shonest, and scatteredst my blindness. Thou breathedst odours, and I drew in breath and pant for Thee. I tasted, and hunger and thirst. Thou touchedst me, and I burned for thy peace. (Pusey's translation)

Here in Augustine, we have that elevation of mind which, if Longinus is to be believed, holds the foremost rank among all the qualities that constitute the sublime; and the passage I have quoted from the *Confessions* illustrates Longinus's judgement that there is no tone so lofty as that of genuine passion, in its right place, when it bursts out in a wild gust of mad enthusiasm and, as it were, fills the speaker's words with frenzy.[11]

Apart from the sympathy of Augustine with Virgil which I have mentioned—his sharing of a philosophic spirit, their sense of providence, their sense of religion, their sense of the sublime—there are other areas where this sympathy is evinced—their sense of mission, for example; their following of duty, however hard the cost: *Italiam non sponte sequor,* "Give me chastity, but not just now"—yet Augustine did choose chastity; and notably their preoccupation with love—of which I shall be speaking presently. There is so much in common between those two spirits that it is not surprising that Virgil was judged in later times to have been a natural Christian. I suppose it could be said that both Virgil and Augustine, while being in one sense men of their times, transcended them and draw nearer to one another in a longer and larger view of humanity.

I have, I hope, said enough to illustrate the view that the *Aeneid* was symbolical of Rome's achievement at the time of Augustus, that Virgil and his *Aeneid* enjoyed a transcending importance for the contemporaries of Augustine, that Augustine knew the *Aeneid* well, and that he shared much sympathy with its author. I must now go on to consider a few of the ways in which Virgil's *Aeneid* influenced Augustine's *Confessions*.

Ernst Robert Curtius, in the first chapter of his *European Literature and the Latin Middle Ages*, writes:

> "the *timeless present* which is an essential characteristic of literature means that the literature of the past can always be active in that of the present. So Homer in Virgil, Virgil in Dante, Plutarch and Seneca in Shakespeare, Shakespeare in Goethe, the *Odyssey* in Joyce—there is a wealth of figures which literature has formed and which can forever pass into new bodies: Achilles, Oedipus, Semiramis, Faust, Don Juan."[12]

Here I add Virgil's *Aeneid* in Augustine's *Confessions,* and the figure in question is Aeneas.

That Augustine should have thought of himself, given his acquaintanceship and sympathy with the *Aeneid,* from time to time in the course of his *Confessions* as another Aeneas is hardly surprising. Each of the stories of Aeneas and Augustine, the one fictional, the other real, is in its own way the spiritual transmutation which anthropologists such as M. Eliade discover in the myths of man. The mystery of regeneration consists of an archetypal process which is realised in different planes in many ways. It is effected whenever the need exists to surpass one mode of being and to enter upon another, higher mode. The protagonist undergoes a shattering personal experience which precedes a mystic vocation. There has to be the ritual of an agony, a death, and resurrection. The abolition of the merely human, transcendence and freedom, are invariably expressed by some "flight."

In these and other particulars it can be seen that both the *Aeneid* and the *Confessions* approach a usual pattern and to one another. Aeneas in his flight from Troy has many shattering personal experiences, many a trial, and a visit to the underworld from which he emerges regenerated, with a clear vision of his destiny and the strength and confidence to fulfil it. Augustine, likewise, pictures himself as the Prodigal Son fleeing back to the Father (an important related *motif* in the *Confessions*), has equally shattering personal experiences with trials, "dies to his old self" and puts on Christ in a mystic calling from which he emerges regenerated. There are differences of emphasis between the one work and the other—in particular the *Confessions* stress the "flight" in terms of the Neoplatonic flight to the fatherland and the way thither. But broadly speaking each is the story of Everyman in his journey through life. And as Ulysses is something of a model for Aeneas in the *Aeneid* so he lurks behind Aeneas in the *Confessions*.[13]

Let us now consider a passage in the *Confessions* where there is direct quotation from the *Aeneid*. In the first book of the *Confessions* Augustine is comparing the good of reading, writing, and arithmetic with the study of literature, to the disadvantage of the latter: in literature,

> "I was forced to learn the wanderings of one Aeneas, forgetful of my own, and to weep for dead Dido, because she killed herself for love; the while with dry eyes, I endured my miserable self, dying among those things, far from Thee, O God my life. For what more miserable than a miserable being who commiserates not himself; weeping the death of Dido for love of Aeneas, but weeping not his own death for want of love of Thee, O God—all this I wept not, I who wept for Dido slain, and 'seeking by the sword a stroke and wound extreme,' myself seeking the while a worse extreme, the extremest and lowest of Thy creatures, having forsaken Thee, earth passing into earth. And if forbid to read all this, I was grieved that I might not read what grieved me. Madness like this is thought a higher and a richer learning, than that by which I learned to read and write . . . I sinned, then, when as a boy I preferred those empty to those more profitable studies, or rather loved the one and hated the other. 'One and one, two'; 'two and two, four'; this was to me a hateful sing-song: 'the burning of Troy,' and 'Creusa's shade and sad similitude' [both references to the second book of the *Aeneid*] were the choice spectacle of my vanity."[14]

There are other explicit references in the *Confessions* to the *Aeneid*, but this is, I believe, the most significant in relation to the sense in which the *Aeneid* is active in the *Confessions*. The reference to Dido is, of course, to the fourth book of the *Aeneid*. In that book the love affair of Aeneas with Dido, Jupiter's ordering of Aeneas to leave her and proceed to the founding of Rome, and her unhappy consequential suicide are described. Dido represents some literary and perhaps one political figure— the Circe of Homer, the Medea of Apollonius Rhodius for example, and also, perhaps, the historical Cleopatra. But the depiction of her love for Aeneas and its tragic end also derives from a fear of love and its effects seen in such figures as Circe and Medea that was much manifested in ancient classical literature. Lucretius, whose heir Virgil to some extent was considered to be, had reinforced that fear with a profoundly pessimistic and savage indictment of Love. Virgil's depiction of love elsewhere and in connection with Dido remains entirely his own and entirely pessimistic. He was preoccupied with the theme of love and gave all his sympathies to the one that loved—to Dido—but finally he rejects love. Love, for all his sympathy with the lover, is, though alluring, if not almost inescapable, an evil, a wound, madness, a consuming fire, utterly destructive.

Few who have read the Aeneas and Dido episode in the *Aeneid* have not felt that Virgil, despite his seemingly ruthless termination of that affair in his poem, was on the side of Dido. So have been subsequent readers. "Dido," Helen Waddell writes in *The Wandering Scholars*, "was the romantic heroine of the Middle Ages . . . (They took her) to their hearts, wrote lament after lament for her, cried over her as the young men of the eighteenth century cried over Manon Lescaut . . . To come back to Dido after much novel-reading is to recognize a great heroine in the hands of a great novelist."[15] Matthew Arnold placed Dido beside Prometheus and Achilles as outside time and belonging to the domain of our permanent passions. Not a few would share the opinion of Eric Segal that although the *Aeneid*'s "ostensible subject is *arma uirumque,* yet our abiding memories of it are of love and *Liebestod.*"[16]

Helen Waddell states simply that Augustine "broke his heart" for Dido. This in effect is what he himself, as we have seen, declares. He emphasizes that he *indulged* his grief for her: "and if forbid to read all this, I was grieved that I might not read what grieved me." Indeed certain school exercises involved the portrayal of the role of characters, and entering into all their passions of rage and grief. Augustine excelled in these exercises. Reflecting upon his reactions to fiction about this time, Augustine examines at length in the *Confessions* how griefs are indulged and even loved.[17]

There can be no doubt, then, that Augustine luxuriated in Dido's love and her abandonment. He dwells upon this love of love:

> "And what was it that I delighted in, but to love, and be loved? But I kept not the measure of love, of mind to mind, friendship's bright boundary; but out of the muddy concupiscence of the flesh, and the bubblings of youth, mists fumed up which beclouded and overcast my heart, that I could not discern the clear brightness of love, from the fog of lustfulness."[18]

Soon he was to come to Carthage—founded by Dido herself according to the *Aeneid*—

> "where there sang all around my ears a cauldron of unholy loves. I loved not yet, yet I loved to love, and out of a deep-seated want, I hated myself

for wanting not. I sought what I might love, in love with loving, and safety I hated and a way without snares . . . To love then, and to be beloved, was sweet to me; but more, when I obtained to enjoy the person I loved . . . I fell headlong into love, wherein I longed to be ensnared."[19]

If the evidence of the *Confessions* is to prevail, the principal literary love that so affected the young Augustine was the hopeless love of Dido for Aeneas. The fact that it was both lawless and hopeless constituted for him at that stage part, if not the chief part, of its attraction. This is an important point. Augustine *knew* that what he did was, as he describes it, mad, irrational. Even he himself could not and did not seek to justify it.

Then at nineteen years of age he had what has been termed his first conversion, one to philosophy. He described it as follows:

"In the ordinary course of study, I fell upon a certain book of Cicero. . . . This book of his contains an exhortation to philosophy, and is called *Hortensius*. . . . This book altered my affections, and turned my prayers to Thyself, O Lord; and made me have other purposes and desires. Every vain hope at once became worthless to me; and I longed with an incredibly burning desire for an immortality of wisdom . . . the love of wisdom is in Greek called 'philosophy' with which that book inflamed me."[20]

From this point on in the *Confessions*, until the description of his final conversion to Christianity, the emphasis shifts significantly from his preoccupation with carnal love to preoccupation with problems of philosophy and theology—whether there were two Principles, one of Good and the other of Evil, and if only of Good, how was the existence of evil to be explained? And how could there be a Principle of either Good or Evil which was not material: how could one even conceive an immaterial Principle? These were to be his problems, exacerbated by his uneasy membership of the Manichees, until shortly before his final conversion, when Neoplatonism satisfied him both on the nature of a spiritual Principle and the nature of evil. Meanwhile though he found the Manichees devoted to neither reason nor chastity, and his own carnality was excused by the acceptance of the Manichean Principle of Evil which—and not he himself—was responsible for his sins, there is little reference to any preoccupation with love which so characterized his description of the years preceding his reading of the *Hortensius*.

Augustine's description in the *Confessions* of his total preoccupation with love in his teens is, doubtless, partly rhetorical and partly moralistic. But it also represents truth. That truth, I believe, must be related—as indeed he relates it himself—to his literary and imaginative perception of love. It was not only Dido who fed his emotional sensibility, although, according to his account, she made the deepest impression on him. The fictions of the theatre had a similar effect.

In brief what I am saying is that Augustine's teenage loves were heightened by the effect of romantic fiction upon his imagination and sensibility, particularly Virgil's story of Dido's abandonment of herself to a hopeless and lawless love and her willing choice of tragedy and death.

The thought of Dido did not altogether depart with the reading of the *Hortensius*. If Anatole France was haunted all his life by the vision of Dido in the Fields of Sorrow, it is unlikely that Augustine ceased to remember her during all the years, which lasted up to his very baptism, when he taught Virgil to his pupils. The shift in preoccupation from the world of imagination of the teenage years to the problems of theology and philosophy, with which the *Confessions* occupies itself in describing Augustine's twenties, explains the comparative absence of the theme of human love after its third book—but the shadow of Dido remains. Scholars have discerned in his description of his departure when he was 29 years old from Carthage and from his mother (who did not wish him to leave her and did not know that he was then leaving) the influence of Virgil's description of Aeneas's departure from Carthage and from Dido:

> "my mother . . . grievously bewailed my journey, and followed me as far as the sea. But I deceived her, holding me by force, that either she might keep me back, or go with me . . . , And I lied to my mother, and such a mother, and escaped . . . , I scarcely persuaded her to stay that night in a place hard by our ship . . . That night I privily departed, but she was not behind in weeping and prayer. And what, O Lord, was she with so many tears asking of Thee, but that Thou wouldest not suffer me to sail? . . . The wind blew and swelled our sails, and withdrew the shore from our sight; and she on the morrow was there, frantic with sorrow, and with complaints and groans filled Thy ears . . . After accusing my treachery and hardheartedness, she . . . went to her wonted place, and I to Rome."[21]

Aeneas too had firmly left Dido at Carthage and set out for what was to be Rome. And Dido had equally tried to hold him back, was deceived by him and was frantic on his departure. Virgil's Dido has clearly left her mark again.

As one might expect, when Augustine approaches the description of his final conversion the motif of carnal love begins to reappear with growing frequency. He speaks of the deadly sweetness of the flesh, and of drawing along his chain (of the flesh), dreading to be loosed, and of the weight of carnal custom. Still there remained with him an aspiration towards union with God. It was while in this frame of mind, convinced by the truth of Christianity, yet fearing to be freed from his encumbrances, drowsy and dull towards resolution, that the final crisis came. Once again the struggle that Aeneas had, to wring himself free from Dido his clinging mistress, is evoked:

> "my ancient mistresses still held me; they plucked my fleshly garment, and whispered softly, 'Dost thou cast us off? and from that moment shall we no more be with thee for ever? . . .' And now I much less than half heard them, and not openly shewing themselves and contradicting me, but muttering as it were behind my back, and privily plucking me, *as I was departing*, but to look back on them. Yet they did retard me, so that I hesitated to burst and shake free from them, and to spring over *whither I was called.*"[22]

The phraseology here suggests the model of Aeneas's unwilling but effectual abandonment of Dido. This is quickly followed by the final act of Augustine's conversion. Here Augustine describes how he heard

> "a voice, as of boy or girl, I know not, chanting and oft repeating, 'Take up and read; Take up and read.' Instantly . . . I began to think most intently, whether children were wont in any kind of play to sing such words: nor could I remember ever to have heard the like. So checking the *torrent of my tears*, I arose; interpreting it to be no other than *a command from God*, to open the book, and read the first chapter I should find . . . I seized, opened and in silence read that section, on which my eyes first fell: *Not in rioting and drunkenness, not in chambering and wantonness, not in strife and envying: but put ye on the Lord Jesus Christ, and make not provision for the flesh*, in concupiscence . . . Instantly at the end of this sentence . . . all the darkness of doubt vanished away."[23]

The conversion of Augustine was complete.

Augustine explicitly calls the child's voice a command from God, *diuinitus mihi iuberi*: this command led to the reading of the text which delivered him from the flesh. So Aeneas was divinely commanded by Jupiter's son, Mercury (*Aen.* IV. 223): *attonitus tanto monitu imperioque deorum*. Aeneas and Augustine, both, were by these divine commands astounded and galvanized into action. They were resolved to do what they knew should be done.

The context of this scene of Augustine's conversion is full of literary reminiscences: Courcelle declared that it swarmed with them. It looks as if one of these literary reminiscences could well be the divine bidding of Aeneas by Jupiter's child to depart from Dido.

I hope I have made a sufficient case for the view that the *Aeneid* is active in the *Confessions* where matters of human and carnal love are concerned. The treatment, as a matter of fact, of human and carnal love in the *Confessions*, like the episode of Dido and Aeneas in the *Aeneid*, tends for many people to steal the show, so to speak. For this reason the *Aeneid*'s "activity" in the *Confessions* is significant.

It suggests, moreover, that among other models to which Augustine tended to relate himself in the *Confessions* (the Prodigal Son, the Neoplatonist aspiring to union with the One or seeking, after Porphyry, a universal way of salvation) was Aeneas, waylaid by the carnal life, but finally strengthened in his mission to found Rome. Augustine, as we have said, had a strong sense of mission too and never wanted many friends who waited upon him to lead.

The question arises of whether the effect of the Dido and Aeneas episode on Augustine's sensibility significantly influenced his attitude towards human, physical, love. It is commonly believed that Augustine sinned greatly in sexual matters and that after his conversion he adopted, by way of reaction, a very rigorous, not to say hostile, approach to sex. There is doubt at least of the assumption that he was a notorious sinner in sexual matters. There remains, however, the question of whether the ambiguous attitude to love which he shared with Virgil—preoccupation with it on the one hand and the effort to be delivered from it on the other—did not affect his subsequent attitude to physical love. It is inevitable that it did: but the ambiguity extends here too. His attitude is not appreciably more hostile than was normal among contemporary ecclesiastics and in fact he has quite a lot of sympathy for the problems of human love and, what may to some be surprising, shows much tenderness towards it. I have treated this problem elsewhere.[24]

Virgil continued the story of Dido in the *Aeneid* beyond book IV. She reappears briefly in Book VI[25] where Aeneas is described as visiting the underworld and catching sight of her as she wandered in a great wood. He breaks into tears and addresses her with love. He protests that he had been compelled to depart from her by the orders of the Gods. She flies from him, forever more his enemy. But Virgil had sent Aeneas down to the underworld for another purpose—to meet his father Anchises again,

The *Aeneid* in the *Confessions* 115

and see the long line of his descendants who were to emerge into life in due course, to make Rome great, so great as to rule the world. Virgil employed the Pythagorean and Platonic doctrine of the cycle of souls to enable him, who knew the history of all the great heroes of Rome up to the time of the writing of the *Aeneid*, to have shown to Aeneas, who was yet to found Rome, all those heroes, one by one. Meanwhile he described them as deep in a green valley in Elysium, each awaiting his turn to come on to the stage of life:

> "Deep in a green valley stood father Anchises, surveying
> The spirits there confined before they went up to the light of
> The world above: he was musing seriously, and reviewing
> His folk's full tally, it happened, the line of his loved children,
> Their destinies and fortunes, their characters and their deeds."[26]
>   (translation by C. Day Lewis)

Augustine has unmistakably drawn on this passage for his famous passage on memory in Book X of the *Confessions*.[27] There he speaks of the "fields" of memory where ideas are stored until he summons them to come forth. Then they come forward:

> "I come into the fields and spacious palaces[28] of my memory, where are treasures of countless images of things of every manner . . . Hidden away in that place is also whatever we think about . . . When I am in that realm, I ask that whatsoever I want be brought forth. Certain things come forth immediately. Certain other things are looked for longer, and are rooted out as it were from some deeper receptacles. Certain others rush forth in mobs, and while some different thing is asked and searched for, they jump in between as if to say 'Aren't we perhaps the ones?' By the hands of my heart I brush them away from the face of my remembrance until what I want is unveiled and comes into sight from out of its hiding place. Others come out readily and in unbroken order, just as they are called for: those coming first give way to those that follow. 'I will do this or that,' I say to myself within that vast recess of my mind . . . and this deed or that then follows. 'Oh, that this or that could be!' 'May God forbid this or that!'" (translation by John K. Ryan)

This is not the place to study the recurrence of a similar vocabulary in the two passages I have mentioned, the passage in Virgil describing how the heroes await in Elysium their turn to emerge as great heroes on the stage of Roman history; and the passage in Augustine describing the store of memories and how they emerge in due order in this case into consciousness.[29] The last sentences I have quoted from the *Confes-*

sions—"Oh, that this or that could be!" "May God forbid this or that!"—seem to echo one of the most famous and pathetic lines in this part of the *Aeneid*, where Rome's future heroes are being reviewed:

heu, miserande puer, si qua fata aspera rumpas[30]

(*Alas, poor youth! if only you could escape harsh fate!*).

The youth was Marcellus, who had married Augustus's daughter Julia, and was regarded as a likely successor to Augustus: but he died at twenty years of age. Rome had been unusually affected by grief, as Virgil well conveys. And Augustine has proclaimed, in the passage from the *Confessions* that I have just quoted, that he decides on which item of memory he wishes to recall, not by his mind, but according to the prompting of his heart; "by the hand of my heart" "if only you could escape harsh fate!" "Oh!, that this or that could be!"[31]

I have spoken elsewhere of Augustine the Artist and the *Aeneid*.[32] One of the dominating traits of Augustine as a writer is his ability as an artist to draw on several sources of inspiration at the same time. In the *Confessions* he draws upon the Bible (especially the New Testament story of the Prodigal Son), upon Plotinus and Porphyry, and upon a number of literary sources, in particular Virgil's *Aeneid*. He does not draw upon these as it were in succession, finishing with one and then going on to use another. Rather does he draw upon them both together, or on any number of them at the same time, according as he moulds his own artistic creation, which, whatever his dependence on others, remains uniquely and redolently his. He can use the same source in two quite different ways: at times, for example, in the *Confessions*, his mother appears as Dido (when he deserts her), but at other times as Venus the mother who loved and schemed for her son Aeneas. The suggestion is often very subtle, but as Fontaine says in a quotation I have given earlier on, so impregnated was Augustine's literary sensibility by Virgil that a clear quotation from Virgil is sometimes "of less value than an allusion—than the use, hardly conscious, of a word charged with poetry."

Can one say, as has been suggested indeed, that the first nine books of the *Confessions* are a tale of wandering that corresponds to the Odyssean modelled wanderings of Aeneas in the first six books of the *Aeneid*—a history of the external lives of Augustine and Aeneas—while the last three books of the *Confessions* and the last six of the *Aeneid* are an *Iliad*, a struggle to win a new homeland, in Aeneas's case, and, for Augustine, the struggle to understand and live the new life of faith?[33] It is impossible to prove that Augustine set out to structure his *Confessions* in this way, but the thought can come to one that such a structure may in a general way have occurred to him. Some have noted that the first parts of both the *Aeneid* and the *Confessions* end in the description of an underworld, Elysium in Virgil's case, the plains of memory in Augustine's.[34] Was Augustine conscious of this? We cannot know, nor do we need to know. The clear obtrusion of the Dido and Aeneas episode from Virgil's *Aeneid* into Augustine's *Confessions* is by itself alone proof palpable that Augustine was sensitive to inspiration from the *Aeneid*. It is a fact that of the *Aeneid* and the *Confessions* the first parts are by far the more popular, and the reason is that they are tales of love; but tales of duty too. We can safely assume that Augustine knew what he was about, and was conscious of his debt to Virgil.

PART III

AUGUSTINE, PLOTINUS, AND PORPHYRY

9

Neoplatonism in the Conversion of Augustine

Cardinal Newman, in his essay on the conversion of St. Augustine, remarks that "this memorable event . . . has been celebrated in the Western Church from early times, being the only event of this kind thus distinguished, excepting the conversion of St. Paul." Certain it is that the *Confessions,* the work in which Augustine gives the moving account of his untiring search for truth, is one of the world's most cherished books. It has touched the hearts of countless men and women in their journey through life, and given them confidence and peace.

There have been some, however, who have challenged the sincerity, and indeed veracity of the *Confessions.* There was, for instance, Joannes Clericus in the late seventeenth and early eighteenth century, and it was to be expected that the rationalism of the nineteenth century would reach out its coarse thumb to a book that was so sacred. Naville, Boissier, Harnack, Loofs, Gourdon, Becker, Thimme, and many other scholars, one after the other, have piled up charge upon charge against the *Confessions* until in 1918, in Alfaric's monumental book, *L'évolution intellectuelle de saint Augustin,* we are informed that the *Confessions* grossly distort the truth about Augustine's alleged conversion in A.D. 386. Alfaric holds that at that time Augustine was indifferent to the rite of baptism, regarded Christianity as nothing but a popular form of Platonic wisdom fit only for novices or those that were intellectually feeble, adjusted his Christianity to fit in with his Neoplatonism, and was morally and intellectually converted not to Christianity but to Neoplatonism. If he had died then he would have been considered as a convinced Neoplatonist with a taint of Christianity. Little of this appears, Alfaric says, in the *Confessions,* because it is the book of a rhetor turned bishop. Wedded to a cause and sixteen years after the events which he describes, Augustine minimizes the influence of Neoplatonism on him at the time of his conversion, exaggerates the influence of Christianity, and exploits every rhetorical device, not excluding pure fiction. Gourdon had maintained that the *Confessions* were actually in flagrant contradiction with the facts of his conversion in 386. He declares that Augustine was not a sincere Christian until A.D. 400, when he had been a priest for almost ten, and a bishop for four, years.

One cannot deny that the *Confessions* bears the marks of rhetoric. But this is still a long way off from proving that a Christian bishop uses rhetoric to do gross violence to the truth. Nor can one deny the possibility at that time of Augustine's being, although a bishop, more convinced as a Neoplatonist than as a Christian. We have about the same time the interesting case of Synesius of Cyrene, who agreed to become bishop if he were allowed to continue to hold certain views contrary to the faith. It is proper to observe, however, that this is a possibility that is unlikely. The final decision in this matter is determined only by confronting the *Confessions* with the facts of 386. These are said to be found in a number of *Dialogues* written in 386, in the autumn before his baptism. I propose to show here some of the results which can be obtained when the *Confessions* and the most important of these *Dialogues*, the *Contra Academicos*, are set side by side.

Let us resume very briefly the story of his conversion as set out by Augustine in the *Confessions*. We cannot say that either he or we can tease out every element in this complex human story. It is important to stress certain factors, however—ambition, for instance. From his very earliest days his parents and himself had concentrated their energies and sacrificed much in order that he might succeed as a rhetorician. His patron Romanianus used his money and his influence to this end. He himself changed from Thagaste to Carthage, from Carthage to Rome, and from Rome to Milan to the Imperial Court with this end only in view. He so overworked at his profession and in a feverish canvassing of powerful friends, especially the all-powerful Symmachus, who got for him his appointment in Milan, that his health began to give him serious concern just before his conversion. He tells us that he was on the point of bringing off, as so many other rhetor-protégés of Symmachus had done, some big administrative post in the Imperial Civil Service. He had delivered a panegyric on Bauto, who held all power during the minority of Valentinian. He had hardly to wait until a rich reward would be proffered to him, as it had been proffered to the many fellow-rhetoricians that had preceded him.

Suddenly, in the autumn of 386, he gave up all. Why? *Some* conversion had occurred. The influence of Manicheism, of which he had been not merely a follower but an ardent apostle for nine years, had prejudiced him against any kind of intellectual or spiritual reality. His disillusion with it threw him into a violent scepticism, so that he joined the New Academy, which taught that nothing whatever could be perceived; that one must therefore assent to nothing; but that one might follow the probable or what was like the truth (*ueri simile*) in action. The teaching of Ambrose undid some of the evil work of both Manicheism and the New Academy, and shook him in his doubt about the possibility of spiritual reality and an immaterial deity. There was the constant struggle against the flesh. No sooner had he put away from him the mother of the child whom he called Adeodatus (God-given) than he relapsed, but not in absolute despair, into his former sin. There were the stories that he heard of the lives of the monks in Egypt. They sharpened his desire for a purer, a higher, life. There were the ever-present example, affection, and prayers of his mother, Monnica. All these factors and more, working upon his overwrought, exhausted and struggling soul, both singly and in combination, were further complicated by the influence of Neoplatonism. It is this that interests us particularly at the moment.

Neoplatonism purported to be a revival of Platonism, but was in fact a synthesis of Platonic, Aristotelian, Stoic, and Pythagorean elements. It dominated the pagan philosophical world from the middle of the third to the beginning of the sixth century A.D. Its great master was Plotinus, who lived and taught at Rome at the end of the third century. Its great popularizer was Porphyry, who published the notes of Plotinus as the *Enneads*, and wrote many other popular treatises of his own. Neoplatonism was at once a set of doctrines and a way of life. The central doctrine was that only what was intelligible was. Intelligence, since it seemed to be necessarily dual, inasmuch as it implied in its very notion not only a subject that "intellects" but also an object that is "intellected," could not be the primary principle, and had to have its source, therefore, in a unity that was not intellectual, and that, therefore, by definition, was not. This principle received the name of the One, or the God which is beyond being. It is, as it were, the unmarked centre of a circle. Related to it by emanation is intelligence, which is and which only is. This is the second principle. There is a third principle called the Soul. It arises, as it were, on the fringe of being, of intelligence: it is a link between intelligence and material things. Now we are all of the order of intelligence, but we find ourselves in composition with matter. Our *true* life is the life of intelligence, of nous, of immediate intuition of all truth, and not the life of discursive reason. We need but recollect ourselves and remember that we are Gods, and already we *are* Gods. Matter does make this almost impossible for some of us, and difficult for nearly all of us. Hence our effort must always be directed to purgation, to ridding ourselves as far as possible of the matter which is the vesture of our decay, and to asserting the Godhead in us, until we are altogether freed from the body and resume our union with the all-intelligent, from which we can rise ultimately to the mystical union with the one, the good, or as he is sometimes called the Father.

In the course of the seventh and beginning of the eighth book of the *Confessions,* Augustine tells us that just before his conversion he read certain books of the Platonists. He does not mention any particular Platonist, even though he refers to the matter three times in this short section. We know, however, from his works as a whole that Plotinus or Porphyry or both were chiefly in his mind. In recent years Theiler has maintained that he could have read only Porphyry, while Henry holds that he could have read only Plotinus. These books were translated from Greek into Latin by Victorinus, who had been a rhetor and had been converted to Christianity. Although we do know that Victorinus did translate at least one work of Porphyry—the famous *Isagoge*—we have no independent evidence that he translated anything of Plotinus. Victorinus had, moreover, certain relations with demon-worshippers—a point, as we shall see, which suggests that his interests were more in common with those of Porphyry than Plotinus. These Platonist books taught, Augustine tells us, a doctrine equivalent to that found in the Prologue to St. John's Gospel: "In the beginning was the Word: and the Word was with God: and the Word was God." Augustine marvelled at the similarity, as he thought, between the Neoplatonic principles, sometimes called the Father and the Father's mind, and the Christian Father and Word. He goes on to say that the Platonists did not recognize the Word when he became incarnate. Their pride could not accept the humiliation of birth of a woman, and still less death on a cross. Consequently their foolish heart was darkened, and they became fools. They saw whither they were to go, but did not see the way, that is Christ. He himself, however, although he at first shared their pride and consequently their foolishness, did accept Christ, and in that acceptance found strength to overcome all difficulties. Moreover, when he read the Scriptures again in the light of what the Platonists had taught him, and especially when he read St. Paul, not only did all previous difficulties in understanding the Scriptures vanish, but the truth that he had learned from the Platonists became much clearer through the reading of the Scriptures.

The passages in the *Confessions* just referred to give at once the history of his conversion and at the same time a statement of an idea, a theme, or τόπος, to which he is ever recurring and which reveals to us the germs of the master-ideas of the great Doctor Gratiae. One of the most successful methods of enquiry employed by students of Hellenistic and Post-Hellenistic philosophy and religion is the study of such a recurring theme. It can, I think, be employed to some good effect here.

If we turn to the *City of God*, for instance, to the tenth book, a section written about 415–417, we find the topic in question but with certain precisions that are lacking in the *Confessions*:

> "But Porphyry, being under the dominion of these envious powers (demons) whose influence he was at once ashamed of and afraid to throw off, refused to recognize that Christ is the principle by whose incarnation we are purified . . . a great mystery, unintelligible to Porphyry's pride . . . and this we carnal and feeble men . . . could not possibly understand, unless we were cleansed by him . . . You (Porphyry) say, indeed, that ignorance, and the numberless vices resulting from it, cannot be removed by any mysteries, but only by the πατρικὸς νοῦς, that is the Father's mind or intellect conscious of the Father's will. But that Christ is this mind you do not believe; for him you despise on account of the body He took of a woman and the shame of the cross . . . Though your expressions are inaccurate, you do in some sort, and as through a veil, see what we should strive towards . . . You see in a fashion, although at a distance, although with filmy eye, the country in which we should abide; but the way to it you know not. Yet you believe in grace, for you say that it is granted to few to reach God by virtue of intelligence . . . It is, I suppose, a degradation for learned men to pass from the school of Plato to the discipleship of Christ, who by his spirit taught a fisherman to think and to say: 'In the beginning was the Word: and the Word was with God: and the Word was God.' . . . Porphyry lived in an age when this universal way of the soul's deliverance—in other words, the Christian religion—was exposed to the persecutions of idolaters and demon-worshippers." (X, 24–32)

This passage repeats the same range of ideas and employs very many of the same phrases that we have found in the *Confessions*. It speaks of the existence of the Father and the Word, and of the failure of a Platonist to recognize the Word incarnate. The only Platonist mentioned, however, is Porphyry, whose name is repeatedly and exclusively used in connection with this idea throughout this and many other of the later sections of the *City of God*. One important additional reason given for Porphyry's refusal to recognize Christ is found here: his being involved with demon-worshippers, who attacked the Christian religion. One other matter: the books of Porphyry mentioned by Augustine here in connection with this theme are the *De regressu animae* and the *Letter to Anebo*. Could they have been the Platonist books of the *Confessions*?

Let us turn to another instance of the recurrence of this theme, this time to *Letter* 118 (FOTC 18.278f.), written a few years before the tenth book of the *City of God*. The passage is too long to quote. He writes that the Platonists before the time of Christ had not sufficient authority to impose their true spiritual doctrine on the masses of men who were sunk in ignorance and sin. Consequently they decided to conceal that doctrine and hand it on secretly from one initiate to another. But publicly they taught that nothing whatever could be perceived: they had become the New Academy. However, when the Word became flesh, men were elevated and were given a way and an authority which they could follow. Then it was that the school of Plotinus at Rome began to teach the true spiritual doctrine of Plato once again. There were many clever and learned men (*acutissimi et sollertissimi*) in this school, but some of them were corrupted by curious enquiries, while others recognized Christ as the saviour. From that time all conflict had ceased, and now the whole supremacy of authority and light of reason resided in the name of Christ.

It will be seen that in this last passage the theme is linked to a theory about the Platonists which will not surprise anyone acquainted with the stock-in-trade of Hellenistic philosophy and religion—the theory of a secret doctrine within the sect. The teaching of the Platonists on the Father and the Word could not be revealed to the masses until the Word had come with authority and example to lead to the Father the many who could not follow the way of reason that was for the few. Here, as in the text from the *City of God* and as discovered by Augustine himself in his own experience as set out in the *Confessions*, the cardinal thing for any man and for all men was to accept Christ, the Word incarnate. Here again also we are told that some of the *schola Plotini*, clever and learned men (*acutissimi et sollertissimi*) were prevented by pride and curious inquiries from accepting Christ. There is not a shadow of doubt but that here in this *Letter*, as in the *City of God*, and, we may now say, the *Confessions*, the member of the *schola Plotini* most in mind is also the most famous member of that school, Porphyry.

So far we have indicated part of the history of a single well defined topic in the *Confessions*, the *City of God*, and *Letter* 118. It has gained in precision as we have had the opportunity to observe its use in different contexts. It is employed very frequently in many parts of the *City of God*, in the *De Trinitate*, and in several of the later works. But you may ask, what relevance this has to the confronting of the *Confessions* with the early *Dialogues* with which it is said to be in conflict? I answer that the theme which we have discussed is used so often and to such purpose in the early *Dialogues*, precisely because they were written at the time when Augustine was discovering from his own experience the various elements in the theme, that it is quite impossible to understand the *Dialogues* fully, and one of them, the *Contra Academicos*, hardly at all unless one is aware of the rôle of this theme in Augustine's life. Thus, for example, the theme is found in *De ordine* II, 16, 27; *Soliloquia* I, 2–6, 24 (with which, through *Retractationes* I, 4, 2, we can directly connect the name of Porphyry); *De quantitate animae* LXXVI; *De uera religione* II–VII; and *De doctrina Christiana* II, 40. It is impossible to analyse here these various occurrences of the theme. I shall content myself with a short analysis of its occurrence in the first and most important of these early *Dialogues*, the *Contra Academicos*.

The three books of the *Contra Academicos* were composed in order, as Augustine tells us, to rid his mind of the New Academic teaching about the impossibility of certitude, a view to which he had but lately subscribed. The chief adversary in this work is Cicero, whose *Academica* supplies almost all the subject matter in the book. Augustine's own contribution to the work has escaped much notice, although it is the only point that makes the work interesting, important, or even clear in its argument. For the work is puzzling. It is called by Augustine and the Manuscripts not only *Contra Academicos* (Against the Academics), but also *De academicis* (About the Academics), and simply *Academicorum liber* (the Book of the Academics). He says himself that he rather agrees with the Academics than disagrees with them. And from the following passage you will see why:

> "And so shortly after those times (that is, of Cicero and his contemporaries) Plato's doctrine . . . the clouds of error removed, shone forth especially in Plotinus . . . At last after many generations and many conflicts there is strained out, as it were, one system of true philosophy. For that philosophy is not of this world—such a philosophy our sacred mysteries most justly detest—but of the other, intelligible, world. To this intelligible world the most subtle reasoning would never recall souls

blinded by the manifold darknesses of error and stained deeply with the slime of the body, had not the most high God, because of a certain compassion on the masses, bent and submitted the authority of the divine intellect even to the human body itself. By the precepts and deeds of that intellect souls have been awakened and are able, without the strife of disputation, to return to themselves, and see once again their fatherland . . . This theory about the Academics I have sometimes, as far as I could, thought probable. If it is false I do not mind. It is enough for me that I do not any longer think that truth cannot be found by man. But if any one thinks that the Academics really did hold this view (namely, that truth could *not* be found) let him listen to Cicero. For he says that the Academics had a practice of hiding their own opinions and of not revealing them to anyone except to those who lived with them up to old age. What these opinions were, God knows! For my part I believe that they were Plato's . . . No one doubts but that we are helped to learning by a double force, that of reason and that of authority. I therefore am resolved in nothing whatever to depart from the authority of Christ—for I do not find a stronger. But as to that which is sought out by subtle reasoning—for I am so disposed as to be impatient in my desire to apprehend truth not only by faith but also by understanding— I feel sure at the moment that I shall find it with the Platonists, nor will it be at variance with our sacred mysteries." (III, 41–43 ACW 12.148–50)

Here, then, is the topic again. It has the same articulation as in *Letter* 118. It will be noted that the incarnation is the pivot of the whole theme; and that while some of the Platonists rejected Christ, Augustine accepts him. The whole book centres around this acceptance of the incarnation: it is the argument of the book, an argument that can be briefly, however roughly, resumed as follows: One can assent to truth, if it is found: But it is found in Christ; therefore one can assent to truth. The force of this argument is of more consequence in proving the sincerity of Augustine's conversion than even the unequivocal declaration "I therefore am resolved in nothing whatever to depart from the authority of Christ." At the same time the Platonists had helped him so much already that it was only natural that, although he might disagree with them in the application of their doctrine, he could still hope to learn much from them. One should note the repetition of the epithets *acutissimi et sollertissimi* which we found applied to members of the *schola Plotini* in *Letter* 118. Indeed the correspondence in idea and phrase between these two treatments of the theme is most striking. Finally one must add that Augustine has no evidence for his theory of a secret doctrine in the Academy. It was the kind of theory all too fashionable in many quarters at that time.

His many hesitations in presenting this theory are, apart from other cogent evidence, sufficiently enlightening. But, as he says, he does not mind whether it is true or not. He believed that it was true in the larger designs of providence; if the Academics had not deliberately suppressed their true teaching until after the incarnation, then God had!

There are two other prominent recurrences of this theme in the *Contra Academicos*. We shall say nothing of one (III, 13), but the other is important, for it is the first account of Augustine's conversion, and since the theme is founded on that conversion, it is the first instance of the theme. It bears out the story of the *Confessions*, almost word for word. He writes, in the preface to the second book of the work, to his patron Romanianus:

> But lo! when certain books had instilled a very few drops of most precious unguent upon the meagre flame (of my enthusiasm for the higher life), they stirred up an incredible conflagration. Swiftly did I begin to return entirely to myself. I looked back, nevertheless, . . . as it were from (the end of) a journey to the religion that is implanted in us as children and is bound up in the marrow of our bones. But she indeed was drawing me unknowing to herself. Therefore stumbling, hastening, hesitating, I seize the apostle Paul . . . And then, indeed, whatever had been the little radiance that surrounded the face of philosophy before then, she now appeared great (indeed). . . . (II, 5, 6 ACW 12.69–70)

As in the *Confessions* we read twice of certain books (*quosdam libros*), so here we read of certain books (*libri quidam*). These are the Platonist books that brought to his notice the Platonist teaching of the Father and the Word. They affected him profoundly. He began, as he says, to return to himself (*prorsus totus in me cursim redibam*, C.A.; *et inde admonitus redire ad memetipsum*, C). He examined the Scriptures and especially St. Paul (*itaque titubans properans haesitans arripio apostolum Paulum*, C.A.; *itaque auidissime arripui uenerabilem stilum spiritus tui et prae ceteris apostolum Paulum*, C). He then adds in both places that the reading of St. Paul illuminated what he had read in the Platonist books.

What did he read in St. Paul? You will have noticed that both in the *Contra Academicos* and the *Confessions* he speaks of the fever of his mind as he opened the book: *itaque titubans properans haesitans arripio . . . itaque auidissime arripui . . .* In another famous passage of the *Confessions* he tells of the actual moment of his conversion:

> I cast myself down, I know not how, under a certain fig tree, giving full vent to my tears . . . and not indeed in these words, yet to this

purpose, spake I much unto Thee: and Thou, O Lord, how long? how long, Lord, wilt Thou be angry? For ever? Remember not our former iniquities, for I felt that I was held by them. I sent up these sorrowful words: How long? how long? "tomorrow and tomorrow?" Why not now? Why not is there this hour an end to my uncleanness? So was I speaking, and weeping in the most bitter contrition of heart, when, lo! I heard from a neighbouring house a voice, as of a boy or girl, I know not, chanting, and oft repeating, "Take up and read; Take up and read" . . . So checking the torrent of my tears, I arose; interpreting it to be no other than a command from God, to open the book and read the first chapter I should find . . . Eagerly then I returned (*itaque concitus redii* . . .) to the place where Alypius was sitting; for there had I laid the volume of the *apostle,* when I arose thence. I seized, opened, and in silence read (*arripui, aperui, et legi* . . .) that section on which my eyes first fell: "Not in rioting and drunkenness, not in chambering and wantonness, not in strife and envying: but put ye on the Lord Jesus Christ, and make no provision for the flesh, in concupiscence." No further would I read; nor needed; for instantly at the end of this sentence, by a light as it were of serenity infused into my heart, lo the darkness of doubt vanished away. (C VIII, 28–29, tr. Pusey)

The text which wrought so great a change on Augustine has often seemed to me a disappointing text to have so dramatic an effect. He must have read it, or many other texts like it, before then and had remained unchanged. But in this reading he had received a light. God had used the Platonist books to bring about, at least in part, that great light. Porphyry had said equivalently, "Put ye on the Word." His very words were 'Only the Father's mind could bring mankind to salvation." Porphyry had failed to accept Christ, but in putting on Christ Augustine had found all, strength in his weakness, truth for his mind, and salvation for his soul. From his own experience he was convinced that all men needed Christ in the same way. They needed grace, illumination, and authority.

In the *Confessions,* he tells us: "Nor was I sated in these early days with the wondrous sweetness of considering the depth of thy counsels concerning the salvation of mankind" (IX, 14). He was indeed fascinated by the idea that had operated in his own conversion: the waiting of Platonist truth upon the coming of the Word before it could be taught to men. He was not sure that the Platonists had intended it so—but God had. In the first of his extant letters, a letter to Hermogenianus, he invites his opinion on this part of his theory. The text has so puzzled the editors that they have changed it. The MS reads *contra huiusmodi homines opinor ego illam utiliter excogitatam Dei ueri artem atque rationem.* Goldbacher, in the CSEL, altered the *Dei ueri artem* to *occultandi ueri artem*. The Benedictines before him had altered it to *tegendi ueri artem*. But if we have studied the recurrence of this all-important topic in St. Augustine we shall have no difficulty in translating the MS as it stands. The suppressing of Platonic truth was an *ars Dei,* a thing arranged most usefully by providence.

The general conclusion that emerges from all of this on the question of the relations of Neoplatonism to Christianity in the mind of St. Augustine at the time of his baptism is pretty clear. The Platonists had convinced him rationally of the existence of an immaterial God the Father and his Word. They had, moreover, seemed to conspire with God's providence in holding this spiritual doctrine back from the mass of mankind which could not possibly profit by it, until the coming of the Word. Porphyry had said that the πατρικὸς νοῦς, the Father's mind, would have to come to help men by showing them a universal way to the Father. Augustine departed from the Neoplatonists on the question as to whether or not Christ was that Father's mind. He accepted the incarnation against the opposition of Porphyry, who had considered and rejected the claims of Christ. There could be no more significant proof of the sincerity of Augustine's conversion to Christianity than this. He protests in his very first work that it is sincere. But he does even more—he makes the argument of that first book—the *Contra Academicos*—so completely pivot around the incarnation that it is clear that it occupied all his thoughts, as indeed it did. There is, moreover, quite remarkable accord between the account of his conversion in this first work and that given in the *Confessions*. Although in later works he was to think less of the Neoplatonists, it was but natural that, although he might disagree with them even in his first work, he still looked to them for much help in what could be learnt by the process of reason. He lets us see in these early *Dialogues* that he believed that as God was the source of illumination both of reason and faith, neither need be subordinated to the other, but both coordinated must issue in the discovery of the truth that could only be one.

10

A Master-Motif in Augustine

It will hardly be disputed that St. Augustine was capable of formulating a synthesis, exploiting its possibilities, and commending it in enthusiastic language to the sympathetic consideration of his fellow men. We have but to point to the *City of God* to win, or at any rate, to encourage belief. The grand sweeping synthesis of this work, however, is not the only one attempted by its author. Rather was it a summary of previous syntheses, a fitting together of many parts previously prepared and mutually related, a magnificent symphony dedicated to God. In fact Augustine had the kind of mind which worked, not meticulously in groping analysis, but universally, if I may say so, in intuitive synthesis. His rhetorical training and profession, moreover, tended to help him in the development of a particular theme, whether by the suggestion involved in antithesis, chiasmus, and alliteration, or the over-elaboration and likewise neglect of detail incidental to hyperbole. If men are to be judged by their fruits—and how else can we rightly judge the men of the past?—then Augustine was a mastermind of his age, and it will not be unprofitable for us to study one of the favourite instruments of that mind, namely synthesis. By "synthesis" in this connection I mean a *theory* about something, a *key* to its understanding—and nothing more.

I propose to discuss briefly the very first instance of synthesis found in his extant works. I hope to reveal the source of its inspiration, the peculiar circumstances of its formulation, and its continued exploitation throughout the whole *corpus* of Augustine's works. I hasten to assure you that I shall not inflict upon you an endless repetition of the same ideas in almost the same words. It would indeed seem more scientific to do so. But even if you did not depart before long, you might well ask me if the method of the humanities cannot dispense with some of the tedium of what is now called science, and use quite properly a little intuition. You shall be given, then, the minimum of repetition, but, I hope, enough of reference.

You will recall that in the *Confessions*—itself a synthesis on the grace of God overcoming all weakness—Augustine tells of the combination of influences that brought him almost to conversion, but yet left him unconverted. The moment of his conversion, a moment that was for him the most significant of his whole life, is described in these words:

> et non quidem his uerbis, sed in hac sententia multa dix tibi: Et tu, domine, usquequo? . . . Et ecce audio uocem de uicina domo cum cantu dicentis et crebro repetentis quasi pueri an puellae, nescio: "Tolle lege, tolle lege." Statimque mutato uultu intentissimus cogitare coepi. . . . Itaque concitus redii in eum locum, ubi sedebat Alypius: ibi enim posueram codicem apostoli, cum inde surrexeram. Arripui, aperui et legi in silentio capitulum, quo primum coniecti sunt oculi mei. . . . *sed induite dominum Iesum Christum et carnis prouidentiam ne feceritis in concupiscentiis.* Nec ultra uolui legere nec opus erat. Statim quippe cum fine huiusce sententiae quasi luce securitatis infusa cordi meo omnes dubitationis tenebrae diffugerunt.

Now listen to the same incident described some fourteen years earlier shortly after the time of its occurrence:

> *Ecce* tibi *libri quidam pleni,* ut ait Celsinus, bonas res Arabicas ubi exhalarunt in nos, ubi illi flammulae instillarunt pretiosissimi unguenti guttas paucissimas, incredibile, Romaniane, incredibile et ultra quam de me fortasse et tu credis . . . incendium *concitarunt.* Quis me tunc honor, quae hominum pompa, quae inanis famae cupiditas, quod denique huius mortalis uitae fomentum atque retinaculum commouebat? Prorsus totus *in me cursim redibam.* Respexi tamen confitebor, quasi de itinere in illam religionem, quae *pueris* nobis insita est . . . *itaque titubans properans haesitans arripio apostolum Paulum.* . . . *perlegi* totum *intentissime* atque cautissime. Tunc uero quantulocumque iam *lumine adsperso* tanta se mihi philosophiae facies aperuit . . . (*Contra Academicos,* 2, 5–6)

It is clear that there is a close relationship between both passages. There is the unmistakable echo of words, and of course the incident is the same. But while both are rhetorical, the one employs rhetoric to give a more religious, the other a more philosophic, atmosphere, although philosophy and religion are absent from neither.

If we turn now to another text of the *Confessions* (7.13 ff.; 8.1 ff.), we shall find that it also describes the same incident, employing again the same words (*quosdam* Platonicorum *libros* (twice) . . . ibi legi *non quidem his* verbis . . . et inde *admonitus redire ad memetipsum* . . . *itaque avidissime arripui* venerabilem stilum spiritus *tui et prae ceteris apostolum Paulum*). The treatment here however is very lengthy and will not bear actual quotation on this occasion. Augustine says that when he had read certain

Platonist books, translated from Greek into Latin, he found there equivalently the doctrine that is taught in the prologue to St. John's Gospel, the doctrine of the existence of the Father and the Word. He did not find however, the teaching on the Incarnation and the Crucifixion. The authors of these Platonist books were too proud to accept such teachings, and consequently fell into gross error. Augustine paid attention to what truth they taught and avoided the error. He began to reflect within himself and to aspire to union with God. But the evil habits of his flesh withheld him. He began to follow the Platonists in their pride. Finally he read the Scriptures and especially St. Paul. Whatever truth there was in the Platonist books was also to be found in St. Paul, but without any admixture of error.

This time there is an even balance between the philosophic and the religious in the tone of the passage, and there is considerably less rhetoric. More information too is given on both sides, the religious and the philosophic. While on the one hand we are told of the 'way' (*uia*) to the heavenly fatherland, of the Incarnation and Crucifixion, on the other there is an enthusiastic account of the Platonic hypostases. The two previous texts placed emphasis on the personal experience of Augustine. But here, while the occasion of the passage is the same experience, the emphasis is on the ideas that were operative in his conversion. It is with these ideas that we shall from now on be concerned. For they constitute a τόπος which is found in almost every work of Augustine.

Put quite briefly, once and for all, the τόπος runs as follows. The Platonists, through the use of reason (*ratio*) could, and did, arrive at the fundamental truth of the existence of the Father and His Word. Independently, however, the mass of mankind, who could not use their reason to such effect, could come to the same conclusion through following authority (*auctoritas*), a way (*uia*) to the fatherland. The Platonists recognized the necessity for this way of authority for the masses. They looked around and examined all the persons or institutions that claimed to be such an authority. They rejected all, among them the claims of Christ and the church which he founded. Augustine disagrees with them only on one point—their failure to see that Christ was the way of authority. He believes that the Platonists failed because of their pride in refusing to accept the incarnation and crucifixion and their being led astray by the demons whom they worshipped.

It is to be noticed that the source for these ideas on Platonism are said to be *libri quidam* (CA II, 5), *quosdam Platonicorum libros* (C VII, 9, 26;

VIII, 3), certain books of the Platonists translated from Greek into Latin by Victorinus. One must insist at this stage that the uncertain reading of DBV IV (*lectis autem Platonis* [*Plotini*] *paucissimis libris*); the fact that Victorinus, so far as we know, did not translate anything of Plotinus; the emphatic repetition three times of the term *Platonicorum* (and not *Plotini*); and the mention of the worship of demons—all these factors make it almost impossible that Plotinus is exclusively, or even in a notable way, the Platonist in Augustine's mind. On the other hand, the fact that we do know that Victorinus did translate at least the *Isagoge* of Porphyry; that Porphyry did place great emphasis on the necessity of a way of authority for the masses (or at least Augustine thought so: which is the important point, cf. DCD X, 32); that he examined and rejected the claims of Christ and his church to be that way (cf. DCD X, 24, 28, 29); that he was notoriously (again at least according to Augustine, cf. DCD X, 26, 27, 32) under the spell of demons; and finally that even if the name of Plotinus were used in this connection, nevertheless Porphyry might still be the person understood (a clear instance of this use of the name of the Master, Plotinus, when a written work of the disciple, Porphyry, is referred to, is found in Macrobius: *In Somn.* I, 8, 3–12 = Porphyry, *Sent.*, XXXII, 1, 7)—all these considerations tend to make it probable that Porphyry was the Platonist most in mind when Augustine speaks of the *Platonicorum libros* which played such a vital part in the synthesis that operated in his conversion.

Only one half, however, of the τόπος has been formulated in these passages where Augustine was immediately concerned with setting forth the account of his own conversion. There is an extension of it which makes it take on a universal aspect, a philosophy of history, and a key to the understanding of the world and life: a synthesis.

In the *Contra Academicos*, the first of his extant books, and written simultaneously almost with *De beata vita, De ordine,* and the *Soliloquia* in the autumn preceding his baptism, there is not only the first account of his conversion, which I have already quoted, but also this significant passage:

> Adeo post illa tempora (sc. Ciceronis) non longo intervallo omni pervicacia pertinaciaque demortua os illud Platonis . . . dimotis nubibus erroris emicuit maxime in Plotino . . . quod autem ad eruditionem doctrinamque attinet et mores, quia non defuerunt acutissimi et sollertissimi uiri qui docerent disputationibus suis Aristotelem ac Platonem . . . sibi concinere . . . multis quidem saeculis multisque contentionibus sed

tamen eliquata est ... una certissima philosophiae disciplina. Non enim est ista huius mundi philosophia quam sacra nostra meritissime detestantur, sed alterius intelligibilis, cui animas multiformibus erroris tenebris caecatas et altissimis a corpore sordibus oblitas numquam ista ratio subtillissima reuocaret, nisi summus deus populari quadam clementia diuini intellectus auctoritatem usque ad ipsum corpus humanum declinaret atque submitteret, cuius non solum praeceptis sed etiam factis excitatae animae redire in semetipsas et respicere patriam etiam sine disputationum concertatione potuissent ... nulli autem dubium est gemino pondere nos impelli ad discendum auctoritatis atque rationis (CA III, 41–43).

The gist of the matter is that the Platonic Academy had a positive spiritual doctrine about the Father and the word, but, because the mass of men were so enmeshed in the toils of the body that they were incapable of understanding and accepting such a doctrine, and were consequently in danger of swallowing wholesale the materialism of the Stoics, they had concealed their true teaching and had pretended to teach a negative doctrine, namely that nothing could be certainly known, and therefore one must not assent to anything—especially not to the sensationalism of the Stoics. With the coming of Christ, however, and the elevation of man which followed upon the acceptance of him as the way of authority, the Platonists once more revealed their true teaching and joined Catholicism in leading man both by the way of reason and authority to the heavenly fatherland. This is the whole argument of the *Contra Academicos,* which is sometimes, significantly, called *De Academicis* or merely *Academicorun liber* (cf. R I, 1; Codex Parisinus; Codex Remensis; Codex Harleianus). In passing we may remark that Augustine advanced his theory with great enthusiasm, but little confidence, and with, of course, no convincing evidence that we know of.

A passage with very close verbal parallelism to the text just quoted is found in *Letter* 118, which was written about 410. I do not propose to quote it, but content myself with drawing attention to the easily ascertainable fact that it sets out the τόπος described in a fully articulated manner. While there is no longer any reference at all to Augustine's own personal experience, there are some few points which help towards the identification of the source from which Augustine derived some of the inspiration for the synthesis. For example, the failure of certain Platonists of the school of Plotinus at Rome, *acutissimi et sollertissimi uiri* (a phrase used in the same connection in a passage already quoted from the CA III, 41–43) because of curious enquiries into magic, to recognize

Christ as the authority for which they were seeking. It is impossible to deny that Porphyry was the leading Platonist of the school of Plotinus at Rome, and as we shall see presently, it is also impossible to deny that his failure to accept Christianity was attributed by Augustine to his subservience to demons. According to Augustine, Porphyry was the Platonist *par excellence* who insisted that there must be a divine authority to lead men to the Father. He was, doubtless, in Augustine's mind when in the *Contra Academicos* III, 13 he also wrote: *Etenim numen aliquod aisti solum posse ostendere homini quid sit verum. . . . Veritatis, inquam, Proteus in carminibus ostentat sustinetque personam, quam obtinere nemo potest, si falsis imaginibus deceptus comprehensionis nodos . . . dimiserit.*

There are many other instances of this synthesis, this master-motif, with here and there a slight variation in detail or emphasis. For example it is to be found very frequently in the earlier works, in DOR II, 16, 27; SO I, 2–6, 24 (with which, in R I, 4–3, he connects the name of Porphyry); DQ LXXVI; DVR II–VII; DDC II, 40. But it is also to be found in the later works, for example in the DT IV, 13–15, 20; 13–24, and above all in DCD, especially in Book X 24–32 (quoted on p. 115 above).

To sum up, the synthesis as it appears in DCD is clearly associated with the name of Porphyry—indeed the names of the works of Porphyry in which the inspiration was found are given. The one with most influence is undoubtedly the *De regressu animae*. The synthesis has a history right back to his earliest works in which all its articulations are clearly found, with indications also that, just as at the end, so too in the beginning, the Platonist who played the major rôle was Porphyry. In my view it was the realization that the Platonists taught a positive spiritual doctrine, and above all that they, or some of them, insisted that the way of reason was available for the few, but that a way of authority was necessary for the many, that made it dawn upon Augustine that in the acceptance of Christ he himself, and all others, would be lead to the Father by a way of authority; they would be elevated so as to be able to lead a life that was not of the flesh, and to understand the loftier flights of the operations of reason. He found this acceptance of Christ operative in himself, and its success in him made him an ardent apostle of this way for the many. When he obeyed the command of St. Paul, "Put ye on the Lord Jesus Christ," he felt that he was obeying a precept of the Platonists also, however much they themselves might fail to apply their teaching in practice. It was this seeming agreement between the teachings of Platonism and the Church which dominated his conversion, suggested to him the absolute importance of grace, of the elevation of man through his acceptance of Christ, and convinced him at the time that there were two coordinated, although independent, ways to the Father, that of *ratio* (represented by Platonism with some adjustments), and that of authority (represented by Christ).

It is hardly necessary to point out that these conclusions run counter to those of Alfaric and others in their belief that Augustine was not sincerely convinced about the truth of Catholicism in 386, when he was baptised. The whole point of the synthesis lies in the full acceptance of the incarnation and the belief in grace, for which he later became so noted. Likewise these conclusions run counter to those of Henry who would hold that Porphyry had no part whatever in Augustine's conversion. I would hold that he played a greater part than any other Platonists—indeed a vital part. But neither would I agree with Theiler, who would deny the influence of Plotinus in any form. It is very easy to discover traces of Plotinus in the early works.

Augustine was very pleased with his synthesis. He was, he tells us, fascinated with it. And that is no wonder, if, as I hold, it was so vital in his conversion. At any rate, he writes to Hermogenianus at the time, asking him for his view on this newly discovered theory (*Letter* I. 3). In the *Confessions* he tells us that "he could not be sated in these early days with the wondrous sweetness of considering the depth of God's counsels concerning the salvation of mankind" (IX, 14). God's plan, of course, is the element in his theory which supposes that the Platonists, however unconsciously, withheld their true spiritual doctrine until men were elevated by the coming of Christ. Providence had arranged it, even if the Platonists had not.

In the very first of Augustine's extant letters there is a phrase which has so puzzled commentators and editors that they have emended the text. Augustine's words are represented in the mss as: *Contra huiusmodi homines opinor ego illam utiliter excogitatam Dei ueri artem atque rationem*. Goldbacher in the CSEL changed the *Dei ueri artem* to *occultandi ueri artem*. The Benedictines had already changed it to *tegendi ueri artem*. But as we now see clearly, no change is needed. The synthesis I have described explains the *ars Dei*.

In a more general way, perhaps the discussion of this synthesis may be of some value. It is clearly affected by the very prevalent late Hellenistic wish to find secret teachings reserved for the elect in almost every sect, religious or philosophic. Furthermore it is another instance of a personal experience being translated into terms of a universal theory, useful for all men. It is, moreover, enlightening to observe that although Augustine himself at the very moment in which he was formulating this theory was diffident about its relation to established facts and did not pursue, at that time, the enquiry, he was captivated by the beauty of the idea and continued to use it. It is important also to observe that it not only affected his conversion vitally, but that it left a mark on all his subsequent thinking wherein the part of grace and illumination, both coming directly from God, is so marked. And not only did it leave a mark, it continued to be exploited until the end of his days. Augustine was a true child of his times in the sources from which he discovered this theory; in its formulation; and above all in its exploitation.

11

Augustine's View of Authority and Reason in A.D. 386

❧

Scholars have from time to time spoken of Augustine's "conversion" in 386 to Neoplatonism in terms which convey the idea that he looked then upon Neoplatonism as later (according even to them) he was to look upon Catholicism, that is to say—as an absolute authority. And indeed it might seem at first blush that Augustine does give grounds for such a view. He says, for instance, that authority is twofold, human and divine.[1] He adds of course that the divine is to be preferred. Nevertheless, it might be thought that he then regarded Neoplatonism as a "human authority" which he would follow. We recall the declaration towards the end of the *Contra Academicos*: "I, therefore, am resolved in nothing whatever to depart from the authority of Christ—for I do not find a stronger. But as to that which is sought out by subtle reasoning . . . I feel sure at the moment that I shall find it with the Platonists."[2] From this he might seem to have held the Platonists as an authority, though lower than the authority of Christ. The impression is not weakened by such remarks as: "philosophy *promises* to demonstrate this opinion";[3] "philosophy *promises* to demonstrate clearly the true and hidden God";[4] and "philosophy *promises* to liberate us."[5]

In spite, however, of the evidence of these texts, it cannot be seriously maintained that Augustine accepted Neoplatonism as any kind of real authority.[6] He undoubtedly looked upon it as a guide, which, as we shall see, he did not always follow. When Augustine speaks of human authority he points out that it often deceives[7]—in fact it is not an authority in the same sense as divine authority which claims to be infallible. Human authority has nothing more to commend it than the reasons which it can advance to justify its claims. Its certitude is reducible to that of rational processes.

If there is besides divine authority another claim on Augustine's allegiance, it can be more properly described as the claim of "reason" (*ratio*), not of "human authority." This he himself indicates in the pas-

Authority and Reason 141

sage from the *Contra Academicos* already quoted.[8] "Reason" is in many places contrasted with "authority."[9] He expresses a great desire not only to believe but also to understand what he believes.[10] Indeed he expresses the fear that he shows undue interest in trying to understand things.[11] It may well be that his reasoning often follows the lines of Neoplatonic doctrine; but this is a far different thing from the acceptance of Neoplatonism as an authority.[12]

This much, then, can be said for the view to which we have referred, that it is based on a certain tension—felt by Augustine himself—between reason (which is not necessarily equivalent to the integrated system of Plotinus, or any other of the Neoplatonists), and authority which is that of Christ: *mihi ergo, certum est nusquam prorsus a Christi auctoritate discedere . . . quod autem subtilissima ratione persequendum est—apud Platonicos me interim, reperturum esse confido.*[13]

If we are to understand this problem at all, it is essential that we should know what Augustine means by the term *ratio*. It may be equivalent, for instance to the Plotinian νοῦς (νόησις), or perhaps to the Plotinian διάνοια[14] or it may fluctuate so as not easily to be clearly defined. It is indeed useless for us to attempt an analysis of this concept until we have first examined Augustine's contemporary idea of the soul, of which the *ratio* is strictly speaking some faculty or function. There is abundant evidence that Augustine was interested above all in questions concerning the soul and God,[15] and also that he had no settled view concerning the former.[16]

Unfortunately, Augustine is not entirely consistent in his terminology. We are lucky, however, in having from the period of Cassiciacum itself one of the clearest statements of his view on all this question. In the *Soliloquia*[17] he institutes a comparison between "sensible"—he instances the process of seeing—and "intellectual" perception and comes to a number of probable[18] conclusions. They are essential to the understanding of the relations between *ratio* and *auctoritas* as propounded in the *Contra Academicos* in the text often quoted but never explained: *mihi ergo certum est . . .*[19]

Sense-perception is the union, in the sense, of the sense and the sensible. Intellectual-perception is the union in that which "intellects" (*intelligens, mens*) of that which "intellects" and the "intelligible" (*quod intelligitur, intelligibile*). For sense-perception there are on the part of the sense three things required: a sense (*sensus, oculus*), a looking (*adspec-*

tus), and vision (*visio*). For intellectual-perception there are on the part of that which "intellects" three things required: a part which "intellects" (*intelligens, mens*), a "looking" (*ratio*), and "vision" (*intellectus*). For sense-perception there are on the part of the sensible two things required: an object and the illumination of that object by the sun. The sun fulfils both requirements in itself. For intellectual-perception there are on the part of the intelligible two things required, an object and the illumination (*illuminatio, illustratio*) of the object by God. God fulfils both requirements in Himself. Our intellection of God is never in this life undisturbed.

The teaching of the passage from the *Soliloquia* may be summed up as in Diagrams 1 and 2:

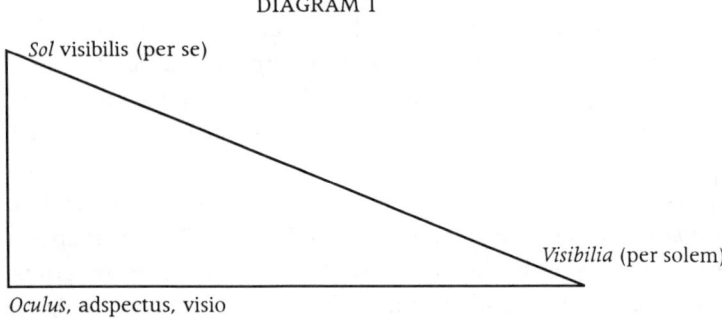

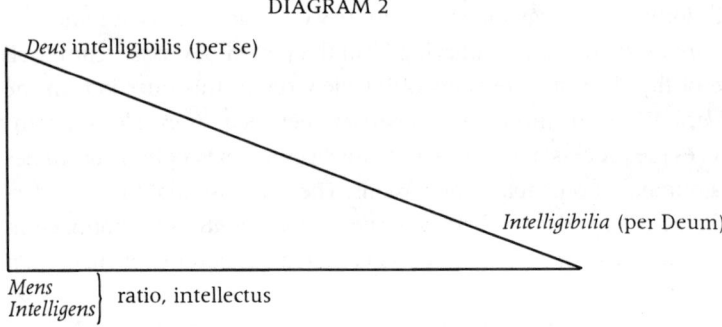

The term *anima* occurs frequently in the course of the passage examined. It is used to designate the subject[20] in which resides the faculty of intellection (*intelligens, mens*) but also, sometimes, that faculty itself.[21]

The term *animus* does not clearly occur in the passage.[22] *Ratio* differs from *intellectus* in the same way as the act of looking differs from the act of seeing. Both are up to a point the same function of the *mens,* and that function is called *ratio.* When the function issues into its completed act it is called *intellectus.*[23]

The scheme set out in the *Soliloquia* is borne out by the testimony of Augustine's later writings[24] and also by the evidence of the contemporary works—the early *Letters* and *Dialogues of Cassiciacum.* In these we find, on the whole, the corresponding significations for the various terms. There is also some additional information given.

Thus, *anima* designates that which together with the body makes up the human composite.[25] It is interchangeable with *animus,*[26] though *animus* is often used as if it applied only to the intellectual (as opposed to the sensitive and vegetative)[27] "parts" of the soul.[28] The *animus* is said to be divine.[29] The *mens* is a faculty of the *animus*[30] (*anima*), and is capable of a discursive function called *ratio,*[31] and also of *"intellection"* (*intellectus*).[32]

There is, of course, a certain fluidity of terminology. It is only natural that a subject should be described in terms of its faculty, and the faculty in its turn in terms of its function. Thus *anima* is occasionally equivalent to *animus,* or to *ratio*:[33] *animus* is sometimes equivalent to *mens*:[34] and both *anima* and *animus* are used instead of a term *intelligentia,*[35] which corresponds to the *mens* or *intelligens* of the passage from the *Soliloquia.* So too, *ratio* is used instead of *mens*[36] and *intelligentia.*[37] Again the term *intellectus,* which strictly applies to the completed function of the *mens,* is used as if it were itself a faculty, a part of the soul.[38] In fact it is, since it is *mens* or *intelligens* in its completed act.

In addition, the *Dialogues* tell us something more of Augustine's speculations on the soul. He has no settled views on many points.[39] Though he does not know the soul's origin,[40] he seems to favour the doctrine of ἀνάμνησις[41] and pre-existence.[42] He is satisfied, too, that the soul is immortal.[43] Though there is early evidence of his belief in the resurrection of the body,[44] the question is not opened in the *Dialogues.* Such indications as there are tend towards an undue disparagement[45] of things sensible, which later he was to regret.[46] The soul was "divine,"[47] was the thing most closely approximating to God,[48] but definitely was not of the same substance as God. This last fundamental and, on the question of Augustine's alleged conversion to Neoplatonism, significant point is quite clearly established from a text where Augustine explicitly considers the view of those who identify the substance of the soul with that of God only to dismiss it as almost blasphemous.[49] The soul, however, could be in constant communion with God,[50] and had always the vision of truth.[51] God's illumination of the *mens* was ever present.[52]

From our analysis of the soul and its processes we can affirm with certainty that Augustine did not think that either the *ratio* or the *intellectus* was as independent in its action as was the νοῦς of Plotinus. *Ratio* in Augustine's early *Dialogues* stands for the discursive function of the *mens* (i.e., *ratio* in the strictest sense), or for the completed act of that function (i.e., *intellectus*) or, by a natural transference, for the truths attained or attainable by such a function. That is to say, *ratio* is the process of the fullest human intellectual perception as Augustine conceived it, and is sometimes used also for the truths perceived. This process and this achievement is impossible without God's illumination. Since, therefore, God is one, and is the source of authority and, ultimately, of reason, authority and reason cannot conflict on what is true. Authority and reason are two approaches to the same truth.

How did Augustine at the time understand their mutual relations? There is plenty of evidence to show that he believed: (1) that authority could dispense altogether with reason; (2) that authority aided by reason was more desirable than authority alone; (3) that reason depended on some authority so that it might begin to operate; and (4) that reason could arrive at an understanding of everything taught by authority.

For the first of these propositions there is incontestable and direct evidence from the text of the *Dialogues*.[53] The second[54] and third[55] are equally supported by the *Dialogues*. The fourth proposition, namely that Augustine believed in A.D. 386 that reason could arrive at an understanding of what was taught by revelation, is perhaps surprising, but is nevertheless certainly to be found many times in the course of the *Dialogues of Cassiciacum*.

The most explicit testimony, that Augustine believed that reason would explain for him what was taught by revelation, comes from a work begun probably within two years after the writing of the *Contra Academicos*. In the *De libero arbitrio*,[56] Augustine says that, first, one must believe, but afterwards one could understand the truth believed: "although I hold these things with an unshakeable faith, nevertheless since I do not *yet* understand them, let us seek, as if all were uncertain. Unless it were one thing to believe and another thing to understand, . . . in vain would the Prophet have said: 'unless you believe, you will not understand.' Even Our Lord promised that we should understand what we believe.'' There are many texts which show that Augustine had already formed this view when he was writing the *Dialogues of Cassiciacum*.

In the *Contra Academicos* we read that "Philosophy promises that she will *clearly* demonstrate the true and secret God."[57] This refers not to the existence of God but to His nature. Again we read that Augustine is so disposed that he desires impatiently not only to believe what is true but also to understand it.[58] Philosophy, he says, alone enables one to understand the sacred mysteries as they ought to be understood.[59] A truly erudite man is not rash in seeking to contemplate, understand, and retain (in mind) the divine mysteries.[60] Finally, Reason in the *Soliloquia* promises to "demonstrate" God as clearly to Augustine's mind (*mens*) as the sun is "shown" to his eyes.[61]

For Augustine, then, in A.D. 386, reason was not to be subordinated to authority. It is true that he conceives of authority as being independent of reason. It is also true that he considers that reason cannot begin to operate until some authority has "opened the door," has proposed the questions, or—as where the authority of Christ was concerned—has guaranteed the answers. Again, reason depended upon illumination from God. Nevertheless apart from these limitations, reason had an independent role to play. It was coordinated with, and perfected, authority. It could never conflict with authority, since both depended on the same infallible source for the same truth.

If, by way of corollary, we are to examine the question in terms of Neoplatonism and Christianity, it will be seen at once that Christianity plays an indispensable role. Neoplatonism, on the other hand, *insofar as Augustine can be satisfied that it expounds truth,* has its own role independent, important and coordinated. This delicately balanced synthesis is based on the primary postulate that God illumines the *ratio*. Obviously, with this illumination the *ratio* can understand even the truths of revelation. Hence it was that the Neoplatonists could, quite independently of revelation, arrive at some idea of the Trinity. "I, therefore, am resolved in nothing whatever to depart from the authority of Christ—for I do not find a stronger. But as to that which is sought out by subtle reasoning—for I am so disposed as to be impatient in my desire to apprehend truth not only by faith but also by understanding—I feel sure at the moment that I shall find it with the Platonists, nor will it be at variance with our sacred mysteries."[62]

12

Augustine and Neoplatonism

The evidence on this question is so difficult to interpret that the ordinary course of giving that evidence and discussing it would on the one hand leave a confused notion on the mind, and on the other fail to bring out the peculiar importance of the matter. While in general it may not be a good thing to approach a topic through a discussion of what various scholars have said about it, in this particular instance the whole question has been so enriched and clarified by the debates of our predecessors and, it is a pleasure to say, our contemporaries, that it seems best to describe the problem as it has unfolded itself over the last three-quarters of a century down to this very day: and the last word has not been said yet.

In 1888 appeared two contributions to Augustinian studies which, with commendable moderation, set the Augustine of the early writings over against the Augustine of the *Confessions*,[1] the philosopher of Cassiciacum over against the Christian Bishop of Hippo. Gaston Boissier[2] was content to explain the obvious element of truth in the contrast by supposing that Augustine changed his point of view. Adolf von Harnack[3] went somewhat further and declared that philosophy was Augustine's primary interest in Cassiciacum, and that the *Confessions* misrepresent his actual development: the *Dialogues* of Cassiciacum do not bear out the idea of a radical conversion to Christianity.

Friedrich Loofs[4] came to the conclusion that even in A.D. 391, five years after his conversion, Augustine was nothing more than a Neoplatonist with a tincture of Christianity. L. Gourdon[5] maintained that the *Dialogues* and the *Confessions* represent two distinct "conversions" and show us "two different men": the *Dialogues* were in flagrant contradiction with the *Confessions*:[6] Augustine was entirely converted to Christianity only about A.D. 400.[7] H. Becker[8] placed the start of Augustine's conversion to Christianity at the death of Monnica. W. Thimme[9] contended that the *Confessions* were quite unreliable; that Augustine in A.D. 386 was neither a Christian, nor free from Academic doubt; and that it was only gradually that he became first a complete Neoplatonist and later a Christian.

These views are well summed up and clearly stated in a work which is regarded with great respect by Augustinian scholars: P. Alfaric's *L'évolution intellectuelle de saint Augustin*.[10] Lest we should seem to exaggerate the seriousness of the attack on the *Confessions* we shall allow Alfaric to speak for himself:

(1) "Quand il a reçu le baptême, il accordait si peu d'importance à ce rite que, dans les écrits de cette époque, où il parle fréquemment de lui-même et de tout ce qui l'intéresse, il n'y fait jamais la plus lointaine allusion. Il était alors assez peu catholique. Sans doute il acceptait la tradition chrétienne, mais il ne la considérait que comme une adaptation populaire de la sagesse platonicienne. Ce n'est que longtemps plus tard qu'il est arrivé à donner à la foi le pas sur la raison" (p. viii).[11]

(2) "Mais il ne l'est devenu définitivement (chrétien) que parce qu'il a cru rester ainsi un pur Platonicien. Même dans la suite, il a tenu quelque temps à la doctrine de Plotin bien plus qu'au dogme catholique" (p. 381).

(3) "Aussi devons-nous . . . représenter (son évolution) autrement que lui-même ne l'a fait au cours des *Confessions*" (p. 382).

(4) "Sa description des combats qui se livraient en lui lors du récit de Pontitien est l'oeuvre d'un rhéteur qui vise constamment à l'effet. Des détails aussi évidemment fictifs que l'apparition des passions et celle de la chasteté donnent lieu de craindre que d'autres, an apparence plus naturels ne soient pas plus exacts" (p. 392).

(5) "Décidément le néophyte qui s'offre ici (dans les *Dialogues*) à nous est bien différent de celui que nous dépeignent les *Confessions*" (p. 398).

(6) ". . . pour connaître l'état d'âme dans lequel il se trouvait quand il les (his first writings) a rédigés, nous devons faire appel à cux bien plus qu'aux *Confessions*. Ainsi nous sommes amenés à le considérer bien moins comme un catéchumène presque uniquement occupé de l'idéal chrétien que comme un disciple de Plotin avant tout soucieux de conformer sa vie à la doctrine du Maître. Moralement comme intellectuellement, c'est au Néoplatonisme qu'il s'est converti, plutôt qu'à l'Evangile" (p. 399).

(7) "Elle (la synthèse faite par Augustin en 386) modifie assez sensiblement la doctrine du Maître (Plotin) pour l'adapter aux enseignements de la foi catholique. Mais elle transforme encore davantage le catholicisme pour le mettre d'accord avec la philosophie plotinienne et

elle ne le considère que comme une forme inférieure de la sagesse, bonne seulement pour les intelligences faibles ou encore novices" (p. 515).

(8) "En lui le Chrétien disparaît derrière le disciple de Plotin. S'il était mort après avoir rédigé les *Soliloques* . . . on ne le considérerait que comme un Néoplatonicien convaincu, plus ou moins teinté de christianisme" (p. 527).[12]

It must be clear from the indications given that the charges levelled against Augustine and his *Confessions* are serious, and are based upon the alleged discrepancies between his early writings and his later work. Whether such fundamental differences exist can be determined only by a careful and unbiased examination of those early documents.

Such charges demand at least a show of evidence. Alfaric does not take refuge behind authority, but sets forth his conclusions on his own responsibility. His analysis of the *Contra Academicos*, though it extends to some six thousand words,[13] is not satisfactory. The preface to the *Contra Academicos* II, which is one of the three really important sections, if not the most important, in the whole work (the other two being the preface of book I and the conclusion of book III), and runs to some two thousand words, is summarized inaccurately in the following remark: "Augustin les (*Contra Academicos* II, III) dédie encore à Romanien, par une ample préface consacrée à l'éloge du Néoplatonisme."[14] The important prefaces to *De beata vita* and *De ordine* fare no better.[15]

So far we have given only one side of the controversy. To Boissier and Harnack replied F. Wörter.[16] J. Martin contested Boissier's views in particular.[17] E. Portalié in a brilliant article on Augustine attempts to offset the attacks of Loofs and Gourdon.[18] Louis de Mondadon joined company with all these in seeking to minimise or explain away the alleged irreconcilability of the *Confessions* and the *Dialogues*.[19] W. Montgomery,[20] A. Hatzfeld,[21] and T. Bret[22] and others have also taken their stand here.

For long, however, the book which was considered to be most successful against Alfaric's thesis was C. Boyer's *Christianisme et néo-platonisme dans la formation de saint Augustin*,[23] a second edition of which was brought out in 1953 in anticipation of the sixteenth centenary of the saint's birth. Of this book E. Gilson has written: "Dans l'ensemble, ce travail est le plus pondéré et, à notre sens, le plus juste que l'on ait consacré à cette délicate question."[24] Certain it is that it put an end to the notion that Augustine's conversion to Christianity in 386 was not fully sincere.

Boyer, however, in adapting his line of argument to meet directly the charge of Alfaric that Augustine was "converted" to Neoplatonism rather than to Christianity in 386 exposed himself to the charge of misrepresenting what actually happened to Augustine at the time. Norregaard[25] criticised him for being so intent on disproving Alfaric's assertions that true methodological principles are overlooked and there is little psychological understanding of the problem. Attention has also been drawn to the fact that Boyer's analysis of the *Contra Academicos*—an analysis in which he places not a little confidence—reduces the distinct Neoplatonic tone of the prefaces almost to vanishing point, and ignores some of the really difficult and important passages.[26] Indeed in recent years scholars have been pronouncing that the problem as conceived by both Alfaric and Boyer is a false problem:[27] one should not speak of Neoplatonism as a kind of authority which must be accepted in full or not at all; and in any case Augustine thought that he could have a synthesis of both Christianity and Neoplatonism, in which, of course, neither was rejected in favour of the other.[28]

As, however, Boyer's position is still by him and a number of others[29] retained with the minimum modification made necessary by the work especially of Courcelle, it may be well to give that position a full statement. Here it is as described by Boyer himself in 1954:[30]

> Saint Augustin est néoplatonicien pour la partie qu'il a vue vraie, il n'est pas néoplatonicien dans la mesure où il a trouvé cette philosophie opposé au christianisme . . . Ayant adhéré au christianisme *avant même de lire les néoplatoniciens* . . . , possédant déjà la foi chrétienne, une foi encore bien imparfaite cependant puisqu'il ne croyait pas à la véritable divinité du Christ, en entendant Ambroise, Augustin était préparé à donner un sens chrétien à bien des phrases qu'il lisait dans Plotin . . . Augustin écoutant Ambroise reçoit en même temps la foi chrétienne dans une expression de pensée néoplatonicienne . . . Augustin y adhère puisqu'il dit *"persuadisti mihi,"* *c'est une question d'autorité*. Ensuite il lit Plotin qui le délivre de ses difficultés métaphysiques. . . . Lisant Plotin, il arrive à concevoir . . . l'existence même de Dieu—Vérité, la Vérité subsistante . . . dès lors peut-on toujours dire qu'il est néoplatonicien?

P. Courcelle[31] and G. Mathon,[32] among others, have given reasons for rejecting this view that Augustine was converted to Christianity as an authority before he read the Platonist books, and these reasons seem to me to fit the evidence supplied by Augustine himself.[33]

The study of Augustine and Neoplatonism was further complicated by a controversy of somewhat similar character to that already described. This time it was—and to some extent still is—not Christianity or Neoplatonism, but of the Neoplatonists, was it Plotinus or Porphyry?

It had been usual to suppose that both Plotinus *and* Porphyry were involved: Bouillet,[34] for example, gives clear expression to this view. But Alfaric[35] and others had begun to speak in terms of almost Plotinus only. A strong reaction came from W. Theiler who in his book, *Porphyrios und Augustin* (Halle, 1933) put forward vigorously the view that there was only one Neoplatonist in question and that was Porphyry.[36] Theiler holds this view almost without modification even still.[37] Courcelle (who is greatly criticized by Theiler) sets out Theiler's position as follows:

> L'on sait qu'un grand auteur, Platon par exemple, est fréquemment cité, à époque tardive, sans qu'on le connaisse directement par ses oeuvres, mais seulement à travers l'interprétation de quelque commentateur. M. Theiler estime qu'il en va de même pour Plotin. Si saint Augustin déclare, dans le *De beata uita,* avoir lu des *Plotini libri,* il faut entendre par là, selon M. Theiler, le commentaire de Porphyre sur les *Ennéades.* Il a systématiquement orienté ses recherches . . . en fonction de *l'Arbeitssatz* suivant, qui se réclame des méthodes de *Quellenforschung*: "S'il apparaît chez un néoplatonicien postérieur à Plotin un morceau doctrinal qui, par son contenu, sa forme, son contexte, se laisse comparer avec un morceau analogue chez Augustin, mais non pas, ou non pas au même degré, avec un morceau analogue chez Plotin, on a le droit de considérer comme porphyrien." L'analogie doctrinale entre saint Augustin et tel Platonicien postérieur (Proclus, Énée de Gaza, Olympiodore ou Damascius) suffit à prouver . . . que, même si Porphyre n'est pas nommé de part et d'autre, nous avons affaire à un vestige porphyrien. Par la suite, chaque fois qu'un érudit a signalé un parallèle entre un Père de l'Église et Plotin, M. Theiler l'a référé régulièrement à Porphyre.[38]

Theiler has applied the same principle to the parallels indicated by Courcelle (later to be discussed) between St. Ambrose and Augustine. Theiler agrees that these parallels are there, but he goes on to maintain that the source is not Plotinus, and not Porphyry directly, but the *lost* work of some Greek Father which in turn depended upon a *lost* work of Porphyry.

H.-R. Schwyzer's remark: "Du fait que la plupart des écrits porphyriens qui viendraient en question comme sources sont perdus, les développements de Theiler ne sont souvent ni démontrables ni réfutables"[39] is apposite—but not in the way taken by Courcelle. It does not mean that Theiler is wrong. Courcelle himself has argued that Augustine had read at least one work of Porphyry now lost, the *De regressu animae*, and probably others about the time of his conversion.[40] Courcelle has also declared that at the time of Augustine "une seule philosophie subsiste, la néoplatonicienne; le maître des esprits est Porphyre."[41] The present writer has put forward a theory which, without denying the roles played by Plotinus and Ambrose in the conversion of Augustine, would give to Porphyry a vital and important place in the conversion and explain the preeminent position of Porphyry in Augustine's later works whenever he refers to Neoplatonism.[42]

The reasons given by Courcelle against Theiler's view[43] do not seem to me convincing. Augustine *did* oppose Porphyry to Plotinus as one of those who had been corrupted by theurgy. In any case this is an irrelevant consideration since Augustine says not merely that he had read a few books of Plotinus, but also, three times, books of Platonists,[44] which if it means anything means Plotinus and at least one other. Porphyry *did* write some kind of a commentary on Plotinus (this again is admitted by Courcelle), and the fact that it is now lost to us does not prove that Augustine could not have read it. Courcelle asks: "N'est-il pas plus vraisemblable que Victorinus ait traduit quelques traites des *Ennéades*, plutôt qu'un commentaire?"[45] The answer to that is that we do not know. What we do know is that Eunapius tells us that Porphyry was a "Godsend" to those who were not able to follow Plotinus;[46] that Victorinus translated at least the *Isagoge* of Porphyry (and we are not certain that he translated anything of Plotinus—although it seems probable that he did) and that even if Victorinus did translate Plotinus, that does not prove that he did not translate Porphyry's commentary on Plotinus also. One might ask in an equally rhetorical way (and with equal lack of force) if Victorinus translated some of the *Enneads*, is it not probable that he translated Porphyry's commentary on them to make them plain? One might urge many other probabilities and ask many other rhetorical questions without bringing the argument one real step forward. Theiler goes too far in denying the influence of Plotinus; he probably claims too much for Porphyry. But he has shown that the influence of Porphyry may well be very great.

Theiler's book was quickly followed by P. Henry's *Plotin et l'Occident* (Louvain, 1934) and *La vision d'Ostie* (Paris, 1938). Henry reacted in a sense to both Theiler and Boyer, but not in any merely controversial spirit: he added to the number of passages in Augustine, particularly in the *Confessions*, claimed as having been inspired by Plotinus, *Enneads*, and brought our interest in Augustine further by advocating the theory, which is still the subject of intense controversy, that Augustine was not only a mystic, but that his mysticism as described in the *Confessions* is intellectual and Plotinian.

His pronouncement against Porphyry was certainly excessive. Recently he has seemed less positive, but is still sceptical: "Je n'ai jamais nié positivement qu'il ait alors lu Porphyre; je disais simplement que j'attendais une preuve péremptoire; cette preuve, je ne l'ai toujours pas."[47] But it is unreasonable to insist upon a peremptory proof in this matter. Most scholars are content to accept provisionally what can be made to seem probable—thus, e.g., Courcelle writes: "Mais s'il me paraît excessif de nier toute influence directe des *Ennéades*, je n'en suis pas moins convaincu que Porphyre a exercé une action considérable et qu'Augustin, en particulier, a lu quantité d'ouvrages de Porphyre longtemps avant de le nommer dans le *De consensu* ou la *Cité de Dieu*. En ce sens, je renchérirais au besoin sur les thèses de M. Theiler . . . j'accorde pleinement à M. Theiler que ce chapitre des *Confessions* (VII, 25) correspond à la phrase autobiographique du *Contra Academicos* (II, 2, 5)."[48] Scholars have been grateful to accept from P. Henry himself opinions for which they have not exacted peremptory proof.

The question of Augustine's mysticism, and even the question of the Neoplatonic elements in that mysticism (which alone concerns us here) had been, of course, dealt with before. Henry, however, set out and interpreted the evidence for the Plotinian elements in a full and compelling way. Since then Courcelle, Pépin, and Mandouze[49] have each added some new details to the list of passages in Augustine's works, especially the *Confessions*, which have overtones that are at once mystical and Plotinian (or, as Theiler would hold, Porphyrean).

M. Mandouze in a brilliant analysis[50] both of the validity of Henry's hypothesis and the wider question[51] of Augustine's mysticism in general seems to the present writer to have made some very helpful observations in reviewing the various theories as to the sources of the vision of Ostia passage in the *Confessions* (X, 23–26).[52]

One of the most encouraging aspects of Augustinian studies during this century is the frequency with which completely new horizons and approaches have been opened up by a succession of brilliant scholars. Many of them have overstated their theses and provoked strong reactions—but this has had a most invigorating effect on our interest in and knowledge of Augustine. The stream of such scholars shows no tendency to slow down and trickle away: on the contrary it has never been in such spate—as was evidenced, for example, by the proceedings of the Augustinian Congress in Paris in 1954 and the publication in three volumes of the communications, reports, and discussions of that Congress under the title *Augustinus Magister.*

Pierre Courcelle, whose very remarkable contribution to our topic we must now discuss, has enriched Augustinian studies enormously, especially by his *Recherches sur les Confessions de saint Augustin* (Paris, 1950).

Courcelle has set out the evidence which leads him to believe that St. Ambrose's sermons, notably the *Hexameron, De Isaac* and *De bono mortis,* showing as they do a demonstrable debt to Neoplatonism (for Courcelle mostly Plotinus, for Theiler altogether some Greek Father and ultimately Porphyry), at one and the same time prepared Augustine for conversion to Christianity and set him on fire with enthusiasm for Neoplatonism. Through the influence not only of Ambrose, but of the Neoplatonist priest Simplicianus and the Neoplatonist layman Theodorus—and probably other Christian Neoplatonists in Milan—and through his own reading of Neoplatonist books, Augustine was intellectually persuaded that he would and should become a Christian and Neoplatonist at the same time.

It can be seen at once that if Courcelle's hypothesis is true, the older controversy as to whether Neoplatonism dominated his Christianity or *vice versa* loses much of its meaning. Courcelle's work has been greatly applauded, as is but just, and his conclusions have been adopted by many. But he has met with a full measure of criticism which is the due honour done to a brilliant scholar.

Apart from Theiler's insistence that Porphyry and not Plotinus is the ultimate source of the alleged Plotinian passages in Ambrose (who, in borrowing the works of a Greek Father, might possibly have been hardly conscious of his being at all Neoplatonic), there are reasons for having certain reserves about Courcelle's conclusions.

If Ambrose did consciously preach a synthesis of Neoplatonism and Christianity, and if he introduced Augustine to a Christian Neoplatonist circle in Milan, then Augustine shows such a reticence about this in the *Confessions* as must surprise us. He breathes not a word about Ambrose in this connection, although he explicitly considers the role that Ambrose did play in his conversion. The efforts of Courcelle who—perhaps to throw greater emphasis on the importance of Ambrose's Neoplatonic *sermons* (on which Courcelle's argument is based)—is at pains to point out that Ambrose did not know Augustine intimately before his baptism, to prove on the contrary that *after* his baptism they became much more friendly seem feeble. Nor am I convinced either that we have grounds for saying that Manlius Theodorus gave Neoplatonist books to Augustine,[53] much less that Ambrose had anything to do with this.

Perhaps because he writes to draw the major attention to the alleged influence of Ambrose on Augustine in helping him to become at once a Neoplatonist and a Christian, Courcelle seems to be at great pains to reduce the importance usually ascribed—and by Augustine himself— to the *tolle lege* scene in the garden. Here again he adduces a mass of parallels (some rather remote) to prove the literary character of the scene.[54] He seeks further to increase the importance of his own theory of a Neoplatonist-Christian conversion effected largely through the sermons of Ambrose by interpreting certain passages in the *Confessions* to mean that Augustine before retiring from his office in 386 made a series of actual but unsuccessful attempts at Plotinian ecstasy and union with the Father. There can be no doubt but that the discovery of Neoplatonism, whether or not it was made possible for him by Ambrose or a Christian Neoplatonist circle in Milan, excited Augustine to a high degree; but this does not justify one in concluding that ecstasies (however unsuccessful) were attempted, or in shifting the emphasis from the central scene in his conversion as described by Augustine himself—the *tolle lege* scene in the garden.

Augustine in the narrative of the *Confessions* clearly ascribes a certain role in his conversion to Ambrose: the rehabilitation of Scripture and Christian belief. He makes no mention of any connection between this and the subsequent reading by him of certain Platonist books, which had tremendous effect upon him. The climax in the narrative, however, comes with the reading in the garden of the text from St. Paul. This is the rhythm of his conversion as described by Augustine: this is the way he saw it and intended others to see it. It is difficult to discover why he might have underplayed the role of Ambrose.

Courcelle's invaluable contribution has been not merely the almost pyrotechnical display of a vast erudition full of the most fascinating suggestions concerned with the whole problem of Augustine and Neoplatonism, but especially the demonstration that Ambrose, consciously or unconsciously, was preaching Christianity in terms markedly Neoplatonic. Since both Simplicianus and Theodorus were Christians and consciously Neoplatonist, were both in Milan at the time, were both either very friendly or at least acquainted with Ambrose and Augustine, *the conditions were evidently present* in which Augustine could become a Christian-Neoplatonist: if he approached Simplicianus, for example, as a Neoplatonist, Christianity would have been commended to him; and if he approached as a Christian, he would likewise have been told of Neoplatonism. Our knowledge of this situation and these conditions is evidently of paramount importance for the understanding of what in fact happened to Augustine—and to Courcelle must be given the immense credit for giving us this knowledge. I disagree with him only where he attempts to fill in the details without sufficient evidence and in a fashion at variance with the ostensible account of the *Confessions*.[55]

The present writer has come independently to conclusions which have many points of contact with those of Courcelle.[56]

In a thesis, *Prolegomena to the Contra Academicos of St. Augustine*, presented to the University of Oxford in 1944,[57] it was concluded that apart from many other possible sources[58] Cicero was a primary source for much of the "Neoplatonism" in the *Dialogues* of Augustine,[59] and that Augustine's circle of friends and acquaintances in Milan must not be overlooked as a source for Augustine's synthesis of Christianity and Neoplatonism. In this synthesis Augustine placed great hope; but in accepting Christ in the Incarnation and rejecting the notion that the human soul was of the same divine substance as the Father he had already bowed to the authority of Christ and put aside the reasoning of the Neoplatonists.

Augustine, nevertheless, considered in 386 that it was possible by reason alone to arrive at the truths revealed by authority, since God was the source of illumination for both coordinated, though independent, sources of knowledge. A list of Plotinian passages was drawn up for the *Contra Academicos*, and a case was made at some length for the theory that Augustine was vitally affected at this juncture by Porphyry. Finally it was argued that not only was there no conflict (as had been supposed by Alfaric, for example) between the *Dialogues* and the *Confessions*, but that there was remarkable accord between them and each threw great light upon the other.[60]

The point concerned with Porphyry is at once novel, and, if true (for I can offer no peremptory proof for it) important. It is based on the occurrence in the *Contra Academicos, De ordine, De quantitate animae, De vera religione, Confessions, De Trinitate, Letter* 118, *City of God,* and other works of a theme which is explicitly associated with Porphyry and Porphyry only in the *City of God*; which is distinctly recognizable in its various elements in all its formulations; with which Porphyry more than any other Neoplatonist can be connected in a number of its formulations even down to a time before Augustine's baptism;[61] and which not only clears up a disputed reading in the first of Augustine's extant letters,[62] but which above all throws great light on the story of Augustine's conversion, on his particular interest in the mystery of the Incarnation and Grace, and especially the text of St. Paul, with which the conversion was finally effected.

The full topic can be stated briefly as follows:

The Platonists, through the use of reason (*ratio*) could, and did, arrive at the fundamental truth of the existence of the Father and his Word. Independently, however, the mass of mankind, who could not use their reason to such effect, could come to the same conclusion through following authority (*auctoritas*), a way (*uia*) to the fatherland. The Platonists recognized the necessity for this way of authority for the masses. They looked around and examined all the persons or institutions that claimed to be such an authority. They rejected all, among them the claims of Christ and the church which he founded. Augustine disagrees with them only on one point: their failure to see that Christ was the way of authority. He believes that the Platonists failed because of their pride in refusing to accept the incarnation and crucifixion and their being led astray by the demons whom they worshipped.

That this topic refers to Porphyry and is already fully present in the *Dialogues* I have argued in a number of places.[63] It is the key, to my mind, to the high point of the *Confessions* from the first mention of the *libri Platonicorum* (VII, 13) to the culmination in the surprisingly significant (on the supposition that Porphyry was close to his thought) text of St. Paul: "Not in rioting and drunkenness . . . but put on our Lord Jesus Christ . . ." (Rom 13.13f.). The challenge here was to accept Christ or follow Porphyry in rejecting Him.[64]

The reader has now, perhaps, been given enough views on Augustine and Neoplatonism to be able to apply his own judgment to the question from a reading of what Augustine says himself in the *Confessions* (VII, 13–8.30).

Addendum

This addendum is intended to supply only some of the textual basis on which the author's position as outlined at the end of the foregoing article is founded. In the first column are given the various elements of a theme which is found in Augustine, to whom it was suggested by the reading of Porphyry. In the second column are given texts from Augustine in which this theme is found. In the third column are given the sources for this theme in Porphyry—*as reported, however, in the words of Augustine*. It will be seen that at a certain stage the ideas of Porphyry and Augustine come into conflict: this conflict marks the later rejection, after an earlier acceptance, of Porphyry's notions of this theme.

	A) Augustine	B) Porphyry
1. The three Principia	1. "ibi legi non quidem his uerbis sed hoc idem omnino multis et multiplicibus suaderi rationibus, quod in principio erat uerbum . . ." C VII, 13.	1. "dicit . . . principia posse purgare . . . i.e. Deum Patrem et Deum Filium." DCD X, 23
	2. "nullumque aliud habet negotium, quae uera . . . philosophia est quam ut doceat, quod sit omnium rerum principium sine principio . . ." DOR II, 16	2. "Praedicas Patrem et eius Filium, quem uocas paternum intellectum seu mentem, et horum medium, quem putamus te dicere Spiritum sanctum . . . Ubi, etsi uerbis indisciplinatis . . ." DCD X, 29
		3. Cf. also DCD X, 28; XIX, 23; XXII, 25.
2. Return to the Father.	1. "in his ipsis libris, ex quibus multa posui, quos de regressu animae scripsit . . ." DCD X, 29	1. "libris, quos de regressu animae scripsit." DCD X, 29
	2. "nescio utrum possent . . . cum istis sordibus viscoque revolare." DVR 7	2. "Dicit etiam ad hoc Deum animam mundo dedisse, ut materiae cognoscens mala ad Patrem recurreret . . ." DCD X, 30
	3. "ne quo . . . visco pennae nostrae impediantur . . . ut . . . evolemus." Sol I, 14 [cf. R I, 4. 3 "ne putaremur . . . Porphyrii . . . tenere sententiam."]	3. "cum Patre constitutam" ibid.

	A) Augustine	B) Porphyry
	4. "nam ut progressus animae usque ad mortalia lapsus est, ita regressus esse in rationem debet." DOR II, 31	4. "reuerti dixit ad Patrem." ibid.
	5. "illa uisco libidinis, detracta caelo suo . . . facile euadit, facile reuolat." CA II, 7	5. "beatae aput Patrem sine fine [animae] teneantur." DCD XIII, 19
	6. "securior rediturus in caelum." CA II, 22 [Cf. R I, 18 "iturus" autem quam "rediturus" dixissem securius propter eos, qui putant animos humanos pro meritis peccatorum suorum de caelo lapsos in corpora ista detrudi (sc. Platonicos)].	6. "cum redierit ad Patrem . . ." DCD XXII, 27
	7. "excitatae animae redire in semet ipsas et respicere patriam." CA III, 42	7. Cf. DCD X, 29–32
3. Purgation of souls a) flight from the body.	1. "omne corpus fugiendum" DCD X, 29 (several times); XIII, 17; XXII, 26 (several times); S 241.7 (5 times), 8.	1. "nec aliquando iam talium polluta contagione [anima] teneretur." DCD X, 30
	2. "ab hoc corpore omnimoda fuga." DQ 76	2. "Porphyrius propter animae purgationem dicit corpus omne fugiendum." DCD XII, 27
	3. "penitus esse ista sensibilia fugienda cavendumque dum hoc corpus agimus . . . SO I, 24 [Cf. R I, 4.3: ". . . ne putaremur . . . Porphyrii . . . tenere sententiam, qua dixit: omne corpus esse fugiendum."]	3. "sapientium animas ita [Porphyrium] uoluisse de corporeis nexibus liberari, ut corpus omne fugientes . . ." DCD XIII, 19
	4. "animam remotissiman ab omnibus nugis et magna labe corporis emergentem." DOR 11.45	4. The phrase "corpus omne fugiendum" is attributed to Porphyry several times (DCD XII, 27; XIII, 19; XXII, 12.26, R I, 4.3)
	5. "ab omni corporis labe animum uindicantes" (attributed to Licentius) CA I, 11	
	6. "animas . . . altissimis a corpore sordibus oblitas . . . reuocaret." CA III, 42	

Augustine and Neoplatonism

	A) Augustine	B) Porphyry
	7. Cf. DVR 3; SO I, 3–6, 12, 23; CA III, 20	
b) flight towards intelligence	1. "non corporeis oculis, sed pura mente veritatem videri . . . sanandum esse animum ad intuendam incommutabilem rerum formam . . . mente sola et intelligentia cerni queat." DVR 3	1. "quod [animam] faciat idoneam ad uidendum Deum et perspicienda ea quae uero sunt." DCD X, 9 [Cf. Porphyry ap Procl. in Tim., I, 202, 6: δεῖ πεπαιδεῦσθαι πρότερον τὸ ἦθος, ἵνα ὅμοιον ὂν τῷ κατανουμένῳ συναρμόζηται πρεπόντως εἰς τὴν γνῶσιν τῆς ἀληθείας.]
	2. "mentem purgabit vitae modus . . . et idoneam faciet spiritualibus percipiendis." ibid. 13.	2. "ad Deum per uirtutem intellegentiae peruenire paucis dicis esse concessum . . . secundum intellectum tamen uiuentibus omne quod deest . . . posse compleri." DCD X, 29
	3. "Intueri mente veritatem." ibid. 30	
	4. "Oculi sani mens est ab omni labe corporis pura." SO I, 12	
	5. "regressus esse in rationem debet." DOR II, 31	
	6. "excitatae animae redire in semet ipsas." CA III, 42	
4. This purgation can be achieved by a few through the use of "reason."	A. *Possible for a few.*	A. *Possible for a few.*
	1. "[sapientia] quasi nudam . . . se non sinit, nisi paucissimis et electissimis amatoribus suis." SO I, 22	1. "[philosophiae uirtus] quae ardua nimis et paucorum est." DCD X, 27
	2. "Philosophia rationem promittit et uix paucissimos liberat." DOR II, 16	2. "ad Deum per uirtutem intellegentiae peruenire paucis dicis esse concessum." DCD X, 29
	3. Cf. E I.1; DOR I, 1, 32; II, 26, 30, 44; DBV 1; CA II, 1; III, 42	
	B. *Only to a limited extent.*	B. *Only to a limited extent.*
	1. "non quidem dum hic uiuis, sapiens eris . . . sed . . . post hanc uitam." CA III, 20	1. "nec ipse dubitas in hac uita hominem nullo modo ad perfectionem sapientiae peruenire . . . sed . . . post hanc uitam." DCD X, 29

	A) Augustine	B) Porphyry
	C. Not without God's grace and divine authority.	C. Not without God's grace and divine authority.
	1. "Sine illa [uniuersali uia: auctoritate diuina] nulla anima liberatur." DCD X, 32	1. "Confiteris tamen gratiam, quando quidem ad Deum per uirtutem intellegentiae peruenire paucis dicis esse concessum. procul dubio Dei gratiam . . . confiteris." DCD X, 29
	2. [Platonici], quia sine homine Christo philosophati sunt, in deceptores daemones inciderunt." DT XIII, 24	2. "Ita ei non sufficiebat quidquid de anima liberanda studiosissime didicerat . . . sentiebat enim adhuc sibi deesse aliquam praestantissimam auctoritatem." DCD X, 32
	3. "neque quisquam inveniendo Deo sit idoneus nisi antea crediderit." DLA II, 6	
5. This purgation can be achieved by the *mass of mankind* only in following some "*authority,*" emanating from the Principles.	1. "[Platonici] neque tanta auctoritate apud populos, ut credenda persuaderent." E 118. 20. cf. 17, 33	1. "dicit . . . principia posse purgare . . . dicit enim Deum Patrem et Deum Filium . . . [et] horum medium." DCD X, 23
	2. "Cognoscant Deum et cedant Deo per quem populis iam omnibus haec credenda persuasa sunt." DVR 6	2. "istorum, quos philosophari piget, incomparabiliter maior est multitudo." DCD X, 27
	3. "viderent profecto eujus auctoritate facilius consuleretur hominibus." DVR 7	3. "Ignorantiam certe et propter eam multa uitia . . . purgari dicis . . . per solum πατρικὸν νοῦν, id est paternam mentem siue intellectum . . ." DCD X, 28
	4. "Sed quia hoc [Deum et spiritualia] anima peccatis suis obruta et implicata, per se ipsam videre ac tenere non posset . . . ineffabili misericordia Dei temporali dispensatione per creaturam mutabilem, sed tamen aeternis legibus servientem . . . ipsi hominum generi subvenitur." DVR 19	4. "Sentiebat enim adhuc sibi deesse aliquam praestantissimam auctoritatem, quam de re tanta sequi oporteret . . . Providentiam quippe diuinam sine ista uniuersali uia liberandae animae genus humanum relinquere potuisse non credit." DCD X, 32
	5. "poteris multa legere, quae magni et divini viri de his rebus necessaria quae videbantur, salubriter imperitioribus quasi nutu quodam locuti	

Augustine and Neoplatonism

	A) Augustine	B) Porphyry
	sunt, credique sibi voluerunt ab iis, quorum animis vel tardioribus vel implicatioribus alia salus esse non posset. Tales enim homines, quorum profecto maxima multitudo est . . . facillime decipiuntur . . . His ergo utilissimum est excellentissimae auctoritati credere, et secundum hoc agere vitam." DQ 12	
	Christ is the way.	Where is the way?
6. There is "a universal way for the liberation of souls."	1. "Deus Christus patria est quo imus: homo Christus via est qua imus . . . non recessit a Patre, et venit ad nos." S 123.3	1. "Denique prope ad epistulae [sc. ad Anebontem] finem petit se ab eo doceri, quae sit ad beatitudinem uia ex Aegyptia sapientia?" DCD X, II
	2. "nos, non qua venimus, sed per aliam viam in patriam redire debemus, quam rex humilis docuit." DT IV, 15	2. "uidetis . . . quo nitendum sit . . . sed . . . qua . . . non uultis agnoscere . . . uidetis . . . patriam in qua manendum est, sed uiam qua eundum est non tenetis." DCD X, 29
	3. "quid interesset inter uidentes quo eundum sit, nec uidentes qua, et uiam ducentem ad beatificam patriam non tantum cernendam sed et habitandam." C VII.26–27 passim; cf. VIII.1	3. "Porphyrius uniuersalem uiam animae liberandae nondum in suam notitiam historiali cognitione dicit esse perlatam." DCD X, 32
	4. "Christianis temporibus . . . quae ad veritatem ac beatitatem via est, non esse dubitandum." DVR 3	4. The phrase "uniuersalis uia animae liberandae" occurs about a score of times in DCD X, 32.
	5. "quid prodest superbienti, et ob hoc erubescenti lignum conscendere, de longinquo prospicere patriam transmarinam? . . . quid obest humili de tanto intervallo non eam videre, in illi ligno ad eam venienti, quo dedignatur ille portari?" DT IV, 20 Cf. DBV 1–5; CA II, 1	
	6. "ueneranda mysteria, quae fide sincera et inconcussa populos liberant." DOR II, 16	

A) Augustine	B) Porphyry
Christ is the way.	Where is the way?
7. "gratias ago summo et uero deo patri, domino liberatori animarum." DBV 36	
Acceptance	Rejection

7. Christ's claim to be that divine authority, "the universal way of salvation."

	A) Augustine	B) Porphyry
A.	*Christ came at the time foreknown to be opportune.*	*Christ came too late.*
1.	"non debebit dici: Quare modo? et Quare sero? quoniam mittentis consilium non est humano ingenio penetrabile." DCD X, 32	"si Christus se . . . salutis uiam dicit, gratiam, et ueritatem, in seque solo ponit animis sibi credentibus reditum; quid egerunt tot saeculorum homines ante Christum? . . . is, cui credi posset, nondum aduentum suum hominibus commodarat?" E 102. 8
2.	"tunc uoluisse hominibus apparere Christum, et apud eos praedicari doctrinam suam, quando sciebat, et ubi sciebat esse, qui in eum fuerant credituri." E 102.14; cf. E 118.17; E 226.3	
3.	cf. E 1.	
B.	*Incarnation of the Word the greatest manifestation of God's providence.*	*Incarnation of a Divinity repugnant*
1.	"nullo modo beneficentius consuluit [Deus] generi humano quam cum ipsa Sapientia Dei totum hominem suscipere dignatus est." DVR 30	"noluit intellegere Dominum Christum esse principium, cuius incarnatione purgamur. Eum quippe in ipsa carne contempsit . . . ea superbia non intellegens." DCD X, 24
2.	"Quid potuit pro salute nostra fieri amplius? . . . quid liberalius divina providentia?" DME 1.12	"si . . . Christum Dei uirtutem et Dei sapientiam cognouisses nec ab eius saluberrima humilitate tumore inflatus uanae scientiae resiluisses." DCD X, 28
3.	"quantum autem illud sit, quod hoc etiam nostri generis corpus tantus propter nos deus adsumere atque agere dignatus est, quanto uidetur uilius, tanto est clementia plenius et a quadam ingeniosorum superbia longe alteque remotius." DOR II, 16	"[Christum' contemnis . . . propter corpus . . . et propter crucis opprobrium . . . Christus humiliter uenit et uos superbi estis." DCD X, 29

Augustine and Neoplatonism

A) Augustine	B) Porphyry
Acceptance	Rejection

4. "animas ... caecatas et altissimis a corpore sordibus oblitas numquam ista ratio subtilissima reuocaret, nisi summus deus populari quadam clementia diuini intellectus auctoritatem usque ad ipsum corpus humanum declinaret." CA III, 42	
5. Cf. DCD X, 28, 29.	
C. *Christ was God; His followers are not unworthy of Him.*	C. *Christ was a good man: His followers are perfidious.*
1. "quidue inde in nostram salutem sine ulla degeneratione manauerit, quem unum deum omnipotentem ... veneranda mysteria, quae fide sincera et inconcussa populos liberant ... praedicant. Quantum autem illud sit, quod hoc etiam nostri generis corpus tantus propter nos deus adsumere atque agere dignatus est ... ." DOR II, 16	1. "Dicit etiam bona philosophus iste de Christo ... Christum enim ... piissimum ... et immortalem factum Christianos uero pollutos.... et contaminatos, et errore implicatos ... uiri pietate praestantissimi est illa [Christi] anima ... piissimum igitur uirum [Christum]." DCD XIX, 23
2. "itaque titubans properans haesitans arripio apostolum Paulum. neque enim uere, inquam, isti tanta potuissent uixissentque ita, ut eos uixisse manifestum est, si eorum litterae atque rationes huic tanto bono aduersarentur." CA II, 5	2. "[Platonici] uani Christi laudatores et Christianae religionis obliqui obtrectatores." DCE I, 23
3. DVR 4.5	3. "[discipuli Christi] quos aliud quam ab illo [Christo] didicerunt docuisse contendunt [Porphyrius et sui sequaces]" ibid., I, 24
	4. Porphyry's attack on St. Paul is referred to in E 75.6; 82, 22.
D. *Christ's Church does teach the "way of universal liberation."*	D. *Christ's Church does not teach the way of universal liberation.*
1. "ne de praeteritis loquar, quae potest quisque non credere, si hodie per gentes populosque praedicatur, In principio erat Verbum ... si adhoc percipiendum, diligendum, perfruendum ut anima sanetur, et tantae luci hauriendae mentis acies convalescat, dicitur avaris, nolite vobis condere thesauros in terra ... Si haec	

	A) Augustine	B) Porphyry
	Acceptance	Rejection
	per totum orbem jam populis leguntur . . . si post tantum sanguinem . . . tot cruces Martyrum . . . si tam innumerabiles aggrediuntur hanc viam . . . si denique per urbes atque oppida, castella . . . appetitur a terrenis aversio et in unum Deum . . . conversio, . . . quid adhuc oscitamus?" DVR 4–5	1. "uidebat ergo ista [persecutiones etc.] Porphyrius . . . cito istam uiam perituram et propterea non esse ipsam liberandae animae uniuersalem putabat non intellegens [numerum martyrum] ad eius confirmationem potius pertinere." DCD X, 32
	Rejection	Rejection and Acceptance
8. The claims of demon-spirits to give the divine authority for the liberation of souls.	1. "nequaquam igitur per impias curiositates et magicas consecrationes animae purgantur . . . falsus mediator . . . intercludit viam per affectus, quos tanto maligniores quanto superbiores . . . inspirat." DT IV, 15 2. "in qua metuenda est aeriorum animalium mira fallacia, quae per rerum ad istos sensus corporis pertinentium quasdam diuinationes nonnullasque sententias decipere animas facillime consuerunt." DOR II, 27 3. "astrologia . . . magnum . . . tormentum . . . curiosis." DOR II, 42 Cf. CA III, 13.	A. *Rejection and Acceptance.* 1. "tibi uidelicet tamquam philosopho theurgicae artis purgationes nequaquam necessariae uideantur; sed aliis eas tamen inportas . . . eos, qui philosophari non possunt, ad ista seducis . . . istorum, quos philosophari piget, incomparabiliter maior est multitudo . . . mittis homines ad theurgos." DCD X, 27 B. *Acceptance.* 1. "[Theurgi] . . . a quibus curiositate deceptus ista perniciosa et insana . . . didicisti." DCD X, 26 2. "Tu autem hoc didicisti non a Platone, sed a Chaldaeis magistris tuis." DCD X, 27 Cf. ibid., X, 32. 3. ". . . perniciossimae curiositate [te] commisisses." DCD X, 27

A) Augustine	B) Porphyry
Rejection	Rejection and Acceptance
	4. "[Plotini condiscipulorum] aliqui se magicarum artium curiositate deprauati sunt." E 118, 33
	5. "Illi autem praecipui gentium philosophi, quia sine homine Christo philosophati sunt, in deceptores daemones inciderunt." DT XIII, 24 cf. C VII, 15.
	6. "nam tertio vitio curiositatis in percunctandis daemonibus, quo isti maxime, eum quibus nunc agitur Pagani a Christiana salute revocantur." DVR 7

13

Porphyry's *Philosophy from Oracles* in Eusebius's *Praeparatio Euangelica* and Augustine's *Dialogues of Cassiciacum* and *City of God* X

৺

The study that follows is made up of two parts, originally prepared for separate publications, and a conclusion which originally belonged to the second part. There is therefore some, but on the whole very little, overlapping.

In the first part reason is given for believing that in *Praeparatio Euangelica* III, 13 we have doctrine inspired by Porphyry's *Philosophy from Oracles*, including the theme of Porphyry's vain search for a way to God, which is frequent in the first book of the *Philosophy from Oracles*. This is not only new evidence, but important for identification of the *Philosophy from Oracles* with the *De regressu animae* of *City of God* X.

In the second part I have developed further the evidence for influence of the *Philosophy from Oracles* (*De regressu animae*) on Augustine's *Dialogues of Cassiciacum*. There is still room for much more work on this point, especially in the light of P. Hadot's recent work (see below), which has been of great use to me.

The third part is a short general conclusion on the topic of the *Philosophy from Oracles* being the work of Porphyry which (apart from chapter 11) Augustine is discussing in *City of God* X.

It is now accepted by most Porphyrian scholars that the "Chaldaean Oracles" were used in the *Philosophy from Oracles*. Even more, Hadot especially has killed the view that Porphyry could be neither a serious nor an original philosopher. My thesis of ten years ago encountered these entrenched views which are now demolished. I have written nothing on it since, but now would like to give it another airing.

I accept the opinion of G. Madec (*Chronique Porphyrienne*, R E Aug 15, 1969, p. 175) that the conclusion as expressed in my *Porphyry's Philosophy from Oracles in Augustine* (p. 145) was formulated in terms too precise—especially in view of the sustained and difficult argument which had preceded it. It is hard to expect any scholar, however conscientious, to weigh each text, relate them all together, and relate them to *non-doctrinal items of evidence* (items of great confirmatory value) as painstakingly and alertly as the author had over a number of years. And yet this is absolutely necessary if a sound judgment is to be given. P. Hadot and H. Dörrie, my principal appraisers, were both kind and conscientious to an extraordinary degree.

In the course of the following pages I have not directly confronted O. du Roy's *L'Intelligence de la Foi en la Trinité selon saint Augustin* (Paris, 1966). I have not done so because I have written extensively of it in *Augustinian Studies*. [Ed note: AS I (1970), 277–84, and this volume, chap. 21.] There I have tried to show my appreciation of the wealth of new insights du Roy has given us on the evolution of Augustine's ideas on the Trinity—but I give, I hope, solid reasons for rejecting, with what Hadot calls the almost unanimous support of scholars, his contention that Augustine had not read the *De regressu animae* (*Philosophy from Oracles*) when he was writing the *Dialogues of Cassiciacum*. In the same volume I have also written much in praise, and, of course, a little in criticism of P. Hadot's *Porphyre et Victorinus*, 2 vols. (Paris, 1968). The present articles have greatly profited from the suggestions and criticisms of G. Folliet and G. Madec of Etudes Augustiniennes.

New Light on Porphyry's *Philosophy from Oracles* from Eusebius's *Praeparatio Euangelica*

Eusebius's *Praeparatio euangelica* is the principal acknowledged source upon which we draw for our knowledge of Porphyry's *Philosophy from Oracles*. In the pages that follow I shall recall the terms of the preface to that work as found in Eusebius, and then proceed to elucidate *Praeparatio Euangelica* III, 13 as affording some new evidence on the *Philosophy from Oracles*. I shall then, by way of short corollary, relate what I have discussed to a current problem connected with the *Philosophy from Oracles*.

The Preface to the *Philosophy from Oracles*

It may be well to state at the outset that Eusebius describes the *Philosophy from Oracles* as a compilation made "against us," that is, Christians.[1] The prominence he gives the book in his discussion and his anxiety to controvert it make this abundantly clear.

But the book could be, and was, more than merely anti-Christian. Porphyry's own description of the book in his Preface to it is given by Eusebius as follows:[2]

> Sure, then, and steadfast is he who draws his hopes of salvation from this as from the only sure source, and to such thou wilt impart information without any reserve. For I myself call the gods to witness, that I have neither added anything, nor taken away from the meaning of the responses, except where I have corrected an erroneous phrase, or made a change for greater clearness, or completed the metre when defective, or struck out anything that did not conduce to the purpose, so that I preserved the sense of what was spoken untouched, guarding against the impiety of such changes, rather than against the avenging justice that follows from the sacrilege.
>
> And our present collection will contain a record of many doctrines of philosophy, according as the gods declared the truth to be; but to a small extent we shall also touch upon the practice of divination, such as will be useful both for contemplation, and for the general purification of life. And the utility which this collection possesses will be best known to as many as have ever been in travail with the truth, and prayed that by receiving the manifestation of it from the gods they might gain relief from their perplexity by virtue of the trustworthy teaching of the speakers.
>
> And do thou endeavour to avoid publishing these above all things, and casting them even before the profane for the sake of reputation, or gain, or any unholy flattery. For so there would be danger not only to thee for transgressing these injunctions, but also to me for lightly trusting thee who couldst not keep the benefits secret to thyself. We must give them then to those who have arranged their plan of life with a view to the salvation of the soul.
>
> These things I beg of you to conceal as the most unutterable of secrets, for even the gods did not make a revelation concerning them openly, but by enigmas.

Eusebius comments that the "discourse adopted lofty strains." But he proceeds immediately to encounter a particular point: what character, in the light of the inspired Pythian oracles, ought to be given to the invisible deified powers? Let us, however, for the moment, weigh the implications of Porphyry's Preface to the *Philosophy from Oracles*.

The doctrine of the oracles was intended to be revealed only to those who have arranged their plan of life with a view to the *salvation of the soul*: δοτέον δὴ τοῖς τὸν βίον ἐνστησαμένοις πρὸς τὴν τῆς ψυχῆς σωτηρίαν. The preface opens with an assurance that these doctrines are the most reliable for one who hopes for *salvation*: τὰς ἐλπίδας τοῦ σωθῆναι. They were especially intended for those who, in travail with the truth, prayed for relief from their perplexity through the gods' revelation. Briefly the *Philosophy from Oracles* was intended by its author for those who sought divine revelation on the truth and the salvation of the soul.

The truth revealed in the *Philosophy from Oracles* is described as being a record of *many* doctrines of philosophy: πολλῶν μὲν τῶν κατὰ φιλοσοφίαν δογμάτων ἀναγραφήν as the gods declared the truth to be. It is emphasized that this is the *main content* of the book—hence its title, *Philosophy from Oracles*. In practice this probably included the exposition of doctrines held in common, according to Porphyry, by Platonists and the *Oracles*. The most obvious instance of this common doctrine is the identification of the Porphyrian ὕπαρξις, ζωή and νοῦς with the Πατήρ, δύναμις and νοῦς of the *Chaldaean Oracles*. Both Porphyry and the *Chaldaean Oracles* differed from Plotinus and Jamblichus in that Plotinus posited one hypostasis and Jamblichus two hypostases before the Triad mentioned.[3] There is now reason to believe that the oracles in question in the *Philosophy from Oracles* included *Chaldaean Oracles*; that Porphyry had inherited a system of equivalences between Middle-Platonic and *Chaldaean Oracles* hypostases at the time of his writing the *Philosophy from Oracles*; and that he treated of these hypostases in the *Philosophy from Oracles*.[4]

The *Philosophy from Oracles*, according to its preface, included—but only to a small extent: ἐπ' ὀλίγον δὲ καὶ τῆς χρηστικῆς ἁψόμεθα πραγματείας—a little on the practice of divination, such as would be useful both for contemplation (θεωρίαν), and for the more general purification of life (κάθαρσιν). The reservations should be kept in mind: a little on divination, not any divination, but divination related to θεωρία and κάθαρσις. Worship of demons was condemned.[5]

Porphyry insists twice that the doctrines conveyed are to be treated as most secret, and twice that they may be given without reserve to those who seek and plan the salvation of their soul. It is to be noted that Porphyry is at pains to explain that he had been careful not to incur the charge of impiety in altering the oracles more than was absolutely necessary for the sense and metre. This piety may have exposed him to the charge of *believing all* of the things that *he reported*: certainly Eusebius and Augustine seem to have constantly imposed on him guilt by association.

One must be on one's guard, therefore, against phrases such as Bidez' *le cauchemar démoniaque qui obsède la Philosophie des oracles.*[6] Bidez greatly underrated Porphyry's level as a philosopher[7] (built on an unsupported chronology of his life[8]), and allowed the admittedly peculiar character of extant oracular fragments (while making little if any allowance for their being reported by Porphyry, and not always necessarily approved by him) to dominate his description of the quality of the book.[9] The preface is surely more reliable than Bidez, and a better foundation on which to build.

Praeparatio Euangelica III, 13, 22ff.

I

Porphyry appears early in the *Prae. eu.* as the author of the *Letter to Anebo* (III, 3, 21), the *De abstinentia* (III, 4, 5) and the *De cultu simulacrorum* (which, however, is not named there). The degradation of Greek and Egyptian theology is referred to characteristically (e.g., III, 13, 4) in terms of Rom. I, 22: "professing themselves to be wise, [they] became fools, changing the glory of the incorruptible God for the likeness of an image of corruptible man, and of birds, and fourfooted beasts and creeping things." Porphyry is also, again characteristically, scolded for his arrogance.

But Eusebius had to be fair and admits that Porphyry and others *claimed* to be conveying secret doctrines and conveying metaphorically through the use of material images teaching on incorporeal beings (e.g., III, 13, 4).[10] Still he professes not to understand (III, 13, 22) why they do this: "But if they shall assert that they deify not the visible bodies of sun and moon and stars, nor yet the sensible parts of the world, but the powers, invisible in them (ἐν τούτοις ἀοράτους δυνάμεις), of the very God who is over all (ἐπὶ πᾶσιν)—for they say that God being *one* fills *all things* (τὰ πάντα) with various powers, and pervades *all*, and *rules* over (ἐπιστατεῖν) all, but as existing *in all* and pervading all in an incorporeal and invisible manner, and that they rightly *worship* Him through the things which we have mentioned[11]—why in the world therefore do they not reject the foul and unseemly fables concerning the gods as being unlawful and impious, and put out of sight the very books concerning them, as containing blasphemous and licentious teaching, and celebrate the one and only and invisible *God* openly and purely (καθαρῶς) and without any foul envelopment?

> For this was what those who had known the truth ought to do, and not to degrade and debase the venerable name of God into foul and

lustful fables of things unspeakable; nor yet to shut themselves up in *cells* and dark *recesses* (οἰκίσκοις καὶ σκότου μυχοῖς) and buildings made by man, as if they would find God inside; nor to think that they are worshipping the divine powers in statues (ξοάνοις) made of lifeless matter, nor to suppose that by vapours of gore (γεώδεσιν ἀτμοῖς αἱμάτων) and filth streaming from the earth, and by the blood of slain animals (νεκρῶν ζῴων αἵμασι) they are doing things pleasing to God.

Surely it became these men of wisdom and of lofty speech, as being set free from all these bonds of error, to impart of their physical speculations ungrudgingly to all men, and to proclaim as it were in naked truth to all, that they should adore not the things that are seen, but only the unseen creator (δημιουργόν) of things visible, worship his invisible and incorporeal powers (δυνάμεις) in ways invisible and incorporeal, not by kindling fire (πῦρ ἅψαντας) nor yet by offerings of rams and bulls (κριὸν καὶ ταῦρον), nay, nor yet by imagining that they honour the deity by garlands and statues (ξοάνοις) and the building of temples, but by worshipping him with purified thoughts (λογισμοῖς κεκαθαρμένοις) and right and true doctrines (δόγμασιν ὀρθοῖς καὶ ἀληθέσι), in dispassionate calmness of soul (ἐν ἀπαθείᾳ ψυχῆς), and in growing as far as possible like (ὁμοιώσει) unto him.

But no one ever yet, barbarian or Greek (οὐ βάρβαρος, οὐχ Ἕλλην), began to show all men this truth except only our Saviour; who having proclaimed to all nations an escape from their ancient error, procured abundantly for them all a way of return and of devotion to the one true and only God of the universe (τὴν πρὸς τὸν ἀληθῆ καὶ μόνον τῶν ὅλων θεὸν ἐπιστροφήν τε καὶ εὐσέβειαν). Yet the men perversely wise who boasted (αὐχήσαντες) of the highest philosophy of life, whereby as the inspired Apostle says (Rom. I, 21f.), "Though they knew God, they glorified him not as God, neither gave thanks; but became vain in their reasonings, and their senseless heart was darkened. They professed indeed to be wise, but became fools and worshipped and served the creature rather than the creator, who is blessed for ever."

So after their long and manifold philosophical speculation, and after their solemn systems of meteorology and physiology, they fell down from their high place, as it were from the loftiest mountaintop . . . pretending that they glorified the like deities with the multitude by offering sacrifice (θύειν) and falling down before images (ξοάνοις) . . . Hear at least how Apollo himself teaches men a hymn . . . for these things also are written by Porphyry in a book which he entitled: *Of the Philosophy derived from Oracles.* . . . (III, 13, 23 sv.)

Here then we have introduced in context the first explicit mention of Porphyry's book, *Philosophy from Oracles*. There may be an immediate reason, however, for believing that he has already in the context quoted been referring to it and using it: γράφει δὲ ὁ Πορφύριος καὶ ταῦτα ἐν οἷς ἐπέγραψε Περὶ τῆς ἐκ λογίων Φιλοσοφίας (III, 14, 4). The quotations following would be sufficiently indicated by ταῦτα: but καί *might* suggest that other matters from the book have been dealt with in the preceding context. Lewy and myself[12] independently came to a similar conclusion about the chapter (IV, 5, 1ff.) immediately preceding the more formal later introduction of the *Philosophy from Oracles* in *Prae. eu.* IV, 6, 2ff.

But there are additional reasons. Eusebius would appear to have brought to an end his consideration of Porphyry's *De cultu simulacrorum* at about III, 13, 22. A new aspect of his topic is then begun. The references in III, 13, 23f. to secret doctrines and not speaking openly to all remind one of the preface to the *Philosophy from Oracles*; but there are other details that suggest the influence of that work at this point.

The combination of Augustine *Ciu. Dei* XIX, 23, *Prae. eu.* IV, 5, 1ff. and especially IV, 9, 1ff. makes it almost certain that the καί of Eusebius *does* refer back to the preceding passages, and that the *Philosophy from Oracles* is the book to which Eusebius has been referring just before explicitly mentioning it as containing καὶ ταῦτα (III, 14, 3). This demands careful explanation. Augustine, *Ciu. Dei* XIX, 23 reads:

> In Deum vero, inquit [Apollo], *generatorem* et in *regem* ante *omnia,* quem tremit et *caelum* et *terra* atque mare et *infernorum abdita* et ipsa numina perhorrescunt; quorum *lex* est Pater, quem valde sancti honorant *Hebraei . . . venerari* [inquit] autem magis *caelestes deos* [iubebant], amplius autem *venerari Deum Patrem.* Hoc autem, inquit, et dii *praecipiunt* et in superioribus ostendimus, quem ad modum animum advertere ad Deum monent et illum colere ubique imperant. Verum indocti et impiae naturae, quibus vere fatum non concessit ab dis dona obtinere neque habere Jovis inmortalis notionem, non audientes et deos et divinos viros deos quidem omnes recusaverunt, *prohibitos autem daemones* et hos non odisse, sed *revereri.* Deum autem simulantes colere,[13] ea sola, per quae Deus adoratur, non agunt. Nam Deus quidem, utpote omnium Pater, nullius indiget; sed nobis est bene, cum eum per iustitiam et castitatem aliasque virtutes adoramus, ipsam vitam precem ad ipsum facientes per *imitationem* et inquisitionem de ipso. Inquisitio enim purgat, inquit; imitatio deificat affectionem ad ipsum operando.

Eusebius in *Prae. eu.* IV, 5, 1ff. writes: "First of all they have set apart the first God, saying that they know him to be one *over all* (ἐπὶ πᾶσι), and first, and *Father* and *king* of all gods, and that after him the race of gods is second, that of daemons third, and heroes fourth. All these, they say, participating in the nature of the higher power (τοῦ κρείττονος ἰδέας μετασχόντα) act and are acted upon in this way and in that, and everything of this kind is called light because of its participating in light. But they also say that evil rules the essence of the lower nature; and this evil is a race of wicked daemons . . . and everything of this kind is called darkness . . . they say that the *heaven*, and the ether as far down as the moon, are assigned to the gods; and the parts about the moon and the atmosphere to daemons; and the region of the *earth* and *parts beneath the earth* (ὑπόγεια) to souls . . . they say that we ought to worship first of all the gods of heaven (τοὺς οὐρανίους) and the ether, secondly the good daemons, thirdly the souls of the heroes, and fourthly to propitiate the bad and wicked daemons.

"But while making these verbal distinctions they in fact throw all into confusion, by *worshipping the wicked powers* (δυνάμεις) only."

Apollo's own hymn, found in *Prae. eu.* IV, 9, 1ff., joined with *Prae. eu.* IV, 5, 1ff., clinches the matter. I shall give the hymn in translation marking the relevant terms:

"Friend, who hast entered on this heaven-taught path (τρίβον),
Heed well thy work; nor to the blessed gods
Forget to slay thine offerings (θυσίας ἐναρίζων) in due form,
Whether to gods of earth (ἐπιχθονίοις), or gods of heaven (οὐρανίοις),
Kings of the sky (αἴθρης βασιλεῦσι) and liquid paths of air (ἠέρος)
And sea, and all who dwell beneath the earth (ὑποχθονίοισιν);
For in their nature's fullness all is bound.
How to devote things living in due form (ὡς θέμις ἐστί)
My verse shall tell, thou in thy tablets write.
For gods of earth and gods of heaven, each, three:
For heavenly gods pure white; for gods of earth
Cattle of kindred hue divide in three
And on the altar lay thy sacrifice (θυσίας ἐναρίζων);
For gods infernal bury deep, and cast
The blood (αἷμα) into a trench (βόθρον). For gentle Nymphs
Honey and gifts of Dionysus pour.
For such as flit for ever o'er the earth
Fill all the blazing altar's (περιπληθέα βωμόν) trench with blood (φόνου).
And cast the feathered fowl into the fire.
Then honey mix'd with meal, and frankincense,
And grains of barley sprinkle over all.
But when thou comest to the sandy shore,
Pour green sea-water on the victim's head,
And cast the body whole into the deep.
Then, all things rightly done, return at last
To the great company of heavenly gods.

For all the powers that in pure ether (αἰθερίοις) dwell,
And in the stars (ἀστραίοις), let blood in fullest stream
Flow from the throat o'er all the sacrifice:
Make of the limbs (ἄκρα) a banquet for the gods,
And give them to the fire; feast on the rest,
Filling with savours sweet (ἀτμοῖσιν λαροῖσιν) the liquid air.
Breathe forth, when all is done, thy solemn vows."

". . . Now this is the method of the sacrifices, which are rendered according to the aforesaid classification of gods."[14]

In *Prae. eu.* IX, 10, 1, we have another fragment from the same part, that is, the first book of the *Philosophy from Oracles*:

But Porphyry, in the first book of his *Philosophy from Oracles*, introduces his own god as himself bearing witness to the wisdom of the Hebrew race as well as of the other nations renowned for intelligence.

It is his Apollo who speaks as follows in an oracle which he is uttering; and while still explaining the subject of sacrifices (see quotation from *Prae. eu.* IV, 9, 1ff. above), he adds words which are well worthy of attention, as being full of divine knowledge:

"Steep is the road (ὁδός) and rough that leads to heaven,
Entered at first through portals bound with brass.
Within are found innumerable paths (ἀτραπιτοί).
Which for the endless good (ἐπ' ἀπείρονα πρῆξιν) of all mankind
They first revealed, who Nile's sweet waters drink.
From them the heavenward paths Phoenicia learned,
Assyria, Lydia, and the Hebrew race":

and so forth: on which the author (Porphyry) further remarks: "For the road to the gods is bound with brass, and both steep and rough; the barbarians (βάρβαροι) discovered many paths (ἀτραπούς) thereof, but the Greeks went astray, and those who already held it even perverted it. The discovery was ascribed by the god to the Egyptians, Phoenicians, Chaldeans (for these are the Assyrians), Lydians, and *Hebrews*."

In addition to this Apollo also says in another oracle:

"Only Chaldeans and Hebrews wisdom found
In the pure worship of a self-born God."[15]

We find at least some of the words omitted ("and so forth") above in *Prae. eu.* XIV, 10, 5, as follows:

"Have you heard how much pains have been taken that a man may offer the sacrifices of purification for the body, to say nothing of finding the salvation of the soul?[16] For the road to the gods is bound . . ."

From a perusal of the themes and terms repeated in DCD XIX, 23, *Prae. eu.* IV, 9, 1ff.; IX, 10, 1; XIV, 10, 4 (and isolated items from V, 8,

10; V, 11, 1; V, 16, 1), all of them explicitly said by Augustine or Eusebius to be extracts from the *Philosophy from Oracles*, we can, I submit, conclude that *Prae. eu.* III, 13, 22ff. also is inspired by the same work.

II

One correspondence in theme between DCD XIX, 23, *Prae. eu.* IV, 5, 1ff., and III, 13, 22ff., I have not yet developed, because it needs particular care and is of particular consequence. As far as DCD XIX, 23 and *Prae. eu.* IV, 5, 1ff. are concerned, one need only draw attention to the contention that Porphyry and others not only did not obey the injunction not to worship the wicked demons, but worshipped them, seemingly, alone.

In Augustine, DCD XIX, 23 we have an explicitly named quotation (translated into Latin) from the *Philosophy from Oracles* on the proper method of worshipping the Father: *quibus sit colendus moribus*. We are told *animum advertere ad Deum et illum colere ubique*. We do ourselves good when *eum per iustitiam et castitatem aliasque virtutes adoramus, ipsam vitam precem ad ipsum facientes per imitationem et inquisitionem de ipso. Inquisitio enim purgat . . . imitatio deificat affectionem ad ipsum operando*.

Prae. eu. V, 15, 4f. has: "You see, for instance, how they say that their magic figures and images of that kind hold them fast in certain spots of ground (he has just quoted from the *Philosophy of Oracles* and is about to quote again from it immediately), though they ought, if, as they say, there is any real divinity in them, to set foot in no other place, except only *in the thought of the soul* (ἐν μόνῃ ψυχῆς διανοίᾳ), and that thought too purified *from all filth and from every stain* (παντὸς ῥύπου καὶ πάσης κηλῖδος κεκαθαρμένη), and adorned with *modesty* and *righteousness* and *all the other virtues* (σωφροσύνῃ τε καὶ δικαιοσύνῃ καὶ ταῖς ἄλλαις ἀρεταῖς κεκοσμημένη)[17] . . . nor would souls already prepared by virtuous and godly practice for the reception of the deity (τῶν εἰς ὑποδοχὴν τοῦ θείου κατὰ τὴν ἐνάρετον καὶ φιλόθεον ψυχὴν προηυτρεπισμένων) have any further need of the evil arts of sorcerers."

This passage repeats clearly phrases found in DCD XIX, 23 just quoted. A section of *Prae. eu.* IV, 10, 5f., although it occurs between two fairly close references (IV, 10, 1, and IV, 10, 7) to Porphyry's *De abstinentia*, is both a concluding summary statement to the complete topic that has gone before, and seems aimed directly against the specific doctrine given shortly before (down to IV, 10, 1) from the *Philosophy from Oracles*. It reads: "Hence we who have been taught to worship only the

God who is over all . . . bring with us no earthy or dead (νεκρόν) offering, nor gore and blood (οὐδὲ λύθρους καὶ αἵματα), nor anything of corruptible and material substance, but with a *mind* purified from all wickedness (νῷ δὲ πάσης κεκαθαρμένῳ κακίας), and with a body clothed with the *ornament of purity and temperance* (τὸν ἐξ ἁγνείας καὶ σωφροσύνης κόσμον) . . . and with right doctrines worthy of God (δόγμασί τε ὀρθοῖς καὶ θεοπρεπέσι) we pray . . .'"

Prae. eu. IV, 4, 1, has: "the sacrifices which are worthy of God have been purified from all wickedness (κεκαθαρμένη κακίας ἀπάσης), and in freedom of soul from all passions (ἔν τε ἀπαθείᾳ ψυχῆς), and in the acquirement of every virtue (καὶ πάσης ἀρετῆς ἀναλήψει), according to the divine doctrines of salvation (κατὰ τὰ θεῖα καὶ σωτηριώδη παιδεύματα) are . . . offered up." This passage is again a concluding summary statement, this time occurring between two explicit references to the *Philosophy from Oracles* (III, 14, 4ff. and IV, 6, 3; no other book of Porphyry is referred to within this section). This passage is clearly inspired by the passage found in DCD XIX, 23, as is *Prae. eu.* V, 15, 4f. certainly, and IV, 10, 5f. possibly.

Now let us look again at *Prae. eu.* III, 13, 24: "nor yet by imagining that they honour the deity by garlands and statues and the building of temples, but by worshipping him with purified thoughts (λογισμοῖς δὲ κεκαθαρμένοις) and right and true doctrines (καὶ δόγμασιν ὀρθοῖς καὶ ἀληθέσι), in dispassionate calmness of soul (ἐν ἀπαθείᾳ ψυχῆς) and in growing as far as possible like unto him (καὶ τῇ πρὸς αὐτὸν κατὰ τὸ δυνατὸν τῆς ἀρετῆς ὁμοιώσει)." Apart from the reasons given earlier for believing that this passage is inspired by the *Philosophy from Oracles*, casting its shadow before (from III, 14, 3, where it is implicitly mentioned), the correspondence with the other passages just examined dealing with the theme of the proper method of worshipping the Father, make it likely that *Prae. eu.* III, 13, 24, is also inspired by the *Philosophy from Oracles*. It is to be noted particularly that *Prae. eu.* III, 13, 24, repeats in ὁμοιώσει the *imitatio* of DCD XIX, 23.

III

Finally, there remains to be developed the correspondence between IX, 10, 1; XIV, 10, 4 and III, 13, 22ff.

Let us turn to *Prae. eu.* IX, 9, 1: it will enable us to see that *Prae. eu.* III, 13, 24f. is, like all its other sections and the last section of III, 13, also inspired by the *Philosophy from Oracles* which was just about to be mentioned as containing the following things *also* (καὶ ταῦτα).

In *Prae. eu.* IX, 10, 1, the first book of the *Philosophy from Oracles* quotes Apollo as bearing witness to the wisdom of the Hebrew race: this also is attested by Augustine, doubtless quoting from the same part of the first book of the *Philosophy from Oracles* in DCD XIX, 23. Apollo has been speaking of sacrifices and then adds that the road (ὁδός) to heaven is steep and rough, inside are innumerable paths (ἀτραπιτοί) which for the endless benefit of all mankind (ἐπ' ἀπείρονα πρῆξιν) first the Egyptians revealed, and then the Phoenicians, the Assyrians, Lydians and Hebrews learned.

Commenting straightway on this oracle Porphyry both immediately substitutes Chaldaeans instead of Assyrians and calls *all* of the peoples mentioned by one single name—*Barbari* (βάρβαροι), that is in contradistinction to the Greeks who were said to have gone astray (ἐπλανήθησαν). He adds that those who had known of the way to heaven had perverted it (οἱ δὲ κρατοῦντες ἤδη καὶ διέφθειραν). Porphyry goes on to quote Apollo as saying, more shortly, "Only Chaldees and Hebrews found wisdom in the pure worship of a self-born God (αὐτογένεθλον ἄνακτα σεβαζόμενοι θεὸν ἁγνῶς)."

Porphyry had also, commenting on the steepness and roughness of the road to heaven, remarked on what pains had to be taken (πόσος πόνος), that a man might offer the sacrifices of purification for the body (ὑπὲρ σώματός τις τὰ καθάρσια θύσῃ), to say nothing of finding the salvation of the soul (οὐχ ὅτι τῆς ψυχῆς τὴν σωτηρίαν ἐξεύροι).[18]

Prae. eu. IV, 4, in a section (IV, 4, 1ff.) where we have already seen reasons to detect inspiration from the *Philosophy from Oracles* speaks of the Greeks and Barbarians as having no knowledge of the true God and being dragged down into an abyss by wicked demons. *Prae. eu.* IV, 21, 2, likewise in an explicitly *Philosophy from Oracles* context, reads: "Wherefore also they (that is the bad demons) might justly be called enemies of God and impious, who ruined all human life, and from whom never any save only our lord and saviour Jesus Christ provided the way of escape (τὴν φυγὴν προεξένησεν) for all men, by preaching to all alike, Greeks and Barbarians, a cure for their ancestral malady, and deliverance (ἐλευθερίαν) from their bitter and inveterate bondage.[19]

Keeping these passages, but *Prae. eu.* IX, 9, 1 especially, in mind, let us now look back again at *Prae. eu.* III, 13, 25: "But no one ever yet, barbarian or Greek, began to show all men this truth (πᾶσιν ἀνθρώποις ταύτης κατῆρξεν τῆς ἀληθείας) except only our saviour; who, having proclaimed to all nations an escape from their ancient error (τῆς παλαιᾶς πλάνης πᾶσι τοῖς ἔθνεσιν ἀποφυγὴν προκηρύξας), procured abundantly for them all a way of return (ἐπιστροφήν) and of devotion (εὐσέβειαν) to the one true and only God of the universe. Yet the men perversely wise who boasted (αὐχήσαντες) of the highest philosophy of life . . . became vain . . . served the creature etc." (Rom. I, 21f.)

It can hardly be doubted, firstly, that III, 13, 25, also is inspired by the *Philosophy from Oracles* and, secondly, that the theme of Porphyry's vain search for a way to the gods was frequent in the first book of the *Philosophy from Oracles*.

Prae. eu. IX, 10, 1 quotes Apollo (from the *Philosophy from Oracles*) as saying that the Egyptians were the first to discover paths (ἀτραπιτοί) to the gods and that then the Phoenicians, Assyrians, Lydians, and Hebrews knew of many roads (ὁδούς) to the gods. Apollo is quoted from another oracle as saying that only the Chaldaeans and Hebrews found the knowledge of a self-generated god whom they worshipped purely. Commenting on the first oracle, Porphyry says that not only had the Greeks gone astray, but that those who found (οἱ κρατοῦντες) the way had "perverted" it: *this makes no exception for Chaldaeans or Hebrews* who alone, he has admitted, had found a pure way to a self-generated God. Briefly, Porphyry *was* looking for a way to the gods (ὁδὸς μακάρων) for the benefit of all men (μερόπων ἐπ' ἀπείρονα πρῆξιν). The Egyptians, Phoenicians, Assyrians, (Chaldaeans), and Hebrews had found ways and lost them (διέφθειραν). The Greeks had gone astray (ἐπλανήθησαν). Porphyry insisted that great pains had to be taken even to offer sacrifices of purification for the body (τὰ καθάρσια θύσῃ) to say nothing of finding the salvation of the soul (τῆς ψυχῆς τὴν σωτηρίαν ἐξεύροι). Eusebius in *Prae. eu.* III, 13, 24; IV, 4, 1 and IV, 21, 2, passages, as we have seen, where inspiration from the *Philosophy from Oracles* is present, speaks of Greeks and Barbarians (i.e., the other peoples mentioned in the oracle of Apollo) as having no knowledge of the true god, or freedom (ἐλευθερίαν), or escape (φυγήν, ἀποφυγήν) for all men, or a way of return (ἐπιστροφήν) from error (πλάνης) and bondage (δουλείας): the wicked demons drag men down (καθειλκυσμένοι) and ruin (λυμηνάμενοι) all human life—they are the enemies of God.

Conclusion

Eusebius in *Prae. eu.* III, 13, 24; IV, 4, 1; IV, 21, 2, says that there was no way of escape to the truth until Christ. This is his reaction to part of the first book of Porphyry's *Philosophy from Oracles*. It is also Augustine's at the end of DCD X to part of the first book of a work of Porphyry's which he describes as *De regressu animae*.[20] This latter work has never been referred to elsewhere. It is impossible to believe that Eusebius would not have referred to it in the context which we have been discussing, if it did exist separately from the *Philosophy from Oracles*; for he used *Aduersus Boëthum de anima, Aduersus Christianos, De abstinentia, De cultu simulacrorum, Epistula ad Anebontem, Recitatio philologica* as well as, most frequently of all, the *Philosophy from Oracles*. Lewy has accepted that *De regressu animae* did not exist as a separate work.[21] It is also significant that Eusebius, dealing so extensively with oracles from Porphyry, does not refer to any other alleged work of Porphyry dealing with oracles.[22]

I have given other reasons elsewhere for identifying the *De regressu animae* with the *Philosophy from Oracles* or part of it. Insofar as dating is concerned, my position has improved.[23] Insofar as "ton" and "attitude" are concerned[24]—although one should be very slow to invoke such an argument when one is dealing with fragments—the present article shows how the themes of the *De regressu animae* and the *Philosophy from Oracles on the universal way of the liberation of the soul* are very like indeed:[25] this is of crucial importance.

Porphyry's *Philosophy from Oracles* in Augustine's *Dialogues of Cassiciacum*[26]

In my *Porphyry's Philosophy from Oracles in Augustine* I have indicated briefly by way of corollary to my main topic some passages and details in the *Dialogues of Cassiciacum* which appeared to me to have possible connection with Porphyry's book. I now propose to develop this theme a little more here.

It may be well to say that since 1959 Porphyry's fortunes have prospered. His most recent interpreter[27] has recovered him from the terrible indictment of Bidez,[28] where he appeared as without originality, a mere shadow of Plotinus, a devotee of wicked demons—so that now he appears as having a distinct and original ontology and unsuspected depths of philosophy. In particular he played a special role in relating Middle-Platonism with the teaching of the *Chaldaean Oracles*; in due course the doctrine of the Trinity of Victorinus, according to Hadot,[29] is essentially related to the Triad of Porphyry, which in turn is related to the Triad of the *Chaldaean Oracles*. The fact of the importance of Porphyry at the end of the fourth century is now admitted to be inescapable.

Although a recent book[30] seeks to deny it, there remains general agreement[31] that Augustine had read the book which he (and he only, and twice only—both times at the end of the tenth book of the *City of God*) described as *De regressu animae* before he wrote the *Dialogues of Cassiciacum*. I have sought, in the study referred to above, to relate this book to the well known work of Porphyry on the *Philosophy from Oracles*. It is only logical, therefore, that I should have sought to find traces of the *Philosophy from Oracles* in these *Dialogues* and that, now that the climate of scholarly opinion is more receptive to Porphyry's claims, I should continue to do so.

The field of operation is much extended by the expansion itself of our knowledge, through Hadot and others, of doctrines and expressions, known or suspected to be Porphyrian.[32] It is not my purpose, however, here to employ this extension of our knowledge to detect Porphyrian traces merely in the *Dialogues*, except perhaps incidentally from time to time.

Retractationes

It is well to have a look at Augustine's *Retractationes* where they seek to emend what he later found fault with in the *Dialogues of Cassiciacum*.[33] Some of this might very well be connected with the *Philosophy from Oracles* or the *De regressu animae*. For the most part what he regrets has to do with Platonists and their doctrine. He regrets praising the *Platonici*, Pythagoras and Mallius Theodorus. He regrets the many places in the *Dialogues* where he had adopted quite simply a Platonist view that there were two worlds, one sensible and the other intelligible (*et quod duos mundos, unum sensibilem, alterum intelligibilem, non ex Platonis uel Platonicorum persona, sed ex mea sic commendaui*): this he later saw made difficulty for Christian teaching, especially in relation to bodily resurrection. He found it necessary so often to correct himself in these few chapters on this important point that he finally resorted to the universal formula: *nec assidue repetendum est, quod et superius inde iam dixi, sed hoc recolendum, ubicumque ista locutio in meis litteris inuenitur.*

A few particular details in these chapters of the *Retractationes* bring the matter perhaps a little closer to Porphyry. Twice (I, 1, 2 and I, 2) he regrets excessive emphasis on the *mens* or *ratio* or *animus* as the dominant part of man, the happiness of which can be achieved in this life, quite independently of the body. Too great emphasis on the value of purgation is also regretted (I, 4, 2). While these ideas clearly belong to the general Platonic topic mentioned just above, they come somewhat closer to the notions that philosophy is a way of salvation for the few only, that purgation is indispensable, and that the real "me" is the *mens*—all ideas which are considered to be particularly (but one should immediately add, not exclusively) Porphyrian.

Porphyry, however, is mentioned specifically at *Retractationes* I, 4, 3: *Et in eo quod ibi dictum est, Penitus esse ista sensibilia fugienda, cauendum fuit ne putaremur illam Porphyrii falsi philosophi tenere sententiam, qua dixit: omne corpus esse fugiendum.* The question arises as to whether or not *cauendum fuit ne putaremur* is to be taken to imply that when he was writing the passage in the *Soliloquia* to which this refers, he was aware of the *sententia: omne corpus esse fugiendum* and aware of it as Porphyry's? I believe it does.[34] Curiously enough the immediately preceding item in the *Retractationes* at this point refers to the universal way to Wisdom—a topic equally characteristic and equally important as the *omne corpus fugiendum* in the so-called *De regressu animae* of Porphyry: *Item quod dixi, ad sapientiae coniunctionem non una uia perueniri, non bene sonat; quasi alia uia sit praeter Christum, qui dixit: Ego sum uia. uitanda ergo erat haec offensio aurium religiosarum; quamuis alia sit illa unuiersalis uia, aliae autem uiae de quibus in Psalmo canimus.* The use of *non una uia* and *uniuersalis* probably indicates that when writing the *Retractationes* Augustine associated both *uia* and *omne corpus fugiendum* with Porphyry's *De regressu animae* and feared that its influence would be "seen" in his earliest work. There is even a third echo of the *De regressu animae* in these short chapters of the *Retractationes*: *alio loco de animo cum agerem dixi; securior rediturus in caelum. Iturus autem, quam rediturus dixissem securius, propter eos qui putant animos humanos pro meritis peccatorum suorum de coelo lapsos siue deiectos, in corpora ista detrudi.* But he *had* used the *re-* and this would be natural if he had known the *De regressu animae*. It is too much to believe that these three items in his earliest works, pointing to the *De regressu animae*, were not in fact influenced by an early acquaintance with that work.

In passing it should be noted that in the *Retractationes* (I, 2) Augustine says that when he was writing them, the copy of *De beata uita* before him was incomplete: *istum librum nostro in codice interruptum reperi, et non parum minus habere*. One would like to know if the part referred to as then missing is—as the text suggests—the actual rather Platonic conclusion, and what he would have found to emend here? In this connection, it is also curious to note that in *Soliloquia* I, 1, 4, he had written *Qui gignit, et quem gignit, unum est*. This sounds Porphyrian rather than Plotinian. In any case he emends the *est* to *sunt* in the *Retractationes*.

The topics of Augustine's *Epistulae* that are contemporary cover similar Platonic themes—Nebridius described later (VI, 1) those he received himself as sounding of Christ, Plato and Plotinus.

The *Dialogues of Cassiciacum* in General

A preliminary remark might be made on the first of the *Dialogues*, the *Contra Academicos*. It is a curious work, inasmuch as although there is a lengthy discussion on the possibility of knowing *truth* through seeking (*inquisitio*) it, Augustine in a summary statement declares that he has not yet got human wisdom but that nevertheless he accepts above all others the *truth* guaranteed by the authority of *Christ*.[35] The movement of the tenth book of the *City of God* is similar, in that Augustine follows Porphyry, in the book there described as *De regressu animae*, in seeking for a *universal way of salvation of the soul* and once again accepts Christ as that way, although Porphyry had declared that he had not yet found the universal way. In broad outline, therefore, the movement of Augustine's quest for *truth* in the *Contra Academicos* is parallel to the movement of his quest for *salvation* in the tenth book of the *City of God*. In the *City of God* his philosopher counterpart is Porphyry. In the *Contra Academicos* it is Cicero for the most part—but the *Platonici*, that is Neoplatonists, are involved in the end too.

The passages from the *Dialogues of Cassiciacum*, which I have already suggested[36] may have connection with Porphyry's *Philosophy from Oracles*, are as follows: (R I, 4, 3): CA I, 1, 3, 11; II, 2, 5, 6f., 22, 24; III, 11, 13, 34, 42; DBV 3, 31, 33, 36; DOR I, 10, 13f., 20; II, 16.

To these might now be added for consideration—especially in view of Hadot's work—for example the passages that discuss the Trinity (e.g., CA II, 4; DBV 34ff.; DOR II, 16, 26, 46, 51); the *uia negativa* (e.g., DOR II, 44, 47); purgation (e.g., DOR II, 51f.); and the ascent to God (e.g., CA II, 4–6; DOR II, 43, 51). Consideration might also be given to the significance of the presence of themes such as *esse* and *non esse* (DBV

31f.); *deus non solum agit omnia sed agitur etiam deus ordine* (cf. Eusebius, *Praeparatio Euangelica* IV, 5, 1: πῇ μὲν ἄγειν πῇ δὲ ἄγεσθαι: cf. *Philosophy from Oracles*); the real *ego* being the *mens* (e.g., CA I, 5, 7, 14); happiness being achieved in the search for truth (e.g., CA I, 5: cf. Eusebius, *Praeparatio Euangelica* V, 14, 4: τοῦ κατ᾽ἀρετὴν καὶ φιλοσοφίαν τρόπου πρὸς εὐδαίμονα καὶ μακάριον αὐτάρκους τυγχάνοντος βίον); philosophy liberates only the few (cf. CA II, 7; DOR II, 16).

There are also terms and phrases[37] which might repay examination in this context: for example—CA I, 23 *se ipsum in semet ipsum colligat* (cf. DOR I, 3: *animum in se ipsum colligendi*); II, 4: *illi flammulae*[38] *instillarunt . . . unguenti guttas paucissimas incredibile . . . incendium concitarunt*; 5: *redeo ad me* (cf. II, 5: *totus in me cursim redibam*; DOR I, 3: *sibi animus redditus*; 30: *redire in semet ipsum*); 7: *illa uisco libidinis detracta caelo suo et inclusa cauea populari*[39]; *DBV* 35: *de ipso fonte*[40] *ueritatis emanat . . . iubar sol ille secretus infundit . . . ipso fonte . . . plenitudine saturati nondum ad nostrum modum*[41] *nos peruenisse fateamur . . . DOR I, 4: cui diuina semina committantur*; 20 *scintillae*[42]; II, 44: *stabilis motus*[43]; 46: *potestas*; 47: *quid sit unum*.[44]

While all of these themes and expressions—and the list is not comprehensive in any sense—might be considered as generally Platonic, Hadot has suggested that some of them may be more specifically Porphyrian. This is not to say that, if so, they are again necessarily to be associated in any way with the *Philosophy from Oracles*: but in view of the contentions that Augustine had read the *De regressu animae* at the time of his writing these *Dialogues*, and that the *De regressu animae* is to be identified with part or whole of the *Philosophy from Oracles*, this association may be possible and so these items should be recorded—but no more, I think, is justified.

Specific Considerations

We now come to specific considerations in relation to our topic.

I. Astronomy (astrology), Arithmetic, Geometry and Music as studies preliminary to Philosophy

In Eusebius's *Praeparatio Euangelica*[45] (XIV, 10, 10), in a context introduced by the naming of Porphyry's *Philosophy from Oracles*, we find the following: "they (i.e., the philosophers) go about boasting everywhere of their mathematical sciences and saying that it is altogether necessary for those who are going to attempt the comprehension of truth to pursue the study of astronomy, arithmetic, geometry, music—for that without these a man cannot be accomplished in learning and philosophy, nay, cannot even touch the truth of things, unless the knowledge of these sciences has been previously impressed upon his soul . . ." Augustine, although his first intention was to discuss in *De ordine* the profounder questions related to this topic, in fact found that his interlocutors were not capable of such a discussion. Hence the whole later portion of *De ordine* is taken up with the order of studies essential (cf. DOR II, 15, 25, 44) for philosophic contemplation. These disciplines culminate in astrology, arithmetic, geometry, and music (II, 41, 42) and lead to an ascent of the soul (II, 43). The presence of this theme and list of subjects may be purely accidental—but it *need* not be, as we shall see immediately: it might be explained by reference to Porphyry.[46]

II. *Oracles*

I have already drawn attention to the presence in the opening paragraph of the *Contra Academicos* of what is tantamount to the title *Philosophy from Oracles*: *quam sententiam uberrimarum doctrinarum oraculis editam remotamque longissime ab intellectu profanorum se demonstraturam ueris amatoribus suis ad quam te inuito philosophia pollicetur.* Philosophy promises to demonstrate a teaching made available from *Oracles* of richest doctrines. Apart from the equivalent occurrence of the title in this way, two further items point to Porphyry's own preface to his book: the book *promised*: "Sure, then, and steadfast is he who draws his hopes of salvation from this as from the only sure source . . ." The book warned against communication of its doctrine to the profane: "And do thou endeavour to avoid publishing these above all things, and casting them even before the profane . . . these things I beg you to conceal as the most unutterable of secrets . . ." (Eusebius, *Praeparatio Euangelica* IV, 7f.) Augustine had shortly before spoken of *respiratio* and *libertas mentis*: both terms occur equivalently as ἀνάπαυσις and τῆς ψυχῆς σωτηρία in Porphyry's own preface.

The term *oracula* occurs also in *De beata uita*, 31: *mentes uestras, inquam, cum intenti estis in deum, uelut quaedam oracula non contemnere statui.* Here Augustine would seem to be "realizing" the philosophical oracles delivered by the gods to those attuned to them. *De ordine* I, 10 has the following: *Sic pater ille deus faciat* (Virgil, *Aen.* X, 875). *Perducet enim ipse, si sequimur, quo nos ire iubet atque ubi ponere sedem, qui dat modo augurium nostrisque inlabitur animis. Nec enim altus Apollo* (Virgil,

Aeneid III, 88f.) *est, qui in speluncis in montibus in memoribus nidore turis pecudumque calamitate concitatus inplet insanos, sed alius profecto est, alius ille altus ueridicus*. The inspiration by Virgil's *Aeneid* is beyond doubt. But it is difficult to exclude the oracles of Apollo in the *Philosophy from Oracles*. Here is an extract from the fragments:

> So when the prophet was eager to see the deity with his own eyes, and was urgent, Apollo said that such a thing was impossible before giving ransom to the wicked daemon. And these are his words:
>
>> 'To the dread genius of thy fatherland
>> Bring thou, for ransom meet, libations first,
>>
>>   in order lay
>> Thy entrails, and the rich libations pour.
>>
>> O daemon, crowned king of erring souls
>> Beneath dark caves, and on the earth above . . .'
>>   (Eusebius, *Praeparatio Euangelica* IV, 20, 1f.)

In one of the longest fragments of the *Philosophy from Oracles* (Eusebius, *Praeparatio Euangelica* IV, 9), Apollo describes the sacrifices appropriate to the descending scale of gods—the slaughter of flocks and the offering of incense. But the majority of the existing fragments deal with Apollo, inspiration and sacrifice in shrine or cave.

In *De ordine* I, 14 occurs the phrase: *aliqui uates magnus aut Chaldeus respondere debuerit*. It is a Chaldaean (oracular) response and can only suggest that in Augustine's mind at the time of writing were the *Chaldaean Oracles* which, as we have seen, a number of scholars believe were used both in the *De regressu animae* and *Philosophy from Oracles*.

Apart from other instances of unusual inspiration in the *Dialogues* (CA II, 2: *non erumpet aliquando ista uirtus et multorum desperantium risus in horrorem stuporemque conuertet et locuta in terris quasi quaedam futurorum signa rursus proiecto totius corporis onere recurret in caelum*;[47] DBV 10: *ex quo diuino fonte*; DOR I, 13: *per quem mihi ille respondeat . . . cuius te quidem credo quandoque uatem futurum*; 16: *subito ille quasi mente quadam correptus exclamat*; 20: *quae minus pasta eruditione disciplinarum tantum deum fortasse sustinere non poterit*; 28: *aduenticio spiritu me credis inflatum*) one particular phrase in the passage (DOR I, 14) where the Chaldeus was mentioned brings us very close to the *Philosophy from Oracles* and (if separate) the *De regressu animae*. It reads: *Numquidnam enim talia futura quisquam illorum aut per se dixit aliquando aut a consultore coactus est dicere.*

The *Philosophy from Oracles* has long passages (e.g., Eusebius, *Praeparatio Euangelica* V, 8f.) describing how the gods were constrained against their will by their clients to respond. Augustine himself in the tenth book of the *City of God* (9, 10, 26- and also 11- which is inspired by Porphyry's *Letter to Anebo*) reports similar phenomena.

It is impossible to deny that there is in the *Dialogues of Cassiciacum* an unusual use of the technique of inspiration and possession by a "god" in order to account for certain surprising doctrines being propounded. Whether or not Augustine did believe in this or simply used a *motif* taken from the oracles, it must be concluded that philosophy from oracles, from Apollo, from Chaldaeans was very much in his mind when he wrote the *Dialogues of Cassiciacum*.

III. *Demons*

As for oracles, so for the associated demons—their presence in these *Dialogues* has not been sufficiently observed. They appear very prominently, however, throughout sections 20 and 21 of *Contra Academicos* I: *sentiri possunt ab huius aeris animalibus quibusdam uilissimis, quos daemonas uocant.* They appear again in *De ordine* II, 27: *metuenda est aeriorum animalium mira fallacia, quae per rerum ad istos sensus corporis pertinentium quasdam diuinationes nonnullasque potentias decipere animas facillime consuerunt.* These sentiments correspond with the existing fragments of the *Philosophy from Oracles*, but more particularly with Augustine's remarks about the demons in relation to the *Philosophy from Oracles* in the *City of God* (XIX, 23) and the *De regressu animae* (X), *De beata uita* repeats[48] three times the phrase *spiritum immundum* (*habere*) found in the Porphyrian *City of God* X, 27.

IV. *Omne corpus fugiendum*

I have given my reasons for associating the phrase *omne corpus fugiendum* as found in the *City of God* XXII, 26 with Porphyry's *Philosophy from Oracles*[49]: *Sed Porphyrius ait, inquiunt, ut beata sit anima, corpus esse omne fugiendum.* The precise meaning of *corpus fugiendum* here is made certain by both *ut beata sit anima*—that is, its happiness in *the next life*—and (at the end of chapter 26) *Non ergo, ut beatae sint animae, corpus est omne fugiendum, sed corpus incorruptibile recipiendum*—which again clearly refers to the soul's future life. Porphyry objected to *any* body: the Christians believed that the soul would be joined to an incorrupt body. Throughout the *City of God*, including the tenth book, this is a primary meaning for the phrase omne corpus fugiendum.[50]

Of course the phrase can also be used in an ascetic or purificatory or general Platonic sense—we must avoid the things of the body to cultivate our soul. But even this sense implies the other one. The purpose of asceticism here is escape from the material body in the next life.

It goes without saying that there are many phrases in the *Dialogues* which are similar to the *omne corpus fugiendum,* at least in the ascetic sense. Augustine himself, as we have seen in *Retractationes* I, 4, 3, felt that words of his in *Soliloquia* I, 24 might have been construed in the eschatological sense. In the *Soliloquia* (I, 24) he had written: *unum est quod tibi possum praecipere, nihil plus noui. Penitus esse ista sensibilia fugienda, cauendumque magnopere, dum hoc corpus agimus, ne quo eorum uisco pennae nostrae impediantur, quibus integris perfectisque opus est ut ad illam lucem ab his tenebris euolemus: quae se ne ostendere quidem dignatur in hac cauea inclusis, nisi tales fuerint ut ista uel effracta uel dissoluta possint in auras suas euadere.*[51] Here there is a fairly clear reference to Plato's cave and the phrase *dum hoc corpus agimus* places the sense in relation to this life—but the purpose of the asceticism in this is again linked to escape from the body hereafter. When emending this in the *Retractationes* (I, 4, 3) Augustine wrote: *non autem dixi ego, omnia sensibilia; sed ista, hoc est, corruptibilia.* But his words had, as he acknowledged, a Porphyrian ring and left themselves open to interpretation in an eschatological sense.

Let us look at some—but not all—similar expressions in the *Dialogues. Contra Academicos* I, 3 has: *(philosophia) docet nihil omnino colendum esse . . . quidquid . . . ullus sensus attingit.* Here are the essentials in idiom, words and sense to make a correspondence with *omne corpus fugiendum.* The phrase following again reminds one of the preface to the *Philosophy from Oracles: (philosophia) uerissimum et secretissimum deum perspicue se demonstraturum promittit et iam iamque quasi per lucidas nubes ostentare dignatur.* Again, as in the shortly preceding preface to the *Contra Academicos* there is emphasis on *promise, demonstration, secrecy*—as in Porphyry's preface. *Per lucidas nubes* is altogether in the style of the *Oracles.*

Contra Academicos I, 11, has: *ab omni corporis labe uindicantes*—a purely ascetical sense; 23 has: *cum ab omnibus inuolucris corporis mentem quantum potest euoluit et se ipsum in semet ipsum colligit;* II, 2, has: *proiecto totius corporis onere recurret in caelum,* which, though having *totius* in place of *omnis* and a different idiom, introduces the eschatological sense. *De beata uita* 4 has: *cum de deo cogitaretur, nihil omnino corporis esse cogitandum, neque cum de anima*—essentially an eschatological sense. *De ordine* I,

32 has: *scripturae . . . philosophos huius mundi euitandos . . . praecipiunt . . . quisquis omnem philosophiam fugiendam putat, nihil nos uult aliud quam non amare sapientiam*. Here we have the equivalent idiom *omnem philosophiam fugiendam*. The use of *philosophia* instead of *corpus* does not depart that much from the sense of *corpus*, since there is question here of philosophies based on material or immaterial principles, as elsewhere there is question of material and immaterial bodies. *De ordine* II, 31 has: *admonendus erat homo, et quo sibi redeundum est, et unde fugiendum*. The context supplies *mortal* to go with *fugiendum*: this is an eschatological sense. *De ordine* II, 50 in fact gives the phrase: *a mortali ad inmortale fugiendum est*—clearly eschatological.

It is incontestible that in the *Dialogues* Augustine shows a tendency to use gerundival forms in sentiments, idioms, and expressions very close indeed to Porphyry's *omne corpus fugiendum* both in an ascetical and the related eschatological sense.[52]

V. *Regressus*

We now come to the connected theme of the "return" (*regressus*) of the soul. Again I have pointed out that *regressus* is used in two senses: that of return to one's original state, the Fatherland, the Father; and that of return to body in the cycle of rebirths.[53] It is in fact another version of the *omne corpus fugiendum*—one departs from bodily things in this life to return to the Father, and when in the next life, one does not return to a body in this. As in the *omne corpus fugiendum* either or both senses may be present according to the context; in the main, however, *regressus* is taken in the sense of return to the Father. Leaving the Father for body again is described (DCD X, 30) as *abire*.

The process of descent and return is described briefly twice in *De ordine* II, 30f.: *in istorum sensuum negotia progresso redire in semet ipsum cuique difficile est*—this has the ascetic sense. *Nam ut progressus animae usque ad mortalia lapsus est, ita regressus* (i.e., *animae*) *esse in rationem debet*—this is clearly the eschatological sense. It is to be noted that the expression *regressus animae*—the title used in DCD X—is virtually found here. The term *progressus* is also found in SO I, 25: *quantum autem mersi eramus, et quo progressi fueramus* . . .

It is natural, however, that we should be more concerned with *regressus* than *progressus*. CA II, 2 uses the term *recurrere* while in 7, in a Porphyrian context, it uses *reuolare*.[54] 22 has: *in regionem suae originis rediens . . . securior rediturus in caelum*. It will be recalled that in the

Retractationes[55] Augustine felt that it would have been safer—from a Christian point of view—to use *iturus*. In this context the ascetical sense is combined with that part of the eschatological sense which deals with arrival in the Fatherland—without any reference to the commencement of a new cycle in rebirth. DBV 1f. has: *quaue (sc. uia) redeundum . . . longeque a sua patria peregrinari . . . reducuntur . . . signa respiciunt et suae dulcissimae patriae quamuis in ipsis fluctibus recordantur et aut recto cursu in nullo falsi et nihil morati eam repetunt aut plerumque uel inter nubila deuiantes . . . errant*. Here the theme is related to a journey to the Fatherland over the sea.[56] Elsewhere this favourite theme of Augustine's is related to a journey over land—often delayed by the tricks of demons.[57] DBV 36 speaks simply of *ad deum reditus noster.*

VI. *Index*

One of the favorite mythological figures for revealing something one needs to, but cannot get to, know is Proteus. Augustine in CA III, 11ff. introduces him as a symbol of truth[58] which can be pointed out (*demonstrare*) only by some deity (*numen*): the deity in question is described in DOR II, 43 as *universae ueritatis index* and is clearly Christ.

VII. *Via*

Finally we come to the commonest aspect of the theme of the return of the soul as found in, for example, DCD X and the *Dialogues*—the allegory of the way, *uia*. It is, of course, implicit in *fugiendum*, in *regressus*, and in *index*. It is found in Plotinus. But there are also the precedent of Moses leading his people to the Promised Land, the Wise Men after visiting the newborn Christ returning by another way home to their own country, and of the Prodigal Son finding his way home from a foreign land. All or any of these may have been present on any particular occasion in Augustine's mind as he was writing the *Dialogues*. But in DCD X the way he had in mind was the universal way to liberate the soul (*uia uniuersalis animae liberandae*) which Porphyry had failed to find in Greek philosophy or the Oracles, though they spoke of ways to the Father, and which Augustine identified in Christ.

Let us simply take some relevant texts as they occur in order in the *Dialogues*. CA I, 11, 12 and III, 34 go together. They give the allegory of a journey (in I, 11 and 12 using the so-called Porphyrian example of Alexandria—a distant city visited by the imagination) over land. In the earlier instances the traveller, beset by many difficulties, never arrives. In the second instance two travellers are in question. At a crossroads one trusts a simple shepherd who tells him to take a particular road: he arrives, by this in fact right road, at his destination in good time. The other pridefully doesn't believe the shepherd, but, getting tired of waiting, follows, without believing it, the directions of a pretentious and deceiving mountebank: as a result he takes the wrong road and wanders through woods and trackless mountains to the desired region. It is difficult not to see in this allegory some connection with the same theme as treated often by Augustine in, for example, C VII, 26f., DT IV, 13–20 and DCD X, 29, 32 and also in the *Philosophy from Oracles* (Eusebius, *Praeparatio Euangelica* IX, 10).[59]

CA II, 5,[60] a most important passage which rehearses the story of Augustine's conversion has: *respexi tamen, confiteor, quasi de itinere in illam religionem, quae pueris nobis insita est et medullitus inplicata. uerum autem ipsa ad se nescientem rapiebat.* The intrusion of *itinere* is puzzling and is most easily explained in the context of the *De regressu animae* of Porphyry—for Porphyry refused to accept Christ as the way and accused the disciples of Christ and especially St. Paul of infamy.[61] Hence the words immediately following in CA II, 5: *arripio apostolum Paulum. Neque enim uere, inquam, isti tanta potuissent uixissentque ita, ut eos uixisse manifestum est, si eorum litterae atque rationes huic tanto bono aduersarentur.* The *isti* immediately recalls the *Christiani* of DCD XIX, 23 whom the *Philosophy from Oracles* accused of many crimes and errors.

CA III, 42 has a clear reference to Christ as the universal way of return of souls to the Father: *animas multiformibus erroris caecatas et altissimis a corpore sordibus oblitas numquam ista ratio subtilissima reuocaret, nisi summus deus populari quadam clementia diuini intellectus auctoritatem usque ad ipsum corpus humanum declinaret atque summitteret, cuius non solum praeceptis sed etiam factis excitatae animae redire in semet ipsas et resipiscere patriam etiam sine disputationum concertatione potuissent.* Here the way of philosophy for the few and of a universal way for the return of souls to the Fatherland is undeniably as present as it is in DCD X.

DOR II, 15f. again speaks of the ways to salvation (*liberaret, salutem*) for the few (philosophy) and the many (Christ). The Christian mysteries save all (*populos liberant.* cf. 29: *universos populos*). There is a reference to contempt of the Incarnation which almost certainly refers to Porphyry. 26f. continues the same theme of salvation (*liberari*) at length: here there is much emphasis upon the activities of demons who would deceive men. 50 speaks of the soul (*anima*) following a *deuium iter* in life.

SO I, 3 has: *Deus qui nos reuocas in uiam*; 23 has: *sed non ad eam (sapientiam) una uia peruenitur.* In R I, 4, 3 where, as we have seen, he mentioned Porphyry's *omne corpus fugiendum,* Augustine regretted that he had seemed here to consider a way (i.e., philosophy) other than Christ. SO II, 25, 27 touch lightly upon the present theme.

The *Philosophy from Oracles* and *City of God* X

In the preceding pages I have given some specific reasons and referred to others for concluding that the presence of the *Philosophy from Oracles* and the *De regressu animae* (which I hold to be the whole or part of the *Philosophy from Oracles*) can be discerned in the *Dialogues of Cassiciacum*. The full appreciation of the evidence requires a very careful reading indeed of the other evidence to which I refer.[62] As in my *Porphyry's Philosophy from Oracles in Augustine* I related what I found of Porphyry's *Philosophy from Oracles* in the *City of God* XIX, 23; XX, 24; XVIII, 53–54; XXII, 25–28, the *De consensu euangelistarum* and *Sermo* 241, 7 to Porphyrian remains (exclusive of the *Letter to Anebo*[63]) in the *City of God* X, so now I shall summarily relate, in a similar limited and internal argument, and by way of final conclusion, the traces of the *Philosophy from Oracles* that I have suspected in the *Dialogues* to Porphyrian remains (again exclusive of the *Letter to Anebo*) in the *City of God* X—always using the acknowledged fragments of the *Philosophy from Oracles* as a guide.

There is in the early part of *City of God* X fairly clear references to the *Philosophy from Oracles* in the references to God's need of nothing and our doing ourselves good in sacrificing to him (cf. *City of God* XIX, 23), but Porphyry is not mentioned until chapter 9, and then he is formally mentioned and remains the chief concern of Augustine until the end of the tenth book.

Although the point has not been appreciated[64] Porphyry is introduced in relation to *one* of his books, and in *City of God* X, chapter 29 Augustine tells us that he has quoted much (*multa*) from a book which he refers to as *De regressu animae.* His use of the *Letter to Anebo* in chapter 11 is formally mentioned and formally concluded within the chapter—it is an intrusion. From chapter 9 to the end of the tenth book *one* work of Porphyry's is mainly used and that is the one mentioned in chapter 9 and again in chapters 29 and 32. It is clear from his introduction of the work in chapter 9 that that work is a curious mixture: *Nam et Porphyrius quan-*

dam quasi purgationem animae per theurgian, cunctanter tamen et pudibunda quodam modo disputatione promittit; reuersionem uero ad Deum hanc artem praestare cuiquam negat; ut uideas eum inter uitium sacrilegae curiositatis et philosophiae professionem sententiis alternantibus fluctuare. The *promittit* suggest the terms of Porphyry's preface to the *Philosophy from Oracles*;[65] a restrained reference to purgation through divination is also in that preface;[66] as is the information that divination is of small account in comparison with philosophy for those in travail for the truth. In Porphyry's own preface to the work there is already some conflict—between divination and philosophy—with philosophy gaining the upper hand. In this sense one might say that that preface was hesitating and shamefaced or at any rate ambiguous.

It is clear in any case that there is this kind of conflict within the *disputatio* described in *City of God* X, 9: Porphyry is ashamed of the theurgy[67] in it, but he still says that this theurgy can purge up to a certain point; theurgy, however, he insists cannot give *return* to God to anyone. Here we have combined in one book elements, seemingly discordant, such as we find in the fragments of the *Philosophy from Oracles* and the *De regressu animae*. The title of the former is certain; the title of the latter is not known outside of *City of God* X, 29 and 32. Fragments of the *Philosophy from Oracles* are already acknowledged as being in the *City of God* X.[68] Chapters 9–22 (exclusive of 11) treat of the exact topics found in the fragments of the *Philosophy from Oracles*.[69] The theme of the universal way is said to come at the end of the first book of the *De regressu animae*: likewise the treatment of a way to the gods comes in the first book of the *Philosophy from Oracles*. Other weighty arguments I have developed at length elsewhere.[70] The absence of any reference to the *De regressu animae* in Eusebius's *Praeparatio euangelica* cannot but be highly significant: he could hardly have avoided mentioning it. The objections to the identification of the two works on grounds of discrepancy of "ton" or chronology have no sound base whatever: for it is admitted that the *disputatio* mentioned in Augustine's *City of God* X, 9 and Porphyry's preface (Eusebius, *Prae. eu.* IV, 6, 2ff.) is a curious mixture; and insofar as there are any chronological indications they allow both items to have been written at the same period.[71]

Right through *City of God* X, Porphyry is consistently represented as being ambiguous in his attitude to demonology. If at chapter 9 the term *pudibunda* is used, at 24 and 26 *erubescebat* is employed, and in 27 and 28 Porphyry is still accused of not being clear.

Much of the *Philosophy from Oracles*—and sections of the *Dialogues of Cassiciacum*, as we have seen⁷²—deal with demons and their deceits. In *City of God* X, they are said to demand sacrifice (16), to block men in their efforts at return (19)—themes strongly present in the fragments of the *Philosophy from Oracles*. Of course the arranging of the "gods" in a hierarchy⁷³ (DCD X, 26) and the selection of sacrifices according to their scale of materiality or immateriality, visibility or invisibility (DCD X, 19) is also prominent in the fragments of the *Philosophy from Oracles*.⁷⁴ The discussion of Heroes (DCD X, 21) is allotted by Wolff to the whole of the third book of the *Philosophy from Oracles*.⁷⁵ All in all there seems no reasonable ground for refusing any longer to accept that chapters 9–22 (exclusive of 11) of the tenth book of the *City of God* is influenced primarily by the *Philosophy from Oracles*. The phrase (DCD X, 23) *dicit etiam Porphyrius diuinis oraculis fuisse responsum* can refer naturally to Porphyry's own plan of giving the responses of the gods συναγωγὴν ἐποιήσατο χρησμῶν τοῦ τε Ἀπόλλωνος καὶ τῶν λοιπῶν θεῶν, or, as he resumes in his preface: "the present collection will contain a record of many doctrines of philosophy, according as *the gods* declared (ἐθέσπισαν) the truth to be.⁷⁶ And when Augustine says (DCD X, 27) that Porphyry learnt his demonology from the Chaldaeans, we can point to the obvious prominence of the Chaldaeans in the *Philosophy from Oracles* and the presence of Chaldaean Oracles there too.⁷⁷

The theme that philosophers can win happiness without theurgy is found in the *Philosophy from Oracles*, in Augustine's *Dialogues*, and in the *City of God* X, 27.⁷⁸ The further important and connected theme that Providence could not leave mankind without some universal way to salvation is likewise present in the *City of God* X, 32: *prouidentiam quippe diuinam sine ista uniuersali uia liberandae animae genus humanum relinquere potuisse non credit*, and in *De ordine* II, 15: *haec . . . cogunt homines plerumque inpie credere nullo nos ordine diuinae prouidentiae gubernari; alios autem pios et bonos atque splendido ingenio praeditos, qui neque nos deseri a summo deo possunt in animum inducere . . . ab his horrendis et inuolutissimis malis liberet ille (Christus)*. Although the special role of the Hebrews in discovering a way of return is prominent in the *Philosophy from Oracles*⁷⁹ and *City of God* X, 32, there is no mention of this in the *Dialogues*.

It is, of course, difficult even to follow carefully the kind of argument given here and to relate to it the writing of others and myself on this point. Clear demonstration in such a field, moreover, is hardly possible.

I submit, however, that there is good ground for the view that the *De regressu animae* and the *Philosophy from Oracles* are to be identified, perhaps the former as part only of the latter; and that the *Philosophy from Oracles* had been read by Augustine at the time of his writing the *Dialogues of Cassiciacum*.[80]

14

Plotinus and Augustine
Exegesis of *Contra Academicos* II, 5

❧

No one, I think, would now dispute some influence of Plotinus on Augustine immediately before his conversion in 386 A.D. Even if the reading *Plotini* in "lectis autem Plotini paucissimis libris" (*De beata uita* 4) is not absolutely certain, there is independent evidence enough in the *Dialogues of Cassiciacum* and Augustine's correspondence of the time to prove it.[1]

There is still some dispute on the extent of Augustine's acquaintance, directly or indirectly through translation, with Plotinus's *Enneads* or doctrine at this or any later time. Some scholars have tended to multiply the number of "loci" in the *Enneads* to which they trace specific items in Augustine. Thus O'Connell[2] recently suggests dependence on some seventeen to twenty-one treatises; Nörregard had indicated twenty-two, and Grandgeorge twenty-six in all. On the other hand Henry would limit the number to two or three.[3] The present writer is inclined to say five or six.

The commonest error in these matters is to attribute to Plotinus specifically doctrine that could naturally have come from the stock-in-trade of ancient philosophy.[4] Neoplatonism, in the words of Dodds, was "really a new synthesis of Platonic, Pythagorean, Aristotelian, and Stoic elements."[5] Augustine, significantly for our present contention, first mentions Plotinus in this way:

> os illud Platonis, quod in philosophia purgatissimum est et lucidissimum, dimotis nubibus erroris emicuit maxime in Plotino, qui Platonicus philosophus ita eius similis iudicatus est, ut simul eos uixisse, tantum autem interest temporis, ut in hoc ille reuixisse putandus sit."[6]

Plotinus, for Augustine in 386, was Plato come to life. It is almost certainly true, moreover, that when he refers to "Platonicorum libri" he is at least including something of the Neoplatonists.

It may also be significant that two scholars who have most convincingly established definite connection between Augustine and the *En-*

neads have both done so in relation to mystical aspirations—Henry in his *La vision d'Ostie* (1938) and Courcelle in the section "Les vaines tentatives d'extases Plotiniennes" of his *Recherches sur les Confessions de saint Augustin* (1950, pp. 157–67) where he adds the important contribution of Ambrose. Again the inclination of the present writer is to think that the dominant influence of Plotinus on Augustine just before his conversion was in this stimulation to mystical ascent. Such mystical aspirations were, of course, known to the world of philosophy long before Plotinus and were not always clearly separated in Augustine's mind from scriptural themes such as the return of the prodigal.[7] Augustine was greatly given to repeated use of a number of themes in various artistic and useful formulations. One of these dominant and oft-repeated themes is that of "ascent," "flight," "return" or "conversion": it recurs so often in short phrases, long passages, whole books and even whole works (such as the "peregrinatio" that is the *City of God*) that one may feel justified in calling it Augustine's "conversion" syndrome. While, as I have said, other elements may enter into this syndrome, a primary element is the stimulation of Plotinus, and principally *Ennead* I, 6, *On Beauty*.

It is not necessary, of course, to believe that Augustine actually attempted Plotinian ecstasy—although it was very much in his essentially ambitious character so to do. But there can be no denying that he loved to describe such orisons:[8] the evidence given by Courcelle from the *Confessions* is proof enough. But it has escaped notice, maybe, that many of the Neoplatonic passages in the *Dialogues of Cassiciacum* are also concerned with what for brevity I call the "conversion syndrome."

There are, as I have said, a number of instances of this syndrome in the *Dialogues*,[9] but here I shall confine myself to that found in the preface to the second book of the *Contra Academicos*. This is the earliest description of his conversion by Augustine. It has very close connection with the account he gives of his first "conversion" by the *Hortensius* of Cicero and his later conversion to Christianity, both to be found in the *Confessions*. It is a very difficult passage to understand. The present study attempts to show that the secret of its understanding is to be found in certain passages of the eighth book of the *Confessions*,[10] and that that understanding places the role of Plotinus on Augustine, perhaps, in a proper light.

It should be remarked that this is an argument internal to Augustine's own works.[11] I believe that, especially in the case of Augustine, this must be used to control the evidence of parallel texts from other authors: Augustine has a disconcerting habit—as we shall see—of using borrowed phrases in senses quite different from their original ones.

It is incontrovertible that according to his *Confessions* Augustine was inflamed by the reading of Neoplatonist books (Book VII), that he then began to read St. Paul (Book VIII, 6, 14) and *then* really "burst into a conflagration," so to speak (VIII, 7, 16ff.). This precise articulation is literally confirmed by the unequivocal evidence of *De beata uita* 4:

> lectis autem Plotini paucissimis libris . . . conlataque cum eis quantum potui, etiam illorum auctoritate, qui diuina mysteria tradiderunt, sic exarsi, ut omnes illas uellem ancoras rumpere, nisi me nonnullorum hominum existimatio commoueret.

This clearly bears out the testimony of the *Confessions* that the real climax came not after reading the Neoplatonist books (though that had provoked a climax of its own), but after the reading of the Christian books. This is an essential point on which to base our argument.

Nevertheless *Contra Academicos* II, 5 has usually been understood to mean that the real climax came after the reading of the Neoplatonist books:[12]

> cum ecce tibi libri quidam pleni, ut ait Celsinus, bonas res Arabicas ubi exhalarunt in nos, ubi illi flammulae instillarunt pretiosissimi unguenti guttas paucissimas, incredibile . . . incendium concitarunt. Quis me tunc honor, quae hominum pompa, quae inanis famae cupiditas, quod denique huius mortalis uitae fomentum atque retinaculum commouebat?

If this passage is to accord with the text just quoted from the *De beata uita* IV and *Confessions* VII and VIII the *libri* referred to are not Neoplatonist but are Christian books.

This, of course, redresses the balance of Neoplatonist as against Christian influence at this time on Augustine—indeed it would remove the seeming evidence of the one text which would give primary emphasis to Neoplatonism. But Augustine's contemporary attitude is certain:

> Mihi ergo certum est nusquam prorsus a Christi auctoritate discedere; non enim reperio ualentiorem. Quod autem subtilissima ratione persequendum est—ita enim iam sum affectus, ut quid sit uerum non credendo solum sed etiam intelligendo apprehendere impatienter desiderem—apud Platonicos me interim, quod sacris nostris non repugnet, reperturum esse credo.[13]

Moreover, it is evident from the *Retractationes* that Augustine was in the end disappointed in his expectations of Neoplatonism, and indeed justifies in the present writer's view[14] Gilson's judgment that "Augustine seems much less concerned with introducing Neoplatonism into Christian theology than with limiting its invasion. The theology of Victorinus shows what would have happened if the genius of Augustine had not kept Neoplatonism within the strict limits of Christian faith."[15]

But in the beginning Augustine did expect a great deal of Neoplatonism.

It would be tedious to outline the contents of *Confessions* VII and VIII. Courcelle in "Les vaines tentatives d'extases Plotiniennes" has quite sufficiently developed and stressed the importance of the influence on Augustine of Plotinus's *Ennead* 1, 6. I am not going to repeat this here. One element in *Ennead* 1, 6 which tends to be underemphasized is the purificatory: this is a connecting link between *Confessions* VII and Plotinus with VIII, Antony and St. Paul. *Confessions* VIII recounts in succession a series of conversions: that of Victorinus (with passing reference to the conversion of St. Paul), that of Antony of Egypt, and that of the companions of Ponticianus and their *fiancées*.

Although the eighth book of the *Confessions as a whole* is a conversion story using the terms[16] of other conversion themes, we must content ourselves here by concentrating on a number of passages which have been rather neglected and are relevant to our present purpose. It will be convenient to indicate (but indicate only) some phrasing interesting especially in connection with *Contra Academicos* II, 4–7: C VIII, 6, 14:

> *Quodam igitur* die—*non recolo* causam, qua erat absens Nebridius—*cum ecce* ad nos domum uenit ad me et Alypium *Ponticianus quidam . . . nescio quid* a nobis uolebat . . . *et forte* supra mensam lusoriam . . . adtendit *codicem: tulit, aperuit, inuenit apostolum Paulum, inopinate* sane . . . cui ego cum indicassem *illis me scripturis curam maximam inpendere,* ortus est sermo ipso narrante de Antonio Aegyptio monacho, cuius nomen clarebat apud seruos tuos, nos autem usque in illam horam latebat. quod ille ubi comperit, inmoratus est in eo sermone *insinuans*[17] tantum uirum ignorantibus et *admirans* eandem nostram ignorantiam. *stupebamus* autem audientes tam recenti memoria et prope nostris temporibus testatissima mirabilia tua in fide recta et *catholica ecclesia* (6, 15). Inde sermo eius deuolutus est ad monasteriorum greges et mores *suaueolentiae tuae* et *ubera deserta heremi,* quorum nos nihil sciebamus, et erat monasterium Mediolanii *plenum* bonis fratribus extra urbis

moenia sub Ambrosio nutritore, et *non noueramus. pertendebat* ille et loquebatur adhuc, et nos *intenti tacebamus.* unde indicit, ut diceret *nescio quando* se et tres alios . . . exisse deambulatum in hortos . . . atque illic, ut *forte* combinati spatiabantur, unum secum seorsum et alios duos itidem seorsum pariterque digressos; sed illos uagabundos inruisse in *quandam* casam, ubi habitabant *quidam* serui tui . . . et inuenisse ibi *codicem,* in quo scripta erat uita Antonii. quam *legere coepit* unus eorum et mirari et *accendi* et inter legendum *meditari arripere talem uitam* et *relicta militia saeculari seruire* tibi . . . *tum subito repletus amore sancto* et *sobrio pudore* iratus sibi coniecit oculos in amicum et ait illi: "dic, quaeso te, omnibus istis *laboribus nostris quo ambimus peruenire?* . . . (much more on these lines) . . . amicus autem dei, si uoluero, *ecce* nunc fio." dixit hoc et *turbidus parturitione nouae uitae reddidit oculos* paginis: et *legebat* et *mutabatur intus,* ubi tu uidebas, et *exuebatur mundo mens eius,* ut mox apparuit. namque dum legit et *uoluit fluctus* cordis sui, *infremuit aliquando* et discreuit decreuitque meliora . . . (7, 16). Narrabat haec Ponticianus. tu autem, domine, inter uerba eius *retorquebas me ad me ipsum, auferens me a dorso meo* . . . ut uiderem, quam *turpis* essem, quam *distortus* et *sordidus, maculosus* et *ulcerosus,* et uidebam et *horrebam* . . . (7, 17). *Tunc uero quanto* ardentius amabam illos, de quibus audiebam salubres affectus, quod se totos tibi *sanandos* dederant, tanto exsecrabilius me comparatum eis oderam. (At this point he recalls the episode of the *Hortensius* "conversion"[18] in his nineteenth year) . . . (18). . . . terminato autem sermone . . . abiit (Ponticianus), et ego ad me.[19] . . . (19) ego *fremebam spiritu* indignans indignatione *turbulentissima,* quod non *irem in placitum et pactum tuum,* deus meus, in quod *eundum esse* omnia *ossa mea clamabant* et in caelum tollebant laudibus: et non illuc *ibatur nauibus* aut *quadrigis* aut *pedibus* . . . nam non solum *ire* uerum etiam *peruenire* illuc nihil erat aliud quam uelle *ire.*[20]

(11.26) *Retinebant*[21] nugae nugarum et *uanitates uanitatum,* antiquae amicae meae . . . et audiebam eas . . . non tamquam libere contradicentes *eundo in obuiam,* sed uelut a dorso mussitantes et discedentem quasi furtim uellicantes, ut *respicerem.* retardabant tamen cunctantem me *abripere* atque *excutere* ab eis et transilire *quo* uocabar, cum diceret mihi consuetudo uiolenta: "putasne sine istis *poteris?*"[22] Sed iam tepidissime hoc dicebat. aperiebatur enim ab ea parte *qua intenderem faciem* et *quo transire trepidabam,* casta dignitas continentiae, serena et non dissolute hilaris, honeste *blandiens,* ut uenirem neque *dubitarem,* et extendens ad me suscipiendum et amplectendum pias manus *plenas* gregibus bonorum exemplorum. ibi tot *pueri* et *puellae,* ibi iuuentus multa et omnis aetas et graues uiduae et uirgines anus, et in omnibus ipsa continentia nequaquam sterilis, sed fecunda mater filiorum gaudiorum de marito te, domine. et inridebat me inrisione hortatoria, quasi diceret: "tu non *poteris,* quod isti, quod istae?" an uero *isti et istae* in se ipsis *possunt* . . . (28) oborta est procella ingens ferens ingentem imbrem lacrimarum . . . (There follows immediately the ultimate climax of the "tolle lege" scene).

If one looks at *Contra Academicos* II, 4–7, which describes, at least in part, the same event, one should not be surprised to discover considerable, and for us here significant correspondence. To begin with the language of Neoplatonist ecstasy, ascent, flight or conversion is present as it is throughout *Confessions* VIII:

a superfluarum cupiditatium uinculis euolaui, quod depositis oneribus mortuarum curarum *respiro resipico redeo ad me* . . . me ad summum ipsum modum peruenturum esse confido . . . sancto huius uitae *inflammatus ardore* . . . omnia mea *uincula* . . . *rupturum.*

Again in Sections 6 and 7 we find the same kind of terminology:

quidquid . . . abiciens et *relinquens* ad huius *pulchritudinem blandus amator* et *sanctus mirans anhelans aestuans aduolaret* . . . *erumpere* in *ueram pulchritudinem nitens tortuose* ac *deformiter* inter *scabra uitiorum* et opinionum *fallacium dumeta frondescit* . . . (7) illa *uisco libidinis detracta caelo* suo et *inclusa cauea populari* uiciniam tamen nominis tenuit ad commonendum aucupem, ne illam contemnit. Hanc igitur sine *pennis sordidatam* et *egentem uolitans libere* soror saepe agnoscit, sed raro *liberat* . . . *ueram pulchritudinem* . . . *sanatis renudatisque oculis posset intueri.* facile *euadit,* facile *reuolat* hoc genus *auium* multis inclusis multum *mirantibus.*

The vital Section, however, is 5. This will have to be quoted in full:

Itaque cum admoto nobis fomite discessisses, numquam cessauimus *inhiantes* in philosophiam atque illam uitam, quae inter nos placuit atque conuenit, prorsus *nihil aliud cogitare* atque id constanter quidem, sed *minus acriter* agebamus, putabamus tamen satis nos agere. Et quoniam nondum aderat *ea flamma,* quae *summa nos arreptura erat,* illam qua *lenta aestuabamus* arbitrabamur esse uel *maximam,* cum *ecce* tibi *libri quidam pleni,* ut ait Celsinus, bonas res Arabicas ubi exhalarunt in nos, ubi illi *flammulae instillarunt* pretiosissimi *unguenti guttas paucissimas, incredibile,* Romaniane, incredibile et ultra quam de me fortasse et tu credis—quid amplius dicam?—etiam mihi ipsi de me ipso *incredibile incendium concitarunt.* Quis me tunc *honor,* quae hominum *pompa* quae *inanis famae cupiditas* quod denique huius mortalis uitae *fomentum* atque *retinaculum* commouebat? Prorsus *totus* in me *cursim redibam. Respexi* tantum, confiteor, *quasi de itinere* in illam *religionem,* quae *pueris nobis insita* est et *medullitas inplicata;* uerum autem ipsa ad se *nescientem rapiebat.* Itaque titubans properans haesitans arripio *apostolum Paulum.* Neque enim uere, inquam, *isti* tanta *potuissent uixissentque* ita, ut eos *uixisse* manifestum est, si eorum *litterae* atque *rationes* huic tanto bono aduersarentur. Perlegi totum *intentissime* atque cautissime.

In this paragraph too there is use of the same Neoplatonist ecstatic phraseology: the recurrence of this terminology in both *Confessions* VIII, and *Contra Academicos* II, 4–7, is, one hopes, quite sufficiently indicated by the italicizing here employed to draw attention to its general correspondence in both places.

The really important question, however, is to identify the *libri quidam pleni* in the *Contra Academicos* passage.

The mention of *libri quidam pleni* and *guttas paucissimas* has been a trap for scholars. Let us consider a little Augustine's use of these terms.

It is patent that Augustine can speak of *libri* that are not Platonist at all. In *Confessions* VIII, for example, he mentions the book in which was written the life of Antony (6, 15: "inuenisse ibi codicem, in quo scripta erat uita Antonii") and, moreover, its reading had an extraordinary effect upon Ponticianus's friend: "et *mirari* et *accendi* et inter legendum *meditari arripere talem uitam* et *relicta militia saeculari seruire tibi* . . . tum *subito repletus amore sancto* et *sobrio pudore* . . . et *mutabatur* intus." In fact he and his companions and their *fiancées* completely and dramatically changed their lives. A second book he mentions, of course, in *Confessions* VIII is the codex of St. Paul which he had been studying at length (6, 14: "illis me scripturis *curam maximam inpendere*").

"Quidam" as used by Augustine has been the occasion of much comment. The word might appear to suggest books that were unfamiliar— but since Augustine uses it of Cicero, for example, and Aeneas[23] (both of whom were quite familiar to Augustine) it does not as a matter of course have such meaning. The combination of "libri" and "quidam," however, is found in C VII, 9, 13 where the books are clearly identified as "Platonic"—"quosdam Platonicorum libros." The same phrase to the same intent recurs in *Confessions* VIII, 2, 3. But this in itself, as we shall presently see, cannot be decisive evidence—it may but underline Augustine's rather indiscriminate use of familiar phrases.

"Plenus" again, which does not mean "substantial," might, in appearing to suggest something very "full" of matter, seem to indicate some very rich material—such as to lead one to think, say, of Plotinus. But it does not as a matter of course have any such implication. In point of fact it is rather a favourite adjective of Augustine's—it is used frequently in *Confessions* VIII: it is used, for example, of the monastery at

Milan which was *"plenum* bonis fratribus" (6, 15) and again (11, 27) of Chastity's hands "plenas gregibus bonorum exemplorum." The "bona exempla" are the edifying lives of Christian boys and girls, the young, the old, and all ages. The use of "plenus" in this connection at this point may possibly be significant for our argument.

We have, moreover, an actual use of *libri plenissimi*[24] in *De ordine* II.28 (contemporary with the *Contra Academicos*). Here again it is used of the precepts of great and almost divine men. The context is concerned explicitly with "authority" ("reason" is explicitly taken up in 30) both divine and human).[25] Divine authority relates to Christ and the authority of the mysteries. Human authority is seen to excel in the case of those who live as they preach—he would appear to be thinking principally of St. Paul but perhaps Ambrose too—especially in the case of those who show themselves great in their use of wealth, or still greater in their contempt of it. This last phrase may refer to the story of Antony, as recounted in *Confessions* VIII, 11, 29, where he followed the injunction to sell all and give to the poor. One should note the emphasis given in this text from *De ordine* II, 27f. to living up to one's precepts: "non *uiuunt* aliter, quam *uiuendum* esse praecipiunt." But we shall return to this passage presently.

"Paucissimus" has been the most misleading word of all. Since in the contemporary *De beata uita* IV mention is made of the "Plotini paucissimis libris" the same books are understood to be referred to by the two superlatives, although the superlative refers to "books" in one case and "drops" in the other. Yet clearly this is in no way necessary. Once again "paucissimus" is rather a favourite word of Augustine. *De ordine* II, 16, for example, has "Philosophia . . . uix paucissimos liberat" which does not refer to books. Another use of this superlative is found in *De ordine* II, 45 where Augustine, addressing Monnica, assures her that from a large range of difficult disciplines only a few are essential to her:

> de omnibus eligentur numero paucissima, ui potentissima, cognitione autem multis quidem ardua, tibi tamen, cuius ingenium cotidie mihi nouum est et cuius animum uel aetate uel admirabili temperantia remotissimum ab omnibus nugis et a magna labe corporis emergentem in se multum surrexisse cognosco, tam erunt facilia quam difficilia tardissimis miserrimeque uiuentibus.

Here the "paucissima" refers to things difficult to be understood by the slow or by people leading bad lives. The context is one dealing specifically with intellectual training—so that the reference to things difficult to understand is inevitable—but there is a remarkable emphasis on right living, if only because of Monnica's being addressed. The "ui potentissima" may well recall, however, the "guttas paucissimas" of *Contra Academicos* II, 5 that had such an incredible effect.

I share the perplexity of many scholars on the identification of Celsinus, and I do not pretend to have anything more to say about "bonas res Arabicas" except that, when explained (as it is) by "exhalarunt . . . instillarunt pretiosissimi unguenti guttas" it must refer to some fragrant "unguent" from Arabia or that region in general or a sandy, desert land: so far as this goes what is referred to might have to do with Plotinus, for example, or Paul, Porphyry, or Antony.

The words "exhalarunt" and "instillarunt," however, are surely curious words to use of books. While Augustine, as we have seen, normally talks about "taking up" or "reading" a book, here he does not do so. It is possible that his mind was so occupied with the image of the scented unguent exploding the flame that he rather unusually personified the books. But one must consider the possibility that Augustine did not say that he had read the books for the simple reason that *he had not read them* or at any rate *all of them*. This alone would account for the phrasing which is so obscure as never to have been satisfactorily explained. Now if we look at *Confessions* VIII we see that, although he read St. Paul, he had only *heard* of the book that described the life of Antony—from Ponticianus. He had not read the life of Antony: it had been passed by word of mouth ("exhalarunt in nos"?) to him.

There is, in fact, in *Confessions* VIII, 6, 15 a phrase which seems to echo the "libri quidem *pleni* . . . bonas res *Arabicas* ubi *exhalarunt* in nos . . . instillarunt *pretiosissimi unguenti* guttas" of the *Contra Academicos*. Ponticianus began to speak of the "monasteriorum greges et mores *suaueolentiae* tuae et *ubera deserta heremi,* quorum nos nihil sciebamus, et erat monasterium Mediolanii *plenum* bonis fratribus . . .'" This is evidence which may help to explain "bonas res Arabicas . . . pretiosissimi unguenti."

This writer is well aware that Augustine appears to have an unlimited capacity for not keeping his sources or the terminology appropriate to them strictly separate. A clear instance of this is his handling of the Plotinian theme of the flight to the fatherland and the scriptural parable of the prodigal son and their separate vocabularies (where separate).[26] I have already indicated that Neoplatonist (or Neoplatonist-seeming) terminology is employed as a matter of course both in *Contra Academicos* II,

4–7 and *Confessions* VIII. I have further indicated that the "guttas paucissimas" may even include a Neoplatonist overtone.

But just as *Confessions* VII deals with the Platonists and VIII with mainly the story told by Ponticianus of Antony and other virtuous Christians, so the earlier part of the section of the *Contra Academicos* in question would seem to deal with the Neoplatonists mainly, and from "cum ecce tibi libri quidam pleni" to the end of 5 *mainly* with the prolonged reading of St. Paul, perhaps of the Neoplatonists and Ambrose, and also the hearing of the report of the life of Antony and the other holy men.

Courcelle has well said: "On voit combien il est arbitraire et artificiel de découper sa conversion milanaise en phases chronologiques ou logiques: influence philosophique exercée par les laïcs, influence religieuse exercée par Ambroise. Par ses sermons *De Isaac* et *De bono mortis*, Ambroise l'initiait en même temps au spiritualisme chrétien et aux doctrines plotiniennes."[27] The general contention of the present study that the *libri quidam pleni* are not or are not exclusively Neoplatonist supports Courcelle's thesis.

The rest of the passage of CA II, 5 bears this out. According to C VIII the story of Ponticianus did set Augustine incredibly on fire. He echoed the self-remonstrations of the friend of Ponticianus on reading from the life of Antony:

> Mirari et accendi . . . meditari arripere talem uitam et relicata militia saeculari seruire tibi . . . repletus amore sancto et sobrio pudore iratus . . . ait . . . "omnibus istis laboribus nostris quo ambimus pervenire?" (the whole passage continues this theme).

This corresponds to the "Quis me tunc honor . . ." of the *Contra Academicos* II, 5. The "Prorsus totus in me cursim redibam" of the *Contra Academicos* II, 5 is paralleled in *Confessions* VIII, 7, 16:

> Narrabat haec Ponticianus. tu autem, domine, inter uerba eius retorquebas me ad me ipsum, auferens ne a dorso meo, ubi me posueram, dum nollem me adtendere.[28]

It would be idle to pretend that the last few lines of *Contra Academicos* II, 5 (from "Respexi tantum" to the end), are easy to decipher. Here again, however, juxtaposition with the account given in *Confessions* VIII clarifies some elements. The "itaque titubans properans haesitans arripio apostolum Paulum" might seem to refer clearly to the *tolle lege* scene (C 12, 29: "arripui, aperui et legi in silentio capitulum"). But the *"perlegi totum"* makes such a simple view impossible—for *Confessions* VIII,

12, 29 says explicitly that he did *not* read the whole of St. Paul *then*: "nec ultra uolui legere nec opus erat." But he had *at an earlier stage* set out to give all his attention to St. Paul. In *Confessions* VII, 21, 27, just after he has described what Courcelle calls "les vaines tentatives d'extases Plotiniennes," he begins: "Itaque auidissime *arripui* uenerabilem stilum spiritus tui et prae ceteris *apostolum Paulum.*" This is later expanded into "illis me scripturis (a few lines earlier identified as Paul the Apostle) *curam maximam inpendere*"—which corresponds to the *"perlegi totum* intentissime et cautissime" of *Contra Academicos* II, 5. The "titubans properans haesitans" of this passage[29] seems to be an overflow from the memory of the scene in *Confessions* VIII, 12, 29: "itaque *concitus* redii ... arripui, aperui, legi" (also echoed in relation to Ponticianus in *Confessions* VIII, 6, 14: tulit, aperuit, inuenit apostolum Paulum). The lines, in other words, in *Contra Academicos* II, 5 refer not at all—except perhaps through overtone in the excitement of the language—to the "tolle lege" scene of *Confessions* VIII, 12, 29. The reason given in the *Contra Academicos* passage for reading St. Paul is not immediate obedience as it were to an oracle but, as he said to himself ("inquam") to see if Christian "litterae" were opposed to the great good of Neoplatonic philosophy ("si eorum litterae atque rationes huic tanto bono aduersarentur"). He wanted to confirm his impression that the Christians could not live as virtuously as they did if in fact their *rationes* and *litterae* were so opposed.

De ordine II, 27f. (contemporary with the *Contra Academicos*) throws light upon these "litterae." We must recall that here is found the significant phrase "magnorum hominum et paene diuinorum *libri plenissimi*" which is the nearest contemporary expression we have found to the crucial *libri* quidam *pleni* of *Contra Academicos* II, 5. These books of the *De ordine* are described as full of "uiuendi praecepta." The context is dealing with the Christian side of human authority (as distinct from "reason," discussed in 30ff.). The passage:

> multa dant indicia doctrinarum suarum et non *uiuunt* aliter, quam *uiuendum esse praecipiunt.* Quibus si aliqua etiam fortunae munera accesserint, quorum appareant usu magni contemtuque maiores, difficilimum omnino est, ut eis quisque uiuendi praecepta dantibus credens recte uituperetur. (DOR II, 27)

in conjunction with 28 refers almost certainly to St. Paul and Ambrose, or both, but also, in its reference to the despising of wealth, possibly to Antony.

At any rate there is here an echo of the *"uixissent* ita, ut eos *uixisse* manifestum est"* of *Contra Academicos* II, 5. For a clear echo of "isti tanta *potuissent"* all we have to do is look at *Confessions* VIII, 11, 27 where *apropos* of Antony we read: "tu non *poteris,* quod isti, quod *istae?* an uero *isti* et *istae* in se ipsis *possunt* ac non in domino suo"?

When one joins all this to the "mores *suaueolentiae* tuae et *ubera deserta heremi* . . . monasterium *plenum"* (which in *Confessions* VIII, 6, 15 explicitly refers to Antony and Christian holy men) we have reason for putting forward the view that *Contra Academicos* II, 5 follows *De beata uita* IV and *Confessions* VIII in introducing the reading of St. Paul and possibly Ambrose and hearing of the life of Antony in the phrase: "cum ecce tibi libri quidam pleni, ut ait Celsinus, bonas res Arabicas ubi exhalarunt in nos, ubi illi flammulae instillarunt pretiossissimi unguenti guttas paucissimas." This is not to be taken as excluding all overtone or reference to the Neoplatonists as well.

There remains to be commented upon the sentence: "Respexi tantum, confiteor, quasi de itinere in illam religionem, quae pueris nobis insita est et medullitus inplicata; uerum autem ipsa ad se nescientem rapiebat" (CA II, 5).

If we seek for enlightenment on this phrase from *Confessions* VIII, we should find it (but Augustine is, of course, not always consistent in the order in which he treats individual terms in separate descriptions) between the end of Ponticianus's story and the seizing of the codex of St. Paul, i.e., between the beginning of 6.16 and the middle of 12.29.

While throughout the whole of *Confessions* VIII there is, naturally in the context of a book dealing with conversion and return, much implied and some explicit reference to journeying, the section beginning with 7.17 reviews Augustine's journey to Wisdom from the time of his reading of the *Hortensius*. He had nothing fixed by which he could direct his course (7, 18 "quo dirigerem cursum meum"') in trying to follow God. The unlearned rise up and seize heaven—but he simply wallowed in filth (8, 9). Then comes a significant borrowing (as we have seen) from Plotinus:

> (8, 19) Ego fremebam spiritu indignans . . . quod non *irem in placitum* et *pactum* tuum, deus meus, in quod *eundum* esse omnia *ossa mea clamabant* et in caelum tollebant laudibus: et non illuc *ibatur nauibus* aut *quadrigis* aut *pedibus,* quantum saltem de domo in eum locum *ieram,* ubi sedebamus. nam non solum *ire* uerum etiam *peruenire* illuc nihil erat aliud quam uelle *ire.*

"Irem in placitum et pactum tuum, deus meus, in quod eundum esse omnia ossa mea clamabant" echoes to some degree the "in illam *religionem, quae pueris nobis insita est et medullitus* inplicata; uerum autem ipsa ad se rapiebat."

The journey theme reappears again prominently in 11, 26: "audiebam (antiquas amicas meas) . . . non tamquam libere contradicentes *eundo in obviam,* sed uelut a dorso mussitantes et discedentem quasi furtim uellicantes, ut *respicerem. retardabant* tamen cunctantem me *abripere* atque excutere ab eis et *transilire quo* uocabar." It will not be surprising to anyone familiar with Augustine's uncanny practice of returning to nearly identical phraseology to observe that in the text just quoted from *Confessions* VIII, 11, 26 we find *respicerem, quasi, eundo in obuiam* and *discedentem* to echo the *"respexi . . . quasi de itinere"* of the *Contra Academicos* II, 5—but they are used to an entirely different purpose. The essential point to be made, however, is that the theme of the *iter,* the journey, is so prominent in C VIII, 6, 16 to 12, 29 that its occurrence in CA II, 5 can thus probably be understood.

The *"respexi"* tantum confiteor, *quasi de itinere* in *illam religionem,* quae *pueris* nobis insita est et *medullitus inplicata* follows, according to our interpretation of *Contra Academicos* II, 5, immediately after the self-confrontation of Augustine that followed the end of Ponticianus's story. In *Confessions* VIII it follows (7, 17) in exactly the same place, and begins with the recall of his encounter with the *Hortensius,* as he says, "in exordio ipsius *adulescentiae."* It seems likely indeed that the present reference in the *Contra Academicos* II, 5, is in fact a reference to the *Hortensius* (the description of which in *Confessions* III, 4, 7 is in part a doublet of the description of his final conversion), where he speaks of his then tender age ("inbecilla aetate") and of his tender heart drinking piously and deeply retaining Christ's name with his mother's milk: "in ipso adhuc lacte matris tenerum cor meum pie libebat et alte retinebat." Here again we have something very akin to the *"pueris* nobis insita est et *medullitus inplicata."* Moreover the point and even words of the following phrase in CA II, 5: *"nescientem rapiebat"* is also found in this passage (III, 4, 8): "et *nesciebam* quid ageres mecum . . . quidquid sine hoc nomine fuisset . . . non me totum *rapiebat."* But naturally, since the *Hortensius* passage is a conversion episode, it has many other points of comparison with CA II, 4–7, which are not strictly relevant to our present purpose.

One remaining question in connection with CA II, 5: the sense of the connectives "tantum, confiteor" and the later "itaque." The "confiteor" makes the point to Romanianus that in being affected by the books of St. Paul and the lives of Antony—the "libri pleni" and the "bonae res Arabicae"—he was doing no more ("tantum")—he has to admit ("confiteor")—than returning to the environment of his childhood. The religion of his childhood had, without his being conscious of it,[30] been drawing him. It was, therefore ("itaque"), in accordance with that providence that he turns to St. Paul to see if his doctrine was at variance with that of the Neoplatonists which had just so profoundly affected him. It may well have overtones, too, as I have said, of his recent excited consultation of St. Paul as an oracle at the time of his conversion.

The purpose of this study has been to give one indication at least, from a close examination of one quite crucial text in the *Contra Academicos*, for the author's belief that the extent and importance of the influence of Plotinus on Augustine have been somewhat misconstrued. There is no denying the powerful and lasting impression that Plotinus's *Ennead* I, 6 especially—and almost certainly a few other essays—had upon an impressionable Augustine. This impression affected Augustine's outlook and expectations more, perhaps, than his doctrine, in which even at the time of his conversion he preferred Christ to Plotinus if they should seem to be in conflict. But it has so deeply entered into his mind, emotions, and language that there is danger of mistaking a Neoplatonic terminology and tone for Neoplatonic doctrine. If it is accepted that the "libri quidam pleni" of *Contra Academicos* II, 5 are not so much Neoplatonic as the writings of St. Paul and perhaps Ambrose and the hearing of the Life of Antony, then that danger will have been clearly revealed.[31] This in turn should help in assessing more correctly the influence of Plotinus on Augustine.

15

The Neoplatonism of Augustine

❧

I have written a good deal on this topic in books and articles, fairly evenly spread out over the last quarter of a century. They bear witness to the inevitable evolution of my ideas on this subject.

During the period there was sustained interest in this field, a great deal of it generated by H. I. Marrou, P. Courcelle, and P. Henry, who, with others, contributed an Augustinian dimension to the remarkable school of late Hellenistic religion and philosophy at Paris, deriving from F. Cumont and J. Bidez, and more recently associated with the names of, for example, A. J. P. Festugière and Ch. H. Puech. There were, of course, others, both in France and far from its confines, who regarded Paris as the center of their studies in this field. And, naturally, I must allude very discreetly indeed to the reigning generation—to such as J. Pépin and P. Hadot—not to say to the very promising group of younger scholars whose formation has been directly or indirectly affected by what I call the Neoplatonic and Augustinian school of Paris.

A great support in more recent times for this scholarly movement was the existence of the Etudes Augustiniennes maintained by Père G. Folliet and his community in the rue François Ier (now in rue de l'Abbaye). Not only have they continued to publish their *Revue des Etudes Augustiniennes*, which contains also an exhaustive bibliography of what is published on Augustine and, of course, Augustine and Neoplatonism, but they arranged a famous Augustinian Congress in Paris in 1954 that was dominated by the topic to which we are now addressing ourselves. The intense interest and controversy that appeared in relation to this subject on that occasion may be seen in the pages of the third volume of the proceedings, *Augustinus Magister* (Paris, 1954), which reports the more than lively discussions. I shall never forget the interjection of F. Chatillon: "Quant à Plotin, votre Plotin, eh bien! flûte pour Plotin!"

This vigorous remark was one of the last protestations on one side in an embattled dispute with which you may not all be familiar. In 1888 A. Harnack and G. Boissier had put forward a view, expounded in its heyday by P. Alfaric in his *L'évolution intellectuelle de saint Augustin* (Paris,

1918), which in effect said that it was not until *long after* his "conversion" that Augustine accepted the Christian faith in opposition to Neoplatonism. In the context of the time and in the light, for example, of the career of Synesius, the professing Neoplatonist bishop of Cyrene, such a view is not extravagant. From the time of C. Boyer's counterattack in 1920, however, this view became gradually untenable—hence F. Chatillon's inelegant remark. Still the majority of scholars by 1954 would have agreed that at the time of his conversion, Augustine's acceptance of Christianity was sincere and that he was also deeply impressed by Neoplatonism. He, with many others, thought (fondly as it proved later) that there could be a synthesis between the Christian faith and Neoplatonic reason since indeed the one God had to be the source for both authority and reason. It would, I think, be true to say that since 1954 we are no longer interested in what is now called the "false" problem of whether Augustine at any particular time was a Christian rather than a Neoplatonist or vice versa. To us he now seems to have been a Christian of his time who held certain views that were abhorrent to Neoplatonism but nevertheless had been much influenced by Neoplatonism in not unimportant ways.

A second problem had in the meantime emerged: which Neoplatonist—Plotinus (204/5–269/70) or Porphyry (232/3–ca. 305) was responsible for this Neoplatonist influence on Augustine? W. Theiler (whose death occurred early in 1977) was breast high for Porphyry; P. Henry for Plotinus. In my own introduction to the *Contra Academicos* I had already made it clear that in my view "both Plotinus and Porphyry are well represented"[1] in that work. To that point, claims for the dominating influence of Plotinus were standard. Since then and, I am happy to say, since my own *Porphyry's Philosophy from the Oracles in Augustine* (Paris, 1959), P. Hadot's very long review of it in the *Revue des Etudes Augustiniennes* (VI.3 [1960], pp. 205–44) and his own subsequent work, *Porphyre et Victorinus,* and the Entretiens held on Porphyry at the Fondation Hardt in Geneva (1966), Porphyry has gained enormously in his reputation as a philosopher and is allowed an important role, alongside his master Plotinus, in influencing Augustine.

So much by way of a *status quaestionis.* But there are some other preliminary remarks which it may be useful to make.

Recently Edward Booth has drawn attention to the eclectic character of Neoplatonism. It was in fact the most influential of the "eclectic contemplative philosophies, with their triple ultimate beings and their doctrines of salvation (which) were the background of Christian Trinitarianism."[2] The spirit of the Roman world, in which Plotinus and Porphyry lived, may have been responsible for some—though hardly all—of the eclectic character of Neoplatonism. The Roman spirit was profoundly sceptical, embracing only the probable, pragmatic and necessarily, therefore, eclectic. I recall vividly how startled I was when I read the opinion of the great Latinist Ernout that Lucretius was not concerned with how true the physical theory of Democritus was on which he based his system: it seemed to work; that was enough.[3] Now I am not saying that Plotinus's approach to truth is the same as that of Lucretius. But I am saying that the Neoplatonists were eclectic.

So was Augustine who was on this point strikingly Roman. Listen to this tidy example from chapter 28 of the twenty-second book of the *City of God*. The topic is the Christian doctrine of the resurrection of the body which the Neoplatonists refused absolutely to countenance:

> The Platonists agree with us that even blessed souls will return to bodies, as Plato says, but will nevertheless not return to any evils, as Porphyry says, and take this also from Varro, that they will return to the same bodies, in which they were formerly, then their whole difficulty about the resurrection of the flesh for eternity will be solved.

It is to be noticed that Augustine is not writing flippantly, although one suspects that if he were challenged on this piece of jigsawing he would have disengaged himself quickly enough. But a remarkable feature of Augustine's writing is his tendency to use the *ballon d'essai*: "This theory," he writes in his first extant work, "about the Academics I have sometimes, as far as I could, thought probable. If it is false, I do not mind."[4] This inconsequential attitude to doctrine propounded by others or even himself is highlighted even more in his other well known tendency to believe that philosophers propounded one thing to the public but propounded very different and sometimes opposite views to their inner circle: it is the old business of exoteric and esoteric doctrines.

But if Augustine was Roman in his eclectic attitude to the truths of physics and logic, he was also Roman in his passionate attachment to ethics. I have often felt disappointed by his handling of philosophical themes in the earlier part of the *City of God*—though I hasten to add both that the controversial nature of that work offered him some excuse, and he does demonstrate a profound aptitude for philosophical speculation elsewhere—but I have always been impressed by his strong passion for social and moral issues. His praise of the high moral and social qualities of Brutus, Torquatus, Curtius, the Decii, Regulus, Cincinnatus, and others is emphatic and sincere.

Quidquid recipitur recipitur ad modum recipientis. The fact that Augustine borrowed from the Neoplatonists what he borrowed from them, and how he used his borrowings, all these reflect his own character and interests. I have written on this topic fairly comprehensively in, for example, RechAug I (1958, pp. 91–111) and in my *Charter of Christendom* (1961, pp. 62–87) and elsewhere. Very briefly, Augustine accepted the Neoplatonic doctrine of an incorporeal Creator, the immortality of the soul, and the existence of Providence and mediatory salvation. Porphyry appeared to Augustine to espouse something like the Christian Trinity and a rudimentary notion of Grace. Augustine had much to criticize in the precise formulation by the Neoplatonists of their doctrines. His criticisms have been usefully set forth by Edward Booth in the article to which I have already referred.[5]

I should now like to look a little, but, necessarily, very quickly, at the particular points of contact which I judge to be of greatest significance between Augustine on the one hand and Plotinus and Porphyry on the other.

In an article in celebration of a Plotinian centenary in 1970,[6] I stressed what I called the conversion syndrome in Augustine's thought and its inspiration in Plotinus, principally in *Ennead* I, 6: "On Beauty." Here Plotinus truly passes on the mystical spell of Plato's *Symposium* to be taken up again by Augustine in a number of passages of the *Confessions* where, according to Courcelle,[7] Augustine describes his attempts to achieve Plotinian ecstasy. I am convinced that the impression that Augustine received from reading Plotinus I, 6, which made it possible for him to abandon materialism in any explanation of reality, abode with him forever. It was not so much Plotinus's articulation of immaterialist doctrine that affected him, as the profound insight that the emotional, almost mystical concentration on the hypostases afforded him:

> The reasoning faculty drew away my thoughts from the power of habit, withdrawing itself from those troops of contradictory phantasms; that so it might find what that light was, whereby it was bedewed, when, without all doubting, it cried out, "That the unchangeable was to be preferred to the changeable"; whence also it knew That Unchangeable,

which, unless it had in some way known, it had had no sure ground to prefer it to the changeable. And thus with the flash of one trembling glance it arrived at That Which Is. But I could not fix my gaze thereon; and my infirmity being struck back, I was thrown again on my wonted habits, carrying along with me only a loving memory thereof, and a longing for what I had, as it were, perceived the odour of, but was not yet able to feed on. Yet dwelt there with me a remembrance of Thee.[8]

Again, in the so-called vision of Ostia, he speaks about touching on eternal wisdom: "Could this (touching) be continued on, and other visions of kind far unlike be withdrawn, and this one ravish, and absorb and wrap up its beholder amid these inward joys, so that life might be for ever like that one moment of understanding which we now sighed after?"[9]

It will be observed that the elevation here described by Augustine uses the emotions if only to dismiss them. The *practical* aspect of the matter is in fact represented by the purification of the senses. This purification was fully propounded by both Plotinus and Porphyry and in due course by Augustine. The approach, then, changing somewhat from the metaphysical to the moral, becomes a theme congenial to Roman moralism, be it in Sallust, Seneca, or Saint Augustine. The Latin language had (and has) an extraordinary power to seize upon the substance of a complicated consideration and express it pithily, memorably, and emotionally. Greek is more intellectual; but when it comes to expressing the whole of human experience and of the *lacrimae rerum*. Latin speaks grandly for the human heart. Over and over again Augustine sums up the necessity to turn to, to be converted to, the Father and to turn away from the things of this world. One can see this in the argument of a whole work such as the *City of God*: *fecerunt itaque ciuitates duas amores duo, terrenam scilicet amor sui usque ad contemptum Dei, caelestem uero amor Dei usque ad contemptum sui.*[10] Or one can see it in the phrases now hackneyed from too much casual use: *inquietum est cor nostrum, donec requiescat in te: noverim me noverim te, ut amem te et contemnam me.* These phrases are highly rhetorical, but their very jingle is part of their usefulness and appeal to the many. We should not be misled for all that; they enshrine the very core of Plotinus's explanation of the origin of things:

ὂν γὰρ τέλειον τῷ μηδὲν ζητεῖν μηδὲ ἔχειν μηδὲ δεῖσθαι οἷον ὑπερερρύη καὶ τὸ ὑπερπλῆρες αὐτοῦ πεποίηκεν ἄλλο. τὸ δὲ γενόμενον εἰς αὐτὸ ἐπεστράφη καὶ ἐπληρώθη καὶ ἐγένετο πρὸς αὐτὸ βλέπον καὶ νοῦς οὗτος. καὶ ἡ μὲν πρὸς ἐκεῖνο στάσις αὐτοῦ τὸ ὂν ἐποίησεν.[11]

Augustine did not quite follow Plotinus in the explanation of the creation of the *nous*, the first being, by the One, but he did preserve the general structure and vocabulary. In particular the term *conversio*, "turning to," was for him an emotional touchstone of deep and lasting importance. The *Confessions* is the story of his own and of everyman's conversion to God. The *City of God* is the same theme writ large in terms of all angels and humanity that ever was or will be. The intellectual inspiration is in Plotinus.

I have been alluding to the salvational element that Augustine—and others—have discerned in Plotinus. But the other Neoplatonist who influenced Augustine (as we know from Augustine's own testimony), Porphyry, is much more explicit on the theme of salvation—which may well afford some explanation as to why we have until recently tended to rate Porphyry rather less than did Augustine, and why Augustine gives more prominence to him than to Plotinus.

Porphyry was for Augustine not only the greatest of recent philosophers but was one who, although he had abandoned or at least rejected and finally attacked Christianity most forcefully, had also examined its claims and, in his view, came very close to it. Porphyry, Augustine says in the *City of God*,[12] had accepted the God of the Hebrews and had extolled the virtues of Christ—as a man, only, however. Pride and the demons had prevented him not only from accepting the divinity of the Christ who had become incarnate and had died on a cross, but also from appreciating the virtues of Christians and the enduring mission of the Church. But Porphyry's salvationism and eclecticism seemed especially useful to Augustine. Augustine refers to him as follows:

> When Porphyry says that no one system of thought has yet embraced a doctrine that embodies a universal path to the liberation of the soul, no, neither the truest of philosophies, nor the moral ideas and practices of the Indians, nor the initiation of the Chaldaeans, nor any other way of life, and adds that this same path has not yet been brought to his attention in the course of his research into history, he is undoubtedly acknowledging that some such path exists though it had not yet come to his attention. So dissatisfied was he with the results of his devoted study of the liberation of the soul and with what his reputation, higher in the eyes of others than in his own, credited him with discovering and maintaining.[13]

It was the nearness of Porphyry's approach—despite his ultimate fierce hostility—to Christianity that induced Augustine to give more extensive notice to Porphyry than to Plotinus and to praise him more. We must recognize this dominating fact in our assessment of Augustine's *own* admission of Neoplatonist influence on him.

The influences of Plotinus and Porphyry on Augustine as indicated so far could be described as important indeed but, especially, *dramatic*. At any rate Augustine's description of them is dramatic and, certainly in relation to the influence of Porphyry, also rather politic. There was a doctrinal influence involved, but it tends to attract our notice less. Nevertheless, the influence of both Plotinus and Porphyry at the doctrinal level, even if ultimately rejected, was wider and deeper than has so far been suggested here. Some of this may have been imbibed directly from a reading of these authors probably for the most part in translation. Some may have come to Augustine orally through his Christian-Neoplatonist friends and acquaintances in Milan. At any rate we now know, thanks to the fruitful labors of Berthold Altaner,[14] quite an amount on the influence of the Greek Neoplatonist Fathers—Basil, the Gregories, Irenaeus, Athanasius, and Origen—on Augustine, manifesting itself at all stages of his life.

I shall end with some comments on the work of Augustine perhaps best known under the title *Hexaemeron* in the earlier medieval period, and, under the title *De Genesi ad litteram*, very little known in more recent centuries. Only one translation of this work into a modern language, French, has been available and that only since 1972.[15] An English translation by John Taylor (of Seattle) should appear fairly soon. This work, Augustine's fourth attempt to comment (as literally as possible) on the first chapters of Genesis, was finished when its author was about sixty-one years of age. It is, therefore, a rather late and mature work and testifies to the permanent influence of Neoplatonism on his thoughts.

I am discussing elsewhere[16] the extent to which Augustine in DGnL depends upon, for example, Plotinus's doctrine on the λόγος for his fundamental and very philosophical understanding of creation as described in Genesis. Likewise I hope to treat at some future time his use in DGnL of Porphyry's idea of *spiritus* for his equally fundamental and equally philosophical understanding of the afterlife. There are other points of influence, such as that of Plotinus's ideas on Providence or Porphyry's angelology (and this was most significant). Here, however, let me mention briefly one instance only of the influence of Plotinus *and* Porphyry, taking them—as for the most part, perhaps they should be—together, as seen in DGnL.

Fundamental to the Neoplatonist system and elaborated with great emphasis in Plotinus is the doctrine that the Father, the One, is beyond being and beyond not only all sensible but also all rational or even intellectual perception:

> (13) Thus the One is in truth beyond all statement: any affirmation is of a thing; but "all-transcending, resting above even the most august divine Mind"—this is the only true description, since it does not make it a thing among things, nor name it where no name could identify it: we can but try to indicate, in our own feeble way, something concerning it. . . . The Transcendent, thus, neither knows itself nor is known in itself. (14) . . . We have neither knowledge nor intellection of it (οὐδὲ γνῶσιν οὐδὲ νόησιν ἔχομεν αὐτοῦ), . . . we can and do state what it is not, while we are silent as to what it is (καὶ γὰρ λέγομεν, ὃ μὴ ἔστιν ὃ δέ ἐστιν, οὐ λέγομεν).[17]

Porphyry and his translator, Victorinus, may well have been agents through whom the idea of the unknowability of the One was transmitted to Augustine. In his *Sententiae* he writes: θεωρεῖται δὲ ἀνοησίᾳ κρεῖττον νοήσεως.[18]

At any rate Augustine even in the early *De ordine* speaks of God as "known better in not being known": *qui scitur melius nesciendo*.[19] In DGnL he has a remarkable passage stressing how God is not any *thing* but that he is nearer to us, nevertheless, than the many things he made:

> Although, I say, it is not possible to say anything of that substance (i.e., God) and there is no way whatever of one man saying anything about it to another except by commandeering some words related to times and places—whereas he is before all times and before all places—nevertheless he is nearer to us, he who made us, than the many things which were made. For in him we live and move and are. . . . It is a greater labor to find them than him, by whom they were made. To become aware of him with a faithful mind from anything, however insignificant, is better in its incomparable blessedness than to comprehend the whole universe of things.[20]

Augustine's use of the *theologia negativa* is, thus, influenced by the Plotinian "Father" or One, whether directly or through Porphyry, or through the Greek Fathers such as Gregory Nazianzen, orally or through writing. The extent to which Augustine's works are heavily marked by this negative theology has been much obscured by what one might call historical institutional theology in the West. This has tended to play down the influence of Platonism in, for example, Aquinas and even more in Augustine, where its presence is more obvious.

From the few instances of Neoplatonic influence on Augustine that I have given you, you will observe that the topic is by no means a simple one. Nor is there any reason why it should be. Neoplatonism, to begin with, was not one, unaltering doctrine, even in Plotinus. After Plotinus it evolved in various ways and, some would say, in curious directions. But above all, the recipient of the influence, Augustine, was a complicated character. Augustine for most of his life as a writer was a Christian bishop deeply committed in literally a sequence of critical controversies, the heat of which was undoubtedly raised significantly by his own ardent temperament. Over and over again, and notably in the *City of God*, he turns aside from a full discussion of some profound problem in order to maintain his general and well-directed polemic. Indeed one can say that the less polemical he is, the more philosophical. It could hardly have been otherwise.

Augustine at the same time was something of an artist and a religious genius. Some have spoken of the warring passions that rent his body. His mind, too, was racked by apparently conflicting loyalties, especially the drive to commend God's claim on us, which appeared to be *absolute*, and at the same time to sympathize with the erring needs of the human heart. In fact he was loyal to both—can be quoted to support both sides—and so can appear to contradict himself.

There is something of that enduring split within him in regard to Neoplatonism too. To the extent—which was in this case quite absolute—that he accepted the incarnation and the resurrection of Christ's and the human body, to that extent he rejected the immaterialism of the Neoplatonists—an absolutely fundamental point. In general, then, I regard Gilson's judgment that Augustine inhibited Neoplatonic influence in the West rather than transmitted it as true.

And yet the traditional practical asceticism of the West, which manifested itself in an actual hostility to the body, however that body is honored in the resurrection of the person, is deeply marked with Platonic dualism. Similarly Augustine sought the rational understanding of the problems and mysteries of Christian theology, perhaps progressively so as time went on, in Neoplatonic sources. Even in the last book of the *City of God*, while opting for the view that in the afterlife our corporeal eyes will see God, he does not omit to give a Neoplatonic view which centers on assimilation of mind with God rather than vision of any kind, however glorified, of corporeal eyes.[21] The matter was not made easier by the knowledge that even Neoplatonic immaterialism was by some understood in a sense involving some kind of matter, however attenuated.

There is no simple statement adequate to describe Augustine's use of the Neoplatonists. I hope, nevertheless, that I have succeeded in conveying to you in some plausible manner how manifold that use might have been.

16

Parting from Porphyry

☙

When Johannes Scottus Eriugena in the ninth century came to discuss in his great dialogue, *Periphyseon* (also known as *De diuisione naturae*), the condition of the saved in the life hereafter, he followed the opinions of Ambrose, Gregory of Nyssa, and Maximus the Confessor, to the effect that the change was not from an earthly into a heavenly body, but, as Ambrose contended, a complete passing into pure spirit, and not into that spirit which is called aether, but into that which is called mind[1]—a characteristically Neoplatonic position. On the other hand he reports Augustine as appearing, in the *City of God*, to have held that it is not the bodies themselves that shall pass away, but their qualities shall be changed into something better: neither the shape nor the size nor the sex of the human body shall pass away, but it shall merely be clothed with spiritual and immortal qualities.[2] Worse still, in his letter to Dardanus, Augustine appears to say that Christ's body after his resurrection is in heaven in a local sense in the same fleshly form and substance as it appeared on earth, with the sole addition of the quality of immortality,[3] when it seems to follow that Christ is not omnipresent as God is, and is not divine beyond all space and time, transcending everything that can be uttered or understood.

Eriugena, claiming that no one has a greater respect for Augustine's teaching than he, or has made a more constant and careful study of this great and most skilled enquirer into all things human and divine, this most copious commentator, quickly comes to the rescue of his Disciple in the Dialogue, who, with an exaggeration which some may see as worthy of the Irishman Eriugena, who actually penned his lines, professes to be staggered, amazed, and horror-stricken—*stupefactus haesito maximoque horrore concussus titubo*—at such a letdown by, of all people, Augustine.[4] He does this in two ways.

First he quotes the *City of God* XX, 13 (*sic*) as agreeing with him (and Ambrose and Gregory of Nyssa): "After the Judgment has been completed, then this heaven and this earth shall cease to exist, and a new heaven and a new earth shall begin to be. For it is not by complete annihilation but by a change of matter that this world shall pass away. . . . Therefore the Apostle also says: 'The shape of this world passes away, but I would not have you anxious.' The shape passes away, not the nature."[5] "Now tell me," says Eriugena, "how this is inconsistent with my words about the passing of this world into its causes, which St. Augustine called its nature? . . . But if anyone is so far from the truth as to say that the nature and substance of the world is sensible and corporeal and extended in space and time . . . , he is not worth answering, for every intelligent physicist accepts as an axiom that the nature and substance of bodies is itself incorporeal." Readers may not be altogether convinced by this argument of Eriugena.

Secondly he contends, especially in relation to the letter to Dardanus and Augustine's appearing to teach that Christ's body after his resurrection is in heaven in a local sense (and therefore not omnipresent, and therefore not divine) that Augustine is giving an exoteric doctrine determined by the exclusively carnal perceptions of his audience, and that his esoteric or real doctrine was quite different.[6]

This traditional distinction between exoteric and esoteric doctrines was extensively employed by Augustine himself in similar situations and it is ironic that Eriugena should use it in relation to him.

Elsewhere[7] Eriugena encounters a similar difficulty when he has to report that Augustine taught in the *De Genesi ad litteram*[8] that man was created animal, male and female, before the fall. The sexual division of man, therefore, was not a consequence of sin. Eriugena followed Gregory of Nyssa in holding that there were two creations of man, one, substantial, in the image of God, the other far removed, namely the division into male and female, a sexuality which, he holds, is not sinful in itself but is a consequence of sin. Eriugena, once again, is amazed at Augustine's doctrine—*mirari non desino.*

It can be seen from the instances that I have cited that Eriugena, looking at the matter from a Greek, Neoplatonic point of view, can hardly believe that Augustine should teach that the body created by God in the beginning was fully animal and sexual (even if its *libido* was fully in control), and the body to be resurrected was also animal and divided into the sexes. To such a Neoplatonic thinker it was something of a scandal, to be explained away however possible. One might note in passing how ironic it is that Augustine, who so conspicuously honoured the body and sexuality in such a fundamental way, should so often be blamed, for other reasons of course, for having helped significantly in bequeathing to the West a negative attitude to sex. One might rather expect to hear from our contemporaries how "modern" he was. But their knowledge of Augustine is at best incomplete.

Be that as it may, I have quoted Eriugena to show that this departure of Augustine from Neoplatonic doctrine had been forcefully remarked upon long before Peter Brown in his paper on *Augustine and Sexuality,* in *Colloquy* 46 (22 May 1983) of the *Centre for Hermeneutical Studies in Hellenistic and Modern Culture* (G.T.U. and Cal-Berkeley), drew attention to this alleged egregious discrepancy in doctrine between Augustine and Ambrose and others. This discrepancy emerged, according to Brown, between 396, about when the *Confessions* were begun, and 416, about two years after the completion of the *De Genesi ad litteram*: it emerged "in the course of a long and tenacious argument on an apparently totally unrelated issue. In those years, the ancient Christian past of Origen, of Jerome, and of Ambrose was pushed aside by Augustine, to clear the ground for his own personal intellectual vendetta with two great pagans—Plotinus, and, above all, Porphyry" (p. 7).

In the Neoplatonic hierarchy of the universe, the "spiritual" was axiomatically superior to its antithesis, the "material." As Brown says "we have here a 'vertical' paradigm of hierarchy. It remains a continuum: higher and lower are joined; but they can be joined only through a hierarchy of subtly mediating states of being . . . it was inconceivable that there should not exist an intermediate form of beings between God and mankind . . . the ethereal *daemones* . . . must necessarily stand between the utterly non-material gods and a human race caught in the dull flesh . . . The incarnation of Christ flattened the sense of a vertical hierarchy based on the axiomatic incompatibility of the fully 'spiritual' and the fully 'material.' It joined the One, High God directly to human flesh, without intermediary. . . . As for the Crucifixion . . . , the *daemones* . . . shuddered and drew back in disgust at the very sign of so obscene and macabre a reminder of physicality at its most malevolently senseless" (p. 8). Hence the "vendetta" with Plotinus, and, above all, Porphyry.

"Vendetta" is in one sense too strong a word to apply to Augustine's attitude to either Plotinus or Porphyry. He almost always speaks with great respect of them and especially of Porphyry, "the most noble," as he proclaims, "philosopher of the pagans," "the most learned of the philosophers,"[9] with whom, and with whose followers in his own day, he had the most extensive discussion. And yet "vendetta" is after all not too strong to suggest the obsessional preoccupation throughout most of his long life that Augustine had with Porphyry's rejection of Christ's incarnation and crucifixion. A full documentation of that obsession is to be found in my own *Porphyry's Philosophy from Oracles in Augustine* (Paris, 1959) and *Porphyry's Philosophy from Oracles in Eusebius's Praeparatio Evangelica and Augustine's Dialogues of Cassiciacum* (Paris, 1969). The constant repetition at length of the same *topos* throughout, for example, the *Confessions, De consensu euangelistarum, Sermo* 241 and especially the *City of God* is not patient of easy analysis, and few indeed, understandably, are those who have so analyzed it. Augustine in the *City of God* relates this obsession to Porphyry's ἐκ λογίων φιλοσοφίας *libri*—the *Philosophy from Oracles*[10]—and to a book which he, and he only, describes in two adjacent chapters of the *City of God* (and there only) as *De regressu animae*, the *Return of the Soul*.[11] H. Lewy,[12] and myself[13] have independently come to the conclusion that no separate work of Porphyry's existed under this, what we take to be merely descriptive, title; and each of us wish to associate it with other works of Porphyry whose formal titles are known. For my part I have argued that the *De regressu animae* is to be related to the *Philosophy from Oracles*, though what I have to say here in no way depends upon any such relation.

The Porphyrian-Vendetta topic runs in its broadest outline something like this. Porphyry recognized that the Father and the Son of the Christian trinity are the principles by whom we are purified. He believed also that the mass of mankind needed a universal way to salvation—a mediator to lead them to God. He examined the claim of Christ to be that mediator. He judged that Christ was a pious man, but that Peter and others of his followers were not good and that Christianity would soon be persecuted out of existence. Porphyry rejected the claim that the man Christ was incarnate God and could not accept the notion that God could submit himself to crucifixion. Porphyry, in spite of his accepting the equivalent to much of the teaching of Christianity, even, it would appear, the teaching on grace, did not succeed in recognizing the incarnation because of his pride before such humility, and also because he was misled by demons. Neither could he accept the resurrection of the human body: the notion of body in heaven was to be abhorred—*ut beata sit anima, corpus est omne fugiendum*.[14] And so the words of St. Paul are verified in Porphyry: "For although they knew God, they did not honour him as God or give thanks to him, but they became futile in their thinking and their senseless minds were darkened. Claiming to be wise they became fools, and exchanged the glory of the immortal God for images resembling mortal men or birds or animals or reptiles."[15]

Margaret Miles and Robert O'Connell in their comments on Brown's paper drew attention to the fact that the Neoplatonic "spiritual" attitude (allegedly characteristic of Ambrose) and Augustine's "material" view are interlaced throughout *the whole* of Augustine's writing: strong expressions of the hierarchical ascetic (that is "spiritual") paradigm (that of Ambrose) can be located in some very late writings, while unambiguous expressions that fit the social ("material") model are to be found in quite early works (pp. 19f.). O'Connell suggests in fact that Augustine did not really reject the Neoplatonic model at all (pp. 22f.). G. Madec also does not accept Brown's thesis.[16]

One should bear in mind that Augustine is a great deal more aporetic than is generally thought, and than his seemingly confident (not to say over-confident) pronouncements on important matters occasionally suggest. This openness to doubt, this failure to find, for the moment at least, satisfying answers to grave problems is most evident in the *De Genesi at litteram*: "I do not seek so much to prescribe," he says, "what each one should believe in relation to things that are obscure, as to show that I myself need instruction in matters on which I have been in doubt; and to restrain the reader from the rashness of coming to firm conclusions where we have been unable to provide knowledge that is certain."[17] Even in the *Retractations,* written about 426–27, he can admit that he still does not know the truth about so important a matter as the origin of the soul.[18] It would be far from surprising if Augustine's early attitudes on the question of the "spiritual" and "material," the "ascetic" and the "social" models, were unsure and somewhat confused.

For the rest of this talk I shall give evidence that the "material" or "social" model to which he refers, is, *pace* Brown, clearly discernible by 388, when Augustine wrote the *De quantitate animae,* and can be seen also in the *Dialogues of Cassiciacum,* his earliest extant works, written in the autumn of 386 after his conversion and before his baptism. It is generally accepted that Augustine had by then read the *De regressu animae,* and both P. Courcelle as well as myself have argued that he had read the *Philosophy from Oracles* (if it is a separate work) also.[19]

What could be clearer than the following: "We shall see also such great transformations and changes (*tantas commutationes et uicissitudines*) of our corporeal nature, in its obedience to the divine dispensation, that we shall hold the very resurrection itself of the flesh (*etiam ipsam resurrectionem carnis*), which partly is reluctantly, and partly altogether not believed, with such certainty, that it cannot be more certain to us than that when the sun sets, it will rise again. In this case death, the ultimate flight and escape from this body, is desired as the greatest boon."[20] Augustine may be employing a manner of speech which is eminently suitable for the carnal and uninstructed, but this he did no less in his last years, and the "social" or "material" model is, for all that, equally to be found in this very early passage.

Augustine goes on to express how we should despise those who scoff at the assumption of humanity by the eternal and unchangeable son of God for our salvation, and of his birth of a virgin, and the other miracles of this story. This whole passage is palpably part of his Porphyrian *topos*-vendetta. There can be no doubt that Augustine by this time (388) had rejected the Porphyrian view that Christ, though man, body and soul, was not God.

This is not to say that Augustine, in 388, had not yet to develop his theology of the incarnation. Miles has summarized this development in her book, *Augustine on the Body*.[21] The background to and occasion for this development, which was uneven, was the chaotic state of incarnational theology in Augustine's time. But Augustine had in 388 accepted the divinity of Christ and his full humanity however he understood their union.[22] He had also accepted the resurrection of human flesh in heaven.

To come to the *Dialogues of Cassiciacum*—one must expect that what Brown calls the "spiritual" (or "ascetic") view of the body is evident by these early works. This is indicated with great regret and much thumping of his breast by Augustine himself frequently in the first four chapters of the first book of the *Retractations*. Most of what he wishes he had not written refers to his praise of the Platonists and his appearing to use their views, especially in relation to the contrast between the "sensible" and "intelligible" worlds. He speaks of their errors as "great." In *De uera religione*, written in 390, however, he had asserted that "with the change of a few words and statements"[23] the Platonists would have become Christians—which shows how optimistic he felt about the Christian uses of Neoplatonism in 390. At the same time, if we are to believe the author of the *Retractations*—and I think we have for the moment no option—Augustine, when he wrote the *Dialogues*, in some at least of the instances that he regrets, held a *differing* opinion from that of the Neoplatonists, *for which opinion his, however, could be mistaken.*

To take one instance, he writes (R I, 4, 3): *Et in eo quod ibi dictum est, "Penitus esse ista sensibilia fugienda"* (SO I, 14, 24), *cauendum fuit ne putaremur illam Porphyrii falsi philosophi tenere sententiam, qua dixit: "Omne corpus fugiendum." Non autem dixi ego, "Omnia" sensibilia; sed, "ista," hoc est, corruptibilia; sed hoc, potius dicendum fuit: "Non autem talia sensibilia futura sunt in futuri saeculi coelo nouo et terra noua."* "And there where it is said, 'One must flee absolutely from those sensibles,' care should have been taken lest I be thought to hold that opinion of the false philosopher Porphyry, by which he says: "all" sensibles; but "those" sensibles, that is sensibles that are corruptible; but I should rather have said: "There will not be such sensibiles in the new heaven and the new earth of the world to come." His final, at least general, position of course was that there could be sensibles and bodies, but incorruptible, in the afterlife, and that these should be welcomed, not fled from. But the implications of the *Retractations* are that at the time of his writing [of] the *Soliloquies*, he *could* consciously have used an expression that *could not* be confused with Porphyry's famous phrase, and, therefore, that he knew that phrase: *omne corpus fugiendum* as Porphyry's and knew what it involved.[24]

Now the phrase *omne corpus fugiendum*, we know from Augustine himself, was referred by Porphyry primarily to body in relation to the afterlife. Porphyry's contention was that the soul could not achieve happiness in heaven if it had any connection with body: *sed Porphyrius ait, inquiunt, ut beata sit anima, corpus esse omne fugiendum*.[25] The conclusion is that Augustine when writing the *Retractations* leads us to believe, presumably in good faith, that when writing the *Soliloquies* he had not accepted Porphyry's teaching that there could be no body in the afterlife.

Augustine explains his carelessness in his use of the term "sense" (and "sensibles") by saying that at the time of writing the *Soliloquies* he still spoke according to the convention (that is, the Platonic convention) whereby the term 'sense' was used properly of the body.[26] But there is, as he points out, a 'sense' of the mind also: *est enim sensus et mentis*,[27] that is sense in heaven, incorruptible and compatible with intelligence. Augustine admits that he would not have used the expression, for example, *mundus intelligibilis* (and correspondingly, *mundus sensibilis*) without qualification if he had been sufficiently instructed in ecclesiastical literature at the time.[28]

Again, in *Contra Academicos* III, 42f., Augustine gives a clear proclamation of his intention to adhere forever to the authority of Christ, in the confidence that he will not find a stronger, and of his adherence to the Christian religion (*sacra nostra*), and of his belief that "God, in his compassion for the mass of men, had *bent and submitted the authority of the divine intellect even to the human body itself.* By the precepts as well as deeds of that intellect souls have been awakened, and are able to return to themselves and see once again their fatherland." This accepts that to Christ's human body had been submitted the authority of the divine intellect and that the masses were led to salvation by Christ's precepts. Although the relation of the Word to Christ's body is not clarified in theological terms, and there is ambiguity about the character of the "intelligible" world hereafter, and, as it appears, some few could make their way there without following Christ as the universal way, nevertheless there is a clear departure from the Porphyrian view of Christ's Incarnation.

In *De ordine* I, 10, 29 there is an emphatic and explicit assertion that Christ, the son of God, is properly called God: *non enim filius* (*Dei*, i.e., *Christus*) *improprie deus dicitur.* It is further said[29] that the Christian mysteries teach us of the one omnipotent God, the tripotent Father, Son, and Holy Spirit. And as to the fact that so great a God took up and lived in our human body for our sakes (*hoc etiam nostri generis corpus tantus propter nos deus adsumere atque agere dignatus est*), the more unworthy it appears, the more full of clemency it truly is and far removed from a certain pride of the clever (*a quadam ingeniosorum superbia*). This clearly is a hit at Porphyry, or such as Porphyry, whose pride, according to Augustine, prevented him from accepting, not Christ's full humanity, but his divinity.

I have indicated elsewhere[30] other texts in the *Dialogues of Cassiciacum* which can be referred in one way or another to Augustine's "vendetta," as Brown describes it, against Porphyry. Augustine did believe that Christ was fully divine and fully human, thus rejecting the Neoplatonic assertion of the incompatibility of the "spiritual" and the "material." To that extent he had already before his baptism embraced the "social" model of which Brown speaks. But, as we have conveyed earlier, we have to accept, too, that there are many texts also in the *Dialogues*, which if taken alone, not to say away from their total context, reflect the "ascetic" or "spiritual" model. In the early days Augustine could justify this double understanding on the ground that there were two ways to the same truth—authority and reason—and that reason could lead independently to the same truth as that proposed by authority. He expected that Neoplatonic reasoning would not conflict with Scriptural truth: as he says himself: "I, therefore, am resolved in nothing whatever to depart from the authority of Christ—for I do not find a stronger. But as to that which is sought out by subtle reasoning—for I am so disposed as to be impatient in my desire to apprehend truth not only by faith but also by understanding—I feel sure at the moment that I shall find it with the Platonists, nor will it be at variance with our sacred mysteries."[31] Not only, he claims, did philosophy not despise the Christian mysteries, but it alone leads one to understand them as they should be understood, and it can address itself to questions posed by the dogmas of authority.[32]

It is clear that, while fully accepting the authority of the Christian Scriptures, Augustine considered himself in the beginning as being among the *paucissimi,* the few, for whom it was more *suitable* that they should make their way through reason alone.[33] He cannot but have underrated at the beginning the difference between himself and such as Porphyry in relation to the compatibility or incompatibility of the "spiritual" and the "material." But by the time he wrote *De quantitate animae* in 388, he commended the way of authority as safer and describes the desire to know by reason as arising from *cupiditas;* nor was he sure that such true and unerring reason was at all discoverable by man (*si tamen ullo modo haec ab homine inueniri potest*).[34]

But from the beginning nevertheless, on the evidence of the *Dialogues of Cassiciacum,* he accepted explicitly the divinity and authority of Christ, the Scriptures, the *ueneranda mysteria* of the Christian community; likewise he accepted the doctrine of the trinity and of the incarnation; and, if we interpret the *Retractations* correctly, he believed in 386, as he certainly did in 388, in the resurrection of the human body. By 388 we have evidence that he believed in the virgin birth and the other miracles of Christ's life, including, it seems clear from the context, Christ's crucifixion and, probably, his resurrection.[35]

Augustine, as we have seen, had always a strong sense of the "economy" of truth, of the esoteric and exoteric in doctrine. After all he was but following St. Paul: "I fed you with milk, not solid food; for you were not ready for it; and even yet you are not ready, for you are still of the flesh."[36] His thoughts on the relations of authority and reason have always this economy in mind.[37] He accepts in *De quantitate animae*[38] that there comes a time when milk is not suitable and should be refused, while at the same time he speaks with passion against those who despise such an economy and with praise of those who practise it.[39] At the same time he leaves us in no doubt in his very earliest works that he fully believed *for himself* in the doctrines I have just listed. Furthermore he is aware that he is parting from Porphyry in accepting the central doctrine of the joining of the "spiritual" and the "material" in the incarnation. Reason, he held, had not misled Porphyry; rather was it his pride and the influence of demons. For himself he continued to explore how far reason could go in understanding the faith: this is to be seen in a remarkable way in a work as late as *De Genesi ad litteram*.

In the early days he suffered much excusable confusion: "What have I held firmly?" he asks in *De beata uita*, whose opinions on the question of the soul are uncertain and ever-changing.[40] It is a question which tormented him at this time, and he appears to complain that he might have got more help on it from Ambrose.[41] It is a question which still confronted him even at the end. Neoplatonism might help; Neoplatonism might hinder. As he said himself he took the "spoils of the Egyptians" wherever he could.

Perhaps he had hoped to find in Porphyry's teaching on the *pneuma*, the *spiritus*, as an intermediary between the soul and the body, a way of bridging the "spiritual" and "material." The *pneuma* was a kind of psychic envelope, or vehicle, ὄχημα, covering the soul during its descent through the planetary orbits. The soul's experience on earth was inscribed on this envelope which accompanied the soul after its separation from the body.[42] Augustine shows himself aware of this idea not only in his *De Genesi ad litteram*, but also in E 13, 2 (dated before 391): there he speaks of a certain enduring body of the soul or quasi-body which some call a "vehicle." But in 391 he seems unsure about this "vehicle."

The *Confessions* indicate clearly that there was a period after his reading of the Neoplatonist books when he followed Porphyry in pride in rejecting Christ. According to the same *Confessions* that period ended on the *intellectual* level when Augustine compared the teaching of the Neoplatonists with that of St. Paul: "Whatever truths I had read in those other works I here found to be uttered along with the praise of your grace."[43] He was now intellectually satisfied about Christ: "The way, the Saviour himself, had become pleasing, but as yet I was loath to tread its narrow passes."[44] The problem of the flesh probably played a part in this hesitation. But there was also, it appears, some embarrassment *vis-à-vis* the Platonists. Victorinus had been likewise embarrassed, and so Simplicianus told the circumstances of his conversion to Augustine to stimulate him to follow Victorinus in becoming formally a Christian.[45]

De beata uita appears to bear out this sequence of events: "Having read a few books of Plato (the books referred to in the *Confessions* as books of the Platonists), and compared with them also the authority of those who have handed on to us the divine mysteries, I became so on fire that I wanted to break all anchors that held me, except that the regard I had for certain men affected me."[46]

There remained only the movement of his will. It happened with the *tolle lege* that led him to this text of St. Paul: "Put you on the Lord Jesus Christ, and make not provision for the flesh in its concupiscences."[47] In putting on Christ, he parted from Porphyry and, however uncertainly, from the "ascetic" or "spiritual" paradigm. This happened, then, not around 386, but at or near the outset of his conversion.

PART IV

AUGUSTINE AND ERIUGENA

17

Augustine's Understanding of the Creation and Fall

❧

Augustine made at least four attempts[1] to expound the story of creation as given in Genesis, of which the best known is the allegorical attempt in the *Confessions*. He was, however, a far greater realist than is commonly believed, and was imbued with something like what we would call the scientific spirit: "le seul Père," to quote Pierre Duhem's famous *Le Système du Monde*,[2] "qui n'ait point dédaigné et passé sous silence les doctrines de la Science profane." He wanted to see how much of the story of Creation in Genesis could be rationally understood. The *De Genesi ad litteram* lets us see how he fared.[3]

Augustine's *De Genesi ad litteram*, "Genesis Understood Literally," was a book of immense influence in the Middle Ages when it was known as the *Hexaemeron*, the "Six Days," that is, the six days of creation; but it has been rather unknown in recent centuries. There had been no separate edition of the work until that in the Bibliothèque Augustinienne, *La Genèse au sens littéral* (Paris, 1972). The first English translation is by John H. Taylor, S.J., *St. Augustine, The Literal Meaning of Genesis*, ACW 41, 42 (New York, 1982). The book and its contents, therefore, have not been familiar to non-Latinists and especially Anglophones until quite recently.

This is a pity, for it is a mature work, written when Augustine was over sixty, and on the whole it is very calm and free from controversy. It is also undogmatic. It makes quite a point of considering various solutions to many problems. Augustine refers frequently to his uncertainty on important matters. Thus, "I have set down in writing, as far as I could," he writes at the beginning of the twelfth and final book, "my exposition of the first part of holy Scripture, which is called Genesis, up to the point when the first man was expelled from Paradise. I do not seek so much to prescribe what each one should believe in relation to things that are obscure, as to show that I myself need instruction in matters on which I have been in doubt." The book in fact leaves many things undecided: it is also profoundly influenced by the secular philosophy of the Neoplatonists.

There are those who contend that in the West we now live in a post-Christian civilisation. Even if this be so, the Hebraic-Christian documents to which Christendom was related remain of great, at least *historical*, interest. The first of these documents gives the story of the creation, including the creation of man and woman, and then their fall: I refer to the opening chapters of the book of Genesis in the Old Testament. I shall confine myself to that account.

Many people, I believe, if they ever reflect on the matter at all, have the impression that the book of Genesis describes first the creation of Adam, the male, in the image of God and later the making of Eve, the female, from a rib of Adam and not in the image of God. This appears to put woman in a position of inferiority from the beginning. But is this, we should ask, what Genesis says?

By way of digression, may I say that a *leitmotif* in this discussion will necessarily be the question of the equality or inequality of the sexes in the creation. One must not expect too much of Augustine who, while striking, as I hope to show, some significant blows on woman's behalf, inevitably passed on some of the long-inherited prejudices of his time against women—some of them not even recognised by women themselves as prejudices. No reader of his *Confessions* can lay down that book and say that Augustine was not subject to woman's charm, or did not respond in affection, if only to the devotion of his mother Monnica. But he inherited a literary and philosophical view from the Greek world—through the Hellenistic Roman world—according to which woman was dangerous to man, a Pandora who brought trouble upon him, and inferior to man. Aristotle classified woman as an infertile male.[4] The philosophical schools not only provided education for men but also companionship, in which women for the most part did not share. Augustine was deeply affected by these philosophical models, as is clear from the *Confessions*, where he describes how he and others, interested in philosophy, formed the project of living in a philosophical community—but such wives as there were would have none of it![5] The Roman world, which touched Augustine more immediately, greatly respected women as mothers, but a woman's legal position was little more than that of a chattel of her husband or some other male of her family. Adultery by her could in early days be punished by death, while a man might go scot-free. The purpose of marriage was procreation, and a woman who was barren could legally be penalised. Roman literature mostly represented woman as dangerous: think of the fierce onslaught of the poet Lucretius on women in the fourth book of his *De rerum natura*,[6] or of Virgil's pronounced interest in, but final discouragement of, the love of women in his *Aeneid*. Or think of the speech attributed by Livy to Marcus Porcius Cato: "Give loose rein to women's uncontrollable nature . . . and expect that they themselves will set bounds to their licence! . . . The moment they begin to be your equals, they will begin to be your superiors!"[7] Apart from the influences on Augustine in this matter from his Greek and Roman backgrounds there was also the influence of the Old and New Testaments. The Hebrew mother, respected for her fertility and the "labour of her hands," remained under the authority of her father or her husband. Jewish men could even cancel the vows that their women made to God. The New Testament holds many texts from St. Paul which on their face relegate women to an inferior state: as the head of every man is Christ, so the head of every woman is her husband; man was not created for woman, woman was created for man.[8]

These are but a few instances of the attitudes towards women which persisted not only in Augustine's day but for very long after, if not indeed until, so to speak, yesterday. There were women who rebelled against them (we meet some of them in the *Satires* of Juvenal),[9] though they can hardly have been such horrors as the virulence of Juvenal depicts. But few spoke for the cause of woman or bothered to mention it at all. This does not mean that individual men did not treat individual women as equals, or that romantic love did not exist then as it does now. But by and large Augustine grew up with inherited ideas of the inferiority of women, whatever the respect owed them in their moral figures as mothers.

In these circumstances it would be an unreasonable expectation to feel that one could exonerate Augustine of all charges of prejudice against woman. Of some prejudices—by our present-day views—he could hardly have been conscious.

To return then to Genesis, we should ask, "What *does* Genesis say on the creation of man and woman?" Here it is, in the version followed by Augustine (the Latin version of the Septuagint): "Et dixit Deus: faciamus hominem ad imaginem et similitudinem nostram; et dominetur piscium maris, et uolatilium caeli, et omnium pecorum et omnis terrae et omnium reptilium repentium super terram. Et fecit Deus hominem, ad imaginem Dei fecit eum: masculum et feminam fecit eos,"[10] "*Let us make man in our image and likeness. And let man have dominion over the fish of the sea, and the birds of the air, and all cattle, and all the earth, and all creeping things that creep upon the earth. And God created man, in the image of God he made him: male and female he made them."* The word used for man here, *homo*, does not refer specifically to male or female. *Homo*, unlike *uir* which is specific to the male, is generic and refers equally to male and female. The text makes this explicit by adding "male and female he made them." According to this text, then, man *and* woman were created in God's image equally, and both given equal dominion over animals and the earth.

But what about the making of Eve from Adam's rib? Augustine saw that there were two accounts, not one, of creation in the first three chapters of Genesis. The first extends down to and, on his calculation, includes the fifth verse in the second chapter. The text I have quoted belongs to this first account. The second account begins in the sixth verse of the second chapter; it includes the reference to the rib.

How can there be two *differing* accounts of the same event? Augustine, following the Neoplatonists, and particularly Plotinus,[11] understands that there was one creation only, of all things together and at the same time, *simul et semel*, but that that creation had, so to speak, two "moments" or aspects. In the first moment or aspect were made the "causal reasons," the *rationes causales*, of all things that ever were to be. The "causal reasons" of man and woman were fully existent in time and fully differentiated as to sex, but they were not yet corporeal. This is the stage of creation to which the text about man and woman being equally created in God's image refers. In the second moment of creation the "causal reasons" of things, including Adam and Eve, are in due and varying time verified in reality—they become the kind of beings we see, corporeal, visible and so on: but they had fully existed from the first moment of creation.

Augustine's theory of "causal reasons" derives ultimately from Stoic doctrine, but more immediately from Plotinus's theory of *logoi* or "reasons." Plotinus sought to account for the existence of things in their emanation from the Father or First Hypostasis or the One. From the One emanates "logos" or intelligence or *nous* which implies the duality of thinker and thought. From "logos" in its turn emanates the soul or spirit which is the point of mediation between the immaterial and the material or sensible world. Plotinus's three hypostases—the One, Logos and Soul—are in a descending order of being. The fancied Christian correspondences, Father, Logos or Word, and Spirit, are on the other hand equal and constitute the trinity. Augustine's "causal reasons," therefore, are a creation not of the *nous*, Logos, word, intelligence, or reason only, but of the trinity. In Plotinus's scheme the *nous* is the model of which the universe is the image.[12] In Augustine the causal reasons are said to be in the Word.

To understand Augustine's concept of the creation of the causal reason of man or woman or, for it was similar, angel, one must look a little more closely at Plotinus's *nous*.[13] The *nous* is a radiance of the one, a *perilampsis*. This radiance, Plotinus tries to explain, looked towards the one from which it has its being, recognised that it was separated from the one, saw reflected in itself the potentiality of the one, and moved in love towards its origin.[14] Thus had *nous* emanated from the Father. Since there is no mention of the creation of the angels in Genesis, the order *Fiat lux*, "Let there be light," refers, Augustine believes, to the creation of the angels. "Immediately on the word of God, light (the angel) was made, and the light created clung to the creating light, seeing it and itself in it, that is the reason by which it was made. It saw itself in itself, that is as being separate, because it was made from him who made it."[15] Such was, in Plotinian/Augustinian terms, the creation of the angel. Since man is also an intellectual creature, Augustine does not think it necessary to explain the creation of the causal reasons of man or woman: he simply refers to that of the angel as being identical. "[Our] nature itself, which is intellectual, is like that light (namely, the angel), and therefore its creation is its knowing the Word of God by which it is made."[16]

The creation of woman in her causal reason, that is as already existing and differentiated as woman from man, is identical, therefore, not only with that of man but also of the angel. With man she is equally the image of God and holds with him equal dominion over all animals. Augustine is confronted with many authorities who opposed him and also with serious difficulties in thus seeking (in Neoplatonic philosophy) some rational understanding of Genesis. St. Basil of Caesarea, for example, whose homily *In verba faciamus* Augustine was probably using in his exposition of Genesis, supposed that the causal reasons of man and woman included only their minds, their *mentes*:[17] he excluded the bodily specification of woman at this stage. Augustine insists that woman specifically existed then. Origen had a different idea. Man and woman were not differentiated in a bodily way in their causal reasons. The differentiation was of function: the male contemplated eternal truth; the female administered temporalities; the one commanding, the other obeying, both related in a quasi-marriage.[18] Augustine will have none of this. He maintains his position unaffected by authorities.

And he has to encounter the greatest of them, St. Paul, who states clearly that "the male is the image and glory of God, but woman is the glory of the male," *uir . . . imago et gloria Dei est, mulier autem gloria uiri.*[19] This on the face of it denies that woman was made in the image of God. Once again Augustine insists on his own position, St. Paul notwithstanding. St. Paul must have been speaking figuratively, he says: by male, Augustine suggested, was meant the contemplation of truth and by woman the administration of temporalities: St. Paul was not talking about man and woman in themselves at all: he was talking in terms of the long-lasting stereotyped roles of man and woman.[20]

Then there was the difficulty of understanding the following text—which was clearly within the account of the first moment of creation: "And God blessed them, saying 'Increase and multiply and fill the earth . . . behold I give you all manner of food.'"[21] How could "causal reasons" whose bodies were invisible reproduce? How could they eat food? Augustine admits that he has no satisfactory solution; he can only remark that whatever the difficulty was about the "causal reasons" of man and woman reproducing or eating, there is in fact no evidence in Genesis that in the first moment of creation they did. Both of these functions could have been fulfilled in the second moment of creation.

And so we come to the second moment of creation: "Then the Lord God formed man of dust from the ground, and breathed into his nostrils the breath of life; and man became a living being. And the Lord God planted a garden in Eden, in the east; and there he put the man whom he had formed. And out of the ground the Lord God made to grow every tree that is pleasant to the sight and good for food, the tree of life also in the midst of the garden, and the tree of the knowledge of good and evil . . . And the Lord God commanded the man, saying, 'You may freely eat of every tree of the garden; but of the tree of the knowledge of good and evil you shall not eat, for in the day that you eat of it you shall die.' Then the Lord God said, 'It is not good that the man should be alone; I will make him a helper fit for him.' . . . So the Lord God caused a deep sleep to fall upon the man, and while he slept took one of his ribs . . . and the rib which the Lord God had taken from the man he made into a woman and brought her to the man. Then the man said, 'This at last is bone of my bone and flesh of my flesh.'"[22]

Augustine pronounces that to take the words of Genesis "the Lord God formed man of dust from the ground" literally is too puerile: one must believe that Genesis is meant figuratively here . . . *translato uerbo usum credere deberemus*.[23] With regard to Eve, he must have allowed the same fundamental position. Yet he appears to be less radical: he tries to see some significance in the figure that Eve was made *from* Adam. He does this, it would appear, to emphasize the intimate bonding of Adam and Eve and all humanity in one and the same flesh. It will be noticed that in this Augustine, far from denigrating the flesh, honours it as much as he can. He may have pastoral reasons too for not dismissing as puerile the forming of Eve from Adam: the image of Eve coming from Adam's side suggested a parallel with both the birth of Christ from the Virgin, and of the Church emerging from the side of Christ pierced by a lance at the Crucifixion.[24] The first of these comparisons at least, far from putting Eve in an inferior position in emerging from Adam's side, sets her beside Christ, who was God as well as man, as born of the Virgin Mary. This is more than merely flattering to Eve and woman.

Augustine does not in fact know how Adam or Eve, from being "causal reasons," equally images of God in their minds, came in the second moment of creation physically to be. He assumes that, as Adam was the first man, he could not have had parents; but he leaves it open as to whether he came to be in this visible world as an infant or a mature man or in any other stage. He discusses the question, however, on the basis of Adam's coming to physical life as a mature man. Similarly, Eve could not have been gestated by Adam, but she could have started this life as an infant or a mature woman. Augustine supposes, however, that, if she came in some way from Adam in the second moment of her creation, she arrived at full maturity later than he did. This has serious consequences, as we shall see presently.

This coming into physical being of Adam and Eve could not in the nature of creation be the same as that which would be ordained as normal for all the other "causal reasons" of men and women that ever were to be: these would be propagated by parents and grow up from infancy to full maturity. When the "causal reasons" of all things were created *simul et semel* at the beginning of time, God did not ordain that Adam and Eve should in the second moment of their creation come into physical being as all other men and women: He made special arrangements in his act of creation for them. In this way there was no infringement of the laws of nature in the manner of their creation, nor any miracle. This too is the explanation, Augustine says, of other seeming "miracles." God does not change his mind: he provided for all such events in the first "moment" of creation.

The man and woman that came to be in the second moment of creation had real animal bodies and inhabited a real physical place. Here Augustine departed from the view of Origen,[25] for example, for whom the Garden of Eden was no more than figurative, and that of others of the Greek Fathers, such as Gregory of Nyssa, according to whom man and woman did not have animal bodies until after the Fall.[26] Augustine indeed did not object even to the notion that Adam and Eve might have propagated before the Fall, either without being subjected to *libido*, or with *libido* (which would not be sinful). He, therefore, honours human nature as it is found in man and woman. For him, there is no association of the sexuality of either man or woman as such with sin. Nor did Augustine even consider the view of some of the Greek Fathers that woman and her sexuality was a declension in being from that of man, and that when, in the end, all things returned to the Father the first step from the lowest level of being was that woman should become man, and so on upwards. Augustine accepted the equal innocent alert sexuality of man and woman before the Fall.[27]

Augustine in *Genesis Understood Literally* does not—although as we shall see he does elsewhere—differ from the understanding of his contemporaries, pagan and Christian, on the end of sexuality and marriage. The text of Genesis said that woman was made to be a helper fit for man. Augustine understands the way she might help as follows: "If woman was not made for the specific aid of begetting children for man, for what aid was she made? Was it to work the land with him? There was no toil then, and he had no need of aid. If he were to need it, a male would have been a better aid. One might relate this aid to companionship in the case where man began to get tired of being alone—but for living and speaking together, would not two men who were friends live with one another more harmoniously than a man and a woman? [Here we see the influence of ancient social and educational factors and notably of the philosophical schools.] And if they had to live together on the basis of one giving orders and the other obeying, lest opposing wills should trouble the peace of those living together, provision had been made for achieving this, since one was created before, the other after [he is referring to the second moment of creation] and especially since the second was created from the first, as woman was created. No one would claim that God could have made a woman only and not also, if He so willed, a male from the rib of man. And so I can discover no aid for man for which woman was made, if childbearing is eliminated."[28]

One knows, of course, that Augustine was not the first to make such a pronouncement, and so cannot be said to be primarily responsible for it. It is important, however, to bear in mind that he had a tendency to make absolute statements which were never meant to be more than theoretical. In practice he recognised that life was not led on absolutes. Thus in the *City of God* he declares that a state which does not pay worship to the true, that is Christian, God fails in true justice; and, therefore, since justice belongs to the definition of a state, is not a state. In practice, however, he accepts that Rome for example is a state since it does possess justice as this is normally understood. Similarly in his book *On the Good of Marriage*, to which he refers for guidance on such questions in this section of DGnL, he states equally clearly: "Marriage seems to me to be a good not exclusively on account of the procreation of children, but on account also of the natural bonding of the two sexes in itself."[29] That natural bonding, in his view, is not without significance; otherwise, he says, one could not properly speak of marriage between a couple too old to produce children.

When we come to the story of the Fall, we find Augustine at his wits' end to excuse both Adam and Eve. Eve, according to Genesis, was found by the serpent to be the weak point. It was impossible, Augustine thought, that one endowed with spiritual intelligence, as was Adam, should believe the Devil when he represented that God would be jealous of Adam's knowledge if he ate of the fruit of the tree of knowledge. It was possible that Eve, being in her second aspect created later than Adam and therefore not *yet* having attained a full level of knowledge, for that reason did succumb to the Devil's temptation. Augustine puts this forward as no more than a possible explanation. He is at pains, though, to indicate that Eve would in due course have attained the same level of spirituality and intelligence as Adam, and therefore, presumably, would not have been deceived by the Devil.[30] Augustine suggests that, when Adam consented to eat the apple on Eve's invitation, he knew he was doing wrong but—and here comes the romantic touch—was undone, as was Solomon later, by his great love for Eve.

"Can one believe," Augustine asks, "that Solomon, a man of remarkable wisdom, thought that there was any use in the cult of idols? No, he was unable to resist the love of women which brought him to this evil, doing what he knew should not be done, lest he should disappoint the mistresses whom he loved to distraction and who destroyed him. Likewise Adam, after the woman had been seduced and had eaten of the forbidden tree and had given to him to eat with her, could not bring himself to disappoint her. He felt sure that she would waste away if she did not have his support and were alienated from his mind. The disagreement would be the end of her. He was . . . overcome . . . by a certain loving benevolence through which it usually happens that for fear of turning a friend into an enemy we offend God."[31] In short, Adam's love of Eve was greater than his fear of God.

This idea—which is associated with Theophilus of Antioch—Augustine advances as no more than a suggestion. In fact he says quite clearly that he does not know what the temptation of the apple was for either Eve or Adam or what really happened.

There are few basic considerations relevant to the status of women which do not come up in one way or another in a discussion of the account given in Genesis of the creation of Adam and Eve and of their status *vis-à-vis* one another before the Fall. In a post-Christian world belief in the story of Genesis is not to be presumed. Nevertheless, the status of women up till now has been profoundly affected by that story. In spite of the enormous prejudices against women in the Greco-Roman and Hebraic world, which I have attempted to outline, Augustine on almost every point defends the equality of woman with man. Her making is equal; her endowments are equal. She is not something that had to be made because of sin: she was made as Adam was made and both had ordinary human bodies that felt as human bodies feel. Such feelings were not sinful in themselves. Procreation was not the exclusive end of marriage. Augustine did not of course encounter the problems of the twentieth century, and one can hardly be confident in deciding what his views would be on any present issue; but he tended to take an evolutionary view of the world and humanity, which is not to say that he was a full scientific evolutionist. But just as he held that the Patriarchs did not sin in having many wives so that the population of the world might be built up to a sufficient number, whereas his contemporaries would have sinned in having many wives, so we should not assume that he was adamant in his opinions. Indeed he is remarkably unsure of his opinions on many crucial issues even in advanced years.

Augustine was undoubtedly attracted to women and could sympathize with the uncontrollable love of women such as Dido in the *Aeneid*. Even when he had been converted and embraced chastity, he confessed how at times the thought of women occupied his mind. If he denied his senses, however, that did not mean that he lost sympathy. I have the impression indeed that, whether because of his remarkable relations with his mother Monnica or not, he had an especial understanding of and sympathy for women. This may not be what one has heard about the Church Father. One should read the *Confessions*, the story of his youth, and then DGnL, a work of his sixties, and only then come to a firm conclusion for oneself.

18

Eriugena's Use of Augustine in His Teaching on the Return of the Soul and the Vision of God

ào

Eriugena's use of and attitude towards Augustine is a matter of great importance in the study of the ninth century Irish philosopher.[1] For the moment—until all Eriugena's works have been scientifically edited—one has to content oneself with limited essays into this difficult field. Yet there is one general question to which we should be able to supply some fairly clear answer: does Eriugena's thought essentially reflect the thought of Augustine or does it not? Are we to believe Bett, for example, who declares: "It is not too much to say that some of Augustine's treatises, especially the *City of God*, the *Confessions*, and *On the Trinity*, count for more, in Eriugena's essential thought, than the whole of the Dionysian writings, with the *Ambigua* of Maximus thrown into the scale."[2] Or are we to believe Mathon: "Il faut admettre que le ressort profond de la pensée d'Érigène n'est plus d'inspiration augustinienne"?[3]

Bett's claim does not appear to be supported by the statistics of the sources indicated by Eriugena himself.[4] The ratio between Eriugena's citations in *De diuisione naturae*,[5] for example, of Augustine and of all Greek authors combined is roughly 1:3 in Book I; 1:2 in Book II; 2:3 in Book III; 1:1 in Book IV; and 1:2 in Book V. This averages out for all the work as about two to one in favour of all the Greek authors combined against Augustine alone. But, of course, such a result may be of absolutely no significance whatever: quality can not be judged by quantity. Augustine might still, as Bett claims, dominate Eriugena's essential thought—nor would it be surprising if he did, in view of his general domination in philosophy and theology in the West down at least to the time of Eriugena.

Mathon, on the other hand, appears to be supported by the major Eriugenian scholar of our time, Cappuyns. For him there is a *contraste frappant*, for example, between the treatment of the topic of the beatific vision found in Eriugena's near contemporaries who depended mostly on Augustine, and Eirugena himself who followed the Greeks: "S'il arrive à S. Augustin de ne pas envisager un problème, ses disciples également l'ignorent. Et c'est ainsi, sans doute, que ceux qui s'enflammaient pour le mode, corporel ou intellectuel, de la vision béatifique, ne songèrent pas même, sauf Jean Scot disciple des Grecs, à en scruter la nature intime."[6] It is clearly implied here that Augustine had not envisaged aspects of the problem which became known to Eriugena from the Greeks and, moreover, that these aspects were significant, indeed of striking contrast. In essence what is being said is that Augustine does not adopt a Neoplatonic line of doctrine in the matter in question, and Eriugena, following the Greeks, does, which affects the whole tone of his treatment. In this Cappuyns appears to be on the same side as Gilson,[7] who feels that the extent and importance of Augustine's Neoplatonism *in general* are greatly exaggerated and their significance misunderstood.

We have, then, two apparently diametrically opposed views regarding Eriugena's essential thought. The problem, however, is more complicated than I have so far represented it. Not only did Augustine's thought evolve in response—in a degree more than usual—to his experiences; not only did he, as do all other sensible thinkers, admit that he had not solved to his satisfaction many of the great problems of existence; but Augustine had a strong impulse, which was partly artistic and perhaps also on occasion political, to believe that authors can profess one view for popular consumption while at least entertaining, or at any rate not dismissing, another and perhaps contradictory one.

We must dwell on this matter a little more, for it plays—according to Eriugena, as we shall see—an important role in the present enquiry. This attitude of Augustine derives from the well-established practice of antiquity of distinguishing between doctrines that were esoteric and exoteric, secret and popular, on which it is unnecessary to expatiate here. This is related to the belief, greatly favoured by Augustine in his earlier days, that there were two ways to salvation, the way of philosophy for the few and the way of authority for the many, and that the few, especially while following their philosophical way, would at the same time profit from the way of authority.[8]

Augustine was also deeply impressed by the paradoxical role of providence in his own life and in the life of mankind: things which one anticipated would be to one's great disadvantage turned out to be greatly to one's advantage; one sought a certain thing in a certain place and instead found its opposite: Augustine himself read Porphyry, who attacked Christianity, only to be convinced by his reading of Porphyry of the truth of Christianity: *uenena ipsa, quae per inconuenientiam perniciosa sunt, conuenienter adhibita in salubria mediacamenta uertantur.*[9] Things are truly seldom what they seem! Professions are not always to be taken at their face value.

There are probably other factors concerned, but, whatever the explanation, Augustine's fondness for believing that others did not mean what they said is remarkable. I have given elsewhere a list of instances of this occurring in the first half of the *City of God*:[10] they concern Posidonius, Varro, Numa, Socrates, and Apuleius. These are supposed to have at least tolerated popular opinions while hinting, to those who might know, their real belief: *neque hoc aperte dicere uoluisse, sed intelligentibus reliquisse . . . ciuilem (religionem) uero reprehendere quidem non audeat* (Varro);[11] *eorum malitiae . . . pepercerit* (Apuleius) *significauit tamen prudentibus, quid de illis sentire deberent.*[12] Augustine's *Contra Academicos* advances the hypothesis that the New Academics only pretended to be sceptics: in reality they carefully transmitted to the few the true positive doctrine of Plato.[13]

If Augustine had such marked fondness for so benignly interpreting doctrine of an opponent inconvenient to him, one is perhaps justified in raising the question if Augustine himself gives grounds on occasion for equally benign interpretation of himself? Did Augustine, in short, profess popular doctrine, which he might or might not hold to be true, while hinting his true opinion, or at least an opinion that he did not dismiss, to those who could read, so to speak, between the lines? This is a very serious question which one might discuss on a more suitable occasion. I do not propose to face it now, if only because here we are concerned, as we must be, with *Eriugena* more than Augustine.

The interesting thing is that Eriugena *does* make this characteristically Augustinian hypothesis about Augustine himself in relation to a fundamental Eriugenian doctrine, that of the return, the *reditus* or *regressus*, of the soul and the *visio Dei*. He purports indeed to reveal the *anti-Augustin chez Augustin*.

I must emphasize, in passing, that there is a world of difference between Eriugena's believing that Augustine, given the undisputed authority of the Pseudo-Dionysius, must have esoterically held similar views to this disciple of St. Paul (although, using the "economy" he was so ready to ascribe to others, he might exoterically profess different ones) and Eriugena's deliberately deforming Augustine's text for the purposes of controversy. Thus, Mathon has written: "Il y a beaucoup plus grave: l'utilisation déformante et arbitraire de ce qu'il a effectivement soutenu. Certes, la polémique et ses exigences excusent bien des choses, mais ces procédés révèlent un état d'esprit, des présupposés et des buts qui n'en demeurent pas moins. Et Jean Scot n'a pas hésité à y recourir pour arriver à ses fins."[14] This, I feel, does no justice to Eriugena's handling of Augustine which, as I shall try to show in the rest of this paper, is on the contrary scrupulous and sensitive.

In *De diuisione naturae* 986Bff. then, Eriugena, having quoted the view that the bodies of the saved will be as now, even to the division of male and female, except that they will be changed to spiritual qualities, professes great surprise that the Fathers—who in the context clearly include Augustine—should teach such doctrine. He can explain it only on the basis that they were sparing those who would not think except in fleshly terms: facilius ducor existimare, non aliam ob causam ad haec excogitanda et scribenda attractos fuisse, nisi ut saltem vel sic terrenis carnalibusque cogitationibus deditos, simplicisque fidei rudimentis nutritos ad spiritualia cogitanda sublevarent . . . Haec itaque, ut opinor, magni divinique considerantes, timidisque fidelium simplicium cogitationibus consulentes, utilius[15] visum est eis praedicare terrenorum sensibiliumque corporum transmutationem in caelestia sprituliaque corpora quam penitus[16] corpora et corporalia et sensibilia omnia nunquam esse futura.

It is in the light of this kind of declaration by Eriugena of the practice of economy by authors such as Augustine that we proceed to examine Eriugena's use of Augustine on the question of the return of the soul and, in due course, the *visio Dei*.

The return of the soul favoured by Eriugena[17] (876Aff.) is that propounded by Maximus and comprises five "returns." The first is the dissolution of the body into the four elements; the second is the recovery by the individual, from the elements, of his own body in the resurrection. According to Eriugena everybody accepts these two returns.

The third return is the change of body into spirit (*quando corpus in spiritum mutabitur*); the fourth, the return of the spirit to the primordial causes (*spiritus in primordiales causas revertetur*); the fifth, the return of nature and its causes to God, as air is moved into light (*ipsa natura cum suis causis movebitur in Deum, sicut aer movetur in lucem*). According to

Eriugena some theologians flatly deny (*penitus negant*) these last three "returns," and some are prudently doubtful (*caute dubitant*). These latter do not dare to assert even that Christ's humanity was changed (*conversam fuisse*) into divinity.

Augustine is quoted and reported as denying that the human soul can be changed to God or the body to soul (*negat animam humanam converti posse in Deum, neque corpus in animam*).[18] Eriugena declares that he willingly follows Augustine (and Boethius) in this (*libenter accipimus*), but is not unaware that the Greeks think differently. The Disciple fears, however, that these Greek views, however probable, may seem to the less instructed like ravings and self-contradictions.

In spite of this report of Augustine as "denying" Maximus's third and fifth "returns," it seems clear from every other indication that Eriugena regards Augustine as being among those who are prudently doubtful of, rather than among those who absolutely deny, these returns. The strongest indication of this is that those who prudently doubt are said to be those who do not dare to assert that Christ's humanity was changed into divinity, and Augustine, in Eriugena's account, is explicitly such a person.

The question of the 'conversion' of Christ's humanity to divinity was, however, for Augustine the most crucial and far-reaching of all. Eriugena reports[19] that Augustine in his *Letter to Dardanus* unhesitatingly affirms that the body of the Lord after resurrection is locally in heaven in the same form and substance of flesh in which he appeared in the world, with the addition only of immortality. Christ was not, therefore, everywhere (as God is), nor changed to divinity beyond all places and times, but would visibly and bodily come down from some place to judge the living and the dead. Eriugena refuses to believe that Augustine can support this view: that Christ's resurrected body is locally in a corporeal heaven (*caelum corporeum*) and simultaneously that that corporeal heaven will absolutely perish (*penitus interiturum*). Augustine, he indicates,[20] cannot believe these contrary propositions (*contraria*). His statement in the *City of God*[21] that this heaven will cease and change into a new heaven (*esse desinet hoc caelum et haec terra quando incipiet esse caelum nouum et terra noua; mutatione namque rerum, non omni modo interitu transibit hic mundus*) Eriugena regards as indicating total destruction of the corporeal: *caelum scilicet corporeum penitus interiturum*. Augustine cannot, therefore, mean that only Christ's humanity will persist in sensible and local form, when all other sensible things will have ceased. The conclusion is, therefore, expressed (992A): "credibilius arbitrandum est secundum capacitatem singulorum quibus scripsit, scripsisse, quam a sanctis Patribus, qui eum praecesserunt ordine temporum, ab Ambrosio dico Gregorioqe Theologo, quorum auctoritate in aliis locis non discrepat, dissensisse." Ambrose is quoted as being very clear that the change at issue is not from an earthly body to a heavenly one, but "omnino transitus in ipsum purum spiritum, in illum, qui intellectus vocitatur." Augustine can hardly have been unaware of such a view of Ambrose.

Eriugena, therefore, decides that Augustine does not at all disagree with the Greeks (993A): "Dic, quaeso, ubi dissonat (Augustinus) ab his, quae diximus, de transitu mundi hujus in suas causas, quas ipse naturam vocavit? Ille dicit, hoc caelum et hanc terram post judicium esse desitura, solam vero eorum naturam immutabiliter manere; similiter et nos docuimus vestigia ejus et aliorum similium sequentes, omne, quod in hoc mundo sensibile et locale et temporale, omneque mutabilitati obnoxium periturum, hoc est, transiturum in ipsam substantiam, hoc est, naturam; naturam vero ejus, quae incorporaliter et intelligibiliter in primordialibus rerum omnium causis immutabiliter et incorruptibiliter continetur, semper mansuram." He thus proceeds to spell out the implications of Maximus's third and fourth "returns," and asserts that he, Eriugena, is following Augustine and others in so understanding them. He implies that he is so sure that Augustine is on the side of Maximus and Ambrose in this that he treats with contempt (*omni responso indignus*) the notion that the nature that persists forever can be corporeal. Equally he accuses anyone who holds that Christ will persist forever in the flesh of not knowing the teaching of the Catholic Church. Only a madman (*amens*) would say that, whereas the celestial powers would escape from the sensible, Christ, already become spirit and God himself, would be detained in it.[22]

These uncomplimentary terms are very unlikely to be employed by Eriugena where he thought there could be any suspicion that they might be applied to Augustine. He, in other words, appears to feel satisfied that, whatever Augustine might say sometimes out of pastoral consideration for the uninstructed, he was at one on this matter with Ambrose and the rest.

The question naturally arises—*en passant*—why Augustine should have been so insistent on the eternal persistence of Christ's flesh, glorified of course, but not changed entirely to spirit? Anyone familiar with the climactic books of either the *Confessions* or the *City of God* will know that his encounter with Porphyry centred on the acceptance or rejection of Christ's becoming flesh. The incarnation was unthinkable to Porphyry, as were Christ's death and his bodily resurrection. Porphyry's touchstone was flight from the body—*omne corpus fugiendum.* One should try to escape from the body in this life; happiness in the afterlife equally depended on the absence of body in heaven and the absence of the prospect of return to it on earth again. Augustine in humility accepted that very incarnate Christ that Porphyry in pride rejected. From the day of his conversion on, Augustine was more and more convinced that he should espouse the way of humility to which Christ's flesh, in the incarnation and resurrection, was inextricably related, and shun the intellectual pride of Porphyry. The acceptance of this position by Augustine halted, if it did not also reverse, so to speak, his appreciation of Neoplatonism, and, because of his role in the West, the impact of Neoplatonism on the Western Church generally. For him Christ's resurrected fleshly body became an *idée fixe,* a touchstone of loyalty to Christ: the block was, therefore, at least partly emotional. Though this *idée fixe* is prominent in Augustine, it is not usually defended with the kind of subtle argument in which Eriugena revelled. Hence it became possible for Eriugena to treat Augustine's protestations on this point with respect, but to suggest that Augustine, nevertheless, agreed, for example, with Ambrose.

But Eriugena can not only interpret Augustine benignly in true Augustinian fashion: he can counter Augustine's pronouncements that are doubtful about, and sometimes hostile to Maximus's third and subsequent "returns," by quoting him often, extensively and, it would appear, convincingly in support of Maximus. Hence it is impossible to believe that Augustine was, as Cappuyns implies, *unaware* of the range of ideas suggested by the Greeks and Ambrose. This is *a priori* unlikely and can hardly now seem true, in view of both our increased knowledge of Ambrose's Neoplatonism and Eriugena's account of things.

Augustine's *actual* attitude to these ideas is more difficult to determine. While one may not feel entirely happy agreeing with Eriugena's conclusion that Augustine wholly accepted these views, one may find it possible to believe that he was prudently doubtful, but perhaps not actually opposed to them. He professed indeed very considerable uncertainty on these matters, as we shall immediately see.

If we now approach the question of the *futura felicitas,* the *visio Dei,* we shall see that Augustine declares openly his state of indecision. According to the *Retractationes* his statement on the matter in the *City of God* XXII, 29, dated to about 426 (the one used by Eriugena in *De diuisione naturae* 447Bff.) is final and definitive.[23]

Augustine starts (XXII, 29) by declaring that if he were to tell the truth he would confess his ignorance on the topic. He can say only what he *believes* (*dico quod credo*). The saints, *without* the use of eyes in their glorified bodies, will see God in spirit. The interesting question, however, is if they shall see him *with* their eyes? If they do, it cannot be because of any refinement of their sight, but simply by virtue of being able to see even *incorporalia: uis itaque praepollentior oculorum erit illorum, non ut acrius uideant, . . . sed ut uideant et incorporalia*. Augustine has to admit that Scripture gives no unambiguous testimony on this point.

He then turns to philosophy, to the philosophy (clearly Platonic/Neoplatonic) which holds that intelligible things cannot be perceived through the body nor corporeal things through the intellect working on its own. If this were true, then he would have to accept that the eyes even of the glorified or spiritual body could not see God. Now whereas in earlier life at least he approved easily of such notions in philosophy, at this point he remarks: *si possit nobis esse certissima* (*ista ratiocinatio*). The suggestion is that he finds it difficult to resist this reasoning—but in absolute terms he can so resist. He adds that *true* reason and, equivalently, Scripture contemns such a view: God, who is incorporeal does know corporeal things. From the Biblical instances of Elisha and Gehazi[24] Augustine assumes also that bodies can be seen by spirit. Why then might not the converse be true: that a spiritual body has the power to see spirit with its body? Surely we know the interior lives of our fellow men, which are invisible, through the body: *aliorum uitas, cum sint inuisibiles, per corpus uidet*. He concludes, then, that it is possible and *ualde credibile* that the spiritual eyes of our spiritual bodies will see through the body the incorporeal God.

In spite of such proclaimed credibility Augustine finally offers no more than the choice of alternatives: either the spiritual bodily eyes will have some assimilation to the intellectual (*aliquid habeant menti simile*) so that they can see incorporeal things, or God will be seen through bodies in every body. The first is difficult or impossible to demonstrate from Scripture; the second is easier to understand. "Aut ergo sic per illos oculos uidebitur Deus, ut aliquid habeant in tanta excellentia menti simile, quo et incorporea natura cernatur, quod ullis exemplis siue scripturarum testimoniis diuinarum uel difficile est uel impossibile ostendere; aut, quod est ad intelligendum facilius, ita Deus nobis erit notus atque conspicuus, ut uideatur spiritu a singulis nobis in singulis nobis, uideatur ab altero in altero, uideatur in se ipso, uideatur in caelo nouo et terra noua atque in omni, quae tunc fuerit, creatura, uideatur et per corpora in omni corpore, quocumque fuerint spiritalis corporis oculi acie perueniente directi" (XXII, 29).

It is significant that Augustine here in his final statement actually allows the possibility of the spiritual body becoming to a certain point assimilated to spirit. *To this extent* at least he himself (as distinct from Eriugena's interpretation of him in *De diuisione naturae* PL 993A) accepts Maximus's third "return," that the body becomes spirit. He always had allowed an open mind on the subject: *qualia sanctorum corpora in resurrectione futura sint, potest aliquanto scrupulosius inter Christianarum scripturarum doctissimos disputari.*[25] Eriugena had, therefore, a genuine opening for interpreting Augustine on this point in a sense acceptable to himself.[26]

When we turn from Augustine's to Eriugena's most formal (and noted as such by Cappuyns)[27] consideration of the topic of the *visio Dei* in *De diuisione naturae* 447A–451C, we are faced with the old problem of the perception of spirit by body. He describes *futura felicitas* as *ipsius diuinae essentiae pura contemplatio atque immediata*. Straightway he quotes Augustine's treatment of the matter, which we have just looked at: *per corpora, quae gestabimus, in omni corpore, quodcunque uidebimus ipsum Dominum perspicua claritate contemplabimur.*[28] It is made clear that the vision will be not directly of God, but of a God seen in another body, a theophany—for the divine essence is not comprehensible to any even intellectual creature. These theophanies (as the Greeks call them) or *apparitiones divinae* will vary according to the varying deserts of the saints, and they are sometimes termed God.

The really profound question, however, is what a theophany is. Here the description of Maximus is given and immediately confirmed in a remarkable way by quotation from Augustine. For Maximus a theophany comes from God, from the condescension of the Word who is the wisdom of the Father down, so to speak, to the purified human nature made by him, and the exaltation upwards of the same human nature to the Word through divine love (449A): "Ait enim theophaniam effici non aliunde nisi ex deo, fieri uero ex condescensione diuini uerbi, hoc est unigeniti filii qui est sapientia patris, ueluti deorsum uersus ad humanam naturam a se conditam atque purgatam, et exaltatione sursum

Return of the Soul 253

uersus humanae naturae ad praedictum uerbum per diuinum amorem."[29] And Augustine describes it in the following manner: the creating wisdom of the Father comes into our souls through an ineffable condescension of his mercy, joining our intellect to him, so that in an ineffable manner a certain conjoined wisdom comes into being, both from his descent to us and habitation in us, and from our intelligence elevated to him by him through love and formed in him (449B): "Sapientia patris in qua et per quam omnia facta sunt, quae non est creata sed creans, fit in animabus nostris quadam ineffabili suae misericordiae condescensione ac sibi adiungit nostrum intellectum, ut ineffabili quodam modo quaedam quasi composita fiat sapientia ex ipso descendente ad nos et in nobis habitante et ex nostra intelligentia ab eo per amorem ad se assumpta et in se formata."[30]

Maximus, following an old tradition, illustrates this conformation of the Word and our intelligence by appealing especially to the similes of air in light and metal in fire (450A): "Absente luce aer est obscurus, solis autem lumen per se subsistens nullo sensu corporeo comprehenditur; cum uero solare lumen aeri misceatur, tunc incipit apparere ita, ut in se ipso sensibus sit incomprehsibile, mixtum uero aeri sensibus possit comprehendi." Later the image of the iron in the fire is given.[31] In both cases the point made is that though the inferior (air, iron) appears to be one with the superior, each in reality remains separate. So are we joined in a theophany, while retaining our substance separate. There is no "confusion" of substances but rather a union, an *adunatio*, involving no composition.[32]

Augustine was familiar with the same images of light and air, of their union and their remaining, at the same time, separate: *in ipsis corporibus aeri lux incorrupta misceatur.*[33] Moreover he had, according to Eriugena (993A), asserted that *hoc caelum et hanc terram post iudicium esse desitura, solam vero eorum naturam immutabiliter manere*. Eriugena goes on to say that if anyone held that this *natura* was corporeal or subject to place and time, generation and corruption, he was outside the pale of reason and unworthy of attention—which Augustine, presumably, was not.

The Disciple in the *De diuisione naturae*, nevertheless, professes not to see clearly how the doctrine of Maximus accords with that of Augustine. The question looks as if it were put simply to give the Master an opportunity of emphasizing the agreement of the two. The Master confidently invites him to listen more closely to Augustine's text (450C): "per corpora quae gestabimus, in omni corpore, quodcunque videbimus, quaquaversum oculos nostri corporis duxerimus, ipsum Deum perspicua claritate contemplabimur."[34] We cannot see God directly—we shall see him through our bodies in every body that we shall see, that is in a theophany. Through our intellects we shall see him in intellects. His excellence will be so great that only he will shine forth.

Eriugena discusses (978Df.) the return of human nature in general. When the world is finished (*finito mundo*) all men will be restored in Christ (*totius humanae naturae in Christo restaurationem*). But some will ascend to God himself, to beatitude and deification. This deification Eriugena describes as *beata vita, pax aeterna in contemplatione veritatis*. Augustine's words are quoted in confirmation: "est enim beata vita gaudium de veritate, quae est Christus." For Augustine Christ is always first and last.

The foregoing enquiry does not seek to demonstrate that Augustine on the one hand, and Gregory, Maximus, and Ambrose on the other, agreed on the return of the soul and the *visio Dei*, or appeared to Eriugena so to agree. Augustine had departed too much from Neoplatonic doctrine, and was too emotionally and pastorally involved in stressing the model humility of Christ's Incarnation—the union of flesh and divinity *par excellence*—to find such agreement easy. It seems also to be true—and this needs to be emphasized—that his mind was not made up on the matter. These resistances and doubts are reflected in Eriugena's reports of his views. Nevertheless it seems likely from our examination that this disciple of Ambrose *knew* the views of Ambrose and, though he may have appeared to do so on occasion, did not simply reject them. It is not a matter of saying with Bett that Augustine dominates the essential thought of Eriugena; or of implying with Cappuyns that Augustine was unaware of significant and striking aspects of a central problem that determine the character of Eriugena's doctrine. The matter is more complicated than that. Augustine does not always dominate, but he is always there; and Eriugena succeeds to a surprising degree in wringing support from him for his favourite theses: this he can do—and in good faith—because of Augustine's own wide sympathies and knowledge, his doubts and economies. Eriugena was not insincere when he spoke of Augustine as his "Father."

19

Eriugena's Use of Augustine in His Teaching on the Soul-Body Relationship

🙢

The use of Augustine in Western Europe is not an insignificant question, nor one wholly without reference to our contemporary world. It is a cliché to describe Augustine as a *pontifex,* a bridge-maker, between the worlds of Greece and Rome and the Bible on the one hand, and Western Christendom on the other. There was indeed much that Augustine did pass on, but "passing on" was not the only function that he fulfilled. There was also much, as Gilson and others have remarked, that he did *not* pass on. His own choices, or apparent choices, among the doctrinal developments of an emerging Church became in large part the choices, or apparent choices, of the West. His word ran, seemingly unchallenged, until Aristotle and Thomas Aquinas gained the centre of the stage. But his influence still continued. It is well to bear in mind that Aquinas not only followed an Augustinian rule, but professed doctrinal allegiance to Pater Augustinus. It is well to bear in mind also that the Reformer Luther bore the religious name of Augustinus. In his characteristic way, he said he had not read Augustine so much as swallowed him whole! Augustine heavily marked the Reformation. And many of the theological and ethical positions being questioned or rejected today are traditionally attributed to Augustine, and to what is now judged his constricting and obscurantist influence. Our contemporaries speak of building bridges between persons and peoples, and a little also of rejecting fathers. It is the role of Augustine as Father of the West (a title sometimes attributed to him and to some others, including Virgil) that is now under attack. It may be useful, therefore, to look closer at one instance of the way in which he and his teaching were treated by his successors.

It is a feature of human life and its institutions that complex personalities and problems are simplified—over-simplified. Myth plays an important role here. But not every such simplification is described or recognized as myth. There is a more ordinary level of myth-making which usually goes by the name of received truth. I am not suggesting that this feature, especially in regard to institutions, is avoidable or altogether without good. Cohesion in society, as we are learning in our time, is as difficult to achieve as it is desirable, related, as it must be to the conflicting, and indeed sometimes noble, aspirations of man.

The process of simplification, however, usually does inadequate justice to the personality or problem so simplified. To choose a secular instance from the past—Julius Caesar (who also, by the way, might fairly lay claim to the title of Father of the West) could not have been the transcendent genius of the famous, but to the initiated, rather amusing portrait given of him by Theodore Mommsen, who was writing, of course, under the influence of a particular political ideology. It is equally unlikely that the same Caesar was the Satanic *Uebermensch* portrayed by Lucan or the simple bloodthirsty destroyer of Rousseau or Boileau.

The "great" men themselves do not always fully analyze their own motives or consider meticulously every aspect of the problem that faces them. They are determined by so many antecedent factors and are swept along, often by the seeming force of circumstances. They may partly determine the course of events, but at times they are determined by it. Soon they become prisoners of an image; and if that image is considered to be successful, they will have difficulty in disowning it. When they are dead, their followers crystallize their teaching, already misinterpreting it, perhaps, for their own reasons, but at any rate inevitably failing to pass on the hesitations, the qualifications, the evolutions and imposed political stances of the master.

I have found it necessary to indulge in these preliminary generalities because they are especially pertinent to the use made of Augustine and his teaching throughout the Christian era. Augustine himself, who lived from A.D. 354 to 430, is known generally from his *Confessions* and from the report that he was the greatest of the Church Fathers in the West, and in particular the one who taught seemingly absolute (if not fully comprehensible) doctrines on grace and predestination. He is the fleshly sinner who reacted too much and sought too much to impose his reactions on others. The title *Confessions* seems to confirm part of such a view.

Augustine is also known as the author of a great work, the *City of God*, which shares the fate of many great books—of being acknowledged to be great but remaining unread. Again its title, and to a certain extent its contents, suggest that it is a political treatise, a Christian version of Plato's and Cicero's *Republics*. Some have discovered in it theories of the relations of Church and State or, more recently, a philosophy (as it is termed) of history. In fact it is mainly about theology.

The real Augustine, however, and his works are not fully represented by these two great books alone, so sketchily understood. With regard to his personality also, it is necessary to be on one's guard against the idea that he ceased to be intellectual and sensitive when he became a bishop: the manner of his life changed and correspondingly there was perceptible evolution of his personality. But the best biography of Augustine, that by Peter Brown, shows some of the author's Irish penchant for the over-dramatic, when he puts into sharp and prolonged contrast the mystical-intellectual follower of Plotinus of Augustine's young manhood, and the bargaining bishop who greased a politician's hand with, if you will allow fact to mix the metaphor, a string of stallions. Augustine undoubtedly progressed from a practical position of tolerance of what he called error to a merely theoretical one, and thence again to practical intolerance. This is most clearly seen in his developing attitude to the schismatic church of the Donatists. He could be so anxious to win that he was unfair to his opponents—as he was in the cases of Felix, Faustus and Fortunatus, the Manicheans. A recent scholar has described his attitude to these as that of the Public Prosecutor. And he could contemplate the damnation of the majority of mankind rather than yield to Pelagius (who, not altogether without reason, professed that he was but following a younger Augustine). But to present matters so succinctly is as unfair as it is to exaggerate the importance of the rather rhetorical descriptions of his mystical ambitions (and he was ambitious) under the influence of a necessarily limited and, perhaps, second-hand acquaintance with Plotinus.

One must read more of Augustine and especially of his non-controversial works if one is to begin to do him justice. In controversy he was, as he said himself, fierce: *atrociter pugnavi*. *De Trinitate*, the various scriptural commentaries, and especially *De Genesi ad litteram* show him more relaxed, more serene, more just to himself and others. It is important too to realize that the last work mentioned, DGnL, often called the *Hexaemeron* in early medieval times, then loomed very large in people's minds. This is not surprising since it and the *imago Dei* were favourite themes of the philosopher-theologians of the early Middle Ages. In his study of the six days of creation Augustine attempts to interpret the

Scriptural account of the most fundamental of all problems, the problem of creation. He essays to do so *literally*, that is to say without much help from allegory, but also not in a fundamentalist sense. The work was written within the period of composition of *De Trinitate* and therefore sometime between, say, 400 and 412 or 415. Without his making many professions about it, *De Genesi* shows a good deal of the philosophic spirit, and in particular a use of some Neoplatonic (or more specifically, Porphyrian) teaching on the soul, which puts a spotlight on Augustine's Neoplatonic approaches and basic uncertainties on a matter of central importance in the relations of soul and body.

Here we may turn to Eriugena, the Irishman at the court of Charles the Bald around the third quarter of the ninth century, who translated Dionysius Areopagiticus and wrote the great treatise *Periphyseon* or *De divisione naturae*. In this work, he describes the externation of being and its return, its *progressus* and *regressus*, seeking his inspiration mainly from Augustine and the Gregories of Nyssa and Nazianzus, Maximus the Confessor, and Ambrose. The last was, you will recall, Augustine's spiritual father if not also, as Courcelle would have it, his guide to a synthesis of Christianity and Neoplatonism.

Among the curiosities of Eriugena's great work is the nature of his dependence on Augustine. Do Augustine's *City of God, Confessions* and *On the Trinity* alone count for more in Eriugena's essential thought than the whole of the Dionysian writings, with the *Ambigua* of Maximus thrown into the scale (as his biographer H. Bett would have it)? Or should one accept the conclusion of G. Mathon that "le ressort profond de la pensée d'Érigène n'est plus d'inspiration augustinienne"? Mathon, nevertheless, cannot ignore Eriugena's evident belief that he was in line with the Great Augustine, and is driven to accuse Eriugena of deforming Augustine's teaching to suit his own purposes—*utilisation déformante et arbitraire de ce qu'il a effectivement soutenu*. The greatest Eriugenian scholar of modern times, Cappuyns, suggests that Eriugena was compelled to go beyond Augustine to the Greek Fathers, because Augustine was simply unaware of their important contributions on the topic, for example, of the beatific vision.

It is true that Eriugena on occasion does admit that the doctrine which he clearly favours does not appear readily reconcilable with that of Augustine, whom nevertheless at least sometimes in these circumstances he professes to follow. Eriugena's embarrassment is also indicated from time to time by his appealing to Ambrose as at least *a* Latin Father who supports the view of the Greek Fathers, which he himself wants to support. Why, we may ask, should Eriugena appeal to Ambrose, if he could have appealed to Augustine? In passing it should be remarked that Eriugena's view of Ambrose accords with the view now entertained of him as a result of the work of Courcelle, Madec, and others and is, therefore, at variance with the "traditional" view of him held in recent times. But if Courcelle and others are right—both about Ambrose and Augustine's relations with Ambrose, could Augustine possibly have been *unaware*—as Cappuyns contended—of the doctrines of Ambrose favoured by Eriugena—seemingly at the expense of Augustine particularly? It seems unlikely. This is not to say that Augustine could not have opposed a doctrine of Ambrose's; but unawareness is a different matter.

It becomes important, then, to try to establish the truth about Eriugena's use of Augustine's teaching, especially in the area in which controversy on this matter has been most concentrated: the relations of soul and body in the beatific vision. If Eriugena's view of Ambrose was untraditional (in our terms, that is) but correct, may not this be true also of his view of Augustine?

Eriugena had two justifications for refusing to believe that Augustine was at variance on the question of the relations of soul and body in the beatific vision, with Ambrose, the Gregories, and Maximus the Confessor. One of these will not detain us for long—the appeal to two sets of teaching, a public one which is intended for the many, and a secret, true, and seemingly contradictory one for the few. This formula for circumventing an adversary's public assertions was often employed in antiquity and was an especial favourite of Augustine himself. It is not surprising, then, if Eriugena applies it to a seemingly recalcitrant Augustine. I shall confine myself to one example.

In *De divisione naturae* 986Bff. Eriugena, clearly with Augustine in mind, supposes that those who taught that the bodies of the saved will be as now, even to the division of male and female, except that they will become heavenly and spiritual, did so for purely *practical* reasons, since fleshly men could not envisage other than fleshly things: "timidisque fidelium simplicium cogitationibus consulentes, utilius visum est eis praedicare terrenorum sensibiliumque corporum transmutationem in caelestia sprituliaque corpora quam penitus corpora et corporalia et sensibilia omnia nunquam esse futura." While one should not insist on the likelihood of Augustine's use of this mythical theology well known to him from Varro, one cannot dismiss it quite out of hand. One can more easily understand why Eriugena was almost compelled to employ this common hypothesis of the ancient and early Christian world: whatever he might say, Augustine *had* to agree with Eriugena, for the simple reason that it was in his time believed that in following the doctrine of Dionysius Areopagiticus one was following the infallible doctrine of Dionysius's master, St. Paul. We know now, of course, that this belief was unjustified.

Wherever possible, however, Eriugena has recourse to the second means of justification—the resort to statements of doctrine by Augustine which could fairly be interpreted as providing agreement, or possible agreement, or at any rate not disagreement with his own convictions. These statements, especially in relation to the soul, were usually inspired by the same Neoplatonic doctrine that lay behind the work of Dionysius and the Greek Fathers too. Augustine in DGnL, while deriving many of his notions on the soul from Scripture, analyzes them in the light of the teaching of the Neoplatonist Porphyry—and DGnL under the title of *Hexaemeron* is for Eriugena possibly the major source for Augustinian doctrine. The twelfth book of this work, with which we shall occupy ourselves presently, though not containing Augustine's final pronouncements on the soul, was nevertheless written when the author was about sixty years of age: its teaching on the soul can, therefore, hardly be said to be immature.

The question of the beatific vision raised for Augustine in the most acute manner possible the problem as to what a glorified body precisely meant. It was a question which always agitated him, and one on which he continued right to the end to be undecided. That the saved soul should see God interiorly, with the eyes of the glorified body closed, was easy to affirm: the immaterial could perceive the immaterial even if, as must happen—since God is invisible even to the angels, whose powers the saved will acquire—only a manifestation of God is perceived. But that the eyes of the glorified body should see a theophany of God in heaven was another matter.

Augustine was definitively negative on the point in a letter of 408: "As for the eyes of the body, they will be no more capable of seeing [God] in heaven than on earth . . . we shall see God by that by which we shall be like him. . . . who would be so mad as to claim that it is by our body that we shall be like him?"¹ He is equally negative in another letter of 413: "God will always be invisible, but his only Son will show him in an invisible manner to eyes worthy of so great a sight."² In still another letter of the same year he maintains his negative stance, but makes two, in relation to our present interest in Eriugena, significant additions.

Firstly, he explicitly invokes in this letter the support of the authority of Jerome and Athanasius and also of Ambrose and a certain, as he writes, Eastern bishop called Gregory. This Gregory may or may not be Gregory of Nazianzus (a favourite authority of Eriugena) but at any rate the mention of Ambrose and Greek authors (explicitly) in the text is highly significant.³

Secondly, apparently out of consideration for an episcopal friend of his episcopal correspondent who was troubled to have heard Augustine's negative views on corporal vision by the glorified body in the afterlife, he does not exclude the possibility that some authority might be found in Scripture to the effect that in heaven there would be such a great change in our bodies that they will be able to see invisible things. It is clear all the same from the context that he does not expect any such authority to be found. Still one must note how he puts Scripture before philosophy, and also how careful he is not to shock the simple, which clearly, at any rate in those days, included bishops. Could not his charity in professing to be willing to be convinced of views which were the opposite of his own not leave him open to the construction of the interested of holding such views?

The two letters just mentioned were written about the same time as the twelfth book of DGnL, the work of Augustine most quoted by Eriugena. This book, seeking to expound St. Paul's description in 2 Cor. XII, 2-4 of his being rapt in vision to the third heaven, distinguishes three kinds of vision—corporeal, spirital, and intellectual. It attributes an unusual meaning to *spiritus*, "spirit," and is strongly revelatory of Augustine's continuing openness, even at threescore years of age to a Neoplatonist, Porphyry, whom elsewhere he condemns roundly.

I shall try to summarize briefly Augustine's account of "spirit" in DGnL.

Augustine distinguishes the *anima spiritalis*, the "spiritual soul" from the *ratio*, which is higher than it, and the *mens*, which is the highest level of the soul.⁴ Here we confine ourselves to what he has to say at the point in question on the *spiritus*.

First the term *spiritus* is applied in Scripture in a generalized way to the risen body—to describe not, significantly, its *corporeal* nature but rather its character as totally *submitted to soul*. The word is also used of the movement of the air, the souls of beasts, the souls of men, man's intellect or *mens*, and finally God himself.[5] The emphasis in these generalized uses of *spiritus* is on the fact of non-attachment to body, but body, so to speak, focusses the meaning.

Augustine attempts to describe it more philosophically as a "certain nature in us where representations of corporeal things are formed."[6] It is not therefore a faculty or a function or any kind of imagination, memory or conscience, but rather a part, so to speak, of our soul where we not only register and store impressions of sense, but where spirits from the outside, for example, can communicate with us through visions they cause there, and where we produce our own dreams and visions when we are in certain states. It is also the part which we employ to envisage our future external actions and so allow us to plan their execution. It is the point of communication between our higher soul and the other spirits and sensibles, which are presented for its judgment by representations and significations retained in the spirit *after* they have been perceived by it.

The *spiritus* has an activity, a vision, which Augustine says is not unsuitably described as a *medium* between the vision of the intellect and the vision of the body: "puto enim non incongruenter medium dici, quod corpus quidem non est, sed simile est corporis, inter illud, quod uere corpus est, et illud, quod nec corpus est nec simile corporis":[7] the vision of the spirit is not body but is like body; the vision of the intellect is not body and is not like body. The *spiritus* is, therefore, once again represented by Augustine as the *locale*, so to speak, of communication between the intellectual and sensible worlds.

It is instructive to notice the correspondence of these ideas about the *spiritus* with those of Porphyry as reported by Augustine himself in the *City of God* and elsewhere.

Porphyry too posits three levels of the soul in which activities are directed either upwards, so to speak, to the intelligibles or to itself or downwards to sensible things.[8] It was the πνευματικὴ ψυχή (of which the term employed by Augustine, *anima spiritalis*, is the exact translation) or πνεῦμα τὸ ψυχικόν which was concerned with the sensibles.[9]

This πνεῦμα of Porphyry is described generally as ἀσώματον—bodiless as being deprived of body. It is pictured in terms of what it has excluded. There are superior types of ἀσώματα—such as νοῦς δὲ καὶ νοερὸς λόγος—which are, improperly, καταχρηστικῶς, so described since they have nothing whatever to do with body. The Porphyrian ψυχή, however, is actually described as the cause of body, αἰτία σώματος.[10]

The πνεῦμα more precisely is an envelope in which the soul was clothed in its descent through the planetary orbits to the body. In it are registered the evidences of its earthly experience. It stays with the soul on the latter's separation from the body. Porphyry also employed the formula πνευματικὸν ὄχημα, "pneumatic vehicle," in this connection.[11] From Augustine's own report on his reading of the book of Porphyry which he calls *De regressu animae* we learn that Porphyry distinguished the *pars spiritalis* of the soul, in which the images of sensible things were registered, from the *pars intellectualis*, by which the truth of intelligible things is perceived.[12] It is possible that here Augustine is interpreting Porphyry rather than using the exact translation of the term used by Porphyry. The terms "part" or "envelope" or "vehicle" can, in any case, be no more than approximations. In this connection, however, it is important to observe that Porphyry appears to differ from Augustine in one essential point: whereas he seems to consider the πνεῦμα as a material reality, Augustine seems to consider the *spiritus* as part of the immaterial soul.[13]

The Porphyrian source of these ideas unusual in Augustine is now admitted, though the significance of this in evaluating the development of Augustine's thought or even his derivatives from Neoplatonism has not yet been sufficiently appreciated. As it happens, these Porphyrian concepts of *spiritus* in Augustine made less impact on subsequent thinkers than did other parts of his philosophical speculation. This may be because they were of less use in church doctrine and were never integrated into Scholasticism. Nevertheless these ideas are found in quite a number of writers from Alcuin to Aquinas himself. The *spiritus* of the *De Genesi ad litteram* is in many ways like the *intellectus passivus* of Averroes and the *spiritus imaginativus* of Robert Kilwardby.[14]

For our purpose here, however, it has been important to show Augustine's teaching on the relations of the soul with the body, in a work of his basic to Eriugena's report on Augustine's doctrine on the soul and body in the beatific vision, as set out in the *De divisione naturae*: that teaching is strongly Neoplatonic in character.

Life after death was a theme on which Porphyry had speculated. According to him, if the πνεῦμα is too deeply impressed with the image of the body, the soul tends to be borne down underneath the earth and is to that extent afflicted.[15]

Surprising as it may seem, Augustine in DGnL XII, 60, 60 asserts that he does not believe that the soul will have any kind of body after death: "Iam utrum (anima) habeat aliquod corpus, cum de hoc corpore exierit, ostendat qui potest; ego autem non puto." It is to be noticed that here he states his own negative belief clearly but, perhaps again not to shock others or for some other reason, he does not exclude the possibility, however unlikely it seems to him, that he may later be proved to be in error.

He sees no reason, nevertheless, why the soul after separation from the body will not bring with it into the next life a likeness of the body, *similitudinem corporis*. It will, therefore, be borne *ad spiritalia*, to the company of "spiritals," where it will rejoice or suffer, because of having the *similitudinem corporis*, according to its merits.[16]

Augustine raises squarely the question of why the spirits of the dead have to receive their bodies back in the resurrection, if they can have perfect beatitude without bodies. He replies that the question is too difficult to be answered perfectly in the present discussion—which, by the way, had gone on for twelve books! He says all the same that there is no doubt but that even when we have abandoned the body and transcended the likenesses of bodies, *transcensis etiam similitudinibus corporalium*, we will not see God as the angels see him. The reason for this is not clear, but it might be, Augustine says, because the soul has a certain natural appetite of governing a body: *inest ei naturalis quidam adpetitus corpus administrandi*. The soul worthy after death of perfect beatitude will receive a body which is not animal but rather rendered *spirital* through the change (*commutationem*) that takes place, and this *spirital* body will, from being a burden, be its glory.[17]

This seems an answer that is far from clear. The terms employed—the meaning of *similitudo corporis*, for example, may or may not be consistently used. It *is* clear, however, that *philosophically* Augustine sees no reason for the teaching on the resurrection of the body which, however, he does not reject. It is also clear that he offers no explanation convincing even to himself of the teaching on the resurrection of the body. Finally he says that we shall not be as the angels: there will remain with us a *spirital* body which will add to our glory or our pain. Hell exists but it is *spirital*, not corporal: "est ergo prorsus inferorum substantia, sed eam spiritalem arbitror esse, non corporalem."[18]

It may be seen that in DGnL Augustine protested that he did not understand what the resurrection of the body meant in terms of its relation to the soul, but for his part attenuated it as far as possible—and in Porphyrian terms. He is careful, however, not to pronounce that other less subtle views are impossible. In the event he himself some ten or twelve years later, in the twenty-first book of the *City of God* declared that the fire of Hell, though material, was mysteriously able to burn the immaterial soul, and that there was no need to enter into a laborious or contentious discussion on the matter.[19]

From all that has been said one observes that Eriugena, in considering the soul-body relationship in the *futura felicitas*, had some difficulty in quoting the support of Augustine without qualification in favour of the teaching of Ambrose, the Gregories, and Maximus, which in reality he himself accepted.

He is compelled to observe that Augustine is either amongst those who flatly deny that the body is changed into spirit: *corpus in spiritum mutabitur (hoc) penitus negant*, or among those who prudently (*caute*) doubt it. These latter hesitate to assert that Christ's humanity was changed (*conversam fuisse*) into divinity.[20] From what we have seen, at any rate, of DGnL Augustine is unlikely to be among those who are described as denying that the body after death would be "changed into spirit" in *some* way or another. He is, however, quoted—and from DGnL—as denying that the body can be changed into soul: *negat converti posse corpus in animam*.[21] But Augustine—if only because of some looseness in terminology—is not necessarily inconsistent: being changed into "spirit" is one thing; being changed into soul is another. At any rate Eriugena professes to follow Augustine on the point, while being aware that the Greeks teach that the body will be changed into soul.

On the whole, however, we have reason to think that Eriugena judged Augustine to have been prudently doubtful on all this matter, if only because even at his most Neoplatonic he explicitly did not exclude the possibility that his views might be wrong. Later in fact he did himself, for whatever reason, express views which at least modified his earlier ones. Moreover he had in any case great difficulty in admitting that Christ's humanity would cease to be with all other material things.

On this last point Eriugena accuses Augustine of holding views that were inconsistent. There were emotional, and maybe ecclesiastical, reasons for Augustine's attitude since Christ's incarnation and resurrection played overwhelming roles in his ever memorable conversion. They were, moreover, the only substantial points on which his hostility to the Christian arch-enemy, Porphyry, focused. Eriugena in effect refuses to believe that Augustine, or any member of the Church, could maintain the eternal persistence of Christ's body, since, in his being circumscribed by the body, he would be inferior to the Father, who was everywhere.[22]

Once again Eriugena supposes that Augustine, in holding such a view on Christ's body, is playing down to the simple: "credibilius arbitrandum est secundum capacitatem singulorum quibus scripsit, scripsisse, quam a sanctis Patribus, qui eum praecesserunt ordine temporum, ab Ambrosio dico Gregorioque Theologo, quorum auctoritate in aliis locis non discrepat, dissensisse."[23]

Eriugena triumphantly concludes, even if he puts his conclusion in the form of a rhetorical question, that Augustine in no way disagrees with the Greeks on the matter: "Dic, quaeso, ubi dissonat [Augustinus] ab his, quae diximus, de transitu mundi huius in suas causas?"[24] His confidence can hardly seem excessive, since even from the last declaration of Augustine's on the matter, found in even the last book of the *City of God* and pronounced by him in his *Retractations* to be final and definitive, and used as his principal text by Eriugena in his principal treatment of the topic in the *De divisione naturae* states once again that, if he were to tell the truth, he should confess his ignorance of the matter. He then goes on to indicate that he would have to accept the philosophical view that the eyes of *no* kind of body, not even *spirital*, can see God, *si posset nobis esset certissima*—if it were certain.[25] But true reason and Scripture go against it. We know that we perceive the lives of others, which are invisible, through seeing their visible bodies, and Scripture refers to instances when bodily eyes look upon the invisible. Finally, even in this last definitive, perhaps even ecclesiastically political text, the *City of God*, he still offers *alternative* solutions to the problem: either the eyes of the spirital body will be assimilated to the intelligence, *aliquid habeant menti simile*, so that they can see incorporeal things, or each of us will see God with our spirit in each of us and in himself: "(Deus) uideatur spiritu a singulis nobis in singulis nobis, uideatur in se ipso."[26]

Not even the Greeks, however, teach that a soul can see God strictly in himself—it sees him in an apparition, a theophany, which is loosely said to be God, as if it were himself. Eriugena once again quotes Augustine in full and detailed support of Maximus the Confessor's description of a theophany which, though interesting, I must spare you.[27] As for Maximus's account of the union of God and the soul—it is like that of light and air: light remains uncorrupted by air but penetrates it and, Maximus says, becomes visible in it. Maximus also uses the image of iron so absorbed in fire that it is indistinguishable from it—yet, though both are united, they are not confused. Likewise God and the soul are united, but retain their separate natures. Augustine used these same images.[28]

Eriugena apparently thought it advisable to make his position clear on whether or not he was satisfied that Augustine was really saying the same thing, taking account of all his statements, as Maximus and the others on the topic in question. Consequently the Disciple in the *De divisione naturae* is represented as saying that he does not perceive with sufficient clarity that the teaching propounded by Eriugena agrees with the words of Pater Augustinus. Eriugena, the Master, invites him to give all his attention and then proceeds to quote again relevant texts from the *City of God*.[29] Eriugena was satisfied that Augustine's teaching supported his. This does not suggest that it dominated it.

John Burnaby, a contemporary Augustinian scholar, has written: "The system which generally goes by the name of Augustinianism is in great part a cruel travesty of Augustine's deepest and most vital thought." Although the influence of Augustine is more extensive than the Augustinianism mentioned, it is still true that Augustine and his work are cruelly travestied. Doctrines are attacked and defended in his name that do much less than justice to his life and works both as they evolved and as they should be judged in their context.

In particular it is important to realize that a certain hardening of Augustine's attitude in doctrinal matters, when he was already in his sixties and felt that he was under attack and may have felt that his life's work was jeopardized, impressed itself upon his last controversies and writings which, in the event, had a dominating effect on the nature of his subsequent influence. Hence it is that the interests of various institutions have constructed an authoritative figure, ever willing to do battle and win, ever willing to hand down clear and sombre doctrines to deliver man from his weakness or banish him to eternal torment. The same figure was known to stress the value of love and lay emphasis on the action, not of the intellect, but of the will. But apart from the burning rhetoric of the *Confessions* (which have redeemed Augustine for many), that love and that will are represented in terms too absolute to appeal strongly to ordinary men apart from their institutional commitments.

The picture given by Eriugena of a man who right to the end professed that he did not know the truth about the soul and body in the afterlife, who allowed alternatives (including one highly tinged with Neoplatonism), who refused to dissociate himself from the public professions of the body of Christians (and so risked misrepresentation), but who, nevertheless, was at one with Maximus in a highly intellectual description of theophany, seems much nearer the evidence of his writings and the probable evolution of his life. Augustine may emerge seeming more hesitant: but the gain is in humanity and intelligence.

Unfortunately Eriugena's work, and so his picture of Augustine, were for the most part overborne as the centuries rolled on and sectarian controversies multiplied. Our days have seen the rediscovery of the Neoplatonism of Augustine and, more recently, important work on the text of Eriugena. The combined operation reminds me, if I may briefly invoke another discipline, of the recovery of an underwater wreck: the task is slow and arduous, but the results can be very well worthwhile.

20

Eriugena's Use of Augustine's *De Genesi ad litteram* in the *Periphyseon*

≈

The *De Genesi ad litteram* and the *De ciuitate dei* of Augustine are each referred to in one way or another about twenty times in the course of the *Periphyseon*. No other work of Augustine receives there any comparable prominence. Both works are used to support one another, and like the two Loves of the *De ciuitate dei* are there somewhat inextricably entwined.

It has seemed to me a helpful exercise, in trying to assess Eriugena's use of Augustine as a source of his doctrine, to concentrate my attention here on *De Genesi ad litteram* rather than *De ciuitate dei*, because its whole subject matter is, broadly speaking, the same—creation, expounded by way of commentary on Genesis by Augustine, and dialectically by Eriugena.

First it is necessary to make some comments on DGnL. To begin with its title: Eriugena in the *De diuisione naturae* refers to it as *Exemeron* except at PL 122.804B[1] where the full title, *De Genesi ad litteram*, is given. Next, one should bear in mind Augustine's own characterization of it as set forth by him at the beginning of its twelfth and final book: "I have set down in writing as far as I could my exposition of the first part of holy scripture, which is called Genesis, up to the point when the first man was expelled from Paradise. I have asserted and defended what I hold as established. I have investigated, given my opinion, and expressed doubts on what I do not hold as established. I do not seek so much to prescribe what each one should believe in relation to things that are obscure, as to show that I myself need instruction in matters on which I have been in doubt; and to restrain the reader from the rashness of coming to firm conclusions where we have been unable to provide knowledge that is certain." (XII, 1, 1)[2]

These observations were no mere literary convention. In the course of the work Augustine has recourse to similar statements: others, he observes, may be able to do better than him in the understanding of

Genesis or even he himself might someday be more successful.³ This modesty of Augustine was sincere and well founded. Was not this book of his, composed between the forty-seventh and sixty-second years of his age, his third serious attempt to understand what could be understood in Genesis? He adjudged his *De Genesi ad Manichaeos* (A.D. 388–89) a failure:⁴ *De Genesi liber imperfectus* (about A.D. 393), as its very title implies, was not completed. His treatment of Genesis in the *Confessiones* was professedly allegorical.⁵ Now he must make another—it proved to be his final—effort to treat Genesis *non secundum allegoricas significationes, sed secundum rerum gestarum proprietatem* (R II, 24, 1): he is treating what is for men an historical event (*res gestae*) with the appropriate historical canons. Augustine accepts that a literal understanding does not exclude a parallel allegorical one also, and moreover that God cannot be accounted for within the limitations of human words. He freely admits the apophatic position which he himself had expressed succinctly in one of the earliest of his works: *deus qui scitur melius nesciendo* (DOR II, 16, 44). But in DGnL he was determined to use to the limits possible all the resources of rational understanding that were available to him. These, and especially the speculations of Plotinus and other Neoplatonists—as the *Notes Complémentaires* of Agaësse and Solignac in the Bibliothèque Augustinienne (vols. 48 and 49) edition of DGnL⁶ reveal—were considerable.

In brief, DGnL is an earnest and subtle attempt at a rational understanding of creation as an historical event described in Genesis. It admits that it does not always satisfy itself; imposes none of its special views on others; and accepts a final apophaticism.

It will help at this point to turn our attention to Eriugena's own formal exposition of the biblical six days of creation in the *Periphyseon*. The beginning of this is to be found in PL 122.690B. The Disciple states that many have expounded many ideas on this topic both in Greek and Latin, and that the discussion of the topic at this point is to be brief and summary. For our purpose here it will be sufficient to comment on his treatment of the meaning of *fiat lux* in 691A–693C. This of course refers to the first and—objectively and apart from man—most important creation.

Here Eriugena gives the opinions of Basil and Augustine and then his own *as his own*. Basil is quoted as holding that the *fiat lux* signified the *conditionem huius lucis corporeae substantialiter in igne*—the establishment of the substance of our corporeal light in fire. This cryptic account of

Basil's view is briefly expounded at 691A, B. Augustine's view of the *fiat lux* is given as signifying *caelestium uirtutum formationem*, the forming of the celestial powers, explained in other words as the creation of the angelic and celestial essence, and again as the establishment of the angelic nature. This view of Augustine Eriugena pronounces to be more correct (*rectius*).

Eriugena himself summarizes the signification he himself wants to give (*uolentes intelligere*) to the *fiat lux* with the formula: the general procession of the primordial causes into their effects. He explains, however, that the scriptural *factumque est uespere et mane, dies unus* means that the procession of the primordial, principal or original causes, though understood to be separated and different from their establishment, as day is from night, is with that establishment but one creation: "non enim alia creatura intelligitur in causis facta, alia in effectibus causarum condita, sed una eademque in rationibus aeternis . . . et in processionibus rationum in effectus."

Eriugena reports, and clearly and fundamentally differs from, Augustine in the interpretation of the biblical *et diuisit deus lucem a tenebris*. For Augustine this signifies, Eriugena says, either the difference between the perfection of form on the one hand and the confusion of "informity" on the other; or the separation of the faithful from the fallen angels. Eriugena here interprets Augustine as understanding that the "reasons" or causes of things are eternal in God and, in being created, from being light become darkness. Eriugena takes, so to speak, a diametrically opposite view of the matter. For him following, he says, Dionysius, darkness signifies the incomprehensibility of the eternal reasons in God as well as God himself; and light signifies the *de-claratio*, manifestation or "theophany" of these reasons in the effects that we can see.

This difference between Eriugena and Augustine, signalled by Eriugena himself, is, as I have said, fundamental. It would not be wholly just to describe Augustine's approach as more philosophical or intellectual, and Eriugena's as more theological or mystical—such a distinction at best could be no more than pragmatic. Yet there is a profound and perhaps revealing difference between looking at darkness as a symbol of something transcendingly superior to light or greatly inferior to it. It may be useful in our present enquiry to take this hint from Eriugena himself and from a context where DGnL, though undoubtedly in Eriugena's mind, is not mentioned.

Finally one should add that Eriugena explains that he is most definitely (*quod absit!*) not preferring the views he has put forward, as if they were discovered by himself, to those of others; but he considers them not to be greatly at variance with true speculation and relevant to the present discussion. As the Disciple says about the three views—i.e., of Basil, Augustine, and Eriugena himself—here given: "Whichever of these interpretations one holds, he will not be far from the truth." As we can see, Eriugena, like Augustine, allows others—and himself—a large discretion.

In concentrating our attention now on the explicit references to Augustine's DGnL in the *Periphyseon* we can have at least the assurance that, even if they do not represent the whole presence, so to speak, of the one book in the other, they give at least the guarantee that we are discussing evidence that is certain and, insofar as we do not choose the passages, objective. It is unlikely, moreover, that the passages from DGnL are not also representative, though one would need a much longer study than can be attempted here to confirm this.

The list of explicit references in the *Periphyseon* to DGnL is as follows: PL 122.446A, 448A, 504C, 640C, 647A, 770C, 781B, 781C, 804B, 809A, 809C, 809D, 814B, 843D, 856C, 877A, 927C, 945A, 954B.[7] You might wish to know the density, so to speak, of their occurrence in the various books of the *Periphyseon*. This is as follows: three in Book I, three in Book III, nine in Book IV, and four in Book V. This preponderance of reference in the fourth and fifth books of the *Periphyseon* may well be of little or even no significance whatever. But it does not *manifestly* accord—though it still may not be in disaccord—with Sheldon-Williams's view that Eriugena was "from the end of Book I onwards, relying heavily on Greek sources."[8]

The majority of these references give actual quotations which in every case but one are strictly or almost strictly accurate: 506C = VIII, 20, 39; 640C and 770C = II, 6, 12; 809A = IX, 4, 8; 809C = XI, 38, 51 (=856C); 809D = XI, 23, 30; 814B = VIII, 1, 1; 843D = XI, 11, 56; 856C = XI, 38, 51 (=809C); 877A = X, 4, 7; and 927C = XI, 20, 27. The quotation in 647A is a somewhat less accurate representation of I, 15, 29. Other references are brief summaries of doctrine: 446A = 448A (cf. IV, 10–12, 39; 23, 40; 25, 42; 26, 43; 28, 45; 29, 46; 32, 49f. (perhaps especially); 34, 53, 55; V, 4, 10; 5, 15); 781C (cf. I, 17, 33ff. and cf. XI, 19, 26); 804B (cf. VI, 19, 30–28, 39); 945A (cf. XII, 33, 60–61); and 954D (cf. XII, 33, 62–34, 67). 781B merely reports that Augustine cleverly argued against the view that the *fiat lux* signified the establishment of a primitive sensible light localized in the higher parts of the universe,[9] a view associated by Eriugena, as we have seen,[10] with Basil.

Citations from DGnL are for us here of little significance in themselves—they can always be read, in themselves that is, in their original setting. What *can* be at varying levels of importance significant for our enquiry is the use to which Eriugena puts them. They can be used, for instance, to indicate that Eriugena has the authority of Augustine. While this use may help to build up our picture of the extent to which Eriugena depended upon Augustine—and this is part of our interest in the question—it will require here little more than a bald statement of the facts. Instances of such citations of Augustine as a supporting authority— sometimes the *ipsissima uerba* without comment, sometimes by way of summary, sometimes with a little manipulation to make them appear to fit in with Eriugena's own preferences (809A, 809C, 809D), once with the complaint that Augustine might have explained more (856C)— are to be found in 504C, 647A, 809A, 809C, 809D, 856C, 927C, 945A and 954D. In 781C the reader who might be curious for further information on a point is simply given a reference to DGnL, and in 781B it is reported merely that in that work Augustine argued against a certain point of view.[11] All of these instances have something to teach us about Eriugena's regard for Augustine's authority, but, as I suggested, they should not detain us here and now.

In 814B and 843D DGnL is quoted, not now as a supporting authority, but simply as representing a statement of a view which Eriugena nevertheless does not favour. This is not such an exercise in independence as it might seem, however, since he can quote (814D) from another work of Augustine a different view on the same topic which he does favour: here he is simply ignoring Augustine in one place only to follow him in another. His embarrassment appears quite strikingly, however, in 877A. Here he quotes the view of Augustine that body cannot be changed into soul. On this he makes the following comment: "(this opinion of Augustine—and Boethius—) not only do we not reprehend: rather we willingly accept it. We are not unaware, however, that the *theologi*, who used the Greek language, thought differently . . . we think it necessary to repeat their views here" (877C). The topic in question is the *reditus inferiorum in superiora*, the possibility, which Ambrose and Maximus are quoted as supporting, that body could become soul in the life hereafter. Eriugena attempted, as I have tried to relate elsewhere,[12] to make it appear that Augustine must have held the view attributed to Ambrose, but out of consideration for the ignorant avoided the appearance of so doing. I do not wish to go over the ground again here. Nor need I. The instance I must now deal with is sufficiently similar to meet our present purpose.

I propose to spend practically all of the remainder of my time considering 446A, 448A, 640C and 770C together, in that all are concerned with one complicated topic outlined principally in 446A; I shall then finally look very briefly at 804B.

In 446A the Disciple expresses a difficulty which arises from what Augustine has said in DGnL. The difficulty centres on the knowability of the eternal reasons or primordial causes in God. Augustine had appeared to say, according to the Disciple, that "the angelic nature was established before every other creature, not in time but in status, and on this account it contemplated the primordial causes, that is, those primary exemplars (*principalia exempla*) which the Greeks call πρωτότυπα, even of others beside its own, first in God, then in itself; then the creatures themselves in their effects." The Disciple objects that the angelic nature "cannot have known its own cause before it proceeded into its proper species." It is to be remarked that Floss limits the reference to Augustine to the initial statement on the precedence of the angel. Sheldon-Williams (whose translation I have used here) extends it (*rectius*, I—to follow Eriugena—would say) to the mention of the primordial causes, but should have taken account of the fact that in doing so he was under the grammatical necessity of continuing the reference to the needed verb (*considerasse*) and the completion of the sense as above indicated. Sheldon-Williams not surprisingly confesses not to have been able to find the quotation in the *De Genesi ad litteram* and suggests the source is to be found in Book I. The words *dictum uidetur*, however, do not imply a quotation, and in fact the doctrine quoted is found mostly in Book IV, especially in 22, 39; 23, 40; 25, 42; 26, 43; 28, 45; 29, 46; 32, 49ff.; 34, 53, 55 and Book V, 4, 10 and 5, 15. The nearest single passage which would have supplied the elements of the report in Eriugena is IV, 32, 49ff. which I shall quote presently.

The Master in 446B widens (as is confirmed in 448A) the difficulty beyond the angel's perception of his own cause in God to that of all causes in God: Saint Paul's text, "For who has known the intellect of the Lord?" (Rom 11, 34), makes it clear that the divine essence, with the reasons which are in it, cannot be comprehensible (448B). The Master later on in 640C quotes Augustine himself in DGnL (II, 6, 12) as saying: "The things that are made by (God) are under (*sub*) him in one way, and the things that are himself are in him in another way." He interprets Augustine as clearly meaning (*tanquam aperte diceret*) that the material things we see are under God in one way, and as understood to be eternally in the primordial causes of things which are not only in God, but are God, in another way. The Master further interprets this to mean not that there are two things in question—one in God (in fact God) and one in this world—but that there is only one thing which, however, is considered in one way in the eternity of the word of God, and in another as temporally constituted in the world. In 770C the Master repeats the same quotation from Augustine in exactly the same substantially accurate words. Floss at this point mistakes as a continuation of the quotation Eriugena's own interpretation of it. This is to the effect that the *intellectus omnium* in divine wisdom is the *substantia* of all, indeed is all. The knowledge (*cognitio*) that the intellectual and rational creature has of itself in itself is, as it were, a certain second substance: *ueluti secunda quaedam substantia eius est*, by which it knows itself only to the extent that it knows and is and wills, but does not know *what* it is. The first substance is constituted in the wisdom of God, which is eternal and immutable; the other is temporal and mutable. The former precedes, the latter follows; the former is primordial and causal, the latter is proceeding and "causative"; the former contains all things universally, the latter holds through knowledge the things submitted to it as particulars, insofar as this is allowed it by its superior; the former brings forth the latter; the latter will return into the former.

In this latter interpretation of Augustine's text Eriugena calls the understanding (*intellectus*) of all things in divine wisdom, which is in fact all things, the substance of all. With it he contrasts the knowledge (*cognitio*) that, for example, the angel—as intellectual creature—has of itself in itself as a second kind of substance. He explicitly excludes from that knowledge a knowledge of what it is—a touch which readily suggests the influence of the Greek *theologi*. It is important to realize that two types of knowing are being contrasted: *intellectus* in God and *cognitio* in the angel. Each knowledge is called a substance: but the *cognitio* of the angel is no more than a *kind* of substance: We are in the different "worlds" of real being and theophany.

With this capacity of interpreting Augustine's text "the things that are made by (God) are under him in one way and the things that are himself are in him in another way," Eriugena has no difficulty in also interpreting the doctrine attributed to Augustine by the Disciple in 446A along the following lines (446B):

As he sees it, Eriugena must, as he says, "steer a straight and middle course, avoiding the appearance of either going against the Apostle or of not holding the opinion of a teacher (Augustine) of weighty and sacred authority. That each has spoken the truth must not be doubted, nay rather, must strongly be maintained" (Sheldon-Williams's translation). He accepts without question that the reasons of all things, which exist in God eternally and without change, are completely inaccessible to all things—including the things of which they are the reasons—such as, for example, the angel. This position, which he takes to be consequent on Paul's text, is absolute. Clearly the middle course must be found in interpreting the words of Augustine so that they may be made to appear to accord with this.

And so "anyone who might say that in the intellects of the angels there are certain theophanies (*theophanias quasdam*) of those reasons, that is to say, certain (divine) manifestations which are comprehensible to the intellectual nature, but which are not the reasons, i.e., the primary exemplars, themselves, will not, I think, stray from the truth. And we believe that St. Augustine was not incorrect when he said that these theophanies were beheld in the angelic nature before the generation of all the natures that are below it." Eriugena adds that not only the divine essence but also God's theophany is called "God." He repeats this interpretation in 448B.

The question for us, however, is: *did* Augustine say "that these theophanies were beheld in the angelic nature before the generation of all the natures that are below it: *Quas theophanias in angelica creatura (secundum) sanctum Augustinum . . . uisas non incongrue dixisse credimus.*?[13] The text appears to be not altogether certain here, but it would seem clear, nevertheless, that Eriugena is not asserting that Augustine said what is attributed to him, but only that he, Eriugena, *believes* that he did. One may ask if the wish is father to the thought (*uolentes intelligere*, 692B)?

To answer this question properly we must first attempt to set out as briefly and accurately as possible what Augustine did say on the point.

I have already indicated where Eriugena could have found it in DGnL. Here is perhaps the most useful passage in this connection:

"But the angelic mind, clinging in pure love to the word of God, after it was created in that order that made it precede other things, saw in the word of God the things that were to be made, before they were made; and thus they came to be in its knowledge, when God said that they were to come to be, before they came to be in their own proper nature. And when, again, these things were made in themselves, the angelic mind also knew them with a lesser knowledge indeed, which is called "evening" knowledge. The things that came to be certainly preceded that knowledge of them, since whatever can be known precedes knowledge (of itself); for unless what is known exists beforehand, it cannot be known ... And so in this way, although there are no intervals of time here, nevertheless the reason of the creature to be created preceded in the word of God, when he said: "Let there be light," and the light itself followed, by which the angelic mind was formed and made in its own nature, but it did not follow elsewhere so as to come to be. And so it is not first said: "And so it was made," and afterwards said: "And God made the light," but immediately after the word of God the light was made and the created light clung to the creating light, seeing it and itself in it, that is the reason by which it was made. For it saw itself in itself, that is, separated as created from him who created ... and the light was divided from the darkness and the light was called "day" and the darkness "night." "Evening" too was made, since that knowledge also was necessary by which the creature was distinguished from the creator as known in one way in itself and another way in him (*creatura aliter in se ipsa cognita quam in illo*). And then in the "morning" another thing—which was to be made by the word of God—was to be known beforehand, first in the knowledge of the angelic mind, then in the nature of the firmament itself. And so God said: "Let the firmament come to be." And so it was made in the knowledge of the spiritual creature which knew it before it came to be in itself. Then God made the firmament, that is to say the nature itself of the firmament, of which the angel's knowledge is lesser, an "evening" knowledge so to speak." (IV, 32, 49ff.)

This passage on inspection will be seen to cover the points made by the Disciple in 446A and in the order in which he made them. It can be seen immediately that Augustine's conception of these matters is complicated and subtle, founded ultimately on his theory of creation as having two moments, so to speak, the *prima conditio*—"the first establishing"—and the *administratio*—"the bringing into effect." The use made by Augustine of previous Neoplatonic and especially Plotinian doctrines is expounded at some length by Agaësse and Solignac in the *Notes Complémentaires* to their edition of the *De Genesi ad litteram* to which I have already referred. There is a striking similarity between the details and structure of Plotinus's account of the constitution of *nous* and the *logoi* and Augustine's account of the creation of the angelic nature and its role. I must refrain, however, just now from adverting further to this aspect of our topic, however seductive, impressive, and illuminating it may be. I must keep to Augustine and to him alone.

The *prima conditio* is the original condition, the original establishing of all things, all at the same time and (so to speak) on the same occasion—*simul et semel*—in an order not of time but of the connection of causes (V, 5, 12). The things thus created, the "reasons" of the elements and of what is made from them, were real, although invisible. They had, or rather were "reasons" which, in accordance with the order contained in their establishment, are brought into the effects (*administratio*) we see in time. Existence, therefore, can be predicated of these reasons at three levels—in God, in the *prima conditio*, and as we see them in temporal things (V, 12, 28). They can be described also like this: "not made but eternal"; "made together, later to become"; and "each created in its own time" (VI, 10, 17). These existences are reflected in the knowledge of the angelic nature, which must now engage our attention.

Since there is no mention of the creation of the angels in Genesis, Augustine identifies it with the *fiat lux!* This light was not the true light, coeternal with the Father through which all things were made, but it was that spirital light of which it could be said: "Before all things wisdom (*sapientia*) was created" (I, 17, 32). The angelic nature, with God's *fiat lux!* came to be, still "clinging," as Augustine says, to the creating light, seeing it and itself—that is the reason by which it was made—in it, but also seeing itself in itself, separated, as created, from the creator (IV, 32, 50). When the angelic nature turned to its creator and was illuminated by him, its creation was complete: "cum conuersa[14] autem et inluminata est, factum est, quod in uerbo Dei dictum est: fiat lux" (I, 9, 17).

Augustine's views on the knowledge of the angelic nature is centred on its knowing the creature through the creator, not (as is the case in man) the creator through the creature (V, 5, 14). It knows, therefore, all creatures, including itself, first in the word of God in which are the eternal reasons of all things, including itself (IV, 24, 41); then in its own angelic nature, in which knowledge all creatures come to be: *prius in eius cognitione fit, cum dicitur: et sic est factum* (IV, 26, 43). Finally it knows things as they are.

It is to be noted that according to Augustine the angelic nature plays a definite role in creation—but it is, unlike the role of *nous* in Plotinus, confined to the purely noetic. It must be emphasized too that the angel's knowledge and creation are simultaneous, if preceding in dignity, with that of all other things in the *prima conditio*. Nevertheless the "reasons" that were in God were not created until they were known by the angel.

It would seem from such an analysis[15] then, that the angelic nature, according to Augustine, must have known the mind of the Lord, the reasons in God: this is the king-pin of Augustine's understanding of creation. The words used in this connection are clear and unqualified: *nouerunt* (IV, 24, 41), *contemplaretur* (IV, 34, 53), *uidit in uerbo Dei facienda . . . uidens se in illa . . . praenoscentis* (IV, 32, 49f.) and so on. There is little ground for supposing that Augustine simply omitted to explain that when he said the angel saw the reasons in God, he actually meant that the angel saw only images of them, manifestations, theophanies. It has to be admitted that the simultaneity of all the elements in the creation as insisted upon by Augustine, and the purely noetic nature of the role of the angelic nature, abate somewhat the reality, so to speak, of the angel's seeing its own—or any other—reason as an eternal reason in the word of God. Nevertheless what is seen is said by Augustine to be the eternal reason—never simply its appearance.

If this be so, then Eriugena in relation to this topic as referred to by him in 446A, 448A, 640C, and 770C, in trying to steer a straight and middle course between Paul and Augustine, each of them speaking the truth, does not succeed, so far as we can see, in doing proper justice to Augustine. Was it because he thought Paul the greater authority? Or was it because he found the Greek way more accessible than Augustine's? I shall have something to say on such questions when we come, almost immediately, to a final assessment.

We come now, very briefly, to 804B. Here the disciple insists that in DGnL[16] Augustine most manifestly maintains that before the Fall man was something animal and mortal: *animale atque mortale*. He was bidden to eat the fruits of paradise, so as—being animal—not to grow weak, and to eat of the tree of life so as —being mortal—not to die. The master does not undertake to argue back against Augustine: others may do so, he will not. For his part he is content to read the opinions of the Fathers on man as created before the Fall, and seek carefully and diligently what each one of them wanted to say. It was no part of his business to compose their conflicts or confirm one and refute another. He knew that after the apostles no Greek had greater authority in the exposition of divine Scripture than Gregory the Theologian,[17] no Latin than Augustine. These two great men appeared to be in conflict on the point in question. Perhaps one could contrive some kind of agreement (*quendam consensum uelimus machinari*): the body which Gregory said God in his foreknowledge additionally provided and added as something external[18] (on account of the sin that man would commit) was the same body, one could contend, as that which Augustine called animal. Gregory spoke of the two creations of man: one, substantial, in the image of God, the other far removed, namely the division, arising from sin, into male and female. But could Augustine speak only of the division into male and female, and not of the creation in the image of God, which is without any sex? It was unlikely that Augustine took this view; and if one consulted his works it was impossible to hold that he did. What Eriugena could not, he protests, understand was why Augustine called that body, which he praised as spirital and blessed, animal?

Here Eriugena is clearly anxious to follow Gregory, who, though not seeing evil in sexuality itself, construes sexuality as a consequence of sin, for which, therefore, God in his foreknowledge provided. On the other hand, Augustine had insisted that the sexual division had not only nothing to do with sin but was in fact original and independent of the consequences of the Fall—so that man was sexual—i.e., animal—from the very beginning. Here Eriugena, as he says, admits the uselessness of seeking to reconcile these two Fathers; but he will not seek to argue against or refute Augustine. He simply cannot believe that Augustine could have held that man before the Fall was animal, especially since he had also stressed the spirital character of the body which Adam then had: "sed mirari non desino cur illud corpus appellat animale quod magnis laudibus exaltat tanquam spirituale (spiritale?) atque beatum." Such protestation at failure to understand is not, however, a substitute for explanation of why he followed Gregory and departed from Augustine.

Sheldon-Williams, writing of what he calls the primitive version of the *Periphyseon*, says that "apparently only Latin sources were used." Of the last four books of the final version (as he describes it) he reports that they rely "heavily on Greek sources."[19] Mathon asserts that Eriugena's developed thought is essentially no longer inspired by Augustine.[20] On the other hand, Bett, for example, holds that Augustine counts for more in the thought of Eriugena than the whole of the Dionysian *oeuvre*—with the *Ambigua* of Maximus thrown in.[21] One gets the impression that the Greek and Latin sources are jockeying for the favoured position.

Eriugena himself is, I think, responsible for this situation. His reverence for Augustine—for Pater Augustinus (cf. e.g., 876C)—was immense. He sought the support of his authority whenever he could; he interpreted Augustine's words in favour of the position he himself was following if this were at all possible. This sometimes caused him undeclared embarrassment. When, however, he could not but find himself in disagreement with Augustine, his embarrassment is plainly brought to our notice. Eriugena can no longer effect a consensus—but he will not argue against Augustine, much less seek to refute him. This embarrassment, manifested in things of greater or smaller moment, conveys, I suggest, to readers a sense that Eriugena abandoned Augustine and had *felt some guilt* for doing so.

I hope I will have suggested to you that this way of looking at things—at any rate for the use of DGnL in the *Periphyseon*—may not strictly represent the truth. Augustine is at pains in DGnL to make clear that he is not satisfied with his own suggestions towards the solution of very difficult problems, and easily admits that others may propose different and better solutions: "in quo opere plura quaesita quam inuenta sunt . . . cetera . . . adhuc requirenda sint." Augustine's humility in facing the explanation of creation was founded on previous failure.

Eriugena and Augustine are fundamentally at one in their approach to the problem of creation: both start out from apophaticism: "Deus qui scitur melius nesciendo." Both are inspired by the Neoplatonic account of creation as a *progressus-regressus*. Augustine never reneges on these, even if his life and works developed in him, in relation to the first of them especially, perhaps, a less negative, more positive attitude and practice. Even this Eriugena excuses and discounts on the ground that Augustine practised the economy of exoteric and esoteric doctrines.

The *De Genesi ad litteram* and the *Periphyseon*, though sharing the same basic topic, creation, differ radically in their approach to it. Augustine's work explicitly sets out to be historical; Eriugena's is theoretical. Augustine's work is tied to the text of Genesis; Eriugena's argument is patently dialectical within the pattern of *progressus-regressus*.

If, therefore, Eriugena does not keep in line with Augustine it is partly at least because their works have radically different methods.

There is, I believe, also a profound psychological difference between their personalities as revealed in their writings. Although they start from the same apophatic and Neoplatonic base—and have much else in common—their approach to the understanding of the symbolism of "night" and "day" in Genesis is highly significant. Augustine is tireless in trying to find rational explanations for everything: clarification is for him the greater practical reality. Eriugena is drawn to the Greek Fathers in finding in incomprehensibility itself a practical means of handling many problems. Can we say after all that, though Augustine had mystical tendencies, the rational element is more pronounced in his writings, and that, though Eriugena was a master of dialectic, the mystical element affected his work profoundly? One can only speculate if the Dionysian writings would have had so pronounced an effect on him if he had not made acquaintance with them in the very special and personal way he came to know them.

Eriugena, as we have seen, makes open profession that he will follow not any particular authority but the authority that seems *best* to him: "amicus Plato, amicus Socrates, sed magis amica ueritas." "Let it be enough for me," he says (804C) "to read the opinions of the Fathers and seek carefully and diligently what each of them thought." The implication of this is that he feels free not to follow any one of the Fathers—not even the alleged disciple of St. Paul, the Pseudo-Dionysius. It is possible indeed that we have been accustomed to use rather too automatically the argument that Eriugena took everything said by St. Paul as at its face value decisive, and that this applied also to St. Paul's alleged disciple. To begin with, the special authority of the Apostle could not be extended to his disciple without qualification. Moreover, both he and the Apostle needed on occasion some interpretation. Hence Eriugena's profession that he studied the opinions of *all* the Fathers—not just Dionysius or the Greeks or Ambrose or Augustine. And there can be no doubt that he was most careful to have all possible support always from Pater Augustinus. Eriugena, it might be said—in fact Gilson has implied it[22]—was peculiarly anxious to follow some authority in everything: this may unfavourably affect our opinion of his originality—but, if it be necessary, we must accept it. He does not always give rational grounds for his preferring one authority to another, and he notably accepts that a reader may think his choice "incredible": *neque cuiquam suademus cred-*

ere, quod ei incredibile uidetur (876C). His throwing up his hands in amazement that Augustine should call Adam's body before the Fall "animal," though he had treated it as very "spirital," hardly takes the place of the kind of reasoning practised by Augustine.

In this connection it is necessary to stress that Eriugena believed that the truth could be viewed from a number of (perhaps even apparently conflicting) angles. Thus in relation to the opinions of Basil and Augustine and his own on the meaning of *"fiat lux"* he remarks (693C): "qualemcunque horum intellectuum quis obtinuerit, non longe a ueritate distabit." One could oversimplify such an approach by saying that to Eriugena there seemed to be a *choice* of truths rather than *one* truth only, though, of course, there was only one truth ultimately. Such an attitude would tend to put more emphasis on authority than reason.

And so it must finally be said, in relation to the enquiry I have reported to you here, that Eriugena felt free, and acted accordingly, to choose the authority he should follow. For a large part if not most of his matter he could rely on, and did rely on, Pater Augustinus. But although he could find directly in Augustine authority for many of the views that he espoused, or interpreted Augustine as holding those views either openly or secretly, he found it *more convenient,* perhaps, to follow Ambrose, Augustine's spiritual and intellectual master, and the Greeks, whose exposition of such views was lengthy and explicit. There is, therefore, it should be remembered, a considerable overlapping between what is implicit or briefly to be found in Augustine, even as reported by Eriugena, and what is openly and extensively quoted from the Greeks in the *Periphyseon*.

The extent of this overlapping is the measure of the balance to be redressed in favour of Augustine vis-à-vis the Greeks in our assessment of Eriugena's use of sources of doctrine in that great work.

PART V

METHOD AND CRITICISM IN THE STUDY OF AUGUSTINE

21

Research Techniques in Augustinian Studies

୬୧

I shall be concerned here principally with *Quellenforschung* and its application to our knowledge of the *development* of Augustine's outlook. I shall be concerned with raising as instances for discussion with you the statements of method of working, and their application, by Olivier du Roy, in his *L'intelligence de la foi en la Trinité selon saint Augustin* (1966), and Pierre Hadot, in his *Porphyre et Victorinus* (2 vols. 1968), both published by Etudes Augustiniennes in Paris. Since my time is very limited, and I must attempt to provoke discussion on at least one or two important issues—but I hope to deal in passing with quite a number of related ones—and I must give a fair exposition of the positions of du Roy and Hadot, I must be both abrupt and condensed.

Quellenforschung is as old as folk-tales, certainly as old as Virgil whose "thefts" from Homer were a matter of pride to him and not reproach, as old as Schopenhauer, as old as Goldschmidt[1] dealing with Plato, and as new as Hadot dealing with Porphyry. I have left out many famous names. And if I were to indicate the like history of derivation in painting, music, and in almost all human activities, I should still but remind you how *inevitable* the study of sources is, and by implication how *valuable*. But *Quellenforschung* within the field of Classical Philology, to the high standards of which we must aspire, has had a chequered and erratic history, a pattern of too much confidence and too little, of excessive admiration and of none. It is not surprising, therefore, that in the recent impressive development of Augustinian studies, particularly in France, *Quellenforschung* is beginning to be an acute question—as indicated, for example, by its formal and emphatic consideration as something fundamental or necessarily implied in the two books I have mentioned.

Let me say at once that if I discuss these two scholars, writing in French, it is because French scholars so dominate our field that it is their work which will almost inevitably come up for consideration in a topic such as ours; because these two scholars formally raise these questions;

and [because] their books are recent. The inconvenience of being Carian Slaves is compensated for, I hope, by the compliment implied in taking their views with respect and seriousness, and by our assurance of that friendship which I like to think exists among us, students of Augustine. As it happens, there is this justification for *my* opening this discussion in that Hadot suggested in his article *à propos* of my *Porphyry's Philosophy from Oracles in Augustine*[2] that an *étude génétique des schémas augustiniens* should be attempted (he was polite enough to imply that I should or could do it); and G. Madec reported to the Rencontre du 12 février 1966 at the Centre Le Nain de Tillemont that du Roy was following Hadot's suggestion in relation to the *schèmes trinitaires* in Augustine's thought, and that Hadot was pursuing the matter himself. *Eh bien, voilà!* Others have done the work and I must be the guilty referee.

I should make one final preliminary point clear: in the case of neither book do I propose to outline its contents or make any evaluation here. I shall keep strictly to their discussion and application or non-application of research techniques. But I hope I may be allowed to say that I found both books very illuminating indeed.

Du Roy's succinct formulation of his method of work is given as follows: "Cette méthode se voudrait à la fois phénoménologique, génétique et structurale. Méthode phénoménologique, c'est-à-dire visant à atteindre l'intuition qui meut la pensée augustinienne et qui, ne s'épuisant dans aucune formulation successive, relance perpétuellement sa recherche. Comme nous l'avons déjà dit ailleurs, notre attention se portera aux tâtonnements et aux hésitations, indices d'une visée qui ne s'épuise pas dans ses expressions. Méthode génétique, puisqu'il s'agit de saisir le jaillissement de cette pensée et son intuition directrice dans une élaboration progressive. Méthode structurale enfin, car il s'agit bien d'une puissante synthèse dont les matériaux, d'origines très diverses, sont intégrés dans un plan d'ensemble sans cesse remanié."[3] You might wish a shorter, perhaps clearer, summary also: "Retenons pour le moment qu'il est impossible de comprendre la pensée d'Augustin sans saisir à la fois sa cohérence (ses structures), son mouvement (sa genèse) et son sens (à la fois son enracinement dans une expérience et sa visée).[4]

The first question, quite a preliminary one, that I would put to you is: does terminology such as *méthode phénoménologique, méthode génétique, méthode structurale* help to clarify matters? I have some difficulty, I confess, in knowing exactly what is here meant by *phénoménologique* and *génétique*. I feel that *génétique* alone would, if intelligently understood (and that should be assumed), do for the two (in fact du Roy in practice hardly exploits his *méthode phénoménologique*—perhaps because it is difficult to define in many cases as against the *méthode génétique*). Indeed I am persuaded that *méthode structurale* alone, if intelligently understood, would do for the whole three. Du Roy himself has perhaps betrayed his position by the phrase: *sans cesse remanié*, which clearly implies that the *méthode structurale* concerns itself not only with coherence, but also with what is dynamic, with movement, which is said to be the specific concern of the *méthode génétique*. And again in using the phrase *synthèse dont les matériaux, d'origines très diverses, sont intégrés*, he cannot but imply that the *méthode structurale* involves necessarily the impetus of new experience, new knowledge, which is said to be the specific concern of the *méthode phénoménologique*. If my own unpretentious outline of method in my *Porphyry's Philosophy from Oracles in Augustine*[5] is consulted it will be seen that I understood that this method provided for "development" and the new experience of confrontation with an author. Is it not true that one can only separate these three methods by excluding from each of them artificially the content of the other? If structural must mean static, then there is room for the *méthode génétique*. But is this not excessive formalism and against experience?

While I am on the question of terminology might I just ask if terms such as *problématique, anagogie trinitaire, synchroniques*, and *diachroniques, démarche rédactionelle* are more clarifying than plain statements of little greater length?

But du Roy has some interest in emphasizing the *méthode génétique*, which for him implies evolution of thought as against *structurale*, which implies for him merely coherence of pattern. For his theme is the genesis or evolution of Augustine's thought: it is related to a "succession chronologique qui lui à fait décourvrir l'intelligence de la Trinité chrétienne dans Plotin . . . et ensuite seulement la nécessité de l'Incarnation comme voie d'humilité vers Dieu. On a voulu voir dans ce schème l'influence de Porphyre."[6] Du Roy thinks that Porphyry's influence here was both partial only and late. On the precise question of the fact of Augustine's knowing Porphyry at the time of the *Dialogues of Cassiciacum* I might be allowed to say that du Roy inconsistently both admits that Augustine might have known Porphyry's *Sententiae*[7] and at the same time fails[8] to deal at all adequately with the mounting evidence from Courcelle to this last book of Hadot[9] that Augustine knew the book referred to, at least descriptively, as *De regressu animae*, at the time of his conversion. His insistence on the incarnation as being both secondary and of later realization than the trinity[10] in the period of his conversion and for some time afterwards is surprising,[11] and ultimately rests on the assumption that Augustine did not think of the incarnation as a mediation but as a lesson in humility and a purification at this time.[12] This, of course, is to forget what elsewhere du Roy so rightly asserts of Augustine, that he had a mind that was both active and able to arrive at the implications of his thought. The incarnation by its very concept of God-taking-man's-nature-while-keeping-his-own implies mediation. It is again to be excessively formalistic, to limit the meaning of words so unwarrantably so that the *méthode génétique* will discover a succession, an evolution.

A seeming implication of the *méthode génétique* is that one may not use texts of a later period of an author's works in relation to earlier ones. Thus du Roy follows Solignac in his criticism of my own practice.[13] There is great confusion in such a view. The *méthode génétique* exposes a scholar to various unwarranted assumptions: (1) that an author has committed to writing his new thought as soon as he has had it; (2) that if it is inspired by a source, that source is sufficiently indicated in this writing. These ideas can be expressed in another way: (1) that if an author doesn't refer to a theme in his writing, he doesn't know it; and (2) that if we cannot see a derivation from a source in a piece of writing, it isn't there. Du Roy in point of fact constantly solicits the evidence of later texts himself and notably in what he describes as the prehistory of his problem: the *Confessions* are used to "place" and illustrate his thesis.[14] It is undeniable that a later text can illuminate one that is earlier and obscure. One thinks, for example, of CA II, 5 which in spite of the help from the *Confessions* is still obscure. As Mandouze says: "Je considère que les parallèles entre Augustin et Augustin permettent de déceler, sinon toujours la permanence d'un état d'esprit, tout au moins une certaine continuité d'inspiration."[15]

Let us now, having considered, however briefly, the *méthode génétique* which Goldschmidt describes as abandoning fact for imagination, as arbitrary and as likely only to paralyze research,[16] pass over to consider the purely structural method as employed by Hadot.

One of the most serious barriers to research is misplaced dogmatism. E. R. Dodds has complained that Creuzer bequeathed a misleading picture of Neoplatonism.[17] Likewise Bidez has passed on a misleading picture of Porphyry.[18] When Hadot was considering my book on the

Philosophy from Oracles in Augustine nearly ten years ago he was still under the influence of that received picture. Now he writes that Porphyry professed a very original doctrine: "Ce sont des aspects insoupçonnés de la doctrine de Porphyre que notre présente recherche a dégagés. Par là même l'histoire du néoplatonisme postplotinien se dessine mieux, et la place que Porphyre y tient se précise considérablement."[19] Hadot asks if we should not now renounce the simple transmission Plotinus–Victorinus–Augustine?[20] That Porphyry, a declared enemy of the Christians, should nevertheless have been used by them is now accepted.[21] Significantly we are told that the merit of Willy Theiler's work has not been sufficiently recognized,[22] and his much contested principle in *Quellenforschung* is now declared to be *bon, mais son application délicate, et même dangereuse*.[23]

Hadot insists (1) that "dans l'étude des écrivains latins de la fin de l'Antiquité, la recherche des sources me semble absolument indispensable. (2) D'autre part, la reconstitution d'une source perdue est possible et légitime, à condition que les éléments qui entrent dans cette reconstruction ne soient jamais séparés de structures littéraires et conceptuelles dont ils font partie."[24] To all of this I can only say, hear hear!— especially to these last few words—a theme must be taken in its total context and compared with another in its total context.[25] Hadot lays down three conditions which have to be fulfilled before one can legitimately conclude that such a passage is derived from such another passage. First, there must be a reason to suspect derivation, either because the author conveys this or a "foreign body" seems to be present (badly integrated, uncharacteristic vocabulary); secondly, enough of the characteristic doctrinal and literary elements of the source must be extant to make discussion possible; and thirdly, and most importantly, "que l'on puisse reconnaître une identité entre l'emprunteur et sa source sur des points qui soient absolument caractéristiques ... une combinaison d'éléments typiques, liés ensemble de manière à former une configuration unique et se retrouvant à la fois et uniquement dans l'emprunteur et dans sa source ... 'structure conceptuelle.'" Hadot considers that such a structure could be the equivalent sometimes of a textual parallel. But it must not be separated from its literary characteristics.[26]

Using such methods Hadot claims to have identified the Palimpsest of Turin as part of Porphyry's commentary on the *Parmenides* of Plato; and building upon this as a basis for further comparison and identification, he claims to discover the Porphyrian elements that dominate in Victorinus's thought and through him profoundly influenced the West. It is a magnificent structure; it throws an immense and welcome light not only on Porphyry's and Victorinus's thought, but also on the development of theology in the West; but can it be taken, as Hadot takes it and prints it, as established? I fear not.

Hadot seems to me to aim at too much certainty and too much precision. In spite of the substantial change in his own appreciation of Porphyry's thought over the last ten years, his attitude is still dogmatic, and his appreciation of what is and what is not exclusively characteristic of Porphyry is still too definite. This on the one hand allows him to identify the bricks, so to speak, of the Porphyrian system, to be recovered from elsewhere, and so build up the whole imposing evidence; but on the other it leaves other scholars somewhat uneasy. There is too much emphasis on coherence in structure, and not enough on genesis. External indications, where they exist, must be treated with the greatest respect, and *prior* to arriving at any conclusion on purely conceptual lines. If, for example, it is incontrovertible that the work referred to informally by Augustine and only twice in the same context as *De regressu animae*[27] is not referred to ever by anyone elsewhere; if moreover one cannot distinguish one work of Porphyry from another on the basis of being chronologically before or after Porphyry's own sojourn with Plotinus—Hadot now writes: "Venu d'Athènes où il avait été le disciple de Longin, qui était encore un moyen-platonicien, il ne sera l'élève de Plotin à Rome que pendant six ans: peut-être n'aura-t-il pas le temps de comprendre toute la nouveauté de la doctrine plotinienne. Il peut avoir eu l'impression que Plotin et les Oracles enseignaient la même chose sous des formules différentes"[28]—then one should take more account of these external factors than of a coherence of *ton* or *attitude*.[29] If, for example, Virgil's *Eclogues* were lost and two fragments were discovered separately, one being the Epicurean description of the origin of the world in *Eclogue* VI and the other the immediately following mythological account of the origin of man, one might have some difficulty in deciding that both had the same author, Virgil; that both came from the pastoral *Eclogues*; and finally that they came from the same poem, following one upon the other without any transition whatever.[30]

It must be clear that I favour the flexible, restrained and intelligent employment of the *méthode structurale* (as including the *méthode génétique*) but rigidly controlled by external evidence.

I must presently leave the discussion to those present. But allow me to mention a few counsels of perfection, applicable to us all:

1. Don't write unless you have something useful to say.
2. Don't include in your bibliographies the names of books which you have not used.
3. Don't discuss another scholar's view on something if you have not read it in his original exposition, probably in his own language.
4. If you are writing for scholars, don't translate original texts unless you are making a point of interpretation.
5. If you feel you are forcing the evidence, stop.
6. If you find yourself coming to the conclusion that your author didn't know what he was saying—but you do—stop.

I can give instances of abuses, by myself and others, on all these matters.

At this point, *I* must stop. But let me end with a quotation: "Of making books there is no end. The growing mass of scholarly publications can keep us from getting to the texts themselves or lure us like Sirens to ostentatious displays of erudition. Specialism, narrowing professionalism, the acquisition of the techniques of scholarship as ends in themselves block the way to an authentic encounter with the ancient work as a creation of the human spirit."[31] As Augustine says: "modus ubique servandus est, ubique amandus;[32] nam modus procul dubio diuinus est."[33]

22

Studies[1] Preparatory to an Understanding of the Mysticism of Augustine and His Doctrine on the Trinity

๛

Of the two studies before us, that of Olivier du Roy has, at least professedly, a single aim: it studies the earlier evolution of Augustine's Trinitarian thought. It makes profession, moreover, of a special technique in research. It requires, as a result, careful assessment of its method and some at least of its results. These results can have far-reaching consequences. André Mandouze's book, on the other hand, does not insist that it profits from any special technique, and its canvas is the whole of Augustine's life and every aspect, but especially the mystical aspects of it. Here we may be content with a more general appraisal. Both books start once again from the *Dialogues of Cassiciacum* and naturally overlap in certain areas. They are widely different in approach—Mandouze's being much more personal than the other—but they have two things in common: they are both very long and both are preparatory to second volumes where it is hoped they will come to grips with their ultimate subjects—Mandouze with mysticism in Augustine and du Roy with Augustine's doctrine on the Trinity. Hence our title.

The subtitle of Olivier du Roy's book is: *Genèse de sa Théologie Trinitaire jusqu'en 391*, that is, as manifested in the *Dialogues of Cassiciacum* (including the *Soliloquia*), *De moribus ecclesiae catholicae et de moribus Manichaeorum, De libero arbitrio, De quantitate animae, De Genesi contra Manichaeos, De musica, De diuersis quaestionibus LXXXIII, De uera religione*, and *Epistula* XI. The most crucial text for du Roy's thesis is *De uera religione* which he considers on pp. 309–388, that is, for between one-fourth and one-fifth of his discussion (as apart from Introduction and lengthy Conclusion).

This discussion is preceded by a consideration of what du Roy calls *la préhistoire de l'intellectus fidei d'Augustin dans la gnose manichéenne* as described in *Confessions* III and VII. In *Confessions* VII, according to du Roy, we are given the key to Augustine's *intellectus fidei* and evolution: "Augustin a découvert Dieu et plus précisément la Trinité grâce à la lecture de livres néo-platoniciens et ensuite seulement le Christ, incarné grâce à la lecture des Epitres pauliniennes. Cette succession des événements est à l'origine d'une structure fondamental de la théologie augustinienne: antériorité de la connaissance de la Trinité sur celle de l'incarnation."[2] The anteriority (if I am coining the word) of his knowledge of the Trinity to his knowledge of the incarnation is the fundamental point du Roy sets out to demonstrate. His enucleation on pages 537–540 of some one hundred and fifty principal Neoplatonic triads which he finds in Augustine and other authors gives some idea of the alertness of du Roy's interest, his subtlety in interpretation, and (to complete another triad in hackneyed rhetorical tradition) perhaps his over-insistence upon his theme. But there are other interesting and important considerations which are related to his fundamental point—among them is his contention that Augustine did not get to know Porphyry until after not only his conversion, but after his return to Milan before his baptism.[3] This last point is in direct conflict with what Hadot calls a view *presque unanime*.[4] But the mere contradiction of a received opinion should not prejudice one's assessment of the view put forward: what is important is the argument advanced.

Here I report briefly[5] du Roy's account of the research technique which he applies in this study. This he describes as *une méthode neuve*.

> Cette méthode se voudrait à la fois phénoménologique, génétique et structurale. Méthode phénoménologique, c'est-à-dire visant à atteindre l'intuition qui meut la pensée augustinienne et qui, ne s'épuisant dans aucune formulation successive, relance perpétuellement sa recherche. Comme nous l'avons déjà dit ailleurs, notre attention se portera aux tâtonnements et aux hésitations, indices d'une visée que ne s'épuise pas dans ses expressions. Méthode génétique, puisqu'il s'agit de saisir le jaillissement de cette pensée et son intuition directrice dans une élaboration progressive. Méthode structurale enfin, car il s'agit bien d'une puissante synthèse dont les matériaux, d'origines très diverses, sont intégrés dans un plan d'ensemble sans cesse remanié.[6]

Augustine's thought is evolutionary and, therefore, must always be related to what is an unusually well-established chronology. His terminology, however, is *flottant*, as H. I. Marrou has pointed out.[7] Du Roy insists, nevertheless—and I would agree with him—that the structures of his thought remain relatively stable. Hence the structural method is the only suitable method for the analysis of Augustine's thought. The structures or schemas are found in the phrase, the paragraph, or a section or the whole of a work. "Au lieu de procéder par multiplication de rapprochements, notre étude s'attardera donc de préférence à des textes longs, traduit intégralement et commentés ligne après ligne. Lorsqu'on interroge l'oeuvre d'Augustin avec cet instrument nouveau qu'est la méthode structurale, elle apparaît admirablement cohérente."[8] I myself have outlined a similar method as follows: "The argument is one internal to certain texts of Augustine. Augustine was no modern scientific philologist and did not consider it necessary when reporting, or referring to, a passage in an author to do so either accurately or even, if he used the passage often, in identical terms. He did, however, tend to repeat topics, and in reading him we soon begin to recognize them, get to know their characteristic details, and watch their development and later entry into a larger synthesis. Here the economical and effective method of parallel texts cannot be employed, not only because of the number of texts involved, but especially because the repetition of words and phrases is here less significant. Each text must be scrutinized carefully in itself and its context and in relation to the others. This necessarily leads to much quotation and repetition: some of this the reader may omit, but at least the evidence will always be there before him."[9]

It is evident that such a method demands very great efforts from the reader, efforts which few will or can afford to give, and certainly not the *lecteurs pressés,* as Hadot calls them,[10] who are in the majority. Indeed it is unfortunately clear that those who refer to and pass judgment on books based on such methods have frequently not read them. One should, therefore, try to limit the application of this method to as small a canvas as possible.

Let us now look at his treatment of *De uera religione.* Since he insists, as he is entitled to, that R I, 13, 1: *tunc* (that is between *De magistro* and *De utilitate credendi,* or 389–391) *etiam de Vera Religione librum scripsi* means that the work was then *written,* he is under no necessity to concede that any part of it is earlier than 388 when he accepts that Augustine had read the *De regressu animae.*[11] Nevertheless his *méthode à la fois phénoménologique, génétique et structurale* is employed to expose *deux couches successives* in the work. Du Roy feels that we should not speak about *plan* in this connection: Mais c'est justement cette notion moderne de "plan" qu'il faut habituellement récuser dan le cas d'Augustin, surtout dans ses ouvrages de recherche. Nous lui substituons la notion de "structure rédactionnelle," plus souple et respectant mieux le mode de composition d'Augustin, fait généralement de plusieurs reprises d'un même thème, selon un schème directeur dont l'intention ne parait pas s'épuiser dans les réalisations successives.[12]

Not only were there *deux intentions superimposées* (p. 310) in the *De uera religione* (an anti-Manichaean and an anti-Porphyrian) but there are distinguishable three *essais* in the anti-Manichaean part. Du Roy summarizes his construction of DVR as follows:[13]

Introd.:	1,1–8,15:	*Dernière introduction (antiporphyrienne).*
	9,16–10,20:	*Première introduction (antimanichéene).*
I.:	11,21–17,34):	*Deux essais successifs pour décrire la chute de l'âme et sa remontée par la "medicina*
II.:	18,35–25,51)	*temporalis"* (cf. 16,30, *ibid.*, 21,29; 24,45, *ibid.*, 32,3; 26,48, *ibid.*, 34,3). *Il faut cependant en excepter deux insertions antiporphyriennes*: 13,26–14,28 et 25,46–47.
	29,52–38,69:	*Le second essai se termine par une anagogie, qui est le développement de celle du De lib. arb.*
III.:	38,69–55,107:	*Triple concupiscence et triple redressement.*
Concl.:	55,108–113:	*Antiporphyrienne.*

While it is abundantly clear that the work is divisible into sections in conformity with the description given of it in the *Retractationes*, it is somewhat too convenient to be able to suggest that one can tease out the sections which show that the work is one in which although it begins: "par pressentir une voie moyenne, la philosophie de la ressemblance ou des analogies, la perspective créationniste finit par l'emporter et culmine dans l'expression de "Trinité créatrice" qu'on y rencontre pour la première fois" (p. 309). This kind of separation of parts of a work which assumes the total and exact separability of themes is highly subjective and is exposed to great error. The anti-Manichean and anti-Porphyrian themes are not in fact so separable here. For example, du Roy writes:[14] "L'intention première du *De vera religione* parait être antimanichéene. Elle exprime au §9, 16 et ouvre l'exposé qui compose le corps de l'ouvrage jusqu'au §55, 107. Son thème général peut être caractérisé par la citation de Rom. 1, 25 ("seruierunt creaturae potius quam creatori") qui intervient dans l'introduction et deux fois au cours de l'exposé." But the same citation is nearly always present in his anti-Porphyrian themes in many other places.[15] Likewise du Roy's assignment of the theme of demons as between the anti-Manichean and anti-Porphyrian themes cannot but leave many unconvinced.[16]

The essential purpose behind du Roy's treatment of DVR is to establish that the Porphyrian theme of Christ the mediator, the way, was not present in Augustine's mind in 386. If, as many scholars think,[17] Augustine had read the work of Porphyry to which he referred twice as *De regressu animae*, then du Roy's thesis on the abrupt change of Augustine's mind from a Plotinian to a Porphyrian mode is seriously endangered. And du Roy does not deal adequately with these scholars' views. I do not think that R I, 13, 7: "*nam ego ipse quando istum ipsum librum* (DVR) *scripsi, ad Mediolanensium corpora martyrum in eadem ciuitate caecum illuminatum fuisse iam noueram*," a text not mentioned by du Roy, can be used to prove a date of writing shortly after the dramatic events of the discovery of the remains of Gervasius and Protasius in June 386—but the text of CA II, 8: "cum tibi aliquam inter nos disputationem de religione misero" puts it beyond doubt that Augustine had a work such as that known as the *De uera religione* in mind just then. I do not accept the argument that whereas *De religione* as a title might refer to, for example, an anti-Manichean work, *De uera religione* explicitly implies an anti-Porphyrian work. This is an argument *ex silentio* and assumes a total consistency in the use of perhaps merely descriptive titles. One text is interesting in connection with the title: "De uera religione: uerum etiam de ipsa religione concordant, quod est ueri amici manifestissimum iudicium."[18]

Du Roy makes two specific statements to support his view that Augustine did not know the *De regressu animae* in 386. He asserts: "Point de traces non plus de ce mot inductio dans les premiers écrits d'Augustin." The term *inductio* is taken by du Roy in relation to the *inductione Chaldaeorum* of the *De regressu*.[19] But in fact traces of *inducere* appear at least once in each of the three *Dialogues of Cassiciacum*.[20] In the first of these Romanianus is informed that the present disputation is being sent to him as an *inductorium* to incite him to taste philosophy. The second of these reads: "Illa est igitur plena satietas animorum, hoc est beata uita, pie perfecteque cognoscere, a quo inducaris in ueritatem, qua ueritate perfruaris, per quid conectaris summo modo." This surely corresponds to du Roy's own description of "anagogie" (*inductio*) as *type d'ascension réflexive et mystique,* here in relation to the Trinity and in a context which is possibly Porphyrian, if not actually related to the *De regressu animae.*[21]

The second statement is as follows: "Aucun texte, au cours de la même période (i.e., before 391), n'emploie à ce propos l'exemple soi-disant porphyrien d'Alexandrie, ville lointaine que visite l'imagination."[22] Alexandria is in fact, as du Roy is aware,[23] mentioned twice in the same context in the *Contra Academicos.*[24] It is given as the name of a town that is (1) distant and (2) at which the wayfarer, though he sets out directly for it and travels until death, *never arrives*: "fac quemquam ex quo tempore iter agere uel aetate uel negotio sinitur, pergere accipere illam uiam atque, ut supra dixi, cum deuiet nusquam, antequam perueniat, tamen uita excedere. . . ." In both instances the distance of Alexandria and the fact that it was an unrealized and therefore only conceived goal are the essential points in the example. It would be excess of formalism to reject this text as irrelevant. The phrase *uariis impeditus causis longo agat tempore et in ea morte praeueniatur* of CA I, 11 may well be connected with CA III, 34[25] and thereby to *De regressu animae* itself.

Apart from matters of detail[26] there are one or two further general remarks that might be made. Du Roy has a tendency to deal inadequately with evidence that endangers his thesis. Thus he seems satisfied to deal with the arguments of Courcelle and myself for the influence of the *omne corpus fugiendum* on the *Dialogues of Cassiciacum* by concluding: "Il reste difficile d'en décider"[27]—but it is a matter quite vital for his thesis. Again he can write: "Toute-fois il faut reconnaître que ce premier trait de la métaphysique d'Augustin . . . coïncide de façon troublante avec les positions I et IV que W. Theiler donne pour caractéristiques du système porphyrien. Nous ne sommes pas encore en mesure de trancher la question."[28] His subsequent suggestions of possible explanations look much like a flight from evidence. He suggests[29] that the presence of the word *ratiuncula* of DI I, 7, 12 *pourrait expliquer en partie l'emploi de oracula* which in any case (formalism again) refers to the Scriptural, not Chaldean *oracula* used by Porphyry. How would he have explained, if he had taken account of it, "quam sententiam uberrimarum doctrinarum oraculis editam remotamque longissime ab intellectu profanorum se demonstraturam ueris amatoribus suis ad quam te inuito philosophia pollicetur"—which, having explicit mention of both philosophy and oracles and secret doctrine, in my view, shows evidence of the influence of Porphyry's *Philosophy from Oracles*?[30] And how the other reference to oracles in the *Dialogues of Cassiciacum*? Yet again when he has to confront Courcelle's urging of DOR II, 9, 27 as evidence for the influence of *De regressu animae*, he describes it as an *indice sérieux* for the possible influence of *De regressu animae*, engages in no discussion whatever of the matter, but refers the reader to a later note where the point, in fact, is again not discussed.[31]

The other point is in relation to the forcing of evidence. This is, I think, especially noticeable, as is not surprising, in the section where "reason" is being identified as the third person of the Trinity.[32]

I should like to record that, although I have found fault with both the methods and, therefore, the conclusions of Olivier du Roy's book, I have also found it fascinating and full of new (to me) information and views. The argument is always sustained with subtlety; the intellectual vistas opened are always elevating to the spirit and impressive. I wonder what Augustine would think of them! Would he agree with du Roy that he hadn't perceived the unity and coherence of his own thought?[33] Certain it is that he would look forward to the second volume to come with growing excitement.

Those who heard André Mandouze speak at the Congrès International Augustinien in Paris in 1954 will have been waiting eagerly but patiently for the appearance of his book on *les aspects mystiques de la pensée augustinienne*.[34] The present book, however, is not the one he set out to write. Although it does keep the *aspects mystiques* in mind, we shall have to wait for *Saint Augustin II: Aspects mystiques de sa vie et de sa pensée*. We trust it will not be long in coming.[35]

This is a very personal book: *l'aventure de la raison et de la grâce* of Augustine became an *aventure de la raison et de grâce* for Mandouze. We shall speak of this presently. This involvement with his subject has given Mandouze an intensity of interest which he would appear to find some difficulty in controlling: he was so busy, he says, that he hadn't the time to write more shortly. And so he has added to what he well calls *cette bibliographie galopante dont la démesure n'est que trop évidente*.[36]

I can think of no book where one will immediately find as readily as here an up-to-the-minute bibliography and generally sound evaluation of any point, almost, of Augustinian scholarship. The work ranges in three somewhat overlapping sections—*Confessio Vitae, Confessio Fidei* and

Confessio Laudis. The subtitles are challenging: *L'imprévu et l'inévitable, Un tempérament prometteur, L'année terrible, Plaisirs du vice et de l'innocence, Les nourritures terrestres, Un converti difficile, La grâce en ce jardin, Un Evéque malgré lui, La divine surprise, La nuit augustinienne, Un moine malgré tout, Polémiste parce qu'apôtre, L'implacable théologie de l'amour sans limites, Métaphysique de l'ambiguité* and so on, to give but a very few. Many titles sound as if they were for a novel or a film, and each section almost becomes one or the other. Here you will find the number of Augustine's works, all about his letters and sermons, illumination, predestination, the problem of the Neoplatonic books, the *tolle lege* scene, his knowledge of Greek, the meaning of *Cicero quidam*—and such seeming trivialities as his suffering from piles!

While the *Table des Matières* is very full and there are indexes *bibliographique, augustinien, lexicographique* and *nominum,* it is a great pity, in view of the quality and comprehensiveness of the book, that Mandouze did not give us a full index of all topics and the various places where they are treated.

Many passages of this book are written in the first person: "Je n'aurai pourtant pas l'hypocrisie de plaider coupable. Si j'ai cru bon d'intervenir à mon tour, c'est qu'à tort ou à raison (à d'autres, qui me liront, d'en décider) une longue fréquentation de l'oeuvre d'Augustin a fini par me persuader que j'avais après tout, moi aussi, quelque chose à dire à son sujet. . . ."[37] Indeed! Il faut beaucoup de naïveté ou beaucoup d'indécence."[38]

Mandouze very firmly demands that the study of Augustine must be approached with religious sympathy.[39] He would even be more radical yet than Hélène Cros who wrote that a conversion would never be anything other than an incompréhensible phenomenon for those who are not converted themselves.[40] The book is animated, therefore, by a strongly pro-religious and pro-Augustine sympathy. It is even pro-ascetic, if not also pro-monastic: "Je ne pouvais faire autrement que de l'entraîner avec moi dans une marche d'approche présentant elle-même un certain caractère ascétique." He even follows Augustine into his apparent excesses: "Tant pis aussi pour ceux qui ont horreur du prosélytisme."[41] He is prepared to meet those who will judge himself perhaps a little intolerant. Occasionally Mandouze adopts the role of preacher: "Et, surtout, Platoniciens, ne protestez pas. . . . Mais écoutez donc. Ah! si au moins il avait pu en avoir une connaissance exacte." Again: "Soyons sérieux. Ce n'est pas 'prêcher pour son saint' que d'essayer de se représenter le plus exactment possible la situation."[42]

It would be a pity if the reader were put off by these attitudes which are not usually admired in an historian. At times the terms and attitudes used are not really acceptable. But in fact Mandouze is *generally* scrupulous in scientific assessment. There are exceptions, however. One feels that when he speaks of Africa and its problems and its politics[43] (involving ideological overtones with relevance to certain fairly recent events) passion becomes a little strong. It is necessary to say all this and quote all this to give some idea of the moving, somewhat idiosyncratic, deeply passionate but essentially fair, comprehensive, and absorbing character of Mandouze's book.

Perhaps, since one cannot discuss the book as a whole here, one might usefully say something of Mandouze's many comments on Augustine's personality, his interest in monastic life and finally his mysticism. Judgments on these matters come from various parts of the book, but for the first two mainly from the *Confessio Vitae* (first part) and for the mysticism from the *Confessio Laudis* (third part).

Mandouze correctly stresses the exaggeration of the African Augustine's language in his description of his fleshly sins: "La luxuriance verbale est une des caractéristiques essentielles de la luxuriance africaine." He doesn't wish to white-wash him—but one has to keep this matter in perspective in relation, especially, to later assessments of character. The real explanation for what excesses there were was that they were *des compensations désespérées* for an unsatisfied spirit.[44]

He was an intellectual but an artist too—unstable on both accounts.[45] His own temperament and the expectations cultivated in him by Manicheism, Neoplatonism and the desire to live a community life made him ambitious for the best: he could never, as we say, settle for the second best.[46] This made the whole process of his conversion slow, difficult—but, of course, deep and far-reaching in its results. He was combative. Here Mandouze is at pains to explain that "Augustin polémiste est inséparable d'Augustin pasteur. La polémique est pour lui l'envers de l'apostolat, ou plutôt son revers. Apôtre d'un zèle dévorant et d'une orthodoxie intransigeante, Augustin ne pouvait éviter d'entrer en conflit avec ceux qui, insensibles à une vérité pour lui aveuglante. . . . Tant pis pour les tièdes."[47] Mandouze almost admits that Augustine could go too far in his combative zeal—and few will disagree with him![48] He was the implacable defender of the rights of the Church against the Donatists and the even more implacable defender of the rights of God against the Pelagians.[49] But the animating force behind all this was the personality and interior history of Augustine. "C'est là évidemment le foyer qui alimente toute sa théologie. Or, qu'est-ce qui peut être an ce domaine plus intime que la conviction d'avoir en soi et cependant au-delà de soi la raison ultime et la cause mystérieuse de soi-même? 'Interior intimo meo, superior summo meo.'"[50] Here personality and mysticism came together. The picture is not altogether an attractive one.

But we must glance at what Mandouze has to say about Augustine, the monk. F. Bolgiani has declared that the ideal of the monastic life is the central theme of the conversion of Saint Augustine and the programme of his new life on the morrow of that conversion.[51] Mandouze endorses this view and gives a very full account of Augustine's aspirations and practice in this regard. This whole section where he analyses Augustine's purposes in his retreat at Cassiciacum is very well developed and is important.[52] When Mandouze comes to consider van der Meer's description, on the other hand, of Augustine's community life at Thagaste as *égoïste et présomptueux* he leaps to the defence not only of Augustine, but of the monastic ideal, and particularly the monastic ideal of Augustine who, for A. J. P. Festugière, for example, is responsible for adding to the *true* Christian spirituality of the first Christians, which was characterised by serving one's neighbor, another tradition in which pagan wisdom was involved.[53] Augustine progressed from the life of wisdom to that of a monk-priest, then to that of a monk-bishop and finally a bishop-monk.[54]

Augustine the mystic is, after all, the centre of Mandouze's interest. He has no doubt that Augustine's experience at Ostia with his mother, Monnica, shortly before her death was a *grâce exceptionnelle*.[55] Later in life he seemed to give only hints of his mystical experiences—but they were real. One has only to read the *Tractatus in Johannis Euangelium* (XX, 12) to be convinced of Augustine's continuing acquaintance with the spiritual dialectic of the mystical.[56] Some have said he was no mystic; others that he was a mystic more or less; others that he was a mystic.[57] Mandouze takes sides definitely in judging the experiences described in *Confessions* VII and X as mystical in the full technical sense of that term: "Si brève que soit la description et si discrète la confidence, il faut résolument voir dans ce texte (X, 40, 65) l'affirmation d'une expérience authentiquement mystique, au sens précis et restrictif que les théologiens donnent à ce mot. Le caractère infus de cette expérience spirituelle est en effet nettement souligné. . . . Le caractère passif et extraordinaire est aussi mis en relief: affectum multum inusitatum, ce qui semble vouloir dire à la fois que ce 'sentiment' est extraordinaire objectivement, inouï et inaccessible à toute âme humaine, et extraordinaire subjectivement, puisque Augustin le distingue expressément de la douceur qu'il éprouve à trouver Dieu en tout."[58] Mandouze institutes an analysis of Augustine's experiences at Milan (C VII) and Ostia (C IX) and comes to some opinions very much in favour of the authenticity and quality of Augustine's mystical experiences. The first result arising from his analysis, he claims, is that it is undeniable that there was no *différence de nature* between the mystical experiences of Milan and Ostia. "Si celle d'Ostie peut être considérée comme mystique, celle de Milan ne l'est pas moins. Plutôt que de dire . . . que la courbe qui relie l'expérience de 387 à l'Enarratio XLI admet sans erreur de méthode d'être prolongée dans l'autre sens jusqu'aux expériences de Milan, nous pouvons affirmer, preuves à l'appui, que la courbe qui va de l'expérience de 386 au sermon postérieur à 410 passe très normalement—et très surnaturellement—par la vision d'Ostie."[59]

Mandouze demands that the "visions" he has examined be judged as being of "une hauteur exceptionnelle et préfigurant bien d'autres rencontres d'Augustin avec son Dieu . . . jusqu'à des approches plus extraordinaires du face à face final." But this goes beyond the field of history. Even mysticism, as Mandouze wisely says, *échappe aux formules*. But of mysticism much more in Mandouze's next volume.[60]

Mandouze's book covers an unusually large number of facts and problems. He is not afraid to make known his own attitudes that he knows will be unpopular, and come to conclusions—such as that Augustine had no system in either philosophy or theology[61]—which may disappoint those who think in simpler terms. It would, therefore, be surprising if there were not many details on which his interpretation would be challenged.[62] But the book as a whole is fascinating and fair. If the style is occasionally dense: "cette métaphysique de l'ambiguïté intensément vécue par Augustin transcende les occasions qui commandent l'alternance de ses effets,"[63] it is mostly straightforward and flowing. Still I hope the second volume will be shorter!

23

The Conditions of Controversy

≥●

The last paragraph of this book [Ed. note: François Decret, *Aspects du Manichéisme dans l'Afrique Romaine* (Paris: Etudes Augustiniennes, 1970)] reads as follows: "Telles furent les controverses menées, contre des Manichéens, par l'évêque d'Hippone avec une admirable foi, avec une éclatante vigueur aussi, bien digne d'une Église qui, depuis Constantin, pris goût aux triomphe. Telles furent aussi les victoires d'Augustin: incertaines et décevantes. Peut-être faut-il penser que l'ancien Auditeur ne se faisait guère d'illusions sur les conversions qu'il pourrait arracher aux fidèles de Mani. Peut-être, dans ces polémiques, ne recherchait-il pas tant un but curatif et médicinal, pour guérir ceux qui étaient atteints de la "folie perverse," mais se proposait-il d'abord de protéger son troupeau par des mesures prophylactiques. Pour éteindre la 'Religion de la Lumière,' il faudra autre chose en effet que l'intelligence et le coeur d'un homme, fût-il l'évêque saint Augustin. Il faudra des tribunaux et des juges. Et des hommes qui sont certains de connaître la Vérité seront condamnés au nom d'une autre vérité." The author "admires" the faith and vigour of Augustine. He goes on to attribute to him a triumphalism characteristic of the post-Constantine church. He suggests that his victories were uncertain and deceptive; that in any case his aim was not to convert or help his adversaries, but merely to "protect" his "flock," by preventing Manichaean influence from affecting them; and (most serious of all) that Augustine employed neither intelligence nor heart—neither truth nor love—to achieve his purpose, but rather tribunals and judges. Even in defence of Truth, Augustine consciously played the power game cynically.

Quantum mutatus ab illo! Time was when one had difficulty in deciding which preponderated in Augustine, intelligence or heart, Truth or Love? *O aeterna ueritas et uera caritas et cara aeternitas! tu es deus meus, tibi suspiro die ac nocte* . . . (C VII, 10, 16). Now he becomes a cynical manipulator of power! One remembers Peter Brown's paragraph: "Without a qualm, Augustine, Alypius, and their agents turned the laymen at the court against the Italian bishops. Count Valerius, a court general, blocked the

305

Pelagians' appeal to have their case heard in Ravenna, and helped to obtain a law to coerce any bishop suspected of Pelagian leanings. This man, *plus catholique que le pape*, a reader of the works of Augustine, proud to have bishops among his clients, his whole house a deadly enemy of heretics, was related to a great landowner in Hippo. Was he also an African? And if so, had Augustine and his friends put pressure on their fellow-countrymen at the court? In any case, such diplomacy was known to be costly. On one mission, Alypius had carried with him the promise of eighty Numidian stallions, fattened on the estates of the church, as *douceurs* for the cavalry officers, whose views on grace had proved decisive. Once again, the African bishops had the pleasure of knowing that *"the heart of the King is in the hand of God"* (*Augustine of Hippo*, p. 362). Augustine bribed his way to victory over the Pelagians. It is admitted by all that he coerced the Donatists—the ending of the schism justifying the means he employed for victory. Now, to complete the circle of the controversies that absorbed the whole of his life as priest and bishop, he also beat the Manichaeans, not with the weapons of truth and love, but with tribunals and deceit.

Deceit! For the further charge here is that the final submission of Felix the Manichaean, for example, was not only insincere, but known to Augustine to be insincere, who conspired in this charade involving God's truth and man's salvation.

This book limits its interest in Manichaeism not only to Augustine's dealings with it, but even only to his three controversies with Fortunatus, Faustus, and Felix. It is, therefore, concerned mainly not with overall truth or falsity, but rather with the techniques and articulations of these three local controversies. It is well to remember this—for though a scholar's obligation is to truth, and not Augustine, much of Augustine, much of the best of Augustine, escapes observation and judgment in so restricted and necessarily pragmatic a field. Achilles had his heel. No great man is without flaw—at least some petty weakness. Sometimes a man's greatness is evident, but carrying with it a good deal that is not so admirable. It does no service to truth or Augustine to make believe that he had not, at all times, faults. This is to some extent Augustine's own admission in the *Confessions*. This is why he had the penitential Psalms as a background to his death. "Let him who is without sin among you be the first to cast a stone on her" (John 8.7). But Augustine's greatness and passionate involvement with truth and love cannot be disputed. We must add only that he was frequently too passionate, frequently too involved, frequently too determined that (his) truth should prevail.

While it is not to be expected that what has just been written puts M. Decret's book in perspective, it does, I hope, clearly enter a serious and important and necessary *caveat*. Let us now join M. Decret without embarrassment on his own ground.

One of the things that strikes one more and more as one reads Augustine is the evidential importance he attaches to the apparent fact that the whole world was wishing to become Christian. I have myself drawn attention to this in relation to his impatience with Porphyry and other Neoplatonists for not becoming Christian, when everyone else did. Why should they be so singular? Were they not also impressed that a religion started by a few ignorant fishermen in a distant and backward part of the empire should in so short a time come to dominate the world? This *incredible* fact Augustine advanced in the *City of God* as a miracle to compel belief. How account for Porphyry's obduracy except by his pride and subjection to demons? Augustine was fully aware of the fact that many of these Christians were insincerely converted: they simply conformed to the fashion or hoped to profit from, in effect, an established, if not political, church. But his passion was not so pure as not to tolerate such abuses. He remembered the tares and the wheat of the parable. He was like some generals in war—he drove as wide an arc as he could with mobile troops while the campaign was fluid. Later would come consolidation. But in the meantime he allowed himself to be swept along into some insincerities.

It may seem a little shocking to speak in such terms of the controversies of Augustine. Without, however, going into the dense series of the state decrees against paganism in the last decade of the fourth century, or dwelling upon the extent to which Augustine and the Catholics used a more than willing civil power to eradicate Donatism in Africa, let us stir ourselves to consider, with a realistic grasp of its implications, the state's onslaught on Manichaeism towards the end of the fourth century and beginning of the fifth. One may recall that Augustine's own departure from Africa has been interpreted as flight from persecution as a Manichaean.

M. Decret gives sufficient information on this onslaught (p. 331, n. 4). In 372 Valentinian, who was tolerant of other sects, imposed heavy fines and confiscations on the Manichaeans. Theodosius, however, was much more severe. In 381 he deprived them of civil rights, even that of giving evidence. In 382 he punished them with death—the only heretics ever so treated by Christian Emperors. Valentinian II in 389 exiled them and confiscated their goods. More sinister, however, was it that the Manichaeans were considered to be the most detestable of heretics—their very name an abomination. A consequence of this was that they got an exceedingly unfavourable "press"—everyone felt he could say the worst things about them with impunity. This must have led to much exaggeration—and by Augustine too—about their already, in some ways at least, bizarre beliefs. M. Decret remarks that he may have more to say on the edicts of repression of the Manichaeans in the *Theodosian Code* later. One looks forward to this with interest.

There is therefore an important part of the *mis-en-scène* of the controversies considered here. It does not suggest that the arguments between Augustine and his three adversaries could be conducted in a psychological atmosphere of total equality, and concern only rational and theological considerations. In fact, things were actually much worse! In the case of Felix, for example, the Scriptures of Mani, which he might use in his own defence on December 7th, 404, had been confiscated and were not available to him in the debate over which his adversary, Augustine, actually presided in *cathedra*. "Non tantum ego possum contra tuam uirtutem; quia mira uirtus est gradus episcopalis" (C Fel. 1, 12: Decret, p. 83, n. 6). "Your being bishop makes quite a difference!" Augustine protested that his episcopal rank counted for nothing in the situation. But who could believe that? Worse, how could Augustine intelligently or honestly make such a claim? M. Decret not surprisingly finds Augustine's cross-examination of an unwilling controversialist *fort choquante* (p. 85). Elsewhere he speaks of Augustine as a *Procureur Général*. If the dice were then loaded against Felix, they are loaded against Augustine now. It is only fair to add, however, that Augustine was under considerable pressure from lay people to engage in these affairs: this was so, for example, in the case of Fortunatus: a controversy conducted with admirable courtesy.

M. Decret interprets the outcome of the confrontation with Felix in a manner which attributes to Augustine the most cynical of all possible attitudes. Felix has seen that he cannot win in an enforced debate where his adversary presides, the audience is mostly hostile, and the documents to which he might appeal have been confiscated. He asks: "dic iam, quid uis faciam?" This is the point of the whole charade. What does *Augustine want* done? He invites Felix to anathemize Mani—but adds, "magnanimously," that no one will compel him to do so. Of course Augustine had just threatened from his *cathedra*, surrounded by his faithful, to anathemize Felix—with grave possible consequences. Felix, astutely, calls God to witness if he anathemizes Mani *willingly*: "Deus uidet, si ex animo facio; non enim homo potest uidere." If, as he proclaims, men cannot see whether he does it willingly or unwillingly, what he says before men is otiose. Felix clearly indicates that what follows—his anathema of Mani—is a forced outward show. Augustine accepts it as such: for him it had the desired effect of giving him the victory before his people. It might have been enough for the congregation. One can hardly believe that it was enough for the real Augustine.

It is possible that M. Decret has tried too hard to be fair to the Manichaeans, and has ended by being, somewhat at least, unsympathetic to Augustine. It is, of course, not his bounden duty in a monograph such as this to take full account of the wider, and perhaps more telling in the long run, considerations to which I have earlier referred. It is enough if he presents with due evidence and analysis an important preoccupation of Augustine's life. If this took place in circumstances that prejudged the issue in favour of an already impassioned Augustine, we must have sympathy for such as Felix and not be without understanding for Augustine.

Apart from the wider and necessarily interesting, important, and controversial issue on which I have thought useful to concentrate, other matters are competently treated by M. Decret. He very properly draws attention to the absence of reference to the Manichaean scriptures in the three controversies in question, although scriptural questions are central to all three. Only in the *Contra Felicem* is there precise reference to the works of Mani. He also brings out well the point that Mani considered himself not only a Christian, but that his unique role was as paraclete to sift from the New Testament what was worthy of adult belief—to point to the authentic doctrine of Christ now overlaid with Catholic tradition and interpretation. M. Decret also helps to put into context the more fantastic aspects of the Manichaean system—both in theory and in practice. It stands to reason that if, for example, Augustine himself could give allegiance to it even with decreasing involvement over nine years, it cannot have been as bizarre as Augustine on occasion with controversial rhetoric represents it. If there were elements in it more gross than were in Catholicism, there were other elements which, speaking rationally, were more fine: they shared the Platonist intolerance of a real Incarnation. But there was a profound pessimism in it, from which Augustine himself, perhaps, never escaped. We know that the Donatist Petilian said so (Decret, p. 46, n. 5). The Manichaeans saw sin in sexual pleasure itself (CF XXIV, 1, p. 719, 15): so did, to some extent, Augustine—though his belief here may have been affected by other factors and by the desirability for him in the Pelagian controversy to have sin transmitted along with the good of birth.

When one feels inclined to agree with Augustine that he went too far in controversy—*atrociter disputaui*, as he said of his sombre encounter with the Pelagians—one has to bear in mind the logic of the positions he defeated. Which is more considerate of man: to insist that he can face his destiny unaided, succeed or fail and take the full consequences—or assure him that he has a Father who helps him to carry out what he wills? Which is more considerate of man: to say that there is a principle of evil which sins in him, so that he has no control over his deeds—or that he is free to sin or not to sin according as he freely wills? If Pelagius flatters man, Mani degrades him. Augustine refuses to do either. The particular controversies are dead. But the problems and possible attitudes remain.

Afterword

If the essays assembled here had a general subtitle, it would be something like *Texts and Contexts in Augustine*. The author's particular strengths, exhibited in this volume and throughout all of his work, are a close reading of texts and an insistence on seeing those texts in the framework of Augustine's life, his concerns of the moment, or his developing thoughts on a particular issue. This approach is a daunting task in dealing with a prolific author like the bishop of Hippo, and it is the measure of O'Meara's contributions to Augustinian studies that he has consistently met the challenge for more than forty years.

The author's penchant for careful analysis is evident in the opening essays, where he deals with the historicity of Augustine's *Dialogues of Cassiciacum* and with the supposed dependence of Patrick's *Confessio* on the *Confessiones*. These studies argue against any literal reading of the *Dialogues*, and they show that the impact of the bishop of Hippo on the bishop of Ireland is negligible or non-demonstrable. Throughout this first section of the book, which focuses on the theme of conversion and confession, O'Meara provides a salutary warning that we should read Augustine in terms of the literary conventions of his time and that we should be wary of finding literary dependence when the education, interests, and circumstances of an author are strikingly different from those of his "source."

The importance of context in all forms of literary inquiry and the perils of drawing a sharp line between "truth" and "fiction" are demonstrated in masterful fashion in the article entitled "Augustine's *Confessions*: Elements of Fiction." This piece is in many ways a summary of O'Meara's scholarly life, and it is a delight to see themes he dealt with earlier in his career (*e.g.*, Augustine's preoccupation with salvation, conversion, sin, Neoplatonism [especially Porphyry], rhetorical and poetic expression, and the free application of Scripture) coming together in a rich and confident assessment of the bishop's work. It is not surprising that this study is the most recent piece in the volume.

The section "Augustine on Love and Sexuality" is both narrower and broader than readers might at first suppose. Narrower because it really deals with Virgil's impact on the bishop's writings; broader because the seer of Mantua influenced Augustine's personal development more than any other single pagan author. The role that Virgil played in Augustine's thinking is reasonably well documented in scholarly research, but O'Meara has done a particularly good job of capturing the spirit in which the bishop read his classical forebear and the attitudes he gleaned from him. The sympathy that binds poet and bishop together is best illustrated in the article "Virgil and Augustine: The *Aeneid* in the *Confessions.*" Similarities of viewpoint on providence, the spirit of religion, the nature of the sublime, and, perhaps most importantly, the sense of mission come through very clearly. Whatever be the philosophical impact of Cicero, Plotinus, or Porphyry on Augustine, it is hard to escape the fact that Virgil was the bishop's guide in matters that touched him most closely.

One area where the impact of Virgil can be felt is in Augustine's harsh views on sexuality. O'Meara deals with this issue convincingly by showing how those views developed early in Augustine's life in a Roman context that was equally harsh and equally inclined to subordinate love to duty. The bishop's reservations about the dangers of the flesh, despite his own "intense and refined sensuality," are in many ways a product of traditional Roman attitudes, and the texts O'Meara brings to bear demonstrate that Augustine's approach to sex was already well established before his debates with the Manichees and the Pelagians.

The conflict between the spiritual and the corporal appears most saliently in the section "Augustine, Plotinus, and Porphyry." Here O'Meara has the satisfaction of seeing a position that he espoused early in his academic career gradually become accepted by a great many scholars. It now seems clear that, even prior to his conversion, Augustine was familiar with the work of Porphyry and that the latter played a critical role in his conversion. Porphyry's *Philosophy from Oracles,* which contains or is identifiable with the *De regressu animi* mentioned in the *City of God,* helps us to understand how the bishop gradually came to see radical differences between Neoplatonism on the one hand and the Christian doctrine of the resurrection on the other. In fact, the role of the resurrected body in the overall scheme of man's creation and salvation becomes one of the touchstones in Augustine's theology. Ironically, in this context it is the bishop who defends the value of the temporal world against the Neoplatonists' disdain for material creation, and Augustine finds himself in the position of both preaching against the demands of the body and of defending its value against detractors. How often we are reminded that Augustine's thought is a mid-ground between opposing ideas.

The highly technical information found in the section on Eriugena does not easily lend itself to generalizations or to conclusions about the character of Augustine, but here, once again, O'Meara's scholarship teaches us something about the larger dimensions of his subject. What comes through in this section of the book is Augustine's own hesitancy about certain theological issues, such as the relation of body and soul in the afterlife. The bishop's admission of ignorance about such matters runs counter to the image of self-assured intransigence which he projects in his later years and reveals a man who is both more humane and more sensitive than is commonly assumed.

The concluding section, which is taken up with critiques of other scholars' work, gives us a view of O'Meara's own guiding principles. Perhaps the most valuable of these is his tendency to avoid hasty judgments about Augustine's motives and to evaluate the man primarily on his strengths rather than on his weaknesses. O'Meara's approach consistently recognizes the complexities of an individual like the bishop of Hippo and the ambiguities inherent in all human actions. Augustine understood the latter very well, and he has been admirably served in having a critic like John J. O'Meara.

LOUIS J. SWIFT

Notes

Introduction

1. *"Le Confessioni" di Agostino d'Hippone*, J. Rodriguez (Palermo, 1985), 61ff.
2. "Porphyrian Studies since 1913," *Aufstieg und Niedergang der römischen Welt* II, 36,2 (Berlin, 1987) 732ff.
3. Cf. "Un oracle antichrétien chez Arnobe," *Mémorial Dom Jean Gribomont* (Rome: Institutum Patristicum Augustinianum, 1988) 144ff., esp. 120–29; "Quosdam Platonicorum Libros," VigChr 43,3 (1989) 248–81, esp. 254–55.
4. Chap. 13 in this volume examines the role of Porphyry in the *Dialogues of Cassiciacum*—a topic taken up again more recently by Ilsetraut Hadot.

Chapter 1. Historicity of the Early Dialogues

1. This was stressed by M. G. de Plinval in his communication, "La technique du dialogue chez saint Augustine et saint Jérôme," read at the 1er Congrès de la Fédération Internationale des Associations d'Etudes Classiques, Paris, 1950.
2. D. Ohlmann, *De Sancti Augustini Diologis in Cassiciaco scriptis* (Argentorati, 1897). J. H. Van Haeringen, *De Augustini ante Baptismum rusticantis operibus* (1917). R. Hirzel, *Der Dialog* (Leipzig, 1895), Vol. II, pp. 376–80.
3. E.g. A. Gudeman, *Sind die Dialoge Augustins historisch?* (Silvae Monacenses, Munich, 1926, pp. 16–27), and R. Philippson under the same title (Rheinisches Museum für Philologie, 1931, pp. 144–50).
4. Op. cit., p. 79: "in libris in Cassiciaco compositis novo quodam atque proprio dialogorum genere Augustinus usus est. Sermones enim cum discipulis et amicis habitos a notariis excipi iussit; deinde quae in tabulis relata erant, in libros transcribenda librariis dictitavit; permulta tamen omisit, discipulorum verba servatis sententiis passim mutavit atque elimavit, alia contraxit atque summatim breviterque descripsit . . . Itaque de minutulis rebus non est cur pugnemus; licet quae de sorice Licentium e somno excitante referuntur, Augustinus fortasse finxerit (i.e., DOR I, 6, 9)—id quod suspicatus est magister humanissimus Kaibelius—propter versum illum Terenti 9 peropportune laudatum, quem proverbii loco fuisse Donatus testatur. . . ." Cf. op. cit., pp. 8, 9.
5. Cf. CA I, 4, however, where we are promised the actual words of two of the interlocutors. Cf. also DOR I, 5.
6. This weakens Ohlmann's case right from the start; cf. n. 4 supra: "permulta tamen *omisit* . . . discipulorum verba . . . *passim mutavit* . . . *alia contraxit* . . . de *minutulis* rebus non est cur pugnemus (this is an admission that the *Dialogues* are not in the full sense historical) licet quae de sorice . . . fortasse finxerit. . . ." If Augustine invented the mouse-incident, then there does not seem to be any reason why he should not also have invented the improbable

vigil of Licentius which is connected with the mouse; the improbable all-night discussion of philosophical questions; the improbable knowledge of difficult questions shown by Licentius—so profound that his companions thought him to be in some way inspired—who up till then had shown little interest in these matters. To allow Augustine discretion in the invention even of small things detracts definitely from the historicity of the *Dialogues*. It is a forcible reminder that the liberties of the *genre* are being used. P. de Labriolle, in the Introduction to his edition of the *Confessions* (Budé, 1925) and C. Boyer, *La Formation de saint Augustin*, pp. 16–18 rightly insist on this point. Those scholars who prefer the testimony of the *Dialogues* to that of the *Confessions*, where they understand them as conflicting on a point of fact, depend largely (cf. Alfaric, *L'évolution intellectuelle de saint Augustin* [Paris, 1918], p. 400 n. 1), on Ohlmann and Van Haeringen for their assumptions that the *Dialogues* are historically more reliable.

7. CA I, 4: "adhibito itaque notario, ne aurae laborem nostrum discerperent, nihil perire permisi, sane in hoc libro res et sententias illorum (Licentii et Trygetii), mea uero et Alypii etiam uerba lecturus es"; DOR I, 5: "ibi disserebamus inter nos, quaecumque uidebantur utilia adhibito sane stilo, quo cuncta exciperentur, quod uidebam conducere ualetudini meae, cum enim nonnulla loquendi cura detinerer, nulla inter disputandum inrepebat immoderata contentio; simul etiam, ut, si quid nostrum litteris mandare placuisset, nec aliter dicendi necessitas nec labor recordationis esset." Ohlmann also instances CA III, 15; DOR I, 29; DBV 15; DOR I, 30, 31. This list is incomplete, as also is Van Haeringen's. The complete list is: CA I, 4, 15; II, 17, 22, 29; III, 15, 44. DBV 15, 18; DOR I, 5, 14, 20, 26, 27, 29, 30, 31, 33; II, 17, 21. All these assurances are worthless, as will presently be shown.

8. We agree. Augustine rather confusedly gives here a twofold division of his writings at the time: (1) "libri disputati cum praesentibus et cum ipso me solo" (2) "epistulae." The first point to note is that he claims the *Dialogues* as *his* ("egerim") *compositions* ("in litteris"). This he could hardly do if he had made no serious changes in the contributions of the other interlocutors—on the assumption that the debates did take place. Secondly the phrase "libri disputati cum praesentibus," though it could possibly imply that he had discussed the various topics of the books with those present in Cassiciacum (as opposed to "cum absente Nebridio"), is more likely to be merely a description of the books as literary Dialogues with parts attributed to those present in Cassiciacum. In this connection it is useful to quote Augustine's own remarks about the *De libero arbitrio*, which Ohlmann (rightly, we are sure) regards as fictional (op. cit. pp. 16, 17). Augustine is writing to Evodius, who was an interlocutor in the book in question: "quamquam et illa (*sc.* opera mea) relegas, quae tibi (*sc.* Evodio) iam diu nota sunt, uel nisi fallor, fuerunt, quia ea fortasse oblitus es, *quae te conferente mecum ac sermocinante conscripsi.* . . ." (E CLXII, 2). It is unthinkable from the nature of the book itself, and the words here used, that Augustine meant that the *De libero arbitrio* was the written report on a debate actually held, and in which Evodius took part. Therefore we are entitled to regard the phrase: "quae te conferente mecum ac sermocinante conscripsi" as a way of saying that he had composed a Dialogue in which Evodius was an interlocutor. The phrase used of the earlier *Dialogues*: "libri disputati cum praesentibus et cum ipso me solo coram te" is, in itself, if anything, more likely to be just such a description of Dialogues and their

interlocutors. In any case the text does not warrant the assertion that the *Dialogues* are a faithful report of debates actually held.

9. He quotes Poujoulat, *Histoire de saint Augustin*, Paris–Lyon, 3 Vols. 1852; Bindemann, *Der hl. Augustinus*, I Bd. Berlin, 1844; II Bd. Leipzig, 1855; III Bd. Greifswald, 1869, in support of his view. Here the methods of composition of the *De beata vita* and the *Contra Academicos* are regarded by Augustine as being similar: "inter illos ut *scriberem* contigit"; Augustine stakes a personal claim on the book. It is significant that "ortus est" and "conpletus" refer, at least grammatically, to *"liber* de beata vita," and not to any such term as "disputatio" expressed or understood. The phrases "ex occasione . . . diei natalis mei" and "tridui disputatione" are connected to the "contigit," which is factual, by the "quippe." We have some reason, then, for concluding that the two details given are historical. The phrases are qualified by the remark: *"sicut satis* ipse indicat." This too guarantees the general historicity of the two details of the occasion of the dialogue and its duration. But the "sicut" cannot be made to extend beyond these two points—even to other such details—with any safety. There is a warning in the word "satis" which implies that the book is historical *to the extent at least* of the two details indicated. This is a definite guarantee, and, though limited, gives us grounds for supposing that other details given can be generally historical too. Nevertheless no other detail can on this account be assumed to be historical, especially if it gives serious grounds for suspicion or contradicts direct evidence.

10. Op. cit., I, p. 294.

11. Why not? There is every evidence that Augustine was dissatisfied with the *Dialogues*. He changed the interlocutors in the course of the *Contra Academicos*. Two-thirds of the last book of that work is a monologue by Augustine himself. Something similar happens in the second book of the *De ordine*. His subsequent *Dialogues* dispense with all verisimilitude, and are little more than question and answer. In the *Retractationes* he notes that he met with more success as he continued to write: "inuenit enim fortasse quomodo scribendo profecerim, quisquis opuscula mea ordine, quo scripta sunt, legerit" (*Prologus Retractationum*). P. Courcelle, *Recherches sur les Confessions de saint Augustin* (Paris, 1950), pp. 20, 24, stresses the point that Augustine did *not* compose his books very well.

12. Cf. Ohlmann, op. cit., pp. 13ff.: "deinde Licentio quoque et Trygetio experrectis sermone collato . . . quam ad sententiam defendendam promptum se atque paratum esse (Licentius praebet), sed priusquam de hac Licenti sententia disputetur, multa fiunt verba de studio artis poeticae, cui enixe operam Licentium navasse Augustinus tradit. arma 10 capiuntur, sed ad ludendum potius quam ad pugnandum neque 11–13, ubi ad exemplum supra propositum redeunt, philisophos disputantes sed rixantes inter se iuvenes invenies. verba fiunt 15–19. Sed 20–24 rursus disputatione intermissa, quomodo surrexerint et quae sermocinati inter se sint (quae res ad quaestionem minime pertinent), fusius narratur et 25–26, quem de pugna illa gallorum nimis acri habuerunt, sermo refertur. Tum demum . . . in viam reducere . . . quae statim ad prorsus alienam quaestionem evagatur . . . 29–30 iuvenes rixandi (cupidi) . . . 31–32 cum matre blandissime colloquitur (Augustinus); de ordine nihil invenias disputatum. Quae ut paucis verbis comprehendam, nonne in libro De ordine I Augustinus narrasse tantum fusius videtur, quae in diurnos commentarios plerumque referre solemus, rem autem . . . breviter tantum perstringit 11, 12, 14, 15, 18, 19?"

13. Cf. op. cit., pp. 14, 79. Ohlmann cannot have it both ways. If the *Dialogues* are a failure from an artistic point of view when judged by the traditional dialogue model, they cannot, without adequate reason being given, be regarded as an artistic achievement when judged by a type of dialogue form differing only slightly from the traditional. Moreover, to demonstrate that the *Dialogues* are not successful according to the traditional model, is not to prove that they are historical either in general or in detail.

14. Op. cit., p. 16. He does, as a matter of fact. R I, 9: "cum adhuc Romae demoraremur, uoluimus disputando *quaerere*, unde sit malum . . .' this refers to the *De libero arbitrio*.

15. Op. cit., pp. 16, 17.

16. Op. cit., p. 17. "Tantum igitur abest ut Hirzelium secutus dialogos in Cassiciaco scriptos fictos esse censeam, quia dialogi, '*de quantitate animae*' et '*de libero arbitrio*' ficti sunt, ut ex eo, quod dialogi hi ficti sunt, illos fictos non esse *pro certo concludam*." To prove that the *Soliloquia, De quantitate animae*, and *De libero arbitrio* are fictitious does not prove that the *Contra Academicos, De beata vita*, and *De ordine* are historical. This is an open fallacy. Ohlmann is undoubtedly right in believing that the latter *Dialogues* are fictitious (Van Haeringen denies this. Cf. op. cit., p. 18, but his reasons are not convincing).

17. Not necessarily. A purely fictional work can be internally and externally consistent. It will be valuable, however, to go through the discussion in order that it may appear how inconsistent the *Dialogues* are.

18. Op. cit., p. 27.

19. There were two sessions on this day as on the 22nd and 23rd.

20. Ohlmann is aware that this order is not borne out by the following texts: (1) "inter illos quidem, qui de Academicis scripti sunt, *duos* etiam libros de ordine scripsi"—(R I, 3). Ohlmann (op. cit., p. 19) supposes that Augustine's explicit *"duos"* can refer only to DOR I; (2) "post pristinum sermonem (*sc.* CA I) . . . septem fere diebus a disputando fuimus otiosi"—(CA II, 10). Ohlmann (op. cit., p. 20) interprets as follows: "Ergo inter septem illos dies disputationes certe habuerunt, otiosi vero fuerunt a disputationibus *tantum de Academicis institutis.*" Both assumptions of Ohlmann are gratuitous.

21. Cf. DOR I, 22.

22. Cf. DOR I, 29. I do not see much force in this argument.

23. Cf. CA III, 44. Cf. Ohlmann, op. cit., p. 15. But was it not Augustine himself who published the *Dialogues*?

24. *De Augustini ante Baptismum rusticantis Operibus* (Groningae, 1917). P. Knöll, CSEL LXIII (1922), fails to notice Van Haeringen's work. Boyer, *La formation de saint Augustin*, p. 9 n. 4, rejects Van Haeringen's thesis.

25. His list of references to the text of the *Dialogues* to support his statements is less incomplete than that of Ohlmann. On this point, e.g., he instances CA I, 4, 15; II, 29; III, 15, 44; DBV 15, 18; DOR I, 5, 27, 30, 31, 33; II, 21. Cf. n. 7 supra.

26. He refers to CA I, 4; DBV 15; DOR I, 5 (op. cit., p. 15).

27. He refers to CA I, 4, 25; II, 10, 22; I, 5, 14, 26, 30, 33; II, 1 (op. cit., p. 16).

28. He refers to CA I, 4; DBV 15; DOR I, 5 (op. cit., p. 21).

29. He refers to CA I, 4; DOR I, 5, 26 (op. cit., pp. 22–24).

30. Van Haeringen appeals to the work of Th. Dokkum: "de constructionis analyticae vice accusativi cum infinitivo fungentis usu apud Augustinum"

(Sneek, 1900) as support for the view that the *words* attributed to Licentius and the others are Augustine's. The proportion of the analytic to the accusative and infinitive construction for the *Contra Academicos* is 1:80; for *De beata vita* 1:25; for the *Confessions* 1:5; for *De Civitate Dei* 1:18; for the *Epistulae* 1:9; for the earlier works (generally) 1:55; for the later 1:11 (Van Haeringen, pp. 24ff., Dokkum, pp. 67ff.). Van Haeringen supposes that Licentius and the others would have used the analytic in preference to the accusative and infinitive (this is gratuitous), and he explains the use of the latter construction on four occasions in the *Contra Academicos* and *De beata vita* by the companions of Augustine by understanding that Augustine changed the expressions used while not interfering with the sense. This analysis is, even if reliable, unnecessary. Augustine had already declared in CA I, 4 that he did this. (It is interesting to note that judged by Dokkum's analysis, the *Confessions* is the most spontaneous of the works mentioned.)

31. *Mémoires pour servir à l'histoire ecclésiastique* XIII. His order is the same as that of Ohlmann, though it starts a day earlier. P. Knöll (CSEL LXIII, p. 2 n. 1) tends to agree with Ohlmann.

32. Tillemont had already turned down this suggestion (loc. cit., art. XXXVI–XLIII, note v), a fact of which Van Haeringen was fully aware (op. cit., pp. 36–37).

33. Cf. n. 20.

34. Cf. n. 20.

35. Cf. Tillemont (loc. cit., art. XXXVI–XLIII, note v): "Il est certain, que la manière, dont il s'exprime en cet endroit porte à croire qu'ils n'en avaient point fait du-tout." Nevertheless, Tillemont elected for the order adopted later by Ohlmann.

36. Van Haeringen was aware that he himself was faced with difficulties similar to those which beset Ohlmann. Thus we read in CA III, 43: "cum tricensimum et tertium aetatis annum agam," which would seem to demand that CA III occurred after DBV (cf. 6, 9) which took place upon Augustine's birthday. Van Haeringen points out that the text is doubtful in its reading and for other reasons; that XXXIII could easily have been written for XXXII; or that when *writing* up the *Contra Academicos* (admittedly after the *occurrence* of DBV) Augustine inadvertently altered the number (op. cit., p. 44). Again Van Haeringen is forced into the assumption that Alypius twice departed from Cassiciacum and twice returned during the period of the three *Dialogues* (op. cit., p. 37)—an hypothesis which is not convenient, since it leads Van Haeringen to the conclusion that Alypius even at the end of CA III was unconvinced and still held a brief for the Academics. This is contradicted by CA III, 45 itself, by CA II, 27, and by the whole tenor of the debate. In any case the sequence of occurrence CA—DOR I—DBV, adopted by Van Haeringen, is impossible, since Licentius forgoes allegiance to the Academy in CA II, 27 and DOR I, 10, while in DBV 14 he is still an Academic.

37. He instances among other points:

a. The absence of Monnica from the disputations of the *Contra Academicos*; her introduction in DOR I; and subsequent reappearance in DBV and DOR II. This absence of Monnica from some of the debates, if it must be explained, can easily be understood without Van Haeringen's hypothesis: she was to be present "cum abundaret otio" (II, 13).

b. Licentius' changing attitude towards philosophy. He took a great interest in it in *Contra Academicos* (cf. I, 4). Then followed an interval of seven days when he renewed his interest in poetry and lost his interest in philosophy (cf. CA II, 10)—an attitude persisting through CA II and III. He changed back again to philosophy in the course of the night discussion in DOR I (cf. 16). The order suggested by Van Haeringen gives a certain consistency to Licentius' attitude which is impossible in any other sequence.

c. The opening sentences of DOR II suppose that the disputation there outlined took place *immediately* after a return of Alypius. In Ohlmann's sequence both CA II and III (i.e., three days debating) intervene between this return and the beginning of DOR II. Van Haeringen's sequence fits the text exactly: "interpositis deinde pauculis diebus [*sc.* after DOR I] uenit Alypius [he was absent for DBV, cf. 14] et exorto sole, clarissimo inuitauit caeli nitor . . . in pratum descendere." It is obvious that the arguments of Ohlmann and Van Haeringen on all this question of date, even if they were relevant, cancel one another out.

38. Cf. R I, 1. "*Contra Academicos . . . scripsi,* ut argumenta [Academicorum] . . . ab animo meo . . . amouerem . . . in eisdem tribus libris *meis . . .*"; R I, 2. "Librum de beata uita non post libros de Academicis, sed inter illos ut *scriberem* contigit . . ."; R I, 3. "duos etiam libros de ordine *scripsi*"; DT XV, 21: "Aduersus Academicos . . . sunt libri tres *nostri* . . . quos qui potuerit et voluerit legere, lectosque intellexerit, nihil eum profecto quae ab eis contra perceptionem veritatis argumenta multa inventa sunt, permovebunt"; *Enchiridion* 7: "tria *confeci* volumina in initio conversionis meae" [*Contra Academicos*].

39. Cf. DT XV, 21, supra n. 38; *Enchiridion* 7 (supra); E I.

40. Cf. DOR I, 14: Licentius says: "si haec, quae a nobis dicta sunt, litteris, *ut instituisti,* mandata *peruagentur* paulo latius ad hominum famam . . ."; DOR I, 31 (infra n. 41). Moreover in DOR I, 30; II, 17; SO II, 28, it is said that these works will be shown to friends. In those days that meant facing the risk of publication, as Augustine himself, and Galen for example somewhat earlier, experienced.

41. Cf. DOR I, 31: "cuius [matris] et ingressum et rogationem cum scribi nostro more iussissem: Quid agitis? Inquit; *numquidnam in illis quos legitis libris etiam feminas umquam audiui in hoc genus disputationes* [disputationis: AHMP m 2 T edd.] *inductas?*—cui ego [Augustinus] —*mei* autem libri si quorum forte manus tetigerint lectoque meo nomine non dixerint: 'iste quis est?' codicemque proiecerint, sed uel curiosi uel nimium studiosi contemta uilitate liminis intrare perrexerint, me tecum philosophantem non moleste ferent nec quemquam istorum, quorum *meis* litteris sermo misceatur, fortasse contemnent. sunt enim non solum liberi, quod cuius disciplinae liberali, nedum philosophiae satis est, sed summo apud suos loco nati. *doctissimorum autem hominum litterae etiam sutores philosophatos et multo uiliora fortunarum genera continent. . . .*"

42. Cf. C I, 14, 19, 26, 27; II, 4–6, 8; III, 6, 7; IV, 1, 2; VI, 18; VII, 17; DUC I. It is not sufficiently realized how great a part ambition played in the life of Augustine, an ambition strongly inculcated by his parents. This is usually overlooked because of the dominance of the intellectual and moral crisis of his life as presented in the *Confessiones*. It is important, however, to remember that the presence of such ambition is of great psychological significance for the *whole* of his life.

43. C IV, 21, 23; cf. IV, 20, 27.

44. C V, 23. Cf. *Contra litteras Petiliani* III, 30; Possidius, *Vita* c. 1.
45. *Contra litteras Petiliani* III, 25, 30.
46. C VI, 9; Seeck, *Symmachus* cxl, says that there was but one panegyric in all. Gibb and Montgomery, ed. *Conf.* p. 147, n. 16, give reasons for believing that there were two, one for the consulship of Bauto, and this, a separate one. P. Courcelle, op. cit., pp. 79ff. also holds that there were two.
47. Cf. the careers of Ausonius (and all his family), Neoterius, Palladius, Pacatus, Priscianus, Marinianus, Theodorus, Lampadius, Hierius, and especially Flavius Mallius Theodorus. Most of these rose to very high office about the time of Augustine's sojourn in Italy, and through the influence of Symmachus. Cf. Seeck, *Symmachus* sub indice Nominum.
48. C VI, 9, 17, 18.
49. C VI, 19.
50. DOR I, 31.
51. R I, 6. "Per idem tempus quo Mediolani fui baptismum percepturus, etiam Disciplinarum libros conatus sum scribere, interrogans eos, qui mecum erant . . . per corporalia cupiens ad incorporalia quibusdam quasi passibus certis uel peruenire uel ducere. Sed earum solum de Grammatica librum absoluere potui . . . et de Musica sex uolumina. . . .'
52. Cf. W. Bousset, *Jüdisch-christlicher Schulbetrieb in Alexandria und Rom* (Göttingen, 1915), pp. 4–5; Festugière, "Le 'logos' hermétique d'enseignement," REG LV (1942), p. 96.
53. Models are not wanting for the *Soliloquia* and the later "catechism" dialogues (such as *De magistro*). Hirzel (op. cit., I, p. 433) instances the *Bimarcus* of Varro (whose works were well conned by Augustine) as a precedent for the *Soliloquia*. As models for the "catechism" dialogues we have extant the *De partitione oratoria* of Cicero, in which Cicero catechises his son (as Augustine does Adeodatus in *De magistro*); Porphyry's *in Aristotelis Categorias commentarium* (ed. A. Busse: *Comm. in Arist. Graeca* IV pars i, p. 55, Berlin, 1887) which is κατὰ πεῦσιν καὶ ἀπόκρισιν: "Il donne à manier à ses élèves . . . un cahier de répétitions par demandes et par réponses, qui est bien caractéristique" (Bidez, *Vie de Porphyre*, p. 62); and a dialogue with a pupil by way of commentary on Aristotle's *Categories* written by Dexippus (ed. A. Busse: *Comm. in Arist. Graeca* IV pars ii. Berlin, 1888). These and others either were, or could have been, known to Augustine. Cf. A. D. Nock, Prolegomena to *Sallustius* (Cambridge, 1926).
54. Cf. J. Guitton, *Le Temps et l'Eternité chez Plotin et saint Augustin*, p. xi: "Ces genres [littéraires] ne sont pas d'ailleurs un habillement; déjà ils imposent à l'esprit certains tours et certains plis. Il n'est pas indifférent d'exprimer sa pensée sous la forme du soliloque, de la confession, de la leçon magistrale ou sous celle du dialogue, du sermon, de la diatribe. En choisissant un genre, on a déjà reconnu ses maîtres: on se rattache à une tradition; on éveille en soi et dans son lecteur des souvenirs; on accepte une compagnie."
55. Cf. Albinus (ii A.D.): Εἰσαγωγὴ εἰς τοὺς Πλάτωνος διαλόγους I (ed. C. F. Hermann, *Platon* VI, Leipzig (T)): ἔστι τοίνυν οὐκ ἄλλο τι [ὁ διάλογος] ἢ λόγος ἐξ ἐρωτήσεως καὶ ἀποκρίσεως συγκείμενος περί τινος τῶν πολιτικῶν καὶ φιλοσόφων πραγμάτων, μετὰ τῆς πρεπούσης ἠθοποιΐας τῶν παραλαμβανομένων προσώπων καὶ τῆς κατὰ τὴν λέξιν κατασκευῆς; ibid., III. δύο ὄντων ... ὑφηγητικοῦ καὶ ζητητικοῦ, ὁ μὲν ὑφηγητικὸς ἥρμοσται πρὸς διδασκαλίαν καὶ πρᾶξιν καὶ ἀπόδειξιν τοῦ ἀληθοῦς, ὁ δὲ ζητητικὸς πρὸς γυμνασίαν καὶ

ἀγῶνα καὶ ἔλεγκον τοῦ ψεύδους. cf. προλεγόμενα τῆς Πλάτωνος φιλοσοφίας (vi. A.D.?), (ed. C. F. Hermann, *Platon* VI, Leipzig (T), XIV for a similar definition.

56. Cf. III, 45.
57. The third book does not start abruptly; it has a short mise-en-scène.
58. Cf. Cic. *Epist. ad Atticum* IV, 16, 2. Proclus tells us that the same feature was found in the dialogues of Theophrastus and Heraclides Ponticus (Proclus: *In Parmen* I, 659, Cousin.)
59. There are some correspondences in the introductory letters to the *Dialogues of Cassiciacum* with Plato's famous *Seventh Epistle*. In both there is an autobiography by way of an *apologia pro vita sua* (cf. CA I, 3; II, 3f.; DBV 4). The intervention of Providence is noted (cf. E VII, 326E; CA prefaces passim). Life is compared to a sea voyage (351D; CA I, 1; II, 1; DBV 1f.). It is asserted that Philosophy does not reveal herself except to those who dedicate themselves to her entirely (340C, D, E; 431A; CA I, 1; II, 8; "ipsum uerum non uidebis, nisi in philosophiam totus intraueris").
60. Cf. P. Wendland: *Anaximenes von Lampsakos* (Berlin, 1905) pp. 81f.
61. Cf. Cicero's *Hortensius*.
62. Protreptics were written by Antisthenes, Aristotle, Epicurus, Cleanthes, Posidonius, Cicero, Clement of Alexandria, among others. Cf. A. J. Festugière: *la révélation d'Hermes Trismégiste* I (Paris, 1944), pp. 324ff.; A. D. Nock and A. J. Festugière, *Corpus Hermeticum*, 2 Vols. Collection Budé (Paris, 1945), XIV, 1; XVI, 1; *Asclepius* 1 for instances (which may very well have been known to Augustine, cf. Nock and Festugiére loc. cit., pp. 259, 264ff., 277, 279–80) of protreptic-prefaces closely approximating to that of the *Contra Academicos*. Cf. especially: Festugière, "Le 'logos' hermétique d'enseignement," REG LV (1942), pp. 77–78 for an analysis of such a preface: "le traité de l'alchimiste Zosime intitulé *Compte final* s'ouvre sur une sorte de prologue, qui a la forme d'une lettre adressée à une dame, Théosébie. Or on lit dans ce prologue, . . . un court morceau d'instruction spirituelle, une invite au recueillement . . . il faut rentrer en soi-même, faire taire les passions. Nous ne cessons de nous agiter, de chercher en dehors de nous ce qui, en vérité, est en nous. Ce défaut vient de la matière. Que l'âme donc se libère de la matière, se concentre au fond d'elle-même, où Dieu est présent. C'est en cela que réside la perfection . . . alors, se connaissant soi-même, on connaîtra Dieu, . . . qui communique avec Dieu puise à la source même d'ou toute vérité s'écoule." Augustine's invitation to Romanianus (CA I, 1–4; II, 1–9) follows these lines. Festugière's further remark (ibid., p. 78): "certes, rien n'est plus commun à l'époque hellénistique que la courte homélie morale adressée a un ou plusieurs auditeurs et que les manuels nomment *diatribe*" reminds us forcibly that Augustine was following very closely a strongly established literary genre.
63. CA I, 4: "cum eos ad studia hortans atque animans, ultra quam optaueram paratos et prorsus inhiantes uiderem, uolui tentare pro aetate quid possent: praesertim cum Hortensius liber Ciceronis eos ex magna parte conciliasse philosophiae uideretur." Cf. C III, 7, 8; VI, 18; VIII, 17. It is not surprising that fragments of the *Hortensius* have been recovered from the *Contra Academicos*. Nor is it surprising that there are echoes of Aristotle's προτρεπτικός, to which the *Hortensius* was closely related, in the *Contra Academicos*. Cf. Müller, *Ciceronis scripta quae manserunt omnia* IV, vol. III, and Walzer, *Aristotelis dialogorum fragmenta* (Florence, 1934).

64. Cf. V, 6.

65. Cf. Festugière, "Le "logos" hermétique d'enseignement, REG LV, pp. 90–92.

66. The *Theaetetus* is particularly interesting in this connection; for in that work Socrates plays the role adopted by Augustine in the *Contra Academicos*; Theodorus that of Alypius; Theaetetus that of Licentius; and other boys that of Trygetius. Cf. also 168E. ὁρᾷς οὖν ὅτι τάδε πάντα πλὴν σοῦ [Θεοδώρου] παιδία ἐστίν. εἰ οὖν πεισόμεθα τῷ ἀνδρί, ἐμὲ καὶ σὲ δεῖ ἐρωτῶντάς τε καὶ ἀποκρινομένους ἀλλήλοις, σπουδάσαι αὐτοῦ περὶ τὸν λόγον. ἵνα μή τοι τοῦτό γε ἔχῃ ἐγκαλεῖν, ὡς παίζοντες πρὸς μειράκια [cf. CA II, 22: "cum istis adulescentibus prolusimus, ubi . . . nobiscum philosophia quasi iocata est"] διεσκεψάμεθ᾽ αὐτοῦ τὸν λόγον.

67. Cf. CA I, 11, 16, 24, 25; II, 10, 25, 29; III, 1.

68. Cf. CA I, 15, 25; II, 30; III, 14.

69. Cf. II, 10. The necessity of sending an account of a debate to an absent person is used in dialogues as an excuse for giving a summary of a discussion or the whole discussion itself. Cf. CA I, 4, 25; Nock and Festugière, *Corpus Hermeticum* XIV, 1; Ἐπεὶ ὁ υἱός μου Τὰτ ἀπόντος σου τὴν τῶν ὅλων ἠθέλησε φύσιν μαθεῖν ... σοὶ δὲ ἐγὼ τῶν λεχθέντων τὰ κυριώτατα κεφάλαια ἐκλεξάμενος δι᾽ ὀλίγων ἠθέλησα ἐπιστεῖλαι. Festugière, "Le 'logos' hermétique d'enseignement," REG LV, p. 94.

70. The *Dialogues of Cassiciacum*, in this, above all, are convincingly "schoolroom dialogues." τόπος after τόπος is taken up, examined, and then dismissed. Cf. Festugière: "Le 'logos' hermétique d'enseignement," REG LV, pp. 79, 81–84.

71. Cf. CA II, 10–14, 17, 22, 24, 25, 29; III, 4, 14. Cf. DBV 16, DOR I, 5; II, 7.

72. Cf. CA I, 6, 16; cf. *Protagoras* 338A, *Symposium* 175E; Tacitus, *Dialogus de oratoribus* IV.

73. Cf. CA II, 10–14 and n. 71 supra.

74. CA I, 4: "adhibito itaque notario . . . nihil perire permisi." CA II, 17: "ore prorumpentia stilo excipitis." DBV 18: "uerba pueri sicut dicta erant cum conscribi mihi placuisset." DOR I, 27: "instituimus . . . uerba non perdere." DOR I, 30: "omnia scribebantur" (particularly instructive in its context). Cf. CA I, 15; II, 22, 29; III, 15, 44; DBV 15; DOR I, 5, 14, 20, 26, 29, 31, 33; II, 17, 21.

75. DOR I, 31: "cuius et ingressum et rogationem cum scribi nostro more iussissem."

76. CA I, 4: "sane in hoc libro . . . mea uero et Alypii *etiam uerba* lecturus es."

77. DOR I, 5: "si quid *nostrum* litteris mandare placuisset, nec *aliter dicendi necessitas* nec labor recordationis esset." Cf. the episode in DOR I, 29.

78. CA I, 4; "sane in hoc libro—res et sententias illorum . . . lecturus es." Cf. DOR I, 27, and indeed the function of the notary.

79. There are many precedents for this: Cicero's *Tusc. disp.* II, 9 ("eisdem fere verbis, ut actum disputatumque est"); Plato's *Euthydemus* (272D, 275B), *Phaedo* (59C, D), *Phaedrus* (cf. 228A–C, 230E, 234D, 236E, 242D, 243C, 262D, 263E), *Menexenus* (236B, C, 246C, 249), *Symposium* (173E, 174A), *Timaeus* (20Eff.).

80. Cf. Plato's *Theaetetus* 143A–C. For examples more or less contemporary

with Augustine, cf. Macrobius *Sat.* I, 6, 13 and I, 1, 5–6; Sulpicius Severus, *Dialogues* 3 c. xvii. Migne PL XX.

81. *Der Dialog.* II, pp. 376–80.

82. Cf. Festugière, "Le 'logos' hermétique d'enseignement," REG LV, pp. 93 and n. 5, 96.

83. Cf. Liddell—Scott—Jones, *A Greek English Lexicon, s.v.* II, 4, III.

84. Cf. Eusebius, *Hist. Eccles.* VI, 23, 1–3; ἐξ ἐκείνων δε καὶ Ὠριγένει τῶν εἰς τὰς θείας γραφὰς ὑπομνημάτων ἐγίγνετο ἀρχή, ... Ταχύγραφοι γὰρ αὐτῷ πλείους ἢ ἑπτὰ τὸν ἀριθμὸν παρῆσαν ὑπαγορεύοντι, χρόνοις τεταγμένοις ἀλλήλους ἀμείβοντες. ... Augustine himself, later on, sometimes availed himself of the presence of a *notarius* during a theological controversy. Cf. Possidius, *Vita* XVII.

85. Cf. Festugière, "L'expérience religieuse du médecin Thessalos," RBi XLVIII (1939), pp. 45ff.

86. Ibid., p. 62.

87. Nock, *Conversion* (Oxford, 1933), p. 289, cites the case of Lucius, taken from *Apuleius* VI, 25ff., an instance which may well have been known to Augustine, who was well acquainted, of course, with the works of one who had come from Madauros where he had himself been at school.

88. Cf. the preface to the *Contra Academicos* and *De beata vita*; cf. Nock and Festugière, *Corpus Hermeticum,* passim and especially VII, XIII, XIV, XVI, and *Asclepius*.

89. Cf. CA II, 25; *De finibus* II, 39; *De legibus* I, 53, *De natura deorum* I, 16; *Phaedo* 91A; *Republic* 539C, *Sophist* 237B; *Theaetetus* 164C–166B, 167E, 169C.

90. Cf. CA I, 15; Plato, *Epist.* VII, 343B.

91. Cf. CA III, 29, 37; *Republic* 509Cff.; *Sophist* 253C.

92. The *Contra Academicos* repeats many of the lesser topics of Cicero's dialogues, and especially of his *Academica*. It resumes, too, much of the stock-in-trade of the Platonic treatment of epistemology: we can have knowledge only of the "real" (CA III, 26; *Philebus* 59A, *Republic* 534A, *Theaetetus*, passim; the "verisimile" cannot be perceived unless the "verum" has already been perceived (cf. CA II, 19; *Phaedrus* 59E, 260A–E, 262A–C, 273D); sense-knowledge is not "knowledge" but in itself is reliable (cf. CA III, 268ff.; *Theaetetus* 184D–186E); and the relativity of sense-knowledge (cf. CA III, 26ff; *Theaetetus* 157E). The *Phaedo* covers most of the argument of CA I; cf. 64E–69E, 78Eff.

93. Cf. *Gorgias* 447A, *Republic* 327ff. Cf. *Timaeus* 20C: ξυνωμολογήσατ' οὖν κοινῇ σκεψάμενοι πρὸς. ὑμᾶς αὐτοὺς εἰς νῦν ἀνταποδώσειν μοι τὰ τῶν λόγων ξένια ... and DBV 9: "non me prandium paulo lautius corporibus nostris solum sed animis etiam exhibere debere."

94. Porph. *Vita Plotini* 2. Porphyry wrote a poem; ὁ ἱερὸς γάμος [no. 74 in Bidez' list] in honour of the anniversary of Plato's birth, cf. *V. Plotini* 15. Cicero refers in *De fin.* II, 102 to Epicurus's direction that his birthday should be celebrated after his death.

95. DOR I, 8, 10, 11, 13, 16–17, 19, 20, 21, 28; II, 12, 17; *Cratylus* 396D–E; *Phaedrus* 235D, 236C, 238C–D, 244, 262D, 265A–B; *Apology* 22A–B; *Euthydemus* 280A; *Hipp. Min.* 365; *Ion* 542A; *Laws* 888E; *Lysis* 214–15; *Phaedrus* 260A; *Protagoras* 347E; *Theaet.* 152B.

96. CA III, 45; *De finibus* IV, 80; *Theaet.* 171C–D.

97. DBV; *Phaedrus* 279B. Cf. Nock and Festugière, *Corpus Hermeticum* I, 30–31; XIII, 13ff.; *Asclepius* 40–41.

98. Cic., *Epist. ad fam.* IX, 8.
99. CA III, 15; DOR II, 12–17; 23–52.
100. Cf. CA III, 14–15 and Cic., *De finibus* I, 29; II, 17; Plato, *Sophist.* 217D.
101. Even Plato, it would seem, had difficulty in sustaining the dramatic effect. Cf. *Anonymer Kommentar zu Platons Theaetet.*, Berliner Klassikertexte II (1905), p. 28.
102. Cf. II, 11. The change is emphasized by the fact that Alypius soon takes over the part of Licentius.
103. CA II, 30: "quaeritur ergo inter nos, utrum eorum [Academicorum] argumentis probabile sit nihil percipi posse ac nulli rei esse assentiendum."
104. II, 11.
105. One must notice that Augustine's dialogues end with as little reference to the person to whom the account is being sent as does any of Cicero's or Plato's.
106. I, 5–22.
107. Op. cit., p. 79; cf. n. 4.
108. Op. cit., p. 22. Van Haeringen's attempt to prove that Trygetius surpassed Licentius in erudition is not likely to convince: "Trygetius Licentium vituperat (CA II, 18); succedit in locum Licenti iam victi (CA II, 20); laudatur, quod grauiorem sententiam ab Augustino aliquando prolatam memoria tenuit (DOR II, 7). [This is a strange error. It is *Licentius* who is praised; cf. loc.]; Trygetius orat, ut saepius disputent (DBV 36)."
109. The debate ended at dawn (20, 22). It must have begun before any of the interlocutors had any sleep, and this for the following reasons: Augustine usually lay awake for the first half (but sometimes, alternatively, for the second) of the night (6). Licentius could have been wakened by a mouse—but though the incident is mentioned three times (6, 9, 14) there is no mention of the mouse *waking* him but rather of troubling ("importunos sorices terruit," "mus oberrans iacenti homini molestus") him *"uigilantem"* (6 and 9). The phrase used in one place (9) is "mus me tibi *uigilantem detulit,"* which suggests that Licentius was lying awake before the mouse came. Trygetius also "uigilabat" (6). Now if Licentius and Trygetius, both very young men if not actually boys, and Augustine were all three to be awake together (Augustine also says: *"uigilabam"* (6)) then it is likely that this occurred early in the night. One passage makes this almost certain: Augustine says that (usually) he gave himself to reflection in the early part of the night and did not allow himself to be disturbed by his pupils. To this end he had ordered that they should do no book work at this time, but should learn to occupy their minds: "nec me patiebar adulescentium lucubrationibus a me ipso auocari, quia et illi per totum diem tantum agebant, ut nimium mihi uideretur, si aliquid etiam noctium in studiorum laborem usurparent, et id a me ipsi quoque praeceptum habebant, ut aliquid et praeter codices secum agerent et sese habitare consuefacerent animum" (6). Apparently it was some time later than when they should have ceased from this occupation that they were discovered sleepless: the phrase "ubi uidi scholam nostram . . . *etiam illis horis non sopitam"* (7) implies that none of them had been asleep. We must conclude that it is likely that none of the participants in that debate had had any sleep that night.
110. 20: "quo diligentius et copiosius respondere cogerer, etiam carmine prouocaret."
111. It is interesting to note that a phrase used by Augustine in the *preface*

of the *Contra Academicos*: "congruat uniuerso" (I, 1) is echoed by Licentius here: "uniuersitatis congruentiam."

112. 20: "multa concurrunt, cur ei sermo iste mittatur."

113. 20: "ab istarum rerum studio remotissimo."

114. 8: "nulla *umquam* de his rebus inter nos antea quaestione agitata." Cf. 20.

115. 20: "multa concurrunt, cur ei sermo iste mittatur, primum est, quia debetur." The "sermo iste" refers to Licentius' doctrine which has gone before. It apparently was regarded by Augustine as some reply to Zenobius's persistent enquiries.

116. Augustine was at this time thirty-two or thirty-three years of age. Licentius and Trygetius (who had joined the army, CA I, 4) were his pupils. Though they are spoken of as "adulescentes" (cf. DOR I, 6, 8) and in Augustine's terminology this would allow them to be at least as old as thirty (cf. C VII, 1), they can hardly, as his pupils, have been as old as that. Moreover, his references to them and their conduct in the debate would lead us to believe that they were more likely to have been nearer to the lower limit of "adulescentia" (i.e., about sixteen, cf. C II, 1) than to the higher. Cf. CA I, 4: "temtare pro aetate"; 8: "adhuc nutriendi educandique sitis"; 25: "exercere uos uellem neruosque uestros et studia, quae mihi magna cura est, explorare"; II, 17: "haec inter nos disputatio suscepta sit exercendi tui causa et ad elimandum animum prouocandi—Numquidnam, inquit [Licentius], aut Academicos legi aut tot disciplinis eruditus sum?"; 19–20 (by implication), 22: "satis sit quod cum istis adulescentibus prolusimus, ubi libenter nobiscum philosophia quasi iocata est. quare auferantur de manibus nostris *fabellae pueriles* . . . ut isti adulescentes et in haec attendere discerent et aggredi ac subire temtarent," 25, 26, 28, 29: "omnia potius, inquam, Alypi, loqui maluisti quam quem ad modum nobis cum his qui loqui nesciant, disputandum sit"; III, 6: "bene nosti istos *adulescentulos* uix adhuc posse discernere, quae acute ac subtiliter disseruntur"; 45 (by implication); DBV 6, 8: "si hoc obscurius est, quam ut id iam uos uidere possitis"; 29: "Trygetius cum se parum intellexisse diceret"; DOR I, 7: "schola nostra"; 20: "si . . . cesserit imbecillitas tua, qua minus pasta eruditione disciplinarum . . ."; II, 28.

117. CA I, 4.

118. CA III, 45.

119. He recognizes that the doctrine is beyond Licentius's capacity; cf. 8: "quod *rem tantam* et *tam subito heri paene ad ista* [*studia*] *conuersus* adulescentis animus concepisset"; 13: [Lic] "Licentius et Augustinum et ea quae sunt in media philosophia docet?" Cf. II, 12: [Aug.] "ea dicitis, *quae nec quomodo dicantur non uisa nec quomodo ea uideatis intellego*; ita et uera et alta esse suspicor"; 17: "quod modo interroganti tam bene atque apte respondetis, . . . *miror unde sit*." He himself adopts towards Licentius the attitude of a disciple, cf. 12: "non enim iam me necesse est esse doctorem, cum tu, qui iam tantae rei te certum esse professus es, adhuc me nihil docueris nimium discere cupientem et propter hoc solum dies noctesque uigilantem" 13 (supra), 27; cf. II, 7: "nihil, inquam [Aug.], nunc resisto rationibus tuis." There is, of course, a touch of irony about these remarks.

120. DOR 1.16: [Aug.] "tacitus miror et *exaestuo* in gratulatione"; 17: [Aug.] "Ego mirabar et tacebam. Trygetius autem ubi uidit hominem *paululum quasi digesta ebrietate affabilem factum redditumque colloquio*"; 19: "Tacebat ille

[Trygetius] nimis, ut postea retulit, ammirans et *horrens subito condiscipuli et familiaris sui afflatum noua inspiratione sermonem."* Cf. DOR II, 12, 17.

121. Cf. 235D, 236C, 238D.

122. Cf. 10: "Haec modo, inquit [Lic.], omitte quaeso, ne me hoc uafrum quiddam et captatorium *a nescio qua diuina re, quae mihi se ostentare coepit, et cui me inhiantem suspendo, detorqueat atque disrumpat."* Augustine then encourages him as if he were a "uates," Cf. loc. and 11, 13 [Aug.]: "non nimis curo, cum interrogo, per quem mihi ille respondeat, qui me cotidie querulum accipit, cuius te quidem credo quandoque *uatem futurum*; nec hoc "quandoque" forsitan longum est," 16: "subito ille [Licentius] quasi *mente quadam correptus exclamat: O si possem dicere quod uolo! rogo, ubiubi estis uerba, succurrite.* et bona et mala in ordine sunt—*credite, si uultis; nam quomodo id explicem nescio"*; 20: "si . . . cesserit inbecillitas tua, quae minus pasta eruditione disciplinarum *tantum deum fortasse sustinere non poterit"*; 21: [Lic.] "siue *aliquo uere diuino nuto et ordine fit in nobis"*; cf. 28: [Lic.] "Quid hoc est rei? quid quasi tibi uideor, inquit, annuere? nescio, *quo aduenticio spiritu me credis inflatum . . . aut fortasse, ait, aliquid mecum est?"* No matter how we tone down the language of these passages, we cannot eliminate the fact that Licentius' capacity is raised beyond all reasonably *possible* expectations in order to make him a mouthpiece for the doctrine attributed to him.

123. It may be said that here the *notarius* was not at work and therefore that the same claims for historical accuracy are not made. But notes were made on the morning after the debate (26), and in any case we have the same guarantee for the facts of *De ordine* I, as for the fact of the *notarius'* presence itself—viz.: Augustine's word.

124. CA II, 18.

125. Cf. DOR I, 31-32; 14: at this very early stage in the discussion, Licentius refers to their "sermo" as a "liber non ignobilis" which some Chaldean might have foreseen. Augustine writing at the end of *De ordine* might use such a phrase; but it is actually attributed to Licentius, and at a time when very little (10-13) has been said.

126. Cf. CA III, 6; DOR II, 7 (where the incongruity is "explained" by the "fact" that Licentius repeated it from memory: "quam sententiam eius cum admiratione considerans recordatus sum id ipsum aliquando me breuiter illo audiente dixisse"), 19.

127. In particular, details similar to the two indicated. They are to be found mostly in the introductory letters and prefaces. In fact those details fit in with accounts given elsewhere.

Chapter 2. *"Arripui, aperui, et legi"*

1. Cf. *Hermes* 80 (1952), p. 45.

2. Cf. C VII, 27: "itaque auidissime arripui uenerabilem stilum Spiritus tui, et prae ceteris apostolum Paulum." Here again Augustine's account of his prolonged study of St. Paul is described in terms influenced by the memory of his dramatic consultation of him in the garden scene.

Chapter 3. *Confessio* and *Confessiones*

1. Paris, 1963, p. 211.
2. "The Place of Saint Patrick in Latin Language and Literature," *VigChr* VI (1952), pp. 69f.
3. The *Confession* of St. Patrick and the *Confessions* of St. Augustine," *IER* LXXXV (1956), pp. 190–97.
4. Op. cit., p. 213.
5. Op. cit., p. 217; cf. p. 541.
6. P. 93.
7. P. 98.
8. Art. cit., p. 190: "Dr. Bieler was careful not to advance his findings with any show of confidence."
9. *Eigse* X (1962), p. 150: "It is, in fact, impossible to establish any literary connection between Augustine's spiritual autobiography and the 'Confession' of St. Patrick." Cf. *IER* CII (1964), p. 363: "O'Meara shows how little foundation there is for this assertion."
10. Op. cit., p. 211 n. 4: "Il (O'M.) est suivi sur ce point par C. Mohrmann."
11. Dublin, 1961. The topic had been studied already by F. R. Montgomery Hitchcock, *Hermathena* 47 (1932), pp. 202–33; 51 (1938), pp. 65–76; 54 (1939), pp. 93–109; and, of course, by L. Bieler, *Libri epistolarum sancti Patricii episcopi*, Introduction, Text and Commentary, CM II (1950), pp. 1–150; 12 (1951), pp. 82–214—reprinted by the Irish Manuscripts Commission, 1, 2 (Dublin, 1952).
12. Op. cit., pp. 7, 4ff., 34f. Cf. D. Binchy, "Patrick and his Biographers Ancient and Modern," *Studia Hibernica* II (1962), p. 88 and n. 237.
13. She believes (op. cit., p. 47) that Patrick's language shows elements which "cannot possibly belong to early British Latin. They bear all the marks of living fifth-century Continental Latin." Binchy, who quotes (art. cit.) K. Jackson, *Language and History in Early Britain* (Edinburgh, 1953), p. 80 (the significant lack of mention of which by Mohrmann is noted by both Binchy and Bieler: *Eigse* X (1962), p. 149) in relation to the problem, does not follow Mohrmann here.
14. Art. cit., p. 195: "As it would be exceedingly pedantic to mention phrases which occur to one as possible echoes, only to dismiss them immediately, I shall confine myself to the suggestion of others." On this occasion I do not propose to repeat my former arguments or those put forward by Professor Mohrmann.
15. "'L'extase d'Ostie,' Possibilités et limites de la méthode des parallèles textuels," AugM I (Paris, 1954), pp. 67–84.
16. Ibid., III, pp. 35–38, 41–50.
17. Ibid., III, pp. 36f.
18. Op. cit., p. 212.
19. *The Works of St. Patrick*, ACW 17 (1953), p. 22.
20. *Ecl.* I, 27ff.
21. Art. cit., p. 196 n. 1.
22. The evidence alleged on p. 213 n. 1 to support this is, by implication, considered by Courcelle as less convincing than that already examined. While, as always, the dependence *could* exist, it is not *proved*.

23. Op. cit., pp. 212f.
24. The evidence alleged by Courcelle is given in op. cit., p. 213, n. 1:

1. Augustin, C III, 11, 20, 4, p. 61 (à propos du songe de Monique):
"Non, inquit, *non* enim *mihi dictum est*: 'Vbi ille, ibi et tu,' *sed*: 'Vbi tu, ibi et ille.' Confiteor tibi, Domine, recordationem meam, quantum recolo, quod saepe non tacui amplius me isto per matrem uigilantem *responso tuo* . . . etiam tum fuisse conmotum, quam ipso somnio. . . . Et dedisti alterum responsum interim, quod recolo."

VIII, 12, 29, 1, p. 199:
"Flebam amarissima contritione cordis mei. Et ecce *audio uocem* de uicina (diuina *S*) domo cum cantu dicentis et repetentis *quasi* pueri an puellae nescio: 'Tolle, lege' . . . *Et legi* in silentio capitulum quo *primum* coniecti sunt oculi mei . . . *Nec ultra uolui legere* nec opus erat."

Patrick, *Conf.* 29, p. 74, 14:
"Ad noctem illam uidi in uisu noctis (cf. *Dan.*, VII, 13) scriptum erat contra faciem meam sine honore, et inter haec audiui *responsum diuinum* (cf. Rom XI, 4) *dicentem mihi*: 'Male uidimus faciem designati nudato nomine.' *Nec sic praedixit*: 'Male uidisti,' *sed*: 'Male uidimus' quasi sibi se iunxisset."

23, p. 70, 16:
"Et ibi scilicet uidi in uisu noctis uirum uenientem quasi de Hiberione, cui nomen Victoricus, cum epistolis innumerabilibus, et dedit mihi unam ex his. *Et legi principium* epistolae continentem: 'Vox Hiberionacum,' et cum recitabam principium epistolae, putabam ipso momento *audire uocem* ipsorum, qui erant iuxta siluam Vocluti, quae est prope mare occidentale, et sic exclamauerunt *quasi* ex uno ore (cf. *Dan.* III, 5): 'Rogamus te, puer, ut uenias et adhuc ambulas inter nos,' et ualde compunctus sum corde (cf. *Act.*, II, 37) *et amplius non potui legere* et sic sum expertus."

On notera qu'il s'agit ici et là d'une "vocation." Le *responsum* divin est fréquent chez Patrick, *Conf.*, 17, p. 65, 24; 21, p. 70, 4; 35, p. 77, 6; surtout 42, p. 81, 12: "Insinuauit nobis responsum accepisse a nuntio Dei, et monuit eam ut esset uirgo Dei et ipsa Deo proximaret: Deo gratias, sexta ab hac die optime et audissime arripuit illud quod etiam omnes uirgines Dei ita hoc faciunt."

Bearing in mind the comments of Mohrmann on parallel texts given in the body of this article, I can discover no *solid* ground to support Courcelle's inclination here.

25. P. 217: "Patrick seul semble avoir été touché intimement par le maître"; p. 541: "Patrick seul semble avoir été touché intimement par l'ouvrage."
26. Op. cit., pp. 201–21.
27. Cf. C. Mohrmann, op. cit., p. 8: "There are, as far as I can see, in Patrick's works no traces of quotations or borrowings from any other book than the Bible. We can assert that Patrick was, so far as we can gather from his works, a man *unius libri*. His only book was Holy Scripture." An authoritative assessment of the unrelated pronouncements of Jackson and Mohr-

mann (see n. 13 above) on the *linguistic* aspect of the problem would be valuable.

Chapter 4. Elements of Fiction

1. *Recherches sur les Confessions de Saint Augustin* (Paris, 1950), pp. 188–202.
2. I make general use of John K. Ryan's translation of the *Confessions,* Image Books (New York, 1960).
3. *Geschichte der Autobiographie,* I, 11, pp. 482ff.
4. See Paul Aubin, *Le Problème de la conversion* (Paris, 1962).
5. *En.* V.1.7, 5ff. See Augustine, *de Genesi ad litteram* IV, 50.
6. DBV I, 5.
7. Op. cit., pp. 29ff.
8. *Ep. ad Alypium* III, 4.
9. E XXVII, 5.
10. Courcelle, op. cit., p. 32, n. 1.
11. *Augustine the Bishop* (London, 1961), p. 567.
12. (Paris, 1939), pp. 54ff. See also A. Solignac in *Les Confessions,* BA XIII (Paris, 1962), pp. 207–33.
13. Ibid., pp. 226–28.
14. See A. Solignac, ibid., p. 667.
15. *The Young Augustine* (London, 1954), pp. 10f.
16. R I, 1, 3.
17. DCD XXII, 29.
18. E XCII, 2f.
19. CXLVII, 15, 37.
20. "Augustine the Artist and the *Aeneid,*" *Mélanges Christine Mohrmann* (Utrecht, 1963), pp. 253ff.
21. *Periphyseon,* PL 122, 992A; see also 968D.
22. See also C V, 17 and VI, 1.
23. See e.g., ibid., XIII, 26, 29, and 42.
24. See ibid., XII, 11, 12, 18; XIII, 44.
25. S. Day Lewis, *Cecil Day Lewis* (London, 1980), p. 110.

Chapter 5. Augustine the Artist and the *Aeneid*

1. A passage in *Contra Academicos* (II, 2, 5), known to summarize the story of his conversion as outlined in the *Confessions,* contains the following possible echoes of *Aen.* IV: *flamma* (23, 54); *respexi* (225, 275); *commouebat* (438, 449); *retinaculum* (580).
2. Cf. my *Charter of Christendom: The Significance of Augustine's 'City of God'* (New York: Macmillan, 1961).

Chapter 6. Roman Background to Christian Sexuality

1. *Morale Conjugale et Progestogènes,* EthL 39, 4 (1963), 787–826.
2. By *sexuality* is here meant *physical love in act or desire,* or more shortly *love, amor.* Other forms of love, such as love of country, of children, of wisdom, spiritual love, friendship will be sufficiently indicated. It is not assumed, however, that none of these latter have any sexual reference.

3. Cf. O'Meara, J. J.: *The Young Augustine*, London 1954, pp. 1ff., 47ff.
4. Cf. Bailey, D. S.: *Sexual Relations in Christian Thought*, New York 1959, p. 59: "Augustine must bear no small measure of responsibility for the *insinuation* into our culture of the idea, still widely current, that Christianity regards sexuality as something peculiarly tainted with evil."
5. Lucretius: IV 1141–91.
6. Lucretius (ed. by D. R. Dudley), London 1965, pp. 127f. Dudley points out that Arnobius and Lactantius tell us that Lucretius was widely read in Africa in the 3rd and 4th centuries.
7. VI 26.
8. Quinn, K.: *Latin Explorations*, 1963, pp. 144ff.
9. Allen, A. W.: *Elegy and the Classical Attitude towards Love*, in *Yale Classical Studies* 11, 1950, pp. 255ff.
10. *Mélanges offerts à Mademoiselle Christine Mohrmann*, Utrecht 1963, pp. 256–60: = chap. 5 supra; Cf. Marrou, H. I.: *Histoire de l'Education dans l'Antiquité*, Paris 1948, 341; "Virgile avant tous, qui resteront à la base de la culture littéraire latine. Désormais un Roman cultivé est un homme qui possède son Virgile, comme un Grec Homère: trésor de sagesse et de beauté déposé au plus profond de la mémoire, dont les vers remontent à la conscience chaque fois qu'on éprouve le besoin d'exprimer, de souligner ou de cautionner un sentiment ou une idée." Cf. pp. 351, 370, 373, 395f. (careers of Virgil and Augustine compared), 411. Romanelli, P.: *S. Agostino nell' Africa del suo tempo*, in *Augustiniana*, Napoli 1955, 17–35; Holtorf, H.: *P. Vergilius Maro: Die Grösseren Gedichte*, I, 1959, p. 78; Morán Martínez, F.: *El espíritu virgiliano en la "Ciudad de Dios"* in *La Ciudad de Dios* 167, 1955, 433–57; Courcelle, P.: *Les Pères de l'Eglise devant les enfers virgiliens*, in *Archives d'Histoire Doctrinale et Littéraire du Moyen Age* 1955, 5–74; *Interprétations néo-platonisantes du livre VI de l' "Enéide,"* in *Recherches sur la tradition platonicienne* 95–136 (Fondation Hardt 1957); 'Les exégèses chrétiennes de la quatrième Eglogue,' in *Revue des Etudes Anciennes* 59, 1957, 294–319; Schmid, W.: *Tityrus Christianus*, in *Rheinisches Museum für Philologie* 96, 1953, 101–65; Kurfess, A.: *Vergils vierte Ekloge bei Hieronymus und Augustinus*, in *Sacris Erudiri* 6, 1954, 5–13.
11. C I, 27.
12. Aeneas's abandoning of Dido reappears in Augustine's *Confessions* both where he is describing his escape from his mother (V 15) and the separation of his mistress—the faithful mother of his son—from him (VI 25). It must be remembered that both Virgil and Augustine themselves gave us the accounts of these separations without which we could not think hardly on Aeneas or Augustine: *their sympathies were strongly* involved on the side of the women. Augustine sometimes seems to represent his mother rather as Venus is represented in the *Aeneid*: she watches over his career and directs him especially in connection with a proposed marriage (C VI 23: *maxime matre dante operam*).
13. VI 719–67.
14. *Annales Academiae Scientiarum Fennicae*, B 135. 1, Helsinki 1965.
15. Cf. op. cit., p. 34.
16. Cf. Frank, T.: *Vergil*, Oxford 1922, p. 108: "Despite their creed (Epicureanism) Lucretius and Vergil are indeed Rome's foremost apostles of Righteousness."
17. Lilja: op. cit., p. 44.
18. Catullus 51, 13–16.

19. Op. cit., p. 109.
20. Cf. Herescu, N.: *Bibliographie de la Littérature Latine,* Paris 1943, p. 157.
21. But of course the affair of Caesar and Cleopatra in all its circumstances and implications was always in the background . . . "Julius Caesar (was) still the dominant figure in Rome . . . Does it not explain why so many traits in Dido's character irresistibly suggest Cleopatra? Why half the lines of the fourth book are reminiscent of Caesar's dallying in Egypt in 47?"; Frank, T.: op. cit., p. 75.
22. Aeschylus, Ag. 671.
23. As held to be probable, e.g. by Frank, T.: *Vergil* 1922, p. 109.
24. Festugière, A. J. P.: *Epicure et ses Dieux,* Paris 1946, p. 69, Festugière's whole chapter here on *L'amitié Epicurienne* is well worth consulting on this point.
25. Diehl, E.: *Die Vitae Vergilianae,* Bonn 1911, p. 10; cf. p. 41, 1, 4.
26. Poschl, V.: *The Art of Vergil,* Ann Arbor 1962, pp. 53f.
27. Perret, J.: *Virgile,* Paris 1959, p. 38: "L'amour n'est que matière, entre beaucoup d'autres, pour les chants." For a contrary view see Alfonsi, L.: *Dalla II alla X Ecloga,* in *Aevum* 35, 1960, 193–98; Marchesi, C.: *Pastorale virgiliana,* in *Helikon,* 1960, 19–27; Winniezuk, L.: *Corn. Gallus Poet and Statesman,* in *Eos* 50, 1959–60, 127–45; Poggioli, R.: *The Oaten Flute,* in *Harvard Library Bulletin* 2, 1957, 147–84; Oliveira Pulquério, M. de: *A expressao do amor nas "Bucólicas" de Virgilio,* in *Humanitas* 6–7, 1957–8, 1–20; Trisoglio, F.: *Le Bucolische Virgiliane come momento idillico estetico,* in *Rivista di Studi Classici* 8, 1960, 289–310.
28. *Ecl.* X 69.
29. Op. cit., p. 39.
30. Cf. Gow, A. S. F.: *Theocritus,* Cambridge 1950, vol. II, pp. 1ff. In Theocritus Daphnis, who according to Diodorus (4, 84) is connected with Artemis, is an Hippolytus figure—one who resists love and dies for having done so.
31. *Eclogue* V 20–44, although inasmuch as it deals with the decay of fertility it approaches the topic negatively, is reminiscent in details of Lucretius I, 1ff.
32. Cf. *Veneris vincula* in *Ecl.* VIII 79.
33. One wonders if Virgil had any special purpose in portraying, in effect, Lucretius as Silenus.
34. *Eclogue* VI 41–47; 61–66; 74–81.
35. Note that in *Georgics* I 62–63 where the creation of *mankind* is being described Deucalion, not Pyrrha, is the agent:
        Deucalion vacuum lapides iactavit in orbem,
        unde homines nati, durum genus.
36. *Aen.* IV 657ff.
37. Ovid: *Metamorphoses* II 340ff.
38. *Ecl.* VIII 23.
39. *Ecl.* VIII 43.
40. *Ecl.* VIII 17–62.
41. *Ecl.* VIII 47–50.
42. *Ecl.* X 6.
43. *Ecl.* X 69.
44. *Georgics* II 324–29.
45. Ibid., 523–24; cf. Lucretius III 895.
46. Ibid., 242–44; Otis, B.: *Virgil,* Oxford 1963, develops the idea of Virgil's

empathy; cf. p. 189: 'Man is here and for this limited purpose the kin of the animal.'
47. *Georg.* III 127.
48. *Georg.* III 178.
49. *Georg.* III 284–85.
50. This episode is of course reminiscent of the episode of Dido and Aeneas; although the treatment is different, love still leads to disaster.
51. *Aen.* I, 673–75.
52. I, 749.
53. IV 27.
54. Cf. Otis, B.: *Ovid as an Epic Poet*, 1966, p. 219. Byblis is meditating incest with her brother:
"Coget amor: potero. Vel, si pudor ora tenebit . . . ," *Met.* IX 514.
55. Cf. 321f.: *te propter extinctus pudor.*
56. *Aen.* IV 54–55.
57. *Georg.* III 266–83.
58. *Aen.* IV 55.
59. *Aen.* IV 479.
60. *Aen.* IV 169–72.
61. Cf. *Aen.* IV 316: "per conubia nostra, per inceptos hymenaeos."
62. *Aen.* IV 338–39.
63. *Aen.* IV 281.
64. *Aen.* IV 346–47.
65. *Aen.* IV 361.
66. *Aen.* IV 395–96.
67. *Aen.* IV 449.
68. *Aen.* VI 445ff.
69. Cf. Newton, F. L.: "Recurrent Imagery in Aen. IV," TAPA 88 (1957), 31–43.
70. *Ecl.* III 101.
71. C III 1 (tr. Pusey).
72. Cf. the author's *The Young Augustine*, London 1954, pp. 85ff.
73. C VIII 1.
74. Ibid., 29.
75. *Ecl.* I 59–63.
76. *Soliloquia* I 17.
77. It is only right to add that in *Sol.* I 25 we are told that that same night the *complexus femineus* no longer seemed *sordidus, foedus, exsecrabilis, horribilis.* On the contrary *imaginatae illae blanditiae et amara suavitas titillaverit.* This perhaps helps us to trust Augustine the more.

Chapter 7. Augustine's Attitude to Love

1. "Virgil and Augustine: The Roman Background to Christian Sexuality," chap. 6 this volume.
2. Ibid., 73ff.
3. For other aspects, especially concerning his training in rhetoric, see H. I. Marrou, *Saint Augustin et la fin de la culture antique* (Paris, 1938).
4. *The Young Augustine* (London, 1954), pp. 47ff.
5. Cf. A. Solignac, *Les Confessions* in BA XIII (1962), pp. 677ff.

6. B. Legewie, "Die körperliche Konstitution und die Krankheiten Augustins," *Miscellanea Agostiniana* II (Rome, 1931), pp. 5ff. and Marrou, *Saint Augustin et l'Augustinisme* (Paris, 1955), p. 24.
7. *L'Enfant d'Agrigente* (Paris, 1950), pp. 141f.
8. See e.g., the discussion in AugM III (Paris, 1954), pp. 251ff.
9. "Morale Conjugale et Progestogènes," EThL 39.4 (1965), pp. 787–826.
10. *Charter of Christendom* (New York, 1961), p. 96.

Chapter 8. The *Aeneid* in the *Confessions*

1. *Histoire de l'éducation dans l'Antiquité*, 2d ed. (1950), p. 341.
2. *Aen.* VI, 851–53.
3. *Augustine and the Latin Classics* (Göteborg, 1967).
4. AugM 1 (1954), pp. 118f.
5. *Somnium Scipionis* I, 9, 8: II, 10, 11.
6. *Convivio* IV.
7. DVR I, 11f.
8. DCD V, 16.
9. Longinus, *On the Sublime*, c. 8.
10. C X, 38.
11. Loc. cit.
12. Translated by W. R. Trask (London, 1953).
13. J. Pépin points out that, in the story of Ulysses as referred to by St. Ambrose in his *Expositio in Lucam* IV, 3, terms from the *Aeneid* (I, 536; II, 23) are used revealing the identification of Ulysses with Aeneas in Latin authors. Cf. his "The Platonic and Christian Ulysses," *NeoPlatonism and Christian Thought*, ed. Dominic J. O'Meara (Albany, 1982), pp. 13f. W. Hübner, "Die praetoria memoriae im zehnten Buch der *Confessiones*: Vergilisches bei Augustin,' REAug XXVII (1981), p. 262.
14. C I, 21f.
15. P. 24 (Pelican, 1954).
16. *Times Literary Supplement*, 11 June 1982.
17. C III, 2–4.
18. Ibid., II, 2.
19. Ibid., III, 1.
20. Ibid., III, 7.
21. Ibid., V, 15.
22. Ibid., VIII, 26.
23. Ibid., VIII, 29.
24. *The Creation of Man in de Genesi ad litteram*, Augustinian Institute, Villanova University, Penn., 1980. See also "Saint Augustine's Understanding of the Creation and Fall," ch. 17 this volume.
25. II, 450ff.
26. *Aen.* VI, 679ff.
27. 12–14.
28. See W. Schmidt, "Die *aula memoriae* in den *Konfessionen* des heiligen Augustin," REAug XIV (1968), pp. 69–89; W. Hübner, art. cit.
29. See the author's "Augustine the Artist and the *Aeneid*," *Mélanges Christine Mohrmann* (Utrecht, 1963), pp. 255, 260: = chap. 5 supra.
30. VI, 882.

31. For a discussion of the influence also of Virgil, *Georgics* IV on the memory passage in Augustine, C X, 12, 14, see W. Hübner, art. cit.
32. See note 29 above.
33. See W. Hübner, art. cit., p. 262.
34. Ibid., pp. 259ff.

Chapter 11. Authority and Reason

1. DOR II, 27: "auctoritas autem partim diuina est, partim humana, sed vera firma summa ea est quae diuina nominatur." Cf. II, 16: "duplex enim est uia quam sequimur . . . aut rationem aut certe auctoritatem." Citations are given from the CSEL when a text is available in that series. Otherwise they are given from Migne, PL. Hence we have sometimes *diuina, intellegens,* and sometimes *divina, intelligens,* and so on.

2. CA III, 43: "mihi ergo, certum est nusquam prorsus a Christi auctoritate discedere; non enim reperio ualentiorem. quod autem subtilissima ratione persequendum est—apud Platonicos me interim, reperturum esse confido."

3. Ibid., I, 1.
4. Ibid., I, 3.
5. Ibid., I, 9; cf. DOR II, 16.

6. Augustine himself tells us that he did not follow Plotinus as an authority; he was not sure that, even if what Plotinus said was true, Plotinus himself knew that it was true: "(Ratio) Si ea quae de Deo dixerunt Plato et Plotinus vera sunt, satisne, tibi est ita Deum scire, ut illi sciebant? (Aug.) Non continuo si ea quae dixerunt, vera sunt, etiam scisse illos ea necesse est. Nam multi copiose dicunt quae nesciunt . . . scire autem aliud est" (SO I, 3).

7. DOR II, 27: "plerumque fallit."

8. CA III, 43: "nusquam prorsus a Christi *auctoritate* discedere . . . quod autem subtilissima ratione persequendum est."

9. Cf. DOR II, 16, 26, 27.

10. Cf. ibid., II, 44: "illa diuina non iam credenda solum uerum etiam contemplanda intellegenda atque retinenda"; ibid., 50: "non iam sola fide sed certa ratione."

11. Cf. E III, 3 (A.D. 387): "illa ratiocinatio, cui tamquam unicae meae blandiri soleo, et ea me nimis oblectare." SO I, 8: "ego quid sciam quaero non quid credam."

12. The term *philosophia* is not as satisfactory in the contrast with *auctoritas* as is *ratio*. In the early *Dialogues, philosophia* can mean anything from religion (cf. DOR I, 31); religion-philosophy (CA I, 1, 3, 9; II, 7, 8, 9, III, 13, 20, 35, 37, 44; DBV 1, 2, 4; DOR I, 32; II, 48); to philosophy (DOR II, 16, 47). Cf. Boyer, *Christianisme et Neo-Platonisme dans la Formation de saint Augustin*, pp. 156, 159, and nn. for this fluid use of the term among writers shortly before the time of Augustine.

13. CA III, 43.

14. Cf. *Enneads* V, 3, 3. Cf. also Nock & Festugière, *Corpus Hermeticum* IV, 3 and n. 6; IX, 10 and n. 36; *Asclepius* 41 and n. 349.

15. Cf. SO I, 7: "(Ratio) Quid ergo scire vis? . . . (Augustinus) Deum et animam scire cupio. (R) nihilne plus? (A) nihil omnino . . . nunc autem nihil aliud amo quam Deum et animam, quorum neutrum scio." Ibid., 15, 16, 20, 27: "(R) animam te certe dicis, et Deum velle cognoscere? (A) hoc est totum

negotium meum. (R) nihilne amplius? (A) nihil prorsus." Ibid., II, 27, 32; DBV 4; DOR II, 24, 44, 47; CA III, 38. Cf. Nock & Festugière, op. cit., I, 18 and n. 47.

16. Cf. SO I, 7; supra n. 15. DBV 5: "quid enim solidum tenui cui adhuc de anima quaestio nutat et fluctuat?" There are many texts in which he considers a variety of differing views on questions in connection with the soul. Cf. DOR II, 48, 50; SO II, 3–5, 23, 26. Even at the end of his life he was still puzzled: cf. R I, 1, 3 (concerning the phrase *animus securior rediturus in caelum*: CA II, 22): "nam quod adtinet ad eius [animi] originem nec tunc sciebam, nec adhuc scio."

17. I, 12–15.

18. "(Ratio) quomodo haec acceperis, ut probabilia, an ut vera? (Augustinus) plane ut probabilia." SO I, 15.

19. III, 43.

20. Cf. SO I, 12: as the *body* must have eyes to see, so must the *soul, anima*, have a *mens*. He also talks about the *sensus animae* [*animi*? ed.].

21. I, 12, 13: "adspectus animae ratio est"; 14: "tria igitur ad animam pertinent ut sana sit, ut adspiciat, ut videat": i.e., *anima = mens*.

22. It is given as a variant reading instead of *animae* early in 12. Cf. supra n. 20.

23. I, 13: "non sequitur ut omnis qui adspicit videat." *Ratio perveniens ad finem suum* is the *visio* called *intellectus*.

24. Cf. E. Gilson, *Introduction a l'étude de Saint Augustin* (Paris, 1929), pp. 53–54, n. 1. The account in the *Soliloquia* has the advantage of being precise.

25. CA I, 9; DOR II, 6, 19.

26. CA I, 9; DBV 8; DOR II, 17, 19, 48, 50; SO II, 3–5, 23, 32–33.

27. Cf. DOR II, 6.

28. CA I, 1.

29. Ibid.

30. E III, 4 (A.D. 387).

31. DOR II, 30: "ratio est mentis motio . . . distinguendi et connectendi potens." Cf. ibid., II, 38, 48, 50.

32. Ibid., II, 17, 19, 41, 42; E III, 4; VIII, 2.

33. DOR II, 48, 50.

34. Ibid., II, 38.

35. SO II, 33; DBV 8.

36. DOR II, 41.

37. SO II, 33.

38. CA I, 22; DOR II, 5–7.

39. Cf. DBV 5: "adhuc de anima [mihi] quaestio mutat et fluctuat." Cf. CA I, 1; DBV I; DOR II, 17, 43, 44, 50; SO I, 1, 7; II, 26.

40. Cf. CA I, 1; DBV I; DOR II, 17. God is its origin in some way. DOR II, 47.

41. SO II, 35; E VII, 2.

42. Cf. DOR II, 31: "progressus animae usque ad mortalia lapsus est, ita regressus esse in rationem debet." Cf. CA I, 9; II, 22; SO II, 35. Cf. E. Gilson, *Introduction*, pp. 94–95.

43. Cf. SO II, 3–5, 23, 32.

44. Cf. DQ LXXVI (written early in A.D. 388).

45. CA I, 9: "cum hoc corpus . . . dereliquerit." Cf. DOR II, 17, 19.

46. Cf. R I, 2, 4. Yet Ambrose could write in A.D. 392: "anima quae corpore velut calceamento utitur." *De instit. uirginis* LXXXVII.

47. CA I, 1; DOR II, 17, 31, 41. Cf. CA I, 11. The term *divinus* is applied to things other than the Deity. Cf. E II, 1: *diuina philosophia*; DOR II, 46.

48. DBV 4: "[anima] nam id est unum in rebus proximum Deo." Cf. CA I, 9.

49. DOR II, 46: "inexpiabile nefas est deum uiolabilem credere, nec ita saltem, ut uel uirtute prouiderit, ne sua substantia uiolaretur; namque animam poenas hic pendere fatentur, cum inter eius et dei substantiam nihil uelint omnino distare." The passage is reminiscent of Plotinus. Cf. "nihil plus inveniet, quam quid sit unum, sed longe altius longeque diuinius . . . [parens uniuersitatis] cuius nulla scientia est in anima nisi scire, quomodo eum nesciat."

50. Cf. DOR II, 5–7, 19.

51. Cf. CA I, 22; DOR II, 5–7, 41; SO II, 33; E VII, 2.

52. In the passage from the *Soliloquia* we are told that God illuminated the *object*. Here the *mens* is the object. Cf. CA I, 19; DBV 10, 14, 18, 27, 31; DOR I, 4, 10, 13, 14, 19, 20, 28, 33; II, 12, 17, 54. Cf. E. Gilson, *Introduction*, pp. 99ff.; R. Jolivet, *Dieu, soleil des esprits* (Paris, 1934).

53. Cf. DOR II, 26: "qui autem sola auctoritate contenti bonis tantum moribus rectisque uotis constanter operam dederint aut contemnentes aut non ualentes disciplinis liberalibus atque optimis erudiri . . . inconcusse credo . . . eos . . . liberari." Cf. CA III, 42: "numquam ista ratio subtilissima reuocaret, nisi summus deus . . . diuini intellectus auctoritatem. . . ." Cf. CA III, 11, 13, 42; DOR II, 16, 26, 27, 46.

54. Cf. DOR II, 26: "qui autem sola auctoritate contenti . . . (as above) erudiri. beatos eos quidem, cum inter homines uiuant, nescio quo modo appellem, tamen inconcusse credo . . . (as above)"; cf. DOR II, 16: "philosophia rationem promittit et uix paucissimos liberat, quos tamen non modo non contemnere illa mysteria (sc. of Catholicism) sed sola intellegere, ut intellegenda sunt cogit. . . ." Cf. DOR I, 32.

55. Cf. ibid., II, 26: "quia nullus hominum nisi ex imperito peritus fit, nullus autem imperitus nouit, qualem se debeat praebere docentibus . . . euenit, ut omnibus bona magna et occulta discere cupientibus non aperiat nisi auctoritas ianuam. . . ." Cf. SO I, 12–15. Cf. DLA II, 5–6.

56. A.D. (388–(391–395)). II, 5–6 (the dialogue is certainly fictitious); "(Evodius) quamquam haec inconcussa fide teneam, tamen *quia cognitione nondum teneo*, ita quaeramus quasi omnia incerta sint . . . nos id quod credimus, nosse et intelligere cupimus. (Augustinus) nisi enim aliud esset credere, et *aliud intelligere*, et primo credendum esset, quod magnum et divinum intelligere cuperemus, frustra Propheta dixisset: nisi credideritis, non intelligetis. Ipse quoque Dominus noster et dictis et factis ad credendum *primo* hortatus est, quos ad salutem vocavit. Sed *postea* cum de ipso dono loqueretur, quod erat daturus credentibus, non ait: 'haec est autem vita aeterna ut *credant*.' sed, 'haec est,' inquit, 'vita aeterna, ut *cognoscant*. . . .' Deinde jam credentibus dicit: 'quaerite et invenietis': nam neque inventum dici potest, quod incognitum creditur; neque quisquam inveniendo Deo sit idoneus, nisi *ante crediderit*, quod est *postea cogniturus*. . . ."

57. CA I, 3: "[philosophia] verissimum et secretissimum deum perspicue se demonstraturam promittit."

58. Ibid., III, 43: "ita enim iam sum affectus, ut quid sit uerum non credendo solum sed etiam intellegendo apprehendere impatienter desiderem."

59. DOR II, 16: "philosophia rationem promittit et vix paucissimos liberat, quos tamen non modo non contemnere illa mysteria sed sola intellegere, ut intellegenda sunt cogit. . . ."

60. Ibid., II, 44: "eruditi dignissimus nomine non temere iam quaerit illa diuina non iam credenda solum uerum etiam contemplanda intellegenda atque retinenda." Cf. ibid., 50.

61. SO I, 12: "Promittit . . . ratio . . . ita se demonstraturam Deum tuae menti, ut oculis sol demonstratur." Cf. ibid., I, 8: "ego quid sciam quaero non quid credam"; ibid., I, 15: "haec duo (i.e., te ipsum et Deum), ut intelligas, docere te audeo"; E III, 3: "illa ratiocinatio, cui tamquam unicae meae blandiri soleo, et ea me nimis oblectare."

62. CA III, 43.

Chapter 12. Augustine and Neoplatonism

1. The *Confessions* had been assailed by Johannes Clericus (1657–1736); cf. PL XLVII, coll. c. 210, but only on internal grounds. A. Naville, *Saint Augustin* (Geneva, 1872), had anticipated Boissier and Harnack.

2. *Revue des Deux-Mondes* (Jan. 1888); cf. *La fin du paganisme*, pp. 291–325.

3. Cf. *Augustins Confessionen*, 2 Auflag. (Giessen, 1895); cf. p. 17: "So ist es nicht schwer, Augustin aus Augustin zu widerlegen."

4. Art. "*Augustinus*" in *Realencyclopädie für prot. Stud.* 3d ed., vol. II (Leipzig, 1897).

5. *Essai sur la conversion de saint Augustin* (Geneva, 1900).

6. Op. cit., p. 51; cf. p. 45: "En 386, Augustin passa par une crise qui le convertit: 1° aux bonnes moeurs; 2° à la philosophie néo-platonicienne. Ce fut tout."

7. Cf. op. cit., p. 87.

8. Augustin, *Studien zu seiner geistigen Entwickelung* (Leipzig, 1908); cf. p. 57.

9. *Augustins geistige Entwickelung in den ersten Jahren nach seiner Bekehrung (386–391)* (Berlin, 1908). He makes his own a quotation from Scheel, *Die Anshauung Augustins ueber Christi Person und Werk*: "Die Confessionen sind rein historisch betrachtet keine Geschichtsquelle" (p. 11).

10. Paris, 1918.

11. Though we do not wish to interrupt the sequence of texts by any comment, nevertheless this is the most suitable place to observe: (a) that Augustine does not speak "de tout ce que l'intéresse" in the *Dialogues*. Even an ecclesiastic would refrain from airing his theological views in any notable way in a discussion of epistemology; (b) that there is at least one allusion to his impending baptism: "quae omnia sacris, quibus initiamur, secretius firmiusque traduntur." DOR II, 27; cf. context.

12. There is, of course, much else which could be quoted in this connection. Some of it does not need serious refutation. What, for instance, can one who has read the early *Dialogues* think of the following remarks: "Si Plotin fait revivre Platon, lui-même revit en Augustin" (p. 518); "Pour lui (Augustine) le Christ est le Platon des foules" (p. 525)? Cf. also pp. viii, 361, 393.

13. Op. cit., pp. 400–402, 404–5, 415–28.

14. Op. cit., p. 405.

15. Op. cit., pp. 403–6.
16. *Die Geistesentwickelung des hl. Aurelius Augustins* (Paderborn, 1892).
17. "St. Augustin à Cassiciacum," APhC (Dec. 1898), pp. 307ff.
18. Art. "Augustin," in *DThC* (Paris, 1903).
19. "Les premières impressions catholiques de saint Augustin," *Etudes* (May 20 and June 5, 1909).
20. *St. Augustine, Aspects of his Life and Thought* (London, 1914), pp. 32ff.
21. *St. Augustin* (Paris, 1898).
22. *La conversion de saint Augustin* (Geneva, 1900).
23. Paris, 1920 (2d ed., Rome, 1953).
24. *Introduction a l'étude de saint Augustin* (Paris, 1929), p. 313.
25. *Augustins Bekehrung* (German translation, Tübingen, 1923), p. 15 n. 2.
26. J. J. O'Meara, *Against the Academics*, ACW XII (1950), p. 21.
27. Cf. G. Mathon, "Quand faut-il placer le retour d'Augustin à la foi catholique?" *REAug* (1955), vols. I–II, p. 107 n. 3. There is a tendency among certain scholars to describe questions discussed by others (especially when they hold an opposite view!) as false problems. Alfaric and Boyer may have been at fault in method and conclusion: but the problem they were dealing with was a real one—still being debated by Boyer, Courcelle, and many others.
28. Cf. J. J. O'Meara, *IThQ* (1951), pp. 338ff.: = chap. 10 supra.
29. E.g., P. Le Blond and M. Sciacca.
30. AugM III (Paris, 1954), p. 97.
31. "Litiges sur la lecture des 'Libri Platonicorum' par saint Augustin," *Augustiniana* (Nov. 1954), pp. 231ff.
32. Art. cit., pp. 110ff.
33. Cf. J. J. O'Meara, *The Young Augustine*, pp. 131ff.
34. *Les Ennéades de Plotin* (Paris, 1857), vol. II, p. 555.
35. Op. cit., p. 375 n. 3.
36. Op. cit., 2.4f.
37. Cf. his review of Courcelle's *Recherches* in *Gnomon* XXV (1953).
38. Art. cit., pp. 225f.
39. RECA s.v. *Plotin*, p. 586, 65.
40. *Les Lettres grecques en Occident* (Paris, 1943), p. 167; cf. "Litiges," p. 228.
41. Ibid., p. 394: Courcelle again speaks of the problem Plotinus-Porphyry as a false problem; cf. AugM III, 99. But Plotinus and Porphyry were really distinct persons whose teachings are published in distinct books and who, on Augustine's own testimony, affected Augustine in distinct ways.
42. *The Young Augustine*, pp. 143ff.; see n. 49 below.
43. "Litiges," pp. 227ff.
44. C VII, 13, 26: VIII, 3.
45. "Litiges," p. 227.
46. *Vitae Sophist.*, p. 7.
47. AugM III, 98.
48. "Litiges," p. 228. I have myself given arguments in favour of Porphyry (but not to the exclusion of Plotinus) in *Against the Academics*: see index s.v. *Porphyry*. See n. 42 above.
49. Cf. Mandouze, *L'exstase d'Ostie*, AugM I (Paris, 1954), p. 67 n. 1, and following pages. The present writer has indicated some Plotinian passages in the *Contra Academicos* in *Against the Academics*, index, s.v. *Plotinus*.
50. AugM I, 67.

51. Ibid., III, 103–63, to which the reader is referred for a full survey of this hotly controverted question.

52. Ibid., I, 80ff.

53. J. J. O'Meara, *The Young Augustine*, pp. 125f.

54. See J. Pépin, *Chronique d'histoire des Philosophies Anciennes* (Desclée de Brouwer, 1955), p. 245 for a list of articles written by Courcelle to elaborate, defend, or explain his views.

55. In *The Young Augustine*, index s.v. *Courcelle*. Cf. C. Mohrmann in a review of *Recherches* in *VigChr* (1951), pp. 249ff.; H.-I. Marrou, *REL* XXIX (1951), pp. 401ff.

56. C. Mohrmann, loc. cit., p. 254: J. Pépin, *Chronique d'histoire*, p. 246.

57. Courcelle, *Les Lettres grecques* (1943) had not been available because of World War II.

58. Cf. A. Solignac, "La question 'de Ideis,'" AugM I, 312ff. One of the encouraging features of Augustinian scholarship at the moment is the willingness of scholars to extend the range of possible sources for both the Neoplatonic and other information of Augustine: this seems to me to be long overdue.

59. M. Testard has addressed himself to this problem: cf. "Note sur *De civitate Dei* XXII, 24," AugM I (Paris, 1954), 193–200.

60. Most of this matter is to be found through the index and notes of *Against the Academics* and *The Young Augustine*.

61. Cf. R I, 4, 3: *Against the Academics*, p. 181 n. 29.

62. J. J. O'Meara, "A Master-Motif in St. Augustine," *Actes du premier Congrès de la Fédération Internationale des associations d'études classiques* (Paris, 1951), p. 317 [and chap. 10 in this volume].

63. Cf. especially the notes to *Against the Academics* s.v. *Porphyry* and *The Young Augustine*, pp. 143–89. An addendum is added below in which in parallel columns are set forth Porphyry's views (B) according to Augustine and Augustine's varying reaction to them (A).

64. See J. J. O'Meara, *Porphyry's Philosophy from Oracles in Augustine* (Paris, 1959).

Chapter 13. Porphyry's *Philosophy from Oracles*

1. V, 36, 5: τοῦ τὴν συσκευὴν καθ' ἡμῶν πεποιημένον. I use Mras's text. When I quote a word or phrase in Greek, I give it in the form in which it is found in Mras's text without alteration. [Ed. note: See now SC 228.247, n.3.]

2. IV, 6, 3ff. Translation of Eusebius by E. H. Gifford (Oxford, 1903).

3. Cf. P. Hadot, *Porphyre et Victorinus* (Paris, 1968), pp. 95, 257–72, 309–11.

4. (1) Cf. e.g., H. Lewy, *Chaldaean Oracles and Theurgy* (Cairo, 1956), pp. 64f., 8, 44, 47, 51ff. Hadot, op. cit., p. 394. It is interesting to observe that E. R. Dodds now agrees: "New Light on the 'Chaldaean Oracles,'" [*HThR* LIV (1961), pp. 265, 267] that it might seem odd "that an oracle-hunter so learned and diligent as Porphyry should have missed at this time (the writing of the *Philosophy from Oracles*) a collection which had been in circulation for at least twenty years." This is a distinct shift from his position in *The Greeks and the Irrational* (Berkeley, 1951), p. 287.

(2) Cf. P. Hadot, op. cit., pp. 92, 95, 257ff., 309ff., 482.

(3) Cf. Augustine, DCD XIX, 23: "amplius autem uenerari Deum Patrem. Hoc autem, inquit, et dii praecipiunt et in superioribus ostendimus, quem ad modum animum aduertere ad Deum monent et illum colere ubique imperant." Earlier on—in Augustine's text—the Father is called *generator et rex ante omnia* and is said to be worshipped by the Hebrews. *In superioribus* implies previous treatment of the cult of God. See Hadot, loc. cit., for the equivalence of the δὶς ἐπέκεινα with the God of the Hebrews. Cf. H. Lewy, *A Latin Hymn to the Creator Ascribed to Plato*, HThR XXXIX (1946), pp. 243-58: "It is a fair conjecture that Porphyry's *Philosophy from Oracles* was the literary source from which [Tiberianus] drew the hymn ascribed to Plato. This work . . . aimed to demonstrate the philosophical—i.e., Platonic—meaning of Greek oracular poetry . . . [it] did contain, in fact, not only oracles, but also hymns, including one or more to the Ruler of the Universe" (p. 258). Cf. Hadot, op. cit., pp. 475f.

5. Augustine, DCD XIX, 23: "prohibitos autem daemones et hos non odisse, sed reuereri."

6. J. Bidez, *Vie de Porphyre* (Gand, 1913), p. 22.

7. See e.g., Hadot, op. cit., pp. 40, 87, 94, 108, 482, 493.

8. See J. J. O'Meara, *Porphyry's Philosophy from Oracles in Augustine* (Paris, 1959), pp. 33-37. Hadot, op. cit., pp. 482f. stresses more the pre-Plotinian and de-emphasizes the Plotinian periods of Porphyry's career. The acceptance of the presence of *Chaldaean Oracles* in the *Philosophy from Oracles* weakens the case for making it a work earlier than *De regressu animae*.

9. This description has been at the back of various arguments from the *tone* or *attitude* of the work that have been used. Cf. P. Hadot, *Citations de Porphyre chez Augustin*, REAug VI (1960), pp. 209, 243. Use of "ton" in the case of fragments is particularly exposed to error. I have written elsewhere [AS 1 (1970); this volume, chap. 21]: "If, for example, Virgil's *Eclogues* were lost and two fragments were discovered separately, one being the Epicurean description of the origin of the world in *Eclogue* VI and the other the immediately following mythological account of the origin of man, one might have some difficulty in deciding that both had the same author, Virgil; that both came from the pastoral *Eclogues*; and finally that they came from the same poem, following one upon the other without any transition whatever."

10. Cf. III, 13, 4f.; III, 14, 8; IV, 1, 3f.; IV, 9, 5ff.

11. ἕνα γὰρ ὄντα θεὸν παντοίαις δυνάμεσι τὰ πάντα πληροῦν καὶ διὰ πάντων διήκειν καὶ τοῖς πᾶσιν ἐπιστατεῖν ἀσωμάτως καὶ ἀφανῶς ἐν πᾶσιν ὄντα καὶ διὰ πάντων διήκοντα, καὶ τοῦτον εἰκότως διὰ τῶν δεδηλωμένων σέβειν φασί. This parenthesis may contain an actual fragment from the *Philosophy from Oracles*.

12. Cf. op. cit., p. 60 n. 2, and Lewy, op. cit., pp. 509ff.—accepted by Hadot, art. cit., p. 210.

13. XIX, 23: "Judaei suscipiunt Deum magis quam isti (Christiani) . . . quibus sit (Pater) colendus moribus."

14. IV, 9, 1ff. Porphyry's comment which follows clarifies the oracle just quoted: "Gods beneath the earth (ὑποχθονίων, νερτερίων) and on the earth (ἐπιχθονίων, χθονίων) should have black four-footed victims (ἱερεῖα τετράποδα) slaughtered (σφάττειν) over trenches (ἐπὶ βόθρων, ἐν ταφῇ) and on altars (ἐπὶ βωμῶν) respectively. Chthonic deities might have lambs (ἀρνῶν νεοπηγέα ... πρόβατον ἔκφανσιν). To the gods of the air (ἀερίοις) which is

filled with light (πεφώτισται) white birds (πτηνά) should be sacrificed (θύειν) as whole burnt-offerings, and the blood should be let run round upon the altars; to the gods of the sea (θαλασσίοις) black birds cast alive into the waves. To the gods of the heaven (οὐρανίοις) and ether (αἰθερίοις) the limbs of white victims are to be consecrated and, in this case, the remaining parts are to be eaten so that we participate with these givers of good things: the others are but averters of evil. The heavenly gods are also called gods of the stars (ἀστραίους).'' Porphyry then goes on to explain (but this is unnecessary he thinks for the intelligent) the symbolic meaning (τῶν θυσιῶν τὰ σύμβολα) of these sacrifices.

15. More follows from the *Philosophy from Oracles* including a further reference to the "Chaldees and far-famed Hebrews."

16. Ἀκήκοας πόσος πόνος, ἵν' ὑπὲρ σώματός τις τὰ καθάρσια θύσῃ, οὐχ ὅτι τῆς ψυχῆς τὴν σωτηρίαν ἐξεύροι;

17. The same sentiments are found in *Praep. euang.* IV, 14, 8, this time taken from *De abstinentia*. Porphyry, of course, uses the same topics in different works.

18. XIV, 10, 5.

19. Numenius, *On the Good*, apud *Praep. euang.* IX, 7, 1, speaks of the Brachmans, Jews, Magi, and Egyptians holding doctrines in common with Plato.

20. So similar is the apologetic of Augustine's DCD and Eusebius's *Praep. euang.* (e.g., *Praep. euang.* I, 2, 1ff., justification for abandoning ancestral gods, fulfillment of prophecies, Christianizing of whole world, deliverance from demons, reduction of savagery of war) and so similar the prominence they give to Porphyry's *Philosophy from Oracles / De regressu animae* that one cannot but wonder if Augustine had access to the *Praep. euang.*, pace B. Altaner, *Kleine Patristische Schriften* (Berlin, 1967), p. 258.

21. Op. cit., pp. 449ff. He relates it to n. 48(= 48a); see following note.

22. E.g., nn. 48 and 48a in R. Beutler's article, "Porphyry," in RECA. I am doubtful about the existence of these separately from the *Philosophy from Oracles*.

23. Cf. nn. 4. 1; 8.

24. Cf. n. 9.

25. Hadot, art. cit., p. 239, saw only opposition between these two works. He is not so sure now (cf. op. cit., p. 482) of the evolution of Porphyry's thought. The *Philosophy from Oracles* does speak of a way of salvation for all; it does speak of Porphyry's failure to find that way. The absence of the term *inductio* is not important since: (i) we are dealing with sparse fragments and (ii) the very reference to the Chaldaeans implies it. Similarly, one cannot insist that the Indi appear in the fragments; and there is mention of moral purgation. It would appear also from *Praep. euang.* V, 14, 4: "If the path of virtue and philosophy is sufficient for a happy and blessed life" (τοῦ κατ' ἀρετήν, καὶ φιλοσοφίαν τρόπου πρὸς εὐδαίμονα καὶ μακάριον αὐταρκους τυγχάνοντος βίον;); (a text, I would say, from the *Philosophy from Oracles*) that the theme of philosophy, that is for Porphyry Platonic philosophy, as sufficient at least for the few was treated of in the *Philosophy from Oracles*.

26. I quote normally from Porphyry's *Philosophy from Oracles* as found mostly in Eusebius's *Praep. euang.* (ed. Mras). G. Wolff's edition of the work, *Philosophia ex oraculis haurienda* (Berlin, 1856) [Ed. note: recently reprinted], is now inadequate and is not easily accessible. A list of sources, including Eusebius, is given by Wolff on pp. 244f.

27. P. Hadot, *Porphyre et Victorinus*, vols. I, II (Paris, 1968).
28. J. Bidez, *Vie de Porphyre* (Gand, 1913).
29. Op. cit., I, pp. 475f.
30. O. du Roy, *L'Intelligence et la foi en la Trinité selon saint Augustin* (Paris, 1966).
31. E.g. Hadot, op. cit. I, 86, 475f.; A. Solignac, ArPh (Juillet-Septembre, 1968), p. 493.
32. Cf. Hadot, op. cit., I, 26, 89ff., 95–108, 257–72, 309ff.
33. R I, 1–4.
34. See my *Against the Academics*, ACW XII (1950), p. 181 and the reference to Courcelle's supporting view.
35. III, 43.
36. *Porphyry's Philosophy from Oracles in Augustine*, pp. 171–76, including the footnotes. Cf. also *Against the Academics*, pp. 177f. (nn. 24, 26, 29); p. 184 n. 63; pp. 186f. (nn. 10, 11); pp. 193f. (n. 61).
37. Some of these may be consulted (sometimes in the Greek equivalent) in Hadot, op. cit., II; Indices III, IV, and V.
38. Cf. Hadot, op. cit., I, p. 183 n. 4. See n. 42 below.
39. Cf. SO I, 24 and R 1. 4, 3; cf. nn. 51, 54.
40. Cf. DBV 10; DOR II, 51.
41. Cf. Hadot, op. cit., I, 387 n. 4.
42. Cf. ibid., p. 183 nn. 4f. for σπέρμα and σπινθήρ.
43. Cf. ibid., p. 287 n. 3.
44. Cf. ibid., p. 274.
45. Translated by E. H. Gifford (Oxford, 1903).
46. The preparatory training, with much emphasis on numbers, is described as *Pythagorae disciplina* in DOR II, 53. In the *Philosophy from Oracles* the Father is called number (cf. Wolff, p. 147 and n. 2. Cf. DOR II, 43: "suspicari coepit se ipsam fortasse numerum esse eum ipsum, quo cuncta numerarentur." E. R. Dodds, "New Light on the 'Chaldaean Oracles,'" HThR LIV (1961), pp. 269ff., makes a strong case for Numenius, usually called the Pythagorean, a source for the philosophy associated with the Chaldaean Oracles.
47. Cf. Eusebius, *Praep. euang.* V, 8, 12: "an emanation from the heavenly power (Apollo) having entered into an organized and living body uses the soul as a basis, and through the body, as its organ, utters speech"—comments Porphyry on an oracle in the *Philosophy from Oracles*.
48. 12, 17, 19.
49. *Porphyry's Philosophy from Oracles in Augustine*, pp. 80f.
50. Cf. DCD X, 29: "omne corpus esse fugiendum, ut anima possit beata permanere cum Deo; quo modo ergo nec umquam soluetur a corpore nec umquam carebit beatitudine, si, ut beata sit anima, corpus est omne fugiendum; uosque etiam dicatis esse in caelestibus inmortalia corpora inmortaliter beatorum: quid est quod, ut beati simus, omne corpus fugiendum opinamini?" These texts leave no doubt but that the prevailing sense of the *omne corpus fugiendum* in DCD X and XXII, 26 is eschatological.
51. Cf. CA II, 7, for a similar passage; cf. n. 39 supra.
52. Phrases such as *dum hoc corpus ago* are, of course, common in the *Dialogues*: cf. CA I, 9, 23; DOR I, 24; II, 7, 26; SO I, 6, 24.
53. Op. cit., pp. 24f.
54. See nn. 14, 26.

55. See p. 5 and R I, 1, 4.
56. Cf. CA III, 3.
57. See pp. 128, 132.
58. But in DCD X, 10, Proteus is equated with Satan.
59. Cf. J. J. O'Meara, op. cit., pp. 174, 166, 10f.
60. *Unguenti guttas paucissimas* in this passage may be glossed by *quaedam numero paucissima, ui potentissima* of DOR II, 45. Cf. also J. J. O'Meara, op. cit., pp. 173f.
61. Cf. J. J. O'Meara, op. cit., p. 88.
62. *Porphyry's Philosophy from Oracles in Augustine* (Paris, 1959) [and Part I this volume].
63. This is found in DCD X, 11. It is formally introduced at the beginning of the chapter and Augustine specifically states that he is quoting from its end at the end of his own chapter (Eusebius, *Praep. euang.* V, 10, curiously ends his quotation from the *Letter* at this point with the same extract). It is well known that Porphyry repeated themes from one work to another. In DCD X—both in chapter 11 and elsewhere—the phenomenon of the gods being compelled to respond against their will (see p. 128) is reported—but one would not be justified in concluding that every reference to this phenomenon was related to the *Letter to Anebo*. From chapter 9, however, to 32 (exclusive of 11) Augustine seems to be quoting from one *disputatio* (9) from which he quotes much (29). It is sometimes asserted that Porphyry appears more critical of demonology in the *Letter* than in the *Philosophy from Oracles*. It remains true that in the *Letter* he is still ambiguous in his attitude and uncritical.
64. Nor *fully* by me in op. cit., p. 104.
65. Eusebius, *Praep. euang.* IV, 6, 4: ἀρχόμενος ἦ μὴν ἀληθεύειν ἐπόμνυται λέγων οὕτως. βέβαιος δὲ καὶ μόνιμος....
66. ἐπ' ὀλίγον δὲ καὶ τῆς χρηστικῆς ἁψόμεθα πραγματείας, ἥτις πρὸς ... τὴν ἄλλην κάθαρσιν.
67. *Theurgia* is explained almost immediately as *consecrationes theurgicae, quas teletas vocant*. Τελεταί were described by Chrysippus as "discourses about the gods" (Arnim, ed. *Stoicorum Veterum Fragmenta* II, 1008)—which would reduce their unacceptability. Lewy, op. cit., p. 464, writes: "The term theurgy 'designates in the writings of the later Neoplatonists both a practical method of union with the gods and the supra-rational union with the highest order of the divine attainable to a human being.'" Cf. O'Meara, op. cit., pp. 35f., 98, 104, 107, 109, 121, 124f.
68. Wolff, 149 n. 6; O'Meara, op. cit., pp. 101–45; P. Hadot, art. cit., pp. 206–44.
69. O'Meara, ibid., pp. 101–15.
70. Op. cit. and art. cit. Cf. Eusebius, ibid., IV, 6, 3ff.
71. O'Meara, op. cit., pp. 33–37; Cf. Hadot, op. cit., I, 482.
72. Cf. p. 16.
73. Cf. O'Meara, op. cit., p. 123; Wolff, pp. 144–46—he attributes the passage in Augustine at this point to the *Philosophy from Oracles*; but on p. 243, to the *De regressu animae*. It clearly belongs to the *Philosophy from Oracles*.
74. Cf. Eusebius, *Praep. euang.* IV, 9f.
75. Cf. Eusebius, ibid., IV, 5. Cf. O'Meara, op. cit., p. 113f.
76. Cf. Eusebius, ibid., IV, 6, 3ff.
77. Cf. Hadot, art. cit., p. 208. He quotes Lewy to this effect also. E. R.

Dodds, "New Light on the 'Chaldaean Oracles,'" HThR LIV (1961), p. 267 is not convincing.

78. Cf. Eusebius, op. cit., V, 14, 4; DOR II passim.
79. Cf. Eusebius, ibid., IX, 10.
80. This does not mean that I think that this was the only work of Porphyry that Augustine had then read, or that he had not read Plotinus: of course he had read some Plotinus, at least in translation.

Chapter 14. Exegesis of Contra Academicos II, 5

1. Cf. J. J. O'Meara, *Against the Academics*, ACW XII (1950), p. 161 n. 102; p. 170 nn. 11, 14, 15, and the other references given there; O. du Roy, *L'Intelligence de la foi en la Trinité selon saint Augustin* (Paris, 1966), p. 69 n. 5.
2. R. O'Connell, *St. Augustine's Early Theory of Man* A.D. *386–391* (Harvard, 1969). I owe the estimate of the number of treatises to my pupil, F. Van Fleteren, O.S.A.
3. Cf. du Roy, loc. cit.
4. Cf. J. J. O'Meara, op. cit., p. 169 n. 5, and *Charter of Christendom* (New York, 1961), pp. 67ff.
5. *The Oxford Classical Dictionary* (Oxford, 1949), s.v. Neoplatonism.
6. CA III, 41.
7. Cf. *Les Confessions* BA XIII (1962), p. 662. I normally use this edition here.
8. Best known instances are the "Vision of Ostia" in C IX, 10, 23ff. and the "sero te amaui" in C X, 27, 38—but there are many others in the *Confessions*: e.g., VI, 6, 9; 10, 17; 11, 8.
9. Cf. CA I, 1; II, 4–7, 22; III, 4, 42; DBV 1–4, 35; DOR I, 3, 32; II, 31, 51; cf. J. J. O'Meara, "Porphyry's *Philosophy from Oracles* in Eusebius's *Praeparatio euangelica* and Augustine's *Dialogues of Cassiciacum*," chap. 13, this volume, where much the same material is mentioned but from a Porphyrian aspect.
10. I do not accept that material of a later period in a writer's life may never be used for the understanding of an earlier work. I have touched on the matter in a discussion of du Roy's op. cit., in AS 1 (1970) [= chap. 21, this volume].
11. Cf. J. J. O'Meara, *Porphyry's Philosophy from Oracles in Augustine* (Paris, 1959), pp. 1f.
12. Cf. J. J. O'Meara, *Against the Academics*, p. 69 and corresponding notes; du Roy, loc. cit.
13. CA III, 43.
14. Cf. *Charter of Christendom*, pp. 73f.
15. E. Gilson, *History of Christian Philosophy in the Middle Ages* (London, 1955), p. 67.
16. We shall see much of this *en passant*: such phrases as "subito et inopinato" (II, 4) and "exarsi ad imitandum" (V, 10) constantly recur.
17. The BA translation (Trehorel et Bouissou), renders "nous découvrit peu à peu ce grand homme"—significantly, perhaps, almost not allowing an equation of *insinuans* with the *guttas . . . instillarunt* of CA II, 5.
18. This is briefly adverted to on pp. 14f.
19. Other phrases in this section of C VIII interesting to our purpose are: "umerisque *liberioribus* pinnas recipiunt . . . confundebar *pudore horribili vehementer*" (VII, 18); "dixi *nescio qua* talia . . . *taceret attonitus* me intuens. *neque*

enim *solita* sonabam . . . me abstulerat *tumultus pectoris*"; "tu sciebas, *ego* autem *non*" (VIII, 19).

20. This passage owes something to Plotinus, *Ennead* I, 6, 8; cf. CA III, 3; C I, 18, 28 (which also depends on the parable of the prodigal son), and DCD IX, 17. Cf. Courcelle, RechAug pp. 126ff.

21. In the preceding section (25) we find:"*uolens et uersans* me in *uinculo* meo donec *abrumperetur* totum, quo iam exiguo tenebar."

22. Following W. Theiler, *Gnomon* XXV (1953), pp. 113–22. Likewise for "cautissime" at the end of the passage.

23. Cf. C, BA XIII, p. 767. I do not accept the suggestion that "quidam" refers to something "of another (non-Christian) world": this would leave "hortulus quidam" (C VIII, 8, 19) and "sub quadam fici arbore," for example, without meaning. Rather it is a characteristic vagueness in relation to something well known employed to heighten a crisis. Cf. J. J. O'Meara, *The Young Augustine* (London, 1954), pp. 9f.

24. "Libri pleni" is found in C V, 7, 12 and 10, 19 in connection with Manichaean books.

25. Cf. *Confessiones,* BA XIV, p. 535.

26. Cf. n. 7 supra.

27. Cf. Courcelle, RechAug (1950), p. 138. Courcelle tends to date the *De Isaac*, the *Hexameron, In Lucam,* and *In Psalmum* CXVIII to early 386 (cf. pp. 123f.).

28. The themes mentioned in this paragraph are, of course, used in passages that show philosophic or scriptural influence or both together—as may be seen from C III, 4, 7f. and the whole of VIII.

29. But cf. Cicero, *Tusc. Disp.,* I, 73: "itaque dubitans, circumspectans haesitans . . . uehitur oratio."

30. Cf. the emphasis upon his unconsciousness of providential action in C VIII, 8, 19 and especially 12, 28.

31. I myself in "Arripui, Aperui, et Legi" [see supra, chapter 2], although I anticipate some of the points of this present study, have been misled in a number of particulars.

Chapter 15. Neoplatonism of Augustine

1. ACW XII (Washington, D.C., 1950), p. 23.

2. "St. Augustine's '*notitia sui*' related to Aristotle and the early Neoplatonists," *Augustiniana* XXVII (1977), p. 102.

3. A. Ernout, *Lucrèce* (Paris, no date), p. 26: "même si l'explication était fausse, elle est bonne du moment qu'elle procure le résultat cherché."

4. CA III, 43.

5. Ibid., 396f.

6. RIPh XCII (1970), pp. 321–37.

7. *Recherches sur les Confessions de saint Augustin* (Paris, 1950), pp. 157ff.

8. Augustine, C VII, 17, 23 (slightly rearranged).

9. Ibid., 9, 25.

10. DCD XIV, 28.

11. Plotinus, *Enn.* V, 2, 1 (Henry-Schwyzer).

12. DCD XIX, 23.

13. Ibid., X, 32 (Loeb translation).

14. *Kleine patristische Schriften,* herausgegeben von Günter Glockmann (Texte und Untersuchungen 83) (Berlin, 1967).
15. P. Agaësse and A. Solignac, BA XLVII, XLVIX (Paris, 1972); J. H. Taylor, ACW 41, 42 (New York, 1982).
16. In the *Saint Augustine Lecture 1977,* Villanova University, Pennsylvania (Villanova, 1981).
17. Plotinus, *Enn.* V, 3, 13 (MacKenna translation).
18. *Sententiae* XXV, 11, 4 (Mommert).
19. DOR II, 16, 44.
20. DGnL V, 16, 34.
21. DCD XXII, 29.

Chapter 16. Parting from Porphyry

1. 987B, 992A.
2. See XX, 16.
3. E 187, 10.
4. 991C–992A.
5. DCD XX, 14; I Cor VII, 31f.
6. 986D: see also 992A.
7. 804B–805B.
8. VI, 19, 30–VI, 28, 39.
9. DCD XXII, 4; XIX, 22.
10. Ibid., XIX, 23; X, 23.
11. Ibid., X, 29, 32.
12. H. Lewy, *Chaldaean Oracles and Theurgy* (Cairo, 1956), pp. 449ff.
13. J. J. O'Meara, *Porphyry's Philosophy from Oracles in Augustine* (Paris, 1959), pp. 1ff.
14. DCD XXII, 26.
15. Rom I, 21ff.
16. *REAug* XXXI (1985), p. 369.
17. XII, 1, 1.
18. I, 1, 3.
19. P. Courcelle, *Les lettres grecques en Occident de Macrobe à Cassiodore* (Paris, 1943), p. 167; "Saint Augustin photinien à Milan" (C. VII, 19, 25), in RicSRel I (1954), pp. 63–71; J. J. O'Meara, op. cit., passim.
20. *An. quant.* XXX, 76.
21. (Scholars Press: 1979), pp. 79ff.
22. In E XI, 2 (c. 390) he adds the term *mystica* to the *susceptio hominis,* found in *De quantitate animae.* In the contemporary *De uera religione* he speaks of Christ as *totum hominem* and *uero homine* (XV, 30) and of his incarnation, death, resurrection, ascension, and sitting (*consessus*) at the right hand of the Father.
23. IV, 7.
24. See Courcelle, op. cit., loc. cit.
25. DCD XXII, 26.
26. R I, 4, 2.
27. R I, 1, 2.
28. R I, 3, 2.
29. II, 5, 16.
30. Op. cit., pp. 171–76; "Porphyry's *Philosophy from Oracles* in Eusebius's

Praeparatio Euangelica and Augustine's *Dialogues of Cassiciacum,"* chapter 13 this volume. See also DOR II, 9, 27.
31. CA III, 20, 43. See chap. 11 this volume.
32. DOR II, 5, 16; 9, 26.
33. Ibid., *ratio aptior eruditis*.
34. DQ VII, 12.
35. Ibid., XXXIII, 76.
36. 1 Cor III, 2; see also Heb V, 12f.
37. DOR II, 5, 15; 9, 26.
38. Loc. cit.
39. See C XII, 27, 37.
40. 5.
41. SO II, 14, 26.
42. See the discussion of the Porphyrian *pneuma* in *La Genèse au sens littéral*, BA XLIX (1972), pp. 559–66.
43. VII, 21, 27.
44. C VIII, 1, 1.
45. Ibid., VIII, 5, 10.
46. I, 4.
47. Rom XIII, 14.

Chapter 17. Creation and Fall

1. In *de Genesi contra Manichaeos* II, in 388; in *de Genesi imperfectus liber*, c. A.D. 391; in C XII and XIII, about 400; and DGnL XII, A.D. 401–15.
2. P. Duhem, *Le système du Monde*, vol. II (Paris, 1954) 411.
3. The text is in PL 34.245–486; CSEL 28/1, 3–435; and BA 48/49, eds. P. Agaësse and A. Solignac.
4. *Generation of Animals* I, 20, 15.
5. VI, 24.
6. 1141f.
7. 34, 2f.
8. I Cor. 11, 3ff.
9. Cf. the famous *Satire* VI.
10. Gen. 1, 26f.
11. See J. O'Meara, op. cit., pp. 42ff.
12. *En.* III, 2, 1.
13. Cf. J. O'Meara, op. cit., p. 44.
14. Cf. Plotinus, *En.* V, 1, 6, 28; 2, 1; 3, 8, 19–23.
15. DGnL IV, 32, 50.
16. Ibid., III, 20, 31f.
17. Cf. DGnL (BA 48), p. 627.
18. Ibid., p. 626.
19. I Cor. 11, 7.
20. DGnL III, 22, 34.
21. Gen. 1, 28ff.
22. Gen. 2, 7ff.
23. DGnL VI, 12, 20.
24. Ibid., IX, 18, 34.
25. Cf. *De prin.* IV, 16; DGnL (BA 49), pp. 497, 694.

26. Cf. DGnL (BA 49), pp. 518f.
27. Ibid., p. 521.
28. DGnL IX, 5, 9.
29. *De bono coniugali* III, 3.
30. DGnL XI, 41, 56.
31. Ibid., XI, 42, 59.

Chapter 18. Return of the Soul . . .

1. In the first instance one might consult the articles of G. Mathon, "L'utilisation des textes de saint Augustin par Jean Scot Erigène dans son *De predestinatione*," AugM III (Paris, 1954), pp. 419–28; and R. Russell, "Some Augustinian Influences in Eriugena's *De diuisione naturae*"; *The Mind of Eriugena*, J. J. O'Meara and L. Bieler, eds. (Dublin, 1973), pp. 31–40.
2. H. Bett, *Johannes Scotus Erigena* (New York, 1964), p. 158; cf. 157 n. 2 and 160 n. 1.
3. Art. cit., p. 428.
4. J. J. O'Meara, *Eriugena* (Cork, 1969), p. 29.
5. I cite according to Migne, PL, but for the first two books of the work I use the text of I. P. Sheldon-Williams, *De diuisione naturae* (Dublin, vol. I, 1968; vol. II, 1972).
6. M. Cappuyns, "Note sur le problème de la vision béatifique au IXème siècle," RThAM I (1929), p. 107.
7. E. Gilson, *History of Christian Philosophy in the Middle Ages* (London, 1955), p. 67. Cf. J. J. O'Meara, ibid., p. 29 and n. 41; and "Plotinus and Augustine," chapter 14 of this volume.
8. DOR II, 16.
9. DCD XI, 22.
10. "Augustine the Artist and the *Aeneid*," *Mélanges offerts à Mademoiselle Christine Mohrmann* (Utrecht/Anvers, 1963), pp. 253f.: chap. 5 this volume.
11. VI, 4; 9.
12. IX, 8.
13. III, 43.
14. Ibid., 425.
15. A favourite term of Augustine in this kind of connection; cf. *De utilitate credendi* X.
16. Another favourite word in Augustine, especially when he is quoting or referring to Porphyry's attitude to the body.
17. The whole subject of return of the soul and *visio Dei* is discussed in, e.g., *De diuisione naturae* PL CXXII, coll. 447–51, 876–82, 926, 977f., 987, 990–94. Gale, 1681 (apud PL CXXII, 96f.), included *De Visione Dei Tractatus* among the works of Eriugena the authenticity of which was unquestioned. Mabillon, 1632–1707 (ibid., 97C), had reported that he had seen a manuscript of Clairmarais near St. Omer of that title ascribed to Eriugena, with the opening words: "omnes sensus corporei ex conjunctione nascuntur animae et corporis." M. Cappuyns, art. cit., 105, and *Jean Scot Erigène* (Louvain, 1933), p. 98, employs a suggestion that the work in question may have been simply an extract of the *De diuisione naturae*. While it is true that there is no report subsequent to Mabillon's on the existence of the manuscript, the suggestion is insufficient reason for setting Gale's and Mabillon's statements aside. The

fact that Eriugena treats of the *uisio Dei* in the *De diuisione naturae* does not exclude his having treated it separately—Cappuyns's own article, after all, and his later book would be instances of precisely this!

18. 877A. "Beatus Aurelius Augustinus in decimo Exemeri sui: Primum, inquit, illud firmissime teneamus, animae naturam nec in naturam corporis conuerti, ut, quae jam fuit anima, fiat corpus, nec in naturam animae irrationalis, ut quae fuit anima hominis, fiat *pecudis*, nec in naturam Dei, ut quae fuit anima, fiat quod est Deus, atque ita vicissim nec corpus, nec animam irrationabilem, nec substantiam quae Deus est, conuerti et fieri animam humanam." *Pecudis* may hint at a common preoccupation of his with Porphyry. Cf. DCD X, 30.

19. 990D.
20. Ibid., 991D.
21. XX, 14.
22. 993B.
23. R II, 67. For a fuller analysis see BA XXXVII: *La Cité de dieu* (Paris, 1960), pp. 853–57. It is to be noted that in his earliest treatment of the problem of the *visio Dei* (E XCII, dated 408) he seemed to exclude, as does Eriugena, *corporal* vision of God of any kind. Later (E CXLVII and CXLVIII, both dated 413) he explained that he had been speaking rather of the non-glorified body—he did not reject the view that the corporal eyes of the glorified body might be so spiritualized as to be capable of seeing God; but he was making no pronouncement on this and insisting rather on the soul's spiritual view of God.
24. 2 Kings 5. 25–26.
25. DCD X, 29.
26. It must be added that Augustine, influenced by Porphyry, entertained for some time an idea of "spirit" and "spiritual" which might open up possibilities of reconciling his view with that of the Greeks. The idea of "spirit" is especially to be seen in *De Genesi ad litteram* (A.D. 401–414), which one observes is a favourite source of reference, under the title of *Hexameron* however, in this part of *De diuisione naturae*. *Spiritus* is there defined (XII, 9) as "uis animae quaedam mente inferior, ubi corporalium rerum similitudines exprimuntur." Its object is a *substantia spiritalis* or *spiritales formae corporalibus similes* (XII, 32). These real substances are neither corporeal nor immaterial: "spiritus" itself, however, is immaterial and is directly affected only by immaterial agents. Augustine does not follow these ideas in the later *De ciuitate Dei* (e.g. XXI, 10). Cf. J. H. Taylor, "The Meaning of *Spiritus* in St. Augustine's *De Genesi* XII," *The Modern Schoolman* XXVI (1949), pp. 211–18.
27. Art. cit., p. 105 n. 29.
28. Augustine's text, however, reads: "Deum . . . per corpora quae gestabimus et quae conspiciemus quaqua uersum oculos duxerimus, clarissima perspicuitate uideamus" (DCD XXII, 29).
29. Dräseke denies that this is a quotation from Maximus: cf. Sheldon-Williams's ed., ad loc. Cf. however J. M. Alonzo, "Teofanía y visión beata en Escoto Erigena," *Rev. Española de Teologia* X (1950), pp. 372f. and n. 40; T. Gregory, "Note sulla dottrina della 'teofanie' in Giovanni Scoto Eriugena," *Studi Medievali* IV (1963), p. 83 and n. 25.
30. Sheldon-Williams, ad loc., failed to trace this quotation in Augustine. He suggests DBV 34 as a possible "source." Cf. C XII, 15, 20; DOR II, 16, 27;

CA III, 42; cf. Alonzo, ibid., n. 41. The extent to which a text of either Maximus or Augustine might be modified by Eriugena has to be kept in mind. Cf. R. Roques on this point: "La méthode selon laquelle un auteur du Moyen Age peut, en toute apparence de bonne foi, 'expliquer avec révérence' des auctoritates dont il s'inspire sans doute, mais qu'il 'façonne' aussi à sa propre image pour une très large part" [Extrait de l'Annuaire de l'E.P.H.E. LXXVII (1969–70), p. 311].

31. For an account of the use of the images of light and fire in this kind of context see J. Pépin, "Stilla aquae modica multo infusa vino, ferrum ignitum, luce perfusus aer. L'origine de trois comparaisons familières à la théologie mystique médiévale," *Divinitas* XI (1967), pp. 331–75(= 1–47). For the use of the image of light in Plotinus, see W. Beierwaltes, "Die Metaphysik des Lichtes in der Philosophie Plotins," *Zeitschrift für philos. Forschung* XV (1961), pp. 334–62.

32. Eriugena cites (881Aff.) the separate unified presence in all substances of *essentia, virtus,* and *naturalis operatio*. He instances also the many species in a genus and numbers in the monad—*sine confusione, vel mixtura, vel compositione*. 879Af. goes over the same ground, but incorporates, in addition, the second mode of being (413D–414C): "inferiora uero a superioribus naturaliter attrahantur, et absorbentur, non ut non sint, sed ut in eis plus salventur, et subsistant et unum sint."

33. E CXXXVII, 3, 11. For the dual aspect of fire—light and burning, cf. DCD XII, 4.

34. As quoted in *De diuisione naturae* 450C. This quotation differs by a word from that given in 447B and both widely (cf. n. 28) from DCD XXII, 29.

Chapter 19. Soul-Body Relationship

1. E XCII, 3.
2. E CXLVII, 37.
3. E CXLVIII, 6f., 10, 12, 15.
4. Cf. DGnL VIII–XII, BA XLIX (1972), p. 565: indebtedness to its authors, P. Agaësse and A. Solignac, is acknowledged, as also to J. H. Taylor's "The Meaning of *Spiritus* in St. Augustine's *de Genesi* XII," *The Modern Schoolman* XXVI (1949), pp. 211–18.
5. DGnL XII, 18f.
6. Ibid., 49.
7. Ibid., 51.
8. Cf. *Aph.* IV, XIII, XVI, XL pp. 35–39 (Mommert); H. Dörrie, *Porphyrios' Symmikta Zetemata,* p. 85.
9. Cf. Synesius, *De insomniis* VII, p. 156, 6–11 (Terzaghi). Porphyry, *Aph.* XXIX.
10. Cf. ibid., I–XI, XXX, XXXI, XL p. 38, XLII.
11. Cf. G. Verbeke, *L'évolution de la doctrine du pneuma* (Louvain, 1945), pp. 364–68 and authorities quoted there.
12. DCD X, 9.
13. Cf. G. Verbeke, op. cit., p. 504.
14. Cf. J. H. Taylor, art. cit., p. 218.
15. Cf. *Aph.* XXIX.
16. DGnL XII, 60.

17. Ibid., XII, 68.
18. Ibid., XII, 61.
19. XXI, 10.
20. *De diu. nat.* 877A.
21. Ibid.
22. Ibid., 990D–991D.
23. Ibid., 992A.
24. Ibid., 993A.
25. DCD XXII, 29. Cf. R II, 67 and Eriugena, *De diu. nat.* 447Bff.
26. DCD XXII, 29.
27. *De diu. nat.* 449Aff.
28. Cf. E CXXXVII, 2; DCD XII, 4.
29. *De diu. nat.* 450Bf.

Chapter 20. *De Genesi ad litteram* in *Periphyseon*

1. I refer normally here to PL rather than to the edition of I. P. Sheldon-Williams (Dublin, vol. I, 1968; vol. II, 1972), only because most of the references are to passages in books III–V, which—apart from III (Dublin, 1981)—have not yet been published in the Dublin edition and since that edition can conveniently be used from references to PL.
2. Cf. R II, 24, 1: "plura quaesita quam inuenta sunt et eorum quae inuenta sunt pauciora firmata, cetera uero ita posita, uelut adhuc requirenda sint."
3. IV, 28, 45.
4. DGnL VIII, 2, 5.
5. C XII, 18, 27.
6. Paris, 1972.
7. The list in M. Cappuyns, *Jean Scot Erigène* (Paris/Louvain, 1933), p. 388, is incorrect in mentioning 931A and 945B.
8. Op. cit. I, 5; cf. n. 19 infra.
9. I, 2, 4ff.
10. P. 3, line 1; cf. PL 693C.
11. Cf. the two preceding notes.
12. "Eriugena's Use of Augustine in His Teaching on the Return of the Soul and the Vision of God," chapter 18 this volume.
13. Text as in Sheldon-Williams.
14. The significance of *conuertere* in e.g., the *Confessiones* and *De ciuitate Dei*, is to be traced back to the series of fundamental ideas here being mentioned and to their background in Plotinus (cf. *Enn.* V, 1, 6, 7; 2, 1; 3, 8).
15. See further BA XLVIII, pp. 657ff. (two moments of creation); pp. 672–74 (the "reasons" in the Word); and pp. 648f. (seeing the "reasons" in the Word).
16. DGnL VI, 19, 30–28, 39.
17. I.e., here, Gregory of Nyssa; cf. M. Cappuyns, op. cit., pp. 176ff.
18. Cf. Gregory of Nyssa, *Orat. Catechet.* PG XLV, 33B–36B.
19. Cf. n. 8 supra.
20. "L'utilisation des textes de saint Augustin par Jean Scot Erigène dans son *De predestinatione*," AugM III (Paris, 1954), pp. 419–28.
21. H. Bett, *Johannes Scotus Erigena* (New York, 1964), p. 158.
22. E. Gilson, *History of Christian Philosophy in the Middle Ages* (London, 1955), p. 127.

Chapter 21. Research Techniques

1. V. Goldschmidt, *Les Dialogues de Platon* (Paris, 1963), pp. xiiiff.
2. "Citations de Porphyre chez Augustin," REAug 6 (1960), p. 244.
3. Op. cit., p. 15.
4. P. 19.
5. Paris, 1959, p. 2.
6. P. 97.
7. PP. 185f.
8. Cf. p. 312, n. 5 especially. He does not take account of my *Philosophy from Oracles in Augustine*, pp. 171ff.
9. P. 476.
10. Cf. e.g., p. 201.
11. Cf. A. Mandouze, *Saint Augustin* (Paris, 1968), p. 535, n. 1: "Je ne pense pas qu'il soit de bonne méthode de partir de l'idée que 'le Christ Incarné tient un rôle secondaire dans les écrits de Cassiciacum.' . . . je dirais alors que j'ai été frappé plus par le caractere à priori de ces analyses que par la force contraignante qui peu se dégager d'un dossier objectif."
12. E.g., pp. 97, n. 1., 323 n. 5, 324.
13. P. 97 n. 1.
14. PP. 11–109.
15. Op. cit., p. 684 n. 1.
16. Loc. cit.
17. The Parmenides of Plato and the Origin of the Neoplatonic "One," *Classical Quarterly* XXII (1928), p. 129.
18. Cf. e.g., as quoted by Hadot, op. cit., pp. 87f.
19. P. 482. Cf. p. 493.
20. P. 22.
21. P. 481.
22. P. 27.
23. P. 25. Cf. W. Theiler, *Porphyrios und Augustin*, p. 4: "Erscheint bei einem nachplotinischen Neuplatoniker ein Lehrstück, das nach Inhalt, Form und Zusammenhang sich mit einem solchen bei Augustin vergleichen lässt, aber nicht oder nicht im selben Mass mit einem bei Plotin, so darf es als porphyrisch gelten."
24. P. 32.
25. Mandouze also emphasizes the necessity for extended extracts: cf. op. cit., p. 33.
26. P. 38.
27. DCD X, 29 and 32.
28. PP. 482f.
29. "Ton" and *attitude* have seriously been used as a deciding factor by Hadot (art. cit., pp. 209, 243—referred to, apparently without dissent by du Roy, p. 71 n. 3 and Mandouze, op. cit., p. 477 n. 1) and du Roy, p. 400. When Mandouze wrote: "Je sais bien que le ton, l'accent, le mouvement sont choses qui, aux yeux des philologues, n'ont pas valeur de preuve" (AugM I [1954] p. 83), he implies great need for restraint in using such evidence.
30. Virgil, *Eclogues* VI, 31–40 and 41ff.
31. Charles Segal, "Some Recent Trends in Classical Literary Studies," *Arethusa* I.1 (1968), p. 19.

32. DBV 36.
33. CA II, 9.

Chapter 22. Mysticism of Augustine

1. Olivier du Roy, *L'Intelligence de la foi en la Trinité selon saint Augustin* (1966), p. 543; A. Mandouze, *Saint Augustin: L'Aventure de la Raison et de la Grâce* (1968), p. 797—both published by Etudes Augustiniennes (Paris).

2. P. 21.

3. A. Solignac writes: "On peut se demander, s'il est de bonne méthode, dans une étude qui se veut rigoureusement chronologique, de commencer par l'analyse de la conversion. Celle-ci en effet ne peut se faire qu'à l'aide des *Confessions*. Or, même si l'on admet l'historicité globale de cet ouvrage, il n'en reste pas moins qu'Augustin y mêle au récit des événements une réflexion d'ordre spéculatif qui correspond aux idées de l'évêque en 397 et non à celles du converti de 387" *ArPh* (Juillet-Septembre 1968), p. 490. Du Roy is aware of this point (p. 105), but this does not make it less faulty in method.

4. P. Hadot, "Citations de Porphyre chez Augustin," *REAug* VI (1960), p. 240.

5. See the report of a Colloquium on "Research Techniques in Augustinian Studies" held at Villanova University, Pennsylvania, on Dec. 6, 1968 [= chap. 21, this volume].

6. P. 15.

7. *Saint Augustin et la fin de la culture antique* (Paris, 1938), p. 245.

8. Cf. du Roy's own references (pp. 17f.) to V. Goldschmidt, *Les Dialogues de Platon, structure et méthode dialectique* (Paris, 1947 and 1963); *Le système stoïcien et l'idée de temps* (Paris, 1953); "Exégèse et axiomatique chez saint Augustin," in *Hommage à Martial Guéroult: L'histoire de la philosophie, ses problèmes, ses méthodes* (Paris, 1965), pp. 4–32; and "Temps historique et temps logique dans l'interprétation des systèmes philosophiques," *Actes du XIe congrès international de philosophie* (Amsterdam/Louvain, 1953), vol. XII, pp. 7–13. Goldschmidt discusses (*Les Dialogues de Platon*) (1963, p. 19), the "history" of the structural method—his quotation from N. Hartmann (*Ontologie* III, p. 118) is à propos: "la connaissance des choses n'attend pas la théorie de la connaissance."

9. *Porphyry's Philosophy from Oracles in Augustine* (Paris, 1959), p. 2.

10. Art. cit., p. 207.

11. It is impossible, however [*pace* du Roy (p. 312 n. 2)] from CA II, 8; R I, 13, 7 (a relevant text to which du Roy makes no reference); and E XV, 1, not to conclude that the work was *projected* (my minimum insistence) in A.D. 386. CA II, 8 and R I, 13, 7 are *compatible* with his having *completed* the book then, but do not prove this against R I, 13, 1. See A. Mandouze, op. cit., p. 492 n. 4: "Quand en effet Augustin s'est trouvé avoir à modifier notablement ses 'intentions rédactionelles' au cours de la composition d'un ouvrage, il n'a jamais manqué de le signaler, en particulier dans les *Retractationes*. Si intellegente soit-elle, l'exégèse que fait du Roy (ibid., p. 315 n. 3) de la rubrique des *Retractationes* consacrée au *De uera religione* me parait solliciter sensiblement le texte. . . ." In the same sense, A. Solignac: "Augustin ne dit pas qu'il ait rédigé cet ouvrage en plusieurs temps" loc. cit., p. 493.

12. Du Roy must concede, however (p. 309 n. 1) that "on trouve *parfois un plan assez ferme* in matters relating to traditional doctrine. But, he says, "Il faut

distinguer la démarche rédactionnelle dans les ouvrages de recherche." There is surely a danger of subjectivism and excessive formalism in such a process. I wonder what *démarche rédactionnelle* means *exactly*?

13. P. 315 n. 3.
14. Pp. 310f.
15. E.g., DT IV, 13ff.; XIII, 24; C VII, 15; S CCXLI, 3. See my *Porphyry's Philosophy from Oracles*, pp. 102, 152, 154, 157, 163, 165, 167, and especially 160f. Cf. in general G. Madec, "Connaissance de Dieu et action de grâces. Essai sur les citations de l'Ep. aux Romains I, 18–25 dans l'oeuvre de saint Augustin," RechAug 2 (1962), 273–309; Mandouze, op. cit., pp. 504f.
16. A. Solignac, loc. cit.: "Je ne suis pas sûr non plus que la distinction des 'couches rédactionnelles' du *De uera religione* soit bien justifiée . . . la distinction d'une section anti-manichéenne et d'une section anti-porphyrienne ne s'appuie pas d'avantage sur des arguments probants." Cf. A. Mandouze, op. cit., p. 492 n. 4.
17. And now Solignac, loc. cit., p. 493.
18. CA III, 13.
19. DCD X, 32.
20. CA I, 4; DBV 35; DOR II, 15, 1.
21. "iubar . . . minus sanis uel repente apertis oculis . . . deum nulla degeneratione impedimente . . . fonte . . . plenitudine . . . liberatori animarum . . . ad deum reditus noster."
22. P. 366.
23. P. 180 n. 7.
24. I, 11; 12.
25. I have already drawn attention to CA III, 34, where there is the story of the two travellers looking for a way, one trustful being guided by a simple shepherd on the right road, the other pridefully careful being deceived by a pretentious *samardocus* and shown the wrong road through woods and trackless mountains to the region desired. It is difficult not to see here a version of the fragments of the *De regressu animae* as found DCD X, 32; and the related C VII, 26ff.; and DT IV, 13–20; and Wolff, *Philosophy from Oracles*, pp. 139ff. See my *Porphyry's Philosophy from Oracles in Augustine*, pp. 174, 166, 10f.
26. E.g., I cannot accept his translation of C IX, 3, 6, which affects the relevant fact of the date of Nebridius's death.
27. P. 132 n. 3.
28. P. 186.
29. P. 213 n. 2.
30. *Porphyry's Philosophy from Oracles in Augustine*, p. 172 and n. 2.
31. P. 312 n. 5.
32. PP. 140–42.
33. P. 180.
34. Cf. AugM I (1954), p. 80.
35. Cf. pp. 11, 35, and 698 n. 9.
36. P. 28.
37. P. 29.
38. P. 44.
39. Pp. 19, 335 n. 1.
40. Pp. 19, 114, 335.
41. Pp. 37, 333.

42. Pp. 506, 513, 376.
43. Pp. 73ff.
44. Pp. 75–79.
45. Pp. 66, 96.
46. P. 176; Cf. my *Young Augustine* (London, 1954), p. 159.
47. Pp. 306 n. 3 and 333f.
48. P. 374.
49. P. 396.
50. Pp. 406f.
51. See Mandouze, p. 176 n. 1.
52. Pp. 200ff.
53. P. 208 and n. 3.
54. P. 219.
55. P. 209.
56. P. 661.
57. P. 671 n. 1.
58. P. 674, n. 5, quoting Solignac.
59. P. 697.
60. Pp. 698f.
61. Cf. p. 248 n. 3.
62. The details are, of course, often discussed in what V. Goldschmidt has called (in another connection) *notes perpétuelles* engulfing on occasions almost two whole pages. One is surprised not to see mentioned anywhere Adolf Holl's book, *Die Welt der Zeichen bei Augustinus* (Wien, 1963). He does not seem to have understood my position, at any rate as expressed in English, on a number of points: e.g., pp. 71 n. 2; 130 n. 3; 471 n. 3.
63. P. 515.

General Index

Adam and Eve, 234, 239, 241–42
Adeodatus, 66, 85, 123, 321
Aeneas (*Aeneid*), 59–68, 81–84, 103–17, 330, 331–35
Agaësse, P., 347, 348, 351
Albinus, 321
Alfaric, P., 121, 138, 147, 148, 149, 155, 209, 316
Allen, A. W., 331
Alonzo, J. M., 350, 351
Altaner, B., 215, 342
Alypius, 42, 45, 46, 66, 130, 305, 306, 320, 323, 325
Ambrose of Milan, 45, 46, 69, 153, 154, 155, 202, 204, 206, 219, 223, 337
Anaximenes, 322
Anchises, 67
Ant(h)ony, St., 39, 42, 198, 201, 203, 204, 205, 208
Apollo's Hymn, 173–74, 185
Apuleius, 61
Aristotle, 19, 91, 123, 234, 322
Arnim, H. F. von, 344
Arnobius, 331
Athanasius, 39, 215
Aubin, P., 330
Augustine: *Confessions*, 1, 24–30, 31–38, 39–56, 103–17, 121, 122, 124, 125, 129–30, 131, 132, 133, 146–148, 200, 228, 256, 316, 320, 321, 330, 338; *Contra Academicos*, 6, 12, 17, 18, 20, 46, 54, 127–28, 129, 131, 133, 134, 135–36, 137, 141, 145, 148, 149, 155, 182, 183, 184, 187, 195–208, 225, 299, 315, 317, 318, 319, 320, 324, 325, 326; *De beata vita*, 13, 15, 19, 27, 44, 135, 148, 150, 184, 192, 197, 218, 229; *De bono coniugali*, 241, 349; *De civitate Dei*, 2, 4, 6, 7, 125–27, 132, 156, 157–65, 175, 211, 219, 246, 256; *De doctrina christiana*, 127; *De Genesi ad litteram*, 3, 53, 215, 221, 233, 240, 243, 257, 269–83, 349; *De libero arbitrio*, 14; *De ordine*, 12, 13, 14, 15, 16, 19, 20, 21, 22, 127, 135, 148, 155, 184, 185, 187, 188, 202, 205, 226, 325, 336, 337; *De quantitate animae*, 127, 155, 227; *De Trinitate*, 127, 156, 161, 257; *De vera religione*, 127, 156, 157–65, 297; *Dialogues of Cassiciacum*, 6, 11–23, 127, 131, 143, 144, 145, 146, 147, 155, 156, 179, 182, 193, 194, 195, 224, 227; *Epistulae*, 46, 128, 138, 143, 156; *Retractationes*, 127, 136, 137, 181, 191, 225, 227, 251, 320, 321; *Soliloquia*, 127, 135, 141, 142, 143, 148, 181, 191, 225, 321, 336
Ausonius, 321
autobiography, 31–33

Bailey, D. S., 331
Basil of Caesarea, 215, 237
Beatrice, P. F., 6
Becker, H., 146
Beierwaltes, W., 351
Bett, H., 349, 352
Beutler, R., 342
Bidez, J., 170, 179, 209, 321, 341, 343
Bieler, L., 31, 32, 35, 328, 349
Binchy, D., 328
Boissier, G., 6, 121, 146, 148, 209
Bolgiani, F., 303
Booth, E., 210, 212
Bouillet, M. N., 150
Bouissou, G., 49
Bousset, W., 321
Boyer, C., 148, 149, 210, 316, 335
Brown, P., 1, 221, 223, 226, 257, 305
Burnaby, J., 267

Callimachus, 59
Cappuyns, M., 244, 250, 258, 259, 349, 350, 352
Carthage, 49, 66, 86, 97, 110, 112, 122
Cassiciacum, 63, 131, 316, 323, 339
Catullus, 71, 73, 74, 101, 331

General Index

Chaldaean Oracles, 166, 169, 180, 185, 299, 345
Chaldaeans, 174, 178, 342
Chatillon, F., 209, 210
Chrysippus, 344
Cicero, 53, 155, 321, 322; *Academica*, 16, 21; *De natura deorum*, 16; *De finibus*, 16; *De oratore*, 16; *De re publica*, 257; *Hortensius*, 17, 21, 28, 29, 45, 85, 111, 112, 199; *Tusculanae Disputationes*, 16, 346
Claudianus Mamertus, 37
Clement of Alexandria, 69, 91, 322
conversion, 35, 43, 140, 146, 330, 338
Corpus Hermeticum, 312
Courcelle, P., 3, 4, 24, 31–38, 39, 45, 55, 56, 149, 150, 151, 152, 153, 154, 155, 196, 204, 205, 209, 212, 223, 259, 299, 317, 340, 343, 346
Cumont, F., 209
Curtius, E. R., 108, 324
Cyprian of Carthage, 43

Dante, 105
Day Lewis, C., 56, 115, 330
Decret, F., 305–10
demons, 168, 186
Dialog(s) as literary genre, 11–13, 317, 318
Dido, 73–76, 82, 84, 86, 100–105, 112, 331, 332
Diotima, 91
Dodds, E. R., 195, 290, 343, 340, 345
Doerrie, H., 167, 351
Dokkum, T., 318, 319
Donatists, 69, 88, 257
Donatus Suetonius *Vita*, 74
Dudley, D. R., 70, 71, 94
Duhem, P., 233, 348

Elysium, 115, 117
Epicurus, Epicureanism, 75, 80, 84, 94, 332
Eriugena, Johannes Scottus, 6, 219–29, 233–83, 349–52
Ernout, A., 211, 346
Eugippius, 37
Eusebius of Caesarea, 45, 324, 345; *Praeparatio evangelica*, 158, 166–75, 178, 179, 342
Evodius, 316

Festugière, A. J., 66, 74, 90, 99, 157, 158, 199, 209, 311, 312, 321, 322, 323, 324, 332, 336
fiction, elements of in *Confessions*, 31–48

Finaert, J., 49
Folliet, G., 167, 209
Fontaine, J., 104, 105
Fortunatus, 306
Frank, T., 331, 332
Fulgentius of Ruspe, 37

Gifford, E. H., 343
Gilson, E., 148, 198, 255, 326, 336, 337, 342, 345, 349, 352
Goldbacher, A., 138
Goldschmidt, V., 287, 353, 354, 356
Gourdon, 121, 146
Gow, A. S. F., 332
Gregory Nazianzenus, 216, 258
Gregory of Nyssa, 219, 240, 352
Gregory, T., 350
Grosjean, P., 31
Gudeman, A., 315
Guitton, J., 321

Hadot, I., 315
Hadot, P., 5, 7, 59, 60, 166, 167, 169, 180, 209, 210, 340, 341, 343, 354
Hagendahl, H., 104
Harnack, A. von, 3, 6, 121, 146, 148, 209
Hatzfeld, A., 148
Henry, P., 114, 151, 152, 209, 210, 336
Herescu, N., 332
Hermogenianus, 130, 138
Hippo, 88, 94, 146
Hirzel, R., 12, 18, 315, 318
Holl, A., 356
Holtorf, H., 75, 331
Horace, 104
Hubner, W., 334, 335

Jackson, K., 328
Jaeger, W., 89
Janssens, L., 69, 91, 100
Jerome, St., 88, 261
Julius Caesar, 256, 332
Juvenal, 104

Kilwardby, R., 263
Knoll, P., 318, 319

Labriolle, P. de, 316
Lactantius, 331
Legewie, B., 97, 334
Lewy, H., 172, 179, 340, 341, 347
Licentius, 19, 46, 63, 78, 315, 316, 317, 319, 320, 325, 326, 327
Lilja, S., 72, 73, 331

General Index

Longinus(?), *On the Sublime*, 106, 107, 334
Loofs, F., 146, 148
Lucretius, 73, 76, 80, 87, 95, 100, 201, 211, 235, 331, 332, 346

MacKenna, S., 93, 347
Macrobius, 104, 105, 135, 324
Madec, G., 166, 167, 223, 355
Mandouze, A., 7, 32, 152, 290, 300–304, 353, 354, 356,
Manichees, (-eans), (-eism), 45, 88, 98, 111, 257, 305, 306, 307, 346
Marrou, H. I., 89, 90, 97, 103, 209, 331, 333, 334, 340
Martin, J., 148
Mathon, G., 149, 244, 247, 258, 339, 349
Maximus, *Ambigua*, 219, 234, 237, 248, 249, 250, 253
Medea, 95
Milan, 3, 39, 45, 54, 78, 86, 112, 202, 215
Miles, M., 223, 224
Misch, G., 31,32, 41
Mohrmann, C., 32, 328, 329, 330, 331, 334, 338, 340, 349
Mondadon, L. de, 138
Mon(n)ica, Augustine's mother, 42, 50, 52, 54, 55, 67, 90, 96, 99, 112, 123, 146, 203, 243, 303, 319
Montgomery, W.,148
Montgomery Hitchcock, F. R., 328

Nebridius, 182, 316
Neoplatonism, 1, 121–31, 133, 146–65, 187, 188, 193
Neo-Pythagoreans, 70, 78
New Academy, The, 54,123, 126, 127, 136, 246
Newman, J. H. Cardinal, 30, 90, 91, 121
Numenius, 342, 343
Nock, A. D., 321, 324, 335

O'Connell, R. J., 195, 223, 345
Ohlmann, 11, 12, 13, 315, 316, 317, 318, 319, 320
O'Meara, D. J., 334
O'Meara, J. J., : *Against the Academics*, 127–28, 129, 201, 334, 345; *Charter of Christendom*, 212, 330, 345; *Eriugena*, 349; *The Creation of Man in De Genesi ad litteram*, 334; *Porphyry's Philosophy from Oracles in Augustine*, 5, 169, 181, 222, 340, 341, 343, 344, 345, 347, 353, 355; *Porphyry's Philosophy from Oracles in Eusebius* (1969), 5, 222, 345, 347; *Prolegomena to the Contra Academicos*, 4, 145; *The Young Augustine*, 4, 331, 333, 356, 339, 340, 346, 356
oracles, 184–86
oracles of Apollo, 185
oracles, Chaldaean, 5, 185, 193, 341, 342, 343, 345
Origen, 69, 205, 230
Orosius, 37
Ostia, 52, 54, 151, 196, 213, 304, 318, 328, 334, 345,
Otis, B., 332, 333
Ovid, 186, 203, 333

Pagels, E., 1
paideia, 90
Patrick, St., 1, 31–38, 328–29
Paul, St., 6, 24, 43, 44, 54, 111, 119, 133, 134, 137, 156, 198, 204, 212, 222, 238
Paulinus of Nola, 37, 45, 46
Pelagius, (Pelagians), (Pelagianism), 86, 88, 100, 102
Pepin, J., 152, 209, 334, 340, 351
Perret, J., 75, 321, 332
Persius, 39
Philippson, R., 315
Philodemus of Gadara, 74
Pistis Sophia, 18
Plato, 36, 54, 127, 324; *Epinomis*, 18; *Republic*, 90; *Symposium*, 91–92, 212
Plinval, M. G. de, 315
Plotinus, 3, 7, 43, 126, 147, 148, 149, 185, 195–208, 346; *Enneads*, 92–93, 141, 151, 195, 206-7, 212, 213
Ponticianus, 198, 204
Porphyry, 3–7, 50, 116, 125–27, 131, 135, 137, 138, 150, 151, 152, 153, 156, 157–65, 166–94, 210, 214, 315, 321, 342; *Adversus Christianos*, 179; *De abstinentia*, 170, 175; *De cultu simulacrorum*, 170; *De regressu animae*, 4, 47, 116, 126, 137, 151, 166, 180,181, 179, 180, 181, 182, 222, 290, 312; *Episula ad Anebonem*, 116, 170, 191; *Isagogue*, 124, 135; *Philosophy from Oracles*, 46, 166–94, 341, 342
Portalie, E., 148
Poschl, V., 75, 332
Posidonius, 60
Poujoulat, 317
Propertius, 71

Prosper of Aquitaine, 37
Protrepticus, 17, 91, 322
Puech, C. H., 209
Pusey, E. B., 97, 107, 130, 333

Quinn, K., 331
Quosdam Platonicorum libros, 47, 133, 134, 135, 156, 315

Rhoades, J., 104
Rodriguez, J., 315
Romanianus, 28, 133, 148, 200, 208
Rome, 73, 103, 105, 106, 107, 112
Roques, R., 351
Roy, O. du, 167, 287, 288, 294–300, 343, 354
Russell, R., 349
Ryan, J. K., 115, 330

Sallust, 2, 95, 213
Schelkle, 104
Schmidt, W., 334
Schwyzer, H. R., 150
Seeck, O., 321
Segal, C., 353
Seneca, 213
Sheldon-Williams, I. P., 349, 350, 352
Silenus, 76, 78
Simplicianus, 42, 153, 154, 155
Smith, A., 6, 315
Solignac, A., 290, 330, 333, 340, 343, 347, 351, 354, 355, 356
Somnium Scipionis, 323, 334
Swift, L. J., 311–13
Symmachus, 112, 321
Synesius of Cyrene, 122, 210, 351

Taylor, J. H., 215, 233, 347, 350, 351
Testard, M., 340
Theiler, W., 114, 150, 151, 152, 153, 200, 335, 346, 353
Theocritus, 68, 332
Theodorus, 153, 154
Theophilus of Antioch, 242
Theophrastus, 322
Thimme, W., 146
Tillemont, 14, 319
Trehorel, E., 49
Trier, 29, 42
Troy, 103
Trygetius, 63, 316, 317, 325, 326, 327

Van der Meer, F., 40, 48, 59,
Van Haeringen, J. F., 315, 316, 318, 319, 320, 325
Varro, 60, 61, 260
Verbeke, G., 351
Victorinus, friend of Augustine, 34
Victorinus, Marius, 46, 114, 124, 135, 151, 180, 198, 216, 343
Virgil, 35, 61–78, 94–108, 175, 331, 332; *Aeneid,* 41, 81–84, 103–17, 175; *Eclogues,* 67–71, 86, 95, 341, 353; *Georgics,* 322

Waddell, H., 110
Watts, 84
Wendland, P., 322
Wolff, G., 193, 332
Wörter, F., 148

Zenobius, 21

Index of Augustinian Texts

Confessiones
I,8: 41
I,13,20: 64
I,17,27: 66
II,1: 97
II,79: 97
III,1: 49, 66, 97
III,7: 28
III, 21: 41
III,42: 158
IV,1,1: 34
IV,16,31: 34
VI,12: 42, 66
VI,17: 43
VI,24: 94
VI,26: 94
VII,9: 4, 134
VII,10: 305
VII,13: 133, 156, 157
VII,17: 93–94
VII,26: 161
VIII,2: 98
VIII,4: 42
VIII,6,14: 198–99
VIII,7,17: 29
VIII,12,29: 24–30, 43, 66
VIII,15: 42, 53
VIII,28: 39, 52
IX,4,12: 34
IX,5: 43
IX,7: 12
IX,18: 42
IX,23: 52
X,3,4: 34
X,8,12: 63
X,12–14: 40, 115
X,23–26: 152
X,27,38: 34, 107
XI,25,32: 34
XI,30: 52
XII,27: 51
XII,35: 51
XII,36: 51
XII,37: 51
XII,41–43: 51

Contra Academicos
I,11: 158
II,4,7: 200
II,4,10: 65
II,5: 6, 24–25, 133, 163, 190, 195–208, 290
II,4–7: 200
II,7: 158
II,8: 298
II,22: 158
III,13: 137
III,20: 159
III,41–43: 135–136
III. 42: 158, 159, 163
III, 43: 54

De beata vita
4: 27, 135
36: 162

De bono coniugali
III,3: 241, 349

De consensu evangelistarum
I,23: 163
I,24: 163

De civitate Dei
IX,4: 66
X,11: 161
X,23: 157, 160
X,24: 162
X,26: 164
X,27: 159, 160, 164
X,28: 160, 162
X,29: 157, 158, 159, 160,161, 162
X,30: 157, 158
X,32: 160, 161, 162, 16
XII,27: 158
XIII,19: 158
XIX,23: 163, 172
XXII,27: 158, 186

De Genesi ad litteram
IX,5,9: 349
XI,41,56: 349
XII,18: 351
XII,60: 264

De libero arbitrio
II,6: 160

De moribus ecclesiae
I,12: 162

De ordine
I,3: 183
I,6,9: 315
I,10,29: 226
I,14: 185
I,26: 64
II,9,27: 300
II,16: 137, 157, 159–161, 162, 163
II,27: 164, 205,335
II,31: 158, 159
II,42: 164
II,45: 158, 202

De quantitate animae
12: 7, 12, 161, 227
76: 158, 161

De trinitate
IV,15: 161, 164
IV,20: 161
XIII,24: 160, 165

De utilitate credendi
X: 52, 60

De vera religione
3: 159, 161
4–5: 163–64

6: 160
7: 157, 160, 165
13: 159
19: 160
30: 159, 162

Epistulae
10,2: 101
13,2: 228
27,5: 46
102: 162
118: 126, 136, 165

Retractationes
1,1: 136
1,1,3: 223
1,2: 12, 182
1,4,3: 157, 181, 191, 225
1,13,1: 296
1,13,7: 298
1,17: 98
1,18: 158
1,24: 187

Sermones
241,7: 191

Soliloquia
1,3: 191
1,12: 159, 336
1,14: 157, 225
1,18: 158
1,22: 159
1,24: 187

Studies in Augustine and Eriugena was composed
in 9.5/13 Meridien by Brevis Press, Bethany, Connecticut;
printed and bound by BookCrafters, Chelsea, Michigan;
and designed by Kachergis Book Design,
Pittsboro, North Carolina.

DATE DUE

FEB 24 1996			

HIGHSMITH 45-220